Strategy for Sustainable Competitive Advantage

T0347369

Routledge Research in Organizational Behavior and Strategy

Strategy for Sustainable Competitive Advantage

Surviving Declining Demand and China's Global Development

Ian Chaston

Taylor & Francis Group

LONDON AND NEW YORK

First published 2012 by Routledge

2 Park Square, Milton Park, Abingdon, Oxon OX14 4RN
711 Third Avenue, New York, NY 10017, USA

Routledge is an imprint of the Taylor & Francis Group, an informa business

First issued in paperback 2016

Library of Congress Cataloging-in-Publication Data
Chaston, Ian.
   Strategy for sustainable competitive advantage : surviving declining demand and China's global development / by Ian Chaston.
       p. cm. — (Routledge research in organizational behaviour and strategy ; 7)
   Includes bibliographical references and index.
   1. Strategic planning.   2. Organizational behavior.   3. China—Commerce.   4. Competition, International.   I. Title.
   HD30.28.C4646 2012
   658.4'012—dc23
   2011043223

ISBN13: 978-0-415-52274-8 (hbk)
ISBN13: 978-1-138-20316-7 (pbk)

Typeset in Sabon by IBT Global.

Contents

Figures and Tables

FIGURES

TABLES

Preface

TOPIC COVERAGE

For the foreseeable future undergraduates, postgraduates and Executive Programme participants having observed the adverse outcomes of the recent global recession and the threat posed by Chinese firms in both their domestic and overseas markets will understandably be concerned about their career prospects. This may cause individuals to question the validity of some of the more conventional theories about strategic management. The purpose of this text is to compliment existing knowledge by examining the strategic issues associated with successfully responding to flattening demand in many Western nation markets and the challenge of defeating new sources of global competition from firms based in emerging nations.

Chapter 1 examines the market demand problems facing the modern organisation. These have been caused by meta events in areas such as massive public sector deficits, population ageing and global warming. What can be concluded is these meta events are likely to severely dampen market demand in many Western economies. Furthermore the culture within China is such that this country will not provide Western firms with a market opportunity capable of providing long term compensation for revenue declines in their traditional markets. The chapter also presents the perspective that over time, especially in world's mature industries, China's rapid globalisation will possible create a new source of potentially unbeatable competition.

Joseph Schumpeter and the Austrian School Economics, on the basis of their analysis of economic cycles and the Great Depression, posited that long term survival is dependent upon organisations recognising and responding to meta-events. The 21st century manager will be facing an unprecedented combination of meta-events. Chapter 2 introduces the concept that survival in the face of meta-events is reliant upon organisations exploiting new knowledge as the basis for developing new forms of competitive advantage. Chapter 3 examines how new knowledge can provide the basis for successful future operations by adopting a zero base orientation towards strategic planning.

Chapter 4 examines the start point in zero base strategy planning involves acquiring an understanding of the knowledge exploitation capabilities of competition and the nature of factors influencing new knowledge trends within the external environment. Chapter 5 examines the nature of alternative new knowledge types and how an RBV assessment can be used for determining internal knowledge exploitation competences.

External and internal knowledge analysis provide the framework for Chapter 6.This chapter reviews how data generated from an external and internal analysis permit identification of knowledge gaps and how identified gaps can provide the basis for a SWOT analysis. Chapter 7 covers the issues of the competences that influence the classification of issues into the opportunities, threats, strengths and weaknesses confronting the organisation.

Chapters 8 and 9 examine the role of competitive advantage in optimising added value performance as the basis of defining organisational objectives and determining the most effective strategy for achieving defined performance objectives. Many of the successes associated with a new organisation achieving national or global market dominance and the ability of some organisations to combat competitive pressures can be attributed to the identification and introduction of a new or an alternative technology. Chapter 9 reviews the implications of technological change and the degree to which this is critical to achieving growth through innovation.

Chapter 10 examines how participation in networks can enhance knowledge acquisition and how the increasing use of collaboration or 'open', innovation enhances the entrepreneurial capabilities of organisations. Repaying mounting public sector debt, a declining corporate tax base and population ageing all have serious implications on the future affordability of the welfare state in many developed economies. Chapter 11 examines how a knowledge based approach to strategic planning in the public sector can assist organisations optimise ongoing service delivery in future years, despite PSOs being required to exist with significantly reduced financial resources.

Chapter 12 reviews the design of the most appropriate organisational structure through which to deliver a business plan. Merely defining a plan which provides a source of competitive advantage is no guarantee of actual business success. Hence Chapter 13 covers the processes associated with successfully implementing a zero base strategy. Implementation of an organisational strategy is rarely a totally free process. Chapter 14 examines how barriers to successful implementation can arise and how these might be overcome.

The advent of electronic convergence and increasingly powerful data management capabilities is providing new opportunities based upon exploiting smart technology. Chapter 15 examines how smart technology offers the prospect of renewed economic growth across a diversity of sectors such as consumer services, supply chain operations and healthcare.

1 A Very Uncertain World

The purpose of this chapter is to cover issues pertaining to:

1. The need for organisations to respond effectively to increasingly turbulent and volatile external environments.
2. The decline in consumer demand in mature Western markets.
3. The problems for Western firms seeking new growth by exploiting the world's potentially future largest market—China.
4. The impact of the growing public sector financial crisis in the Western world on future funding of the welfare state and the impact on consumer disposable income.
5. The growing problems associated with the global resource availability in areas such as oil and agricultural products.
6. The scale of financial impact of the continuing rise in the costs of healthcare provision in Western economies.
7. The inability of Western firms in mature industries to compete in world markets in the face of competition from firms based in emerging economies.
8. The ongoing validity of continuing to utilise conventional strategic planning models.
9. The alternative perspective that Western organisations should accept the Schumpeterian view that ongoing success depends upon the exploitation of innovation.

INTRODUCTION

Ever since the human race began to create formal entities to engage in commercial activities, the fundamental purpose of these organisations is to acquire inputs, add value and to exchange these outputs in return for the efforts expended. In the case of private sector organisations, the primary aim in adding value to inputs is to generate a profit from sales. Within the public and not-for-profit sectors, the main purpose of organisations is usually to deliver outputs at a cost no greater than the input funding received. Unlike the private sector, where payments are provided by the user, these organisations receive payments for their activities from a third party, such as a government agency or charitable donations.

Organisational performance is influenced by interacting external environmental factors. One factor is the cost and availability of inputs. Thus, for example, in 2010 when Russia banned all grain exports due to a poor harvest, this drove up world wheat prices, leading to higher-cost bread. Concurrently not-for-profit organisations, such as the UN, which tend to have inflexible budgets, were forced to reduce the quantity of food supplies which they could afford to ship to disadvantaged people in developing nations.

Ultimately the supply of output is determined by market demand. Should an organisation encounter rising costs while undertaking value added activities, the outcome is likely to be higher prices accompanied by a fall in market demand. In most cases the demand for an organisation's output is also determined by the proportion of total output which customers wish to purchase from the organisation's competitors. An organisation may also face changes in demand should a new competitor such as a new producer based in a developing country decide to enter the market.

Some factors of influence within external environments have become increasingly volatile and uncertain in recent years. Examples include the rising costs of oil and certain agricultural products. Managers then face problems identifying appropriate actions for adapting to the changing market conditions. This is one of the reasons why academics have introduced the concept known as 'strategic complexity theory' (Cunha and Da Cunha 2006). Rising levels of environmental turbulence mean there has been a reduction in orderly competition between organisations, leading to difficulties for managers attempting to predict customers' future needs. As a consequence organisations are required to determine which environmental factors are most likely to undergo major change. This knowledge provides the basis for assessing whether the organisation has the necessary capabilities to remain in existence (Mason 2007). It is scenarios such as these which provide the purpose of this chapter: namely to review environmental change as the basis for questioning whether existing management planning models remain 'fit for purpose' in today's very uncertain world.

CONSUMER DEMAND

The standard strategic assumption within many Western consumer goods companies is that families with children in the age group 18–49 provide the primary source of demand and generate the majority of revenue for multinational giants such as Proctor & Gamble and Nestle. The problem that is now emerging in Western democracies is population ageing. This is causing a rise in the average age of populations as older people are becoming the dominant group within many nations (Johnson 2004). Although the total population in Europe will remain virtually unchanged between now and the year 2050, the number of 65+ individuals is forecasted to increase by 65 percent. Associated with this socio-demographic shift is that older people now own an increasing share of a country's total wealth. In the United States, for example, individuals aged 55+ make up 35 percent of the adult population yet control 70 percent of the net worth of all household assets. The problem for consumer goods companies is that although much wealthier, these older people tend to spend and consume less than their younger counterparts (Chaston 2009a).

In the case of governments, population ageing results in a reverse situation in relation to the demand for services. With people living longer, governments face rising demand for state pensions and healthcare provision (Klaase and Van der Vlist 1990). Long before the 2008 global banking crisis, observers of population ageing were predicting many governments would face a potentially massive fiscal crisis (Jensen et al. 1995). On average the cost of public pensions and healthcare benefits consumes 12 percent of GDP in developed nation economies. Assuming no change in the nature of welfare provision, this figure is forecasted to rise to 24 percent of GDP by 2040. Without significant changes being made in the way governments operate their welfare systems, funding of this increase in welfare provision for older people will require the working population to accept at least a 100 percent increase in their personal tax burden. This in turn will further reduce the spending power of the 18–49 age group.

Recognition of the implications of population ageing has caused many of the world's largest multi-nationals to decide that compensation for declining sales in the West can be achieved by entering rapidly developing markets of countries such as China and Russia. Such perspectives may reflect a somewhat limited understanding of how world history has caused these nations to become highly xenophobic. This attitude has evolved over the centuries because these countries have suffered very severely at the hands of numerous foreign invaders (Fenby 2008). In both countries the political leadership tends to welcome foreign firms in those cases where their presence is seen as an effective strategy for attracting capital or the latest industrial technology or acting as a source of new job creation. However, at the juncture where politicians perceive that domestic firms can fulfil these roles, foreign corporations usually find their ability to remain in the country becomes increasingly difficult (Chaston 2009b).

In the case of Russia, for example, following the advent of perestroika, the Western oil companies were welcomed with open arms to assist the country with modernising existing fields and to open new fields. Once the Russian government felt its own producers had acquired sufficient expertise, the Western oil companies were confronted with problems such as exploration licences being revoked and claims that they were attempting to avoid paying corporation tax (Bucknall 1997). It would appear that few Western corporations learned from the Russian scenario because after failing to achieve commercial success in that country, many of them have re-directed their efforts to enter Chinese markets (Jacques 2009). The attraction of this latter country is that the economy is growing at a rate greater than almost anywhere else in the world. This in turn leads to a massive increase in the size of the all-important consumer market, the middle classes.

Until recently few business leaders were willing to openly express their concerns about the long-term opportunities associated with the Chinese market. One of the first sources of adverse comment was by the CEO of the American GE Corporation, Jeff Immelt. He is quoted (Evans-Pritchard 2010, p. B2) as stating 'It's getting harder for foreign companies to do business there. I am not sure that in the end they want any of us to win or to be successful.' His views have since been echoed by two German corporations, Siemens and BASF, which both feel 'the playing field in China is increasingly tilted against foreigners.' In the same article, Evans-Pritchard also reported that the British multi-national mobile telephone giant Vodafone will probably sell their £4 billion investment in China Mobile because they have concluded it is becoming increasingly difficult to do business in China.

This growing level of concern over the problems of operating in China has also led to the European Chamber of Commerce concluding foreign companies are being actively discouraged from investing in China. In their view this is caused by the Chinese government's policies in areas such as unequal law enforcement and unfair restrictions on operations. The Japanese have traditionally avoided commenting upon adverse trading conditions elsewhere in the world to avoid causing loss of face for foreign governments. However, even the Japanese, who have numerous operations based in China, have recently begun to express concerns about the risks of making further investments in that country (Monaghan 2010).

To generate greater understanding of the attitude to foreign firms in China, Bretnotz and Murphree (2011) undertook an extensive examination of the attitudes and values which overseas firms can expect to encounter. They note that although the Chinese have become more supportive of greater economic freedom and exhibit a willingness to permit overseas firms to enter the country, the government still retains control over the behaviour of the population and the activities of business enterprises. Bretnotz and Murphree's analysis reveals that a significant degree of commercial uncertainty exists because the Chinese government is willing to make abrupt major revisions in policy should this be perceived as beneficial to domestic organisations or is advantageous in frustrating further expansion by overseas firms. Where a sector of industry is deemed as critical to the Chinese economy in terms of supplying domestic markets or expansion into overseas markets, the government has developed a number of mechanisms to influence outcomes. These include granting operating licences only to certain companies, appointing specific firms as the approved suppliers for government contracts and refusing to approve applications from foreign firms to open new plants in China. Foreign companies also face problems created by the country operating a dual track regulatory system. This is achieved by the central government retaining control over certain matters but being willing to delegate relatively autonomous authority over certain other policy issues to regional governments.

Another factor of influence is that China's banks remain under state control. By this means the government can enforce rapid changes in consumer, industrial and financial markets by requiring the banks to respond immediately to new government directives concerning economic policy. An example was provided in 2011 when the government became concerned over rapidly rising house prices. Its solution was to instruct the banks to immediately revise the terms and conditions under which new mortgages could be granted. In relation to commercial credit, although stock markets exist which in theory can provide access to capital, government regulations over the operation of these stock exchanges severely limit the ability of firms to raise capital or engage in merger and acquisitions (M&As).

PUBLIC SECTOR DEMAND

After World War II the appeal of Keynesian economic theory concerning the stimulation of economic growth through deficit spending, linked to the desire of returning military personnel and their families to enjoy a better life, led to the establishment of the modern welfare state (Brown-Collier and Collier 1995). Creation of these new entities caused a massive expansion in public sector spending and public sector jobs as Western governments initiated strategies such as free subsidised services in areas such as education, healthcare, pensions and unemployment benefits. As a consequence the public sector became a critical component of these countries' economies in terms of purchasing products and services from the private sector and providing employment for millions of people. For example, the UK National Health Service (NHS) is now the largest employer of any organisation within Europe.

By the 1980s, the combination of poor economic growth, rising inflation and inflexible attitudes to workplace reform among the public sector unions led to the situation that governments faced increasing problems funding their ever-expanding provision of public sector services. This led to attempts at reform such as the introduction of the New Public Management (NPM) philosophy. This was designed to introduce private sector management practices into the public sector in order to improve efficiency and effectiveness (Chaston 2011). Such initiatives achieved a limited degree of success and hence public sector spending continued to rise (Hood and Jackson 1992). By the beginning of the 21st century most Western nations continued to enjoy economic growth only due the central banks keeping interest rates low, which in turn supported greater consumer spending through higher borrowing (Boyne 2006). The first indication of trouble with this economic model was the emergence of problems in the United States' sub-prime mortgage market. This was followed by banks in both the United States and Europe, due their involvement in complex financial derivative products, being forced to admit their balance sheets contained high levels of toxic debt. In order to avoid a banking collapse on a scale not previously seen since the 1930s, governments were forced to intervene (Anon. 2007a). This resulted in a further massive increase in public sector deficits. The scale of these deficits was exacerbated in some Mediterranean countries because governments had made the mistake of stimulating even faster economic growth through excessive public sector borrowing (Connelly 2008). By 2009 the combined influence of all these events led to the only solution for many developed nation economies of having to implement major cuts in public spending. These cuts will continue to dampen economic growth for some years, severely reduce the scale of public sector purchasing from the private sector and be accompanied by public sector employees being made redundant (Anon. 2009a).

Cutbacks in public sector services will also result in some nations' citizens having to allocate a much larger proportion of their disposable income to self-funding services in areas such as education, healthcare and pensions. Although it is difficult to precisely forecast the impact of these events, it is very certain that private sector organisations can expect a severe decline in sales as the average consumer faces some 5–10 years of significantly reduced personal incomes (Wallop 2010). This forecasted reduction in consumer spending in mature markets is already being felt by the major branded goods companies. David Polman, the CEO of Unilever, perceives slower growth in the face of smaller disposable incomes in the company's mature markets. In his view there are real concerns about social cohesion and unemployment, not just in the peripheral nations of the EU such as Greece, Portugal or Spain but also among other core markets within mainland Europe. Unilever's strategy includes ensuring brands offer consumer choice across different price points and accepting there will be brand switching as consumers seek to purchase products offering the best price/value relationship. However, Polman also believes the company must sustain a focus on innovation in order to develop new or improved products that respond to changing consumer buying behaviour in these mature markets (Lucas 2011).

RESOURCE AVAILABILITY

The ability of organisations to add value and offer prices acceptable to customers is heavily influenced by the cost of raw materials. Energy is a critical cost component for all organisations. In the early years of the 21st century the price of oil began to rise dramatically. To a large degree this rise was fuelled by the rapid growth in the Chinese and Indian economies (Rees 2008). Oil is a non-renewable resource and as the number of cars on the world's roads continues to rise, especially in the emerging economies, this ongoing, ever-increasing demand for petrol will lead to higher oil prices (Moeller 2008). This outcome will concurrently trigger an upward climb in the price of other non-renewable energy resources such as coal and gas, thereby placing upward pressures on global electricity prices (Hartley et al. 2008).

Known and newly identified oil reserves, when linked to ongoing developments in new extraction technologies, will mean that the world is unlikely to run out of oil any time soon. Nevertheless the interaction between supply and demand will result in organisations facing rising costs for carbon-based fuels over the balance of the 21st century. This outcome will impact all other economic activities, from the extraction of minerals to manufacturing of products, production of services and the distribution of goods. Hence most organisations, especially those in engaged in high-energy consumption sectors such as the airline industry, will need to accept rising energy costs as a meta-event requiring careful attention during the development of future strategies.

The other major resource problem is growing shortages in the world's food supplies. The underlying cause of this problem is that demand, especially in underdeveloped economies, is rising at a rate greater than can be sustained from available supplies (Rosen and Shapouri 2009). Currently the United Nations has judged approximately 40 percent of the world's nations to be at risk from serious food shortages or already facing starvation. Although continued growth in the size of the world population is an important factor influencing food shortages, the amplitude of these shortages reflects an inter-action between a number of factors. One factor is that over the last few years there has been a change in eating habits, with rising per capita incomes caus-ing meat to become a more important component of diets in countries such as India, China and Brazil. This switch in eating habits is causing more of the world's cereal output to be directed to the less productive agricultural process of feeding crops to cattle, with 7 kg of grain being required to produce 1 kg of beef. Additional pressure on grain prices has also occurred as countries such as the United States have diverted an increasing proportion of their corn harvest to the highly inefficient process of converting crops into bio-fuels. Together these two factors are considered to be major contributors to what has become known as 'world food inflation' (Hojjat 2009). To this scenario has been added financial investors' speculation in commodities. This has fur-ther aggravated food price volatility (Singh 2009). Although most Western consumers will continue to afford to buy food, the inflation effect will reduce the proportion of disposable income available to spend on other purchases and lead to further increases in public sector operating costs in areas such as caring for patients in hospital (Singh 2009).

A critical issue which is related to both continuing utilisation of hydro-carbon energy sources and the ability of certain nations to grow sufficient food is global warming. The idea that burning ever larger amounts of fos-sil fuels could increase the level of carbon dioxide (or greenhouse gases) in the earth's atmosphere was widely ignored until the publication of reports from the United Nations Intergovernmental Panel on Climate Change (IPCC). Obtaining acceptance of the threat posed by global warning initially proved extremely difficult for the IPCC. Eventually, under the auspices of the United Nations, in 1997 the world leaders met in Kyoto, Japan to discuss proposals about limiting carbon dioxide emissions (Cirman et al. 2009).

It is now accepted by most governments that unless ways are found to reverse current levels of greenhouse gas emissions, the world's climate will become more volatile, ocean temperatures will rise and ice caps will melt at faster rates, eventually resulting in higher sea levels. A significant problem in responding to this threat is the ongoing difficulties in accurately predicting the potential environmental and economic impacts of global climate warming. Nevertheless it seems probable that one very likely outcome is the number of areas of the world experiencing drought will increase. This will be accompanied by more people being threatened by starvation. Furthermore rising sea levels will endanger the deltas of the Nile, Ganges, Brahmaputra and the Mekong. This could lead to millions of people attempting to move away these regions. Additionally some small island countries in the Pacific may disappear under the waves (Bogataj 2009).

The Kyoto Protocol set binding targets for greenhouse gas emissions for 37 industrialised countries and all members of the EU. As developed industrialised economies are historically the biggest emitters of greenhouse gases, the Protocol placed a heavier emissions reduction burden on these countries. The Protocol proposed new mechanisms to help nations achieve their emissions targets, including carbon emissions trading and the use of technology to reduce the production of emissions. There have been significant differences in various nations' responses towards the Kyoto Protocol. A key reason is that any developed economy moving to reduce greenhouse case emissions can expect this action will lead to higher industrial operating costs relative developing countries exempted or refusing to adopt the Protocol. For example, the Bush administration in the United States claimed the Kyoto Protocol would result in a loss of $400 billion in industrial output and 4.9 million US jobs. Attempts to persuade Western nations to accept these higher costs were subsequently frustrated by the Copenhagen Climate Change summit in 2009, where under the leadership of Brazil, China and India, the developing nations refused to commit to an agreement to meet specific global emissions targets by 2025.

Support for the need for greater environmental responsibility by industry tends to decline during economic downturns or when there is growing fear about sustaining competitive advantage in the face of new sources of competition. Even in Europe, where acceptance of the need for a reduction in greenhouse gas emissions is relatively high, the 2008 economic downturn has caused some companies and trade bodies to express concern about being able to compete with firms in China, while this country continues to seek ways of reducing electricity costs by bringing on-line new coal-powered generation capacity. Emergence of this growing resistance to government policy is illustrated by industry's vocal, adverse response to the UK government's 2011 announcement to reduce greenhouse emissions by 60 percent by 2030 (Pickard and Stacey 2011).

THE NEXT RESOURCE CRISIS?

Case Aims: To illustrate how emerging a new raw material shortage could impede plans to manufacture products able to lower greenhouse gas emissions.

First discovered in the 18th century, rare earth elements (or REEs) were long considered chemical curiosities rather than the vital building blocks of technology. Now, however, rare earths have become a boom industry after the invention of a succession of devices such as the iPhone and hybrid cars, which rely on the specific properties exhibited by REEs.

Once extracted and refined, rare earth metals have a vast range of hi-tech uses. Neodymium, one of the most common rare earths, is a key part of neodymium-iron-boron magnets used in hyper-efficient motors and generators. Around two tons of neodymium are needed for each wind turbine. Lanthanum, another REE, is a major ingredient for the batteries used in hybrid vehicles (e.g. each Totoyota Prius uses up to 16 kg). Terbium is vital for low-energy light bulbs and cerium is used in catalytic converters. Worldwide, the industries reliant on REEs, which produce anything from fibre-optic cables to missile guidance systems, are estimated to be worth $3 trillion, or 5 percent of global GDP (Milmo 2010).

The Chinese town of Baotou in Inner Mongolia has become a global capital for the production of rare earths. This is because China, which by an accident of geography holds about 50 percent of the world's rare earth deposits, now produces 97 percent of global supplies. The country's leaders have made no secret of the nature or scale of their ambitions. Global demand has tripled from 40,000 tons to 120,000 tons over the past ten years, during which time China has steadily cut annual exports from 48,500 tons to 31,310 tons. At the beginning of 2010 Beijing announced that it was setting exports at 35,000 tons for each of the next six years, barely enough to satisfy demand in Japan let alone elsewhere in the world. Toyota, for example, annually produces one million hybrid Prius cars, each of which contains 16 kg of rare earths. By 2014, global demand for rare earths is predicted to reach 200,000 tons a year as the green revolution takes hold.

China's move to reduce exports of rare earths has been accompanied by investment in the country's capability to manufacture components containing these materials. The result is that the rare earth industry in China is rapidly moving from a role as a provider of rare earth extracts for export, worth a few hundred million dollars a year, to a producer of finished REE components which will be worth billions. In response to China's reductions in exports, global manufacturers are being forced to consider moving their factories making rare earth–rich components to China to ensure continued access to these key raw materials. Foreign investors are prohibited from establishing rare earth mine enterprises in China. Rare earth smelting and separation projects involving foreign investors are limited to foreign equity joint ventures and foreign cooperative joint ventures. Wholly-owned foreign enterprises are prohibited. Foreign investment in relation to rare earth deep processing, rare earth new material and rare earth applied products is required to be approved by the State Development Planning Commissions. Rare earth smelting and separation projects must also be approved by these same commissions.

(continued)

THE NEXT RESOURCE CRISIS? (continued)

European and North American companies are seeking to open or re-open mines in Canada, South Africa and Greenland. Toyota has effectively bought its own rare earth mine by signing an exclusive supply deal in Vietnam. The problem is that the mining and processing of rare earth is very expensive unless local labour costs are very low and the producers are prepared to ignore the huge pollution problems that are associated with the extraction process for these minerals. Companies are also seeking alternative solutions to reduce their need for rare earths (Hook 2011). For example, Toyota has accelerated its development of an induction motor for hybrid vehicles that uses fewer raw earth magnets. Albermarle, a US chemical company, has launched a new range of catalysts for use in car exhausts that use lower-cost rare earths as a substitute for lanthanum, the cost of which rose by 1,500 percent in just 12 months.

The ability of China to influence the market for rare earths was graphically demonstrated in the early months of 2011, when the government implemented actions that reduced global supplies. Part of the reduction was caused by the government tightening regulations over rare earth mining in an attempt to reduce the high level of pollution which exists in the industry. This action was accompanied by a clamp-down on smuggling and a further reduction in export quotas. This latest move represents a 40 percent reduction over the previous export quota established in 2009. Some observers believe that China wishes to exploit the benefits of being a major supplier of a commodity, similar to the behaviour exhibited by other countries for raw materials such coal, iron ore and wheat (Hook 2011).

HEALTHCARE

For organisations seeking to assess potential changes in declining consumer disposable income, especially in mature Western economies, the other issue of major concern is the rising costs of healthcare. The 20th century saw an exponential increase in further advances in medical knowledge, with the discovery of drugs such as sulphonamide, penicillin and vaccines capable of curing illnesses for which, in many cases, the only previous outcome was death. Concurrently doctors have made major advances in curing other medical conditions by developing new forms of surgery such as organ transplants.

Unfortunately these advances in healthcare represent a significant meta-economic threat as more and more resources are consumed in the provision of increasingly expensive treatments. In 1995 in the United States, annual healthcare expenditures at $1 trillion represented 14 percent of the country's total GDP. Musgrave (1995) estimated that if the current rate of growth for medical spending continues at the same rate, by 2058 America's entire GDP will be required to fund the country's healthcare bills. An added complication is that as medical treatments continue to be even more successful, this increases the average life expectancy of a population, which in turns leads to the emergence of new healthcare problems such as Alzheimer's and dementia (Hudson 1997). The economic implications of how to fund the rising cost of healthcare are not confined just to the developed nations. Emerging economies are finding that changes in lifestyles caused by a rising standard of living are leading to the emergence of obesity and other diet-related illnesses such as hypertension, stroke and diabetes. Popkin (2008) estimated that in China these problems already represent an economic cost in the region of 4–8 percent of GDP.

In the United States, healthcare spending in 2007 reached 16 percent of GDP with the primary increase being in the area of prescription drugs (Zuvekas and Cohen 2007). Many other Western nations are also facing expenditure on drugs requiring an ever-rising proportion of GDP. This trend is unlikely to be reversed as new treatments are discovered and introduced. For those countries where companies and private citizens purchase medical insurance, the inevitable outcome is premiums will continue to rise. The problem over managing rising costs also confronts governments in countries where the public sector provides free or subsidised healthcare services. In these latter countries the likely outcome is either the level of personal taxation will have to be increased or more citizens will be forced to self-fund a much greater proportion of their medical bills.

COMPETITION

Where products or services have been available in a market for many years, all of the potential customers will have become users and no revenue growth opportunities exist from attracting new customers to enter the market. Under these circumstances the only source of future growth will be to persuade customers to switch their loyalty away from their existing supplier. To achieve this aim will usually involve a marketing battle between suppliers based upon up-weighted promotional activity or a price war. Examples of such outcomes are provided by the repeated occurrence of brand wars between brands such as Pepsi versus Coca Cola or McDonald's versus Burger King. In most cases the outcome is very little change in brand shares but a major decline in profitability due to either increased promotional expenditure or a decline in profit margins caused by price wars (Chaston 2009b).

As identified by the Harvard professor Michael Porter (1980, 1985) in his analysis of why American corporations began to lose market share in their domestic markets in the 1980s, the other source of competition is from new market entrants. In many cases these new entrants are from overseas. Their entry usually is a result of the technology used in a sector having become sufficiently widely understood to permit new suppliers based in lower-cost countries to acquire adequate expertise in activities in areas such as manufacturing processes to offer lower priced or higher quality substitute goods. An example of this scenario in the healthcare industry is provided by the entry of India's pharmaceutical companies into the global healthcare industry. While the major Western pharmaceutical companies concentrated on discovering new leading edge technology drugs that could be protected by patents, the Indian firms focused on the development of generic drugs capable of reducing treatment costs. Their success is demonstrated by the fact that in less than 20 years, the Indian firms have become global market leaders in the generic drugs industry (Malhotra and Lofgren 2004).

Possibly the greatest future competitive threat to Western firms in both their domestic and overseas markets is China's rapid rate of globalisation. One of China's key advantages is the country's huge domestic market, which, similar to the United States in the 20th century, provides a stable revenue base during economic downturns elsewhere in the world. There is a tendency for some organisations to underestimate the risk that China poses. This is because they still perceive China as capable of competing only by using prior-generation technology and exploiting lower labour costs. It is worth remembering that similar opinions were formed following Japan's entry into world markets in the 1970s. However, within less than a decade success by firms such as Toyota, Sony and Toshiba by offering superior products based upon exploiting the latest technological advances soon vitiated the accuracy of such perspectives. Furthermore, dismissing China as an immediate threat on the basis of the country lagging behind in the race to exploit the latest technology in areas such as cars and computers is already rendered incorrect in these sectors. Furthermore, in sectors such as telecommunications systems and solar energy, Chinese companies are already achieving global market success on the basis of supplying technologically superior products. To this scenario should be added China's willingness to form close relationships with developing nations, some of which are considered by Western governments as having doubtful human rights policies, in return for being awarded massive construction and engineering contracts to modernise these countries' inadequate national infrastructures.

NO LONGER GOOD FOR AMERICA

Case Aims: To illustrate the dangers of retaining a strategy which no longer provides the basis for competitive advantage.

One of the risks associated with being a founder member firm in an industrial sector located in a developed nation but operating in a globally important industry is the challenge of developing nations' governments wanting to create their own domestic production capability and eventually become dominant players in major overseas markets. Under these circumstances a common outcome is that total world production capacity exceeds global demand. In the face of increasingly competitive market conditions, founder firms may need to reconsider the future viability of their current strategy.

(continued)

NO LONGER GOOD FOR AMERICA (continued)

In reviewing the implications of retaining a strategy possibly no longer appropriate to market conditions, Christensen (2001) points out that General Motors' strategy in the 1960s was to exploit economies of scale and the experience curve effect to become the largest, most profitable car manufacturer in the world. A key assumption underlying this strategy among American manufacturers was that car manufacturing is a high-fixed-cost industry in which success required attainment and retention of a high market share. Founded in 1908 and headquartered in Detroit, GM's original success in overtaking the Ford Motor company was because the latter firm at that time was totally focused on creating an ever larger scale of manufacturing operations. Under the stewardship of Alfred Sloan, GM achieved market leadership by offering a more diverse, broader range of vehicles and wider choice of prices than Ford. After World War II, GM's continued growth was attributable to being a company renowned for regularly introducing new models which appealed to a world where consumers increasingly perceived their purchase of a car as a key aspect of their chosen lifestyle.

In the 1970s, with a 55 percent share of sales and an 85 percent share of industry profits, GM seems to have started losing focus on the importance of meeting consumer needs more effectively than competition. Furthermore in the face of intense pressure from the then very powerful unions in the US car industry, the company agreed to labour contracts providing extremely liberal healthcare and pension benefits to existing and retired employees. Having observed the success achieved by Volkswagen entering the US market, offering high-quality, small cars such as the Beetle, the Japanese car industry strategy began to focusing upon ways of producing small cars offering superior quality while concurrently reducing manufacturing costs. Toyota and Honda achieved these goals through innovative actions such as developing the concept of total quality management (TQM), introducing just-in-time (JIT) manufacturing to dramatically reduce the cycle time from idea through to the launch of a new model.

Finkelstein (2005, p. 21) has proposed that 'mistakes in strategy can be boiled down to two things: a wrong idea and bad stewardship of that idea. An idea that is wrong is not just a bad idea, but an idea that is wrongheaded is worse. It should never have come up in the first place, but it did, usually because of a fundamental misreading of the competitive landscape.' In his opinion this is exactly what occurred within GM during the 1980s, as the company strove to find a way of responding to the Japanese threat of offering higher-quality, lower-cost vehicles. Instead of introducing techniques such as lean manufacturing techniques, just-in-time inventory and supply chain integration, GM decided that the solution to the threat posed by firms such as Toyota was to replace people with integrated, automated robotic manufacturing systems. Unfortunately by not really understanding how to optimise integration of workers with machines, this new strategy was unsuccessful.

(continued)

NO LONGER GOOD FOR AMERICA (continued)

By the beginning of the 21st century, it was extremely clear that the world's largest car company was facing major problems. High operating costs and the need to service an ever-increasing debt mountain meant that profits had shrunk to virtually nothing. Meanwhile Toyota Motor Corporation, by now the world's second-largest car manufacturer, was achieving record sales and profits. GM's response was to implement a survival strategy aimed at dramatically reducing operating costs by shutting plants, laying off thousands of workers and most importantly seeking negotiate a new, lower-cost pension and healthcare deal with the unions (Tong 2006).

A key feature of Totoya's ongoing success was the company's huge commitment to exploiting innovation as the path by which to deliver greater consumer satisfaction than any of their competitors. The company was the first among the large car manufacturers to take seriously the problems associated with global warming and the world's finite oil resources. This led to the development of its highly successful hybrid vehicle, the Toyota Prius. The new product represents just one component of the company's 'Innovation into the Future' global vision of seeking to become a driving force in global regeneration by implementing the most advanced environmentally responsible technologies. The company's development teams are driven by a desire to create automobiles and a motorised society in which people can live safely, securely and comfortably.

With a focus on drastically reducing operating costs and sustaining sales of gas guzzlers such as large SUVs, it was inevitable that GM's response to the threat posed by Toyota and Honda would be totally inadequate following the onset of the downturn in the global economy in 2008. All three of the major US car manufacturers assumed the American government would not be prepared to let their industry fail. Unfortunately the US government's response to avoiding a meltdown in the US financial markets meant that the new Obama administration was unable to fund the scale of financial support being sought by the car industry. In the end the only solution for GM's and Chrysler's massive financial problems was to permit both firms to file for bankruptcy.

PLANNING FUTURES

The industrialisation of society over the last 250 years has led to a growth in the size and scope of organisational entities. These changes mean there is a need for the modern organisation to comprehend the influence on future demand of the interaction of factors, especially those which constitute meta-events. Organisations need to become more effective at developing business plans which accurately define feasible actions to sustain future performance.

One of the earliest examples of the benefits of using a planning philosophy to define the strategy of a multi-divisional manufacturing company was demonstrated by Alfred Sloan, the chief executive officer of General

Motors in the 1930s. His utilisation of a strategic planning philosophy helped the company to overtake Henry Ford, whose introduction of mass production had previously allowed his company to become the car industry's first global brand.

Strategic planning began to be widely accepted as management theory only after World War II. Since that time there has been an ongoing evolution in academic thinking. Nevertheless many of the currently accepted, fundamental principles were in place by the 1960s. Learned et al. (1965), for example, in proposing a process to identify a successful strategy, suggested that the firm needs to develop a set of goals and policies that provided the basis for an appropriate position in the market. To achieve this aim the organisation needs to determine relevant internal strengths and weaknesses in order to specify which distinctive internal competences can best ensure the company's strategy is appropriately aligned with the opportunities and threats which exist in the firm's market environment(s). Accompanying this activity should be actions within the organisation to ensure functional departments such as marketing and manufacturing are acting in an integrated fashion to support the selected strategic positioning. This approach involves asking the three questions: (i) 'where are we now?', (ii) 'where are we going?' and (iii) 'how to get there?'. This basic interrogative approach still provides the basis of strategic planning activity in many organisations and is the standard model taught in most business schools.

STRATEGIC COMPLEXITY

Many strategic planning models currently in use or presented in standard management texts were evolved during a period of economic stability within the Western world. This is because for approximately 40 years after 1945, the West, led by the United States, was engaged in the Cold War, during which the threat of nuclear weapons created a long period of peace. This permitted the Western democracies to create and sustain a society of high employment and to be able to fund the welfare state. By the early 1990s the advent of perestroika in Russia, the collapse of the Berlin Wall and China's acceptance of a need to modernise the country's economy were widely celebrated by Western democracies. This reaction blunted awareness that the end of the Cold War was also a catalyst, eventually resulting in the increasing level of political and economic instability now facing the world.

Academics such as Mintzberg (1990) have raised doubts about the viability of outcomes from conventional strategic planning models. This is because these usually infer that future organisational aims are based upon a simple extrapolation of past events. Mintzberg believes that extrapolation is no longer an appropriate philosophy in an increasingly volatile and turbulent world. The issue of needing to revise strategic management theory in a world where futures are more difficult and problematic to predict has led to the emergence of 'strategic complexity theory' (Cunha and Da Cunha 2006). Mason (2007) proposed that increasing levels of environmental turbulence means there has been a reduction in orderly competition between organisations. He concluded this situation is causing difficulties for managers attempting to accurately predict future customer, product and service requirement trends.

One way of conceptualising this new view of complex markets is to adopt the Schumpeterian perspective that increasingly turbulent events should be seen as offering new opportunities (Schumpeter 1942). To survive and prosper in the face of such environments, organisations need to be increasingly vigilant and develop greater capability in relation to being more effective in implementing rapid responses to environmental change. Strategic complexity theory posits that organisations should be seen as complex adaptive systems. To remain successful demands that these entities learn to align their strategies with their rapidly changing external environments, utilising interaction and proactive response rather than continuing to utilise a philosophy based upon detailed structured analysis providing the basis for defining future actions (Eisenhardt 2002; Eisenhardt and Martin 2000).

Child and McGrath (2001) have posited that in relation to adopting a complexity orientation, simplicity becomes a major feature of new organisational forms. This revised orientation is achieved by permitting operations located near to market to adopt a simpler structure and to be granted semi-autonomous control over their strategic response to environmental change. The role of head office in this situation is to act as a co-ordinating mechanism to ensure retention of an overall common purpose and to support learning that results in knowledge transfer across the organisation. Complexity theory also encompasses the need for organisations to maintain an ability to evolve, a process which Child and McGrath describe as 'continuous morphing.' Structural simplicity is an important facilitator of rapid response because employees are free to tackle problems at the local level. These empowered employees can respond more rapidly to new challenges because they no longer are required to seek permission from head office before implementing actions. Nor do the employees have to wait for actions to be taken or approval of decisions to be provided by others elsewhere within the organisation.

In relation to the application of strategic complexity theory in the public sector, Ferlie (2007) suggests that these organisations are also facing rapid environmental change, which is causing the need to reject a Weberian managerial philosophy. Instead public sector organisations should accept the need for decentralisation, individualisation and support for employees exhibiting entrepreneurial behaviour. An additional source of operational complexity facing public sector organisations is that some governments are adopting a philosophy of involving an increasing number of external stakeholders in decisions concerning service delivery (McAdam et al. 2005). White (1989), in her review of this increasingly popular philosophy of involving external stakeholders in the determination of future public policy, has referred to this new environment as 'public management in a pluralistic arena.'

One of the potential drawbacks with strategic complexity theory is there is very little information in the literature which provides examples of the application of the concept in real-world organisations or offers guidance about what appropriate management tools are available to organisations wishing to utilise the concept. This statement is not one which will inspire confidence among readers, whether the individual is still at university seeking to understand how to be an effective manager following graduation or is a management practioner worrying about sustaining the survival of his or her organisation, or alternatively his or her own career options. For all of these individuals, given the questionable viability of using a traditional, linear sequential strategic planning model of the type in the face of increasingly turbulent external environments, what alternative managerial paradigms exist?

In terms of evolving more relevant managerial solutions for the developer of new theories there are two main options. The first is to utilise quantitative models to evolve a theory that can subsequently be validated by the observation of actual events. This approach has proved extremely successful in fields such as particle physics and astronomy. Rachman (2010) has suggested that economists who have utilised this approach could be suffering from 'physics envy.' He presents the view that recent failures such as predicting the recent global financial crisis raise a fundamental question about whether economics has the ability to discover predictive laws that provide any degree of certainty for forecasting future events.

The influence of uncertainty and non-predictable events is not a problem unique to economists. Scientists in fields such as botany and zoology have long recognised that the interaction of a huge number of variables makes it extremely difficult to define rules which can explain every outcome. Researchers in those areas of science facing variable complexity problems have learned that a more effective philosophy of enquiry is to blend together theories and observations of actual events and evolve paradigms that can evolve and change as new observations become available. Given the huge number of variables associated with the management of organisations, this latter approach is adopted in this text to evolve an alternative approach for firms seeking to survive in a world of depressed domestic demand and the threat posed by China's increasing domination of world markets.

2 Knowledge and Competitive Advantage

The purpose of this chapter is to cover issues pertaining to:

1. An effective response to emerging competition is to focus on innovation to retain market leadership.
2. The inability of M&As to rescue a company facing a decline in market performance.
3. Concepts associated with achieving competitive advantage and the role of the resource-based view (RBV) of the firm in supporting a selected advantage position.
4. The role of new knowledge in sustaining the market performance of Western nation companies.
5. The structures and systems associated with the effective exploitation of new knowledge.
6. The advantages of double-loop learning and the existence of effective organisational learning systems.

THREAT RESPONSE

Kochan (2006) proposed that long-established firms operating in mature markets rarely survive unless there is an ongoing focus on exploiting innovation as the basis for staying ahead of competition. He suggests this orientation is especially critical in those cases where the source of competition is a new market entrant. Support for this perspective is provided by examples such as the Swiss watch industry ignoring Japanese firms using a microchip instead of mechanical movement, Xerox's loss of leadership in the photocopying industry to Canon, and Kodak losing out to firms such as Sony and Panasonic following the introduction of digital cameras.

A failure to recognise the importance of surviving by always remaining ahead of newly emerging competitive threats was identified in a large-scale study of US manufacturing firms (Edmondson and Wheelwright 1989). From their analysis they concluded that in all but a very small number of established firms, the usual response to competition is one of the following:

Mode 1: The focus is on cost reduction through minor process changes and curtailing investment in new capital assets in an attempt to match lower prices being offered by overseas competitors. This solution works for only a short period of time. In some cases survival is extended by persuading governments to implement legislative protectionism of domestic industry by actions such as creating tariff barriers or implementing import quotas.

Mode 2: In this case firms seek to copy the innovation being exhibited by the lead firms in the industry. For example, the US automakers learned from the Japanese and moved to introduce total quality management (TQM) and just-in-time (JIT) techniques into their plants. In this scenario the firms are essentially playing 'catch up.' The problem is that while these new methods are being embedded into their operations, the existing industry leaders are usually developing and implementing new approaches to sustain their leadership position.

In those cases where a long-established firm can perceive no opportunities for growth, a popular alternative for seeking to sustain organisation survival is to engage in mergers or acquisitions (M&As). One would presume the rationale for this strategic activity is to create a larger entity which will be more competitive, efficient and profitable than the performance of the individual participant organisations prior to the M&A. In reality this prospect of increased profitability and market share through an M&A often seems to exercise less of an immediate appeal to many CEOs than the opportunity to be seen as leaders of an even larger organisation, accompanied by an overnight increase in the value of their personal stock options (Cartwright and Cooper 1993). An added concern is that although M&As are predicted as a way to increase market share and shareholder value, in many cases this outcome is not achieved (Nguyen and Kleiner 2003).

Poor outcomes from M&As were also confirmed in a study by KPMG International, which found that 75 to 83 percent of M&As eventually fail (PR Newswire 1999). Given this situation the question must arise about why so many CEOs persist in repeatedly becoming involved in M&A activities given this apparently is a risky strategy. Langford and Brown (2004, p. 5), in commenting on this situation, proposed that:

> There are two reasons for this triumph of hope over experience. First, as is widely acknowledged, it is easy to get carried away by the adrenaline rush of M&A, particularly when M&A waves overwhelm industries. Caught up in the excitement of deal making and urged on by advisers who say they must buy or be bought, acquirers select the wrong targets, overpay and become so distracted by post-deal integration that they neglect their pre-existing businesses. Chief executive ego and excessive self-confidence often play a role.

Other key factors which result in an adverse outcome from M&As include poor due diligence performed on the target company, inadequate pre-purchase planning and insufficient resources being allocated to implementing the post-purchase strategy (Appelbaum et al. 2000a). Simpson (2000) concluded that another important contributory reason is during the post-merger phase there is of a lack of vision, ineffective leadership, culture differences and poor communication. Senior managers often delegate responsibility to middle management, who are not allocated sufficient resources or empowered to make critical decisions. As a consequence there is an increase in employee uncertainty, rising stress levels, a decrease in job satisfaction, declining commitment and reduced loyalty. This outcome is usually accompanied across the workforce by a declining trust in the management's claims of being completely honest in relation to any promises made concerning future job security.Senior managers often also miscalculate or ignore the workforces' priorities by cutting themselves off from relevant information indicating growing employee dissent. Decision-making tends to be centralised. Downward communications may become increasingly formalised. Executives and managers by isolating themselves from employees can eventually cause a massive decline in workforce morale (Appelbaum et al. 2000b).

ACQUISITION FEVER?

Case Aims: To illustrate that growth through acquisition can ultimately lead to business collapse.

The intensity of M&A activity tends to be cyclical, closely following changing economic conditions. During an economic upturn, when stock market prices are rising, interest rates are low and financial institutions are willing to approve large loans, the level of M&A activity rises dramatically. A side effect of increased activity is potential buyers get involved in bidding wars that drive up acquisition costs. It also seems that a certain degree of 'herd behaviour' develops with some CEOs, apparently trying to prove they can buy more firms and pay higher prices than their competitors.

An example of the dangers of becoming excessively enthusiastic about achieving corporate growth through acquisition is provided by the case of Sir Fred Goodwin and the Royal Bank of Scotland (RBS). Goodwin joined RBS in 1998, shortly after the bank had purchased the National Westminster. This was a hostile takeover of an English bank twice its size and was an incredibly audacious move. As the new CEO, Goodwin set about integrating the two businesses and reducing costs, and then used the enlarged business base to move RBS from being a domestic to a global player. The bank spent billions buying banks in America and a stake in the Bank of China. By 2004, RBS enjoyed a market value of $70 billion, outpacing JP Morgan Chase, Deutsche Bank, Barclays and UBS. Goodwin was named Global Businessman of the Year by *Forbes* magazine in 2002 and received his knighthood for services to banking in 2004.

(continued)

ACQUISITION FEVER? (continued)

In October 2007, RBS achieved control of the Dutch bank ABN Amro after shareholders owning 86 percent of the Dutch bank's shares accepted RBS's offer of 70 billion euros. The deal was a milestone in the banking industry, being the world's largest financial services acquisition and the first hostile cross-border takeover of a sizeable mainland European bank (Larsen 2007). A key driver in the acquisition in terms of being prepared to outbid competitors, such as the UK's Barclays Bank, was RBS's chief executive, Sir Fred Goodwin. In the business media he was hailed as an outstanding leader who was assisting the UK banking industry retain the UK's rightful title as being a major player in the world financial services industry (Bevens 2007).

In January 2009 shares in RBS collapsed when the UK government was forced to mount a rescue bid after it became apparent that the bank was facing the worst losses in UK corporate history (Anon. 2009b). The UK government took a 70 percent equity holding in the bank. As part of the government's negotiations, there was the demand for the departure of Sir Fred Goodwin on the grounds that a significant proportion of the blame for the bank's failure could be attributed to his decision to embark on an excessively aggressive acquisition programme as part of his strategy to make RBS one of the largest banks in Europe.Further public acrimony was generated when it was revealed that Sir Fred Goodwin's terms in agreeing to step down as CEO at the age of 50 was to be granted an annual pension from the bank of £693,000.

COMPETITIVE ADVANTAGE

In a mature market, where there is widespread understanding of customer needs and of the base technologies required for the production and distribution of products or services, the issue arises of how any one organisation can stay ahead of competition. One widely accepted theory is that to achieve this goal, the organisation needs to develop and exploit some form of 'competitive advantage.' The term competitive advantage first came to the fore in the 1980s, in large part due to Porter's (1985) text on the subject. As noted by Klein (2002), however, neither Porter nor subsequently some other academics have been willing to offer a definition of competitive advantage which provides sufficient clarity such that the concept is totally understood by students or management practioners. For example, as pointed out by Klein, even Porter (1985, p. 32) in his seminal text on the subject was not prepared to go beyond the statement that 'competitive advantage grows fundamentally out of the value a firm is able to create for its buyers that exceeds the cost of creating it.' Klein expressed the opinion that most people, upon being asked to attribute this definition to a specific business activity, would probably suggest the phrase 'generating a profit.' Hence, in order to assist individuals' greater understanding of the concept of competitive advantage, a simpler definition is hereby proposed—namely:

> Competitive advantage is the long-term tactical philosophy adopted by the organisation through which to outperform other organisations serving the same customer(s) and market sector(s).

One possible reason for the confusion which may exist in the literature over the concept of competitive advantage is that, in an earlier text on strategic management, Porter (1980) proposed there were four alternative, generic, strategic competitive advantage options by which a firm could achieve market success—namely, total market cost leadership, total market differentiation, niche market cost leadership and niche market differentiation. His model has subsequently been widely accepted and utilised. Possibly this confusion over the term competitive advantage would have never emerged if only Porter had referred to his four proposed options as 'alternative strategies through which to gain advantage over competition.'

The Porterian generic alternatives are based upon the two dimensions of (i) product performance and (ii) degree of market coverage. In relation to the latter variable, Porter proposed that a company could opt to offer products or services to the majority of the market or, alternatively, utilise a 'focused' approach of attempting to fulfil only the specific needs of a small group of customers. In relation to product performance, Porter proposed the choice of 'cost leadership' versus delivering 'superior performance' (or 'differentiation'). In his view cost leadership offered a low scale advantage. This is because over time it is probable that another supplier will enter the market offering a product or service at an even lower price. This scenario can emerge when existing firms no longer have access to the resource which provided the original cost advantage. For example, low labour costs may disappear in a developing nation as the country implements a successful modernisation and industrialisation of the nation's economy. Alternatively a company may be utilising a highly accessible mineral, but extraction activities over time may eventually cause this resource to become depleted and operating costs may rise.

Although an elegant, simple tool which has been extremely useful to students and management practioners over the years, the Porterian model does suffer from another potential defect—namely, the term of 'cost leadership.' This typology tends to place too much emphasis on organisational strategies based upon offering the lowest possible price. This may cause users of the tool to believe that unless an organisation can sustain a low price, this option will be unsuccessful. Hence a proposed alternative is to use the terminology of 'superior value.' This latter term may then cause firms to recognise there are other strategic options available in addition to competing purely on the basis of low price. For example, sustaining the mineral extraction example, a firm facing rising labour costs can adopt an entrepreneurial orientation and seek ways of lowering operating costs by using new technology to automate production processes. Alternatively the firm might offer quality-based superior value via the actions of investing in better grading and cleaning systems accompanied by improvements in road and port infrastructure. As demonstrated by Rio Tinto in their Australian iron ore mining operations, these actions have permitted the company to provide customers a product which is of higher quality and requires no further re-grading by the customer after delivery and, because of the infrastructure improvements, disruptions in delivery schedules can be avoided. This package of benefits will offer sufficient added value to customers' operations that they are willing to pay a higher price than that available from the less sophisticated mining operations in countries such as Brazil.

Case materials concerned with how a competitive advantage fails to protect the organisation from losing market share often indicate there has been no significant change in customer behaviour. More usually the leading incumbent firm has not remained alert to the need to continually seek ways of upgrading internal capabilities to sustain their competitive advantage based upon superiority in areas such as productivity or quality. This failure to remain ahead of competition provides other firms with a window of opportunity to develop a superior competitive advantage based upon investing in ongoing upgrading of key internal capabilities (Bate and Johnston 2005).

The strategic philosophy concerning market success based upon exploiting superior internal capability is known as the 'resource-based view of the firm' (or 'RBV'). Although the strategic importance of internal capability has been accepted by management academics since the 1950s, the concept gained much wider acceptance following Prahalad and Hamel's (1990) proposal that market leaders usually achieved and sustained their business performance by consistently exploiting a superior 'core competence.' Their viewpoint is that a core competence provides the basis for supporting two possible strategic options. A company can utilise a core competence to support the entrepreneurial activity of developing and launching new and/or improved products (e.g. Microsoft's original expansion into new areas of software such as their Access database system and regularly updating their existing portfolio of Windows products) or enter new market sectors (e.g. Honda's excellence in engineering capability to support their entry into the marine outboard engine market). Alternatively a firm may have a core competence in the development and implementation of superior operational technologies and processes which permits the organisation to compete on the basis of offering superior value to customers. This latter approach is exemplified by the way major supermarket chains in the United States lost market share to Wal-Mart because this firm exploited capabilities in the areas of procurement and logistics as the basis for offering much lower prices to the American consumer.

MAXIMISING ADDED VALUE

One issue possibly not given sufficient emphasis in the literature on RBV theory is that the competence that provides the basis for competitive advantage must also offer the most effective strategy through which to maximise the organisation's ability to add value when converting inputs into the goods to be sold. One approach for determining which opportunities within an industry offer the highest probability of maximising added value is to identify those firms that enjoy above average long-term profitability. The use of a time specification avoids including organisations where short-term high profitability has occurred due to specific circumstances that may not necessarily be repeated in the future. Thus, for example, it is probably advisable when examining the financial services sector to ignore recent profitability achievements of financial institutions such as a private equity funds that involved post–M&A asset stripping or speculating on neat term shifts in commodity prices.

In recent years some of the most successful performers in terms of consistently generating higher than average profits have been organisations in the software industry (e.g. Oracle) and those engaged in exploiting the opportunities offered by the Internet (e.g. Google, Facebook). The common feature of these organisations is that they are engaged in exploiting advances in knowledge as the basis of achieving and sustaining higher added value better than that achieved by competition. As noted by Drucker (1993) survival strategies in a post-capitalist society will be those Western firms which exploit new knowledge in order to respond to threats of overseas competitors. The current obvious threat comes from firms based in developing nations such as India and China. In the early years of their existence these new market entrants tend to rely upon lower operating costs and using base technology to offer lower-priced products or services. In contrast, as proposed by Gold et al. (2001 p. 186), the knowledge-based firm will 'leverage existing knowledge and create new knowledge that favourably positions them in their chosen markets.'

The importance of exploiting knowledge in today's more uncertain and turbulent world is supported by Kochan's (2006) research. He concluded from his assessment of factors impacting the performance of firms that the most successful organisations are those that exploit new knowledge. These organisations achieve higher levels of productivity, service quality and profitability than their counterparts who continue to base their strategy on the 'twentieth-century tradition' of seeking ways of reducing costs as the basis for remaining in existence. Zack (2003) has proposed that there are three key aims associated with the exploitation of knowledge. These are to ensure that (i) knowledge from one part of a company is made available across the entire organisation, (ii) knowledge is shared between individuals within work teams in order to benefit from past experience and (iii) new knowledge provides the basis for exploiting new opportunities.

An additional aim that might be added is to ensure the correct and most important forms of new knowledge are being exploited. The adverse outcome of failing to achieve this latter aim is illustrated by the demise of the US instant camera company Polaroid Corporation. The founder of the company, Edward Land, had embedded a philosophy into the firm that new knowledge generated through research was the most effective strategy for sustaining organisational performance. As a consequence the company had a long-established heritage of re-investing a high proportion of profits back into research to ensure the company remained ahead of competition. Unfortunately the company failed to invest sufficient funds in acquiring an in-depth understanding of digital imaging. Hence by the time the company eventually launched their own digital camera, other companies were already well entrenched in this new market.

BIG BLUE GOES BACK TO KNOWLEDGE

Case Aims: To illustrate the importance of focusing upon knowledge in order to remain successful.

Tom Watson Snr.'s entry in the world of data processing was via being a salesman for NCR, which sold mechanical cash registers. He joined the Computing Tabulating Recording Corporation (CTR) in 1914. When Watson became general manager, annual sales were $9 million. In 1924, he renamed the company International Business Machines, which subsequently became known as IBM. He went on to build a multi-national business based upon the company's expertise in punch card machines, which were mechanical devices for delivering faster data processing capability. Although achieving a low profit margin on sales, the company continued to expand during World War II through supplying large quantities of data processing equipment to the military.

Tom Watson Jnr. rejoined the company after the war and became president of IBM in 1952. Up until this time IBM's primary commitment was to marketing electro-mechanical punch card systems. Tom Watson Snr. had repeatedly rejected electronic computers as being overpriced and unreliable. Hence the company's involvement in computers was restricted to one-of-a-kind projects such as the IBM SSEC. Tom Watson Jr. took the company in a new direction by exploiting the opportunities he could see in the new world of mainframe computers. Although many within IBM felt that the company should focus on only building a limited number of customised computers for clients such as the US government, Tom Watson Jnr.'s strategy of entering the mainstream market for computers permitted revenue to rise from $214.9 million in 1950 to $734.3 million in 1956.

(continued)

BIG BLUE GOES BACK TO KNOWLEDGE (continued)

As the global leader and the largest computer company in the world, IBM became known as "Big Blue." Unfortunately accompanying phenomenal business growth was a shift towards becoming a highly bureaucratic organisation with numerous layers of management and an increasingly rules-driven internal culture. Commenting in an interview following his retirement, Lew Gerstner, who steered the company back to profitability in the late 1990s, described the IBM he had joined as 'an isolated ecosystem that spawned some exotic life forms that were to be found nowhere else.' He also observed that 'it was amazing to me when I arrived that we could go for hours in meetings and nobody would talk about a customer. I'd never been to a meeting before where we didn't start with a customer' (Hall 2002, p. 7). Innovation and the exploitation of knowledge became sidelined with senior managers believing the company's success was down to being perceived by B2B customers as the leading manufacturer of computer hardware. The downside risks of such rigid thinking had already been exemplified by events such as the company entirely missing the opportunities offered by the microcomputer, minicomputers and worse still, the advent of the PC. Even after the company woke up to the need to avoid failure in the PC industry, it made the major error of agreeing to Bill Gates' proposal that the company should be granted a license for Microsoft's MS:DOS operating system instead of insisting upon outright purchase of the rights to the technology. As the PC industry continued to expand, although IBM machines were perceived as adequate, the company soon encountered competition from IBM clones from companies such as Compaq, which offered IBM performance but at half the price (Anon. 1998).

By the early 1990s it was apparent that Big Blue was in deep trouble and this was reflected by the stock falling to the low $20s in 1993. In what appeared to be an act of desperation the company hired Lew Gernstner. He was a highly successful business leader but somebody who had never previously worked in the computer industry. His initial action was to ignore issues such as vision, innovation or strategy and instead immediately sought a way of resolving the problem that the business was hemorrhaging cash (Anon. 1993). Just four months into the job, Gernstner announced that the company would incur a $8.9 billion restructuring charge in the second quarter of 1993 and in addition to 25,000 already planned job cuts, a further 115,000 employees will be made redundant in 1994. This move would result in IBM's workforce of 225,000 individuals becoming almost 50 percent smaller than in the 1980s.

Initially Gernster made few revisions in IBM's marketing strategy, continuing to permit the company to remain focused on selling mainframes and computer peripherals and attempting to achieve a higher share on the world PC market. Gerstner's leadership style has always been that of listening, most especially to customers and to employees lower down in an organisation. Over time it became apparent to Gernstner that as well as being the CEO of a rigid, rules-driven organisation, the company also thought that its mission was to sell computers.

(continued)

BIG BLUE GOES BACK TO KNOWLEDGE (continued)

In the case of the PC operation, he described these activities as a group focused on 'shifting boxes' (James 1999). His solution was to announce that the company needed to 'return to its roots,' which in his view was a vision based upon providing clients with the solutions involving the management, analysis and exploitation of complex data. He also adopted a somewhat unusual perspective that instead of size being a weakness, IBM'S size and scope actually made it uniquely able to provide customers with solutions which were unavailable from smaller organisations in the IT industry. His new vision was aimed at returning IBM to being a knowledge-based organisation. To support this move, the company expanded into areas such as software development and placed emphasis on marketing data management solutions, not computer equipment. The success of Gernster's decision is reflected by the fact that in only five years following his appointment, the company stock price returned to almost $200.

KNOWLEDGE-BASED ORGANISATIONS

Gold et al. (2001) have proposed that for an organisation to successfully base its future on being a knowledge-based organisation, there is a need for three key infrastructure components—namely, technological, structural and cultural. Technology ensures that new information from within the organisation and from external market systems can provide the basis for constructing 'knowledge maps.' These maps permit the tracking of new knowledge and the identification of emerging new opportunities. Organisations in recent years have been greatly assisted in this activity by advances in technology such as data mining, statistical modelling and network analysis software.

In terms of structure Sanchez and Mahoney (1996) have suggested that organisations need to move away from hierarchical structures and reform into a modular design which can increase flexibility and speed of response. This perspective is similar to that presented by Nonaka and Takeuchi (1995). They proposed the need for the formation of 'hypertext' organisations which are a blend of a formal organisational and self-organised, non-hierarchical entities. These authors also identified the need within organisations to understand the relative importance of 'tacit' versus 'explicit' knowledge in the effective management of innovation. Tacit knowledge is that which is stored in people's minds and can be accessed only through dialogue between employees. In contrast explicit knowledge exists in a formalised, stored form such as a written report or in a data file. This latter type of information is much more readily accessible than tacit knowledge.

Gold et al. believe that although structure is important, the more critical factor in a knowledge-based organisation is the existence of an effective culture. Their proposal is a culture that promotes collaboration and interaction with the emphasis being upon the exploitation of knowledge to optimise innovation. The view of Chaston (2004) is that in addition to these three infrastructure requirements, the organisation also requires systems that support knowledge acquisition, storage, access and scenario modelling.

To gain an understanding of the relative influence of technological versus structural components in the utilisation of knowledge, Gold et al. undertook a survey of senior managers in major US corporations. One of the reasons they were prompted to undertake the study was their perception that possibly the consultancy and IT industries were placing excessive emphasis on the importance of firms investing in the creation of computer-based knowledge management systems without ensuring the concurrent existence of appropriate organisational structures. The researchers analysed acquired data using the LISREL technique, which permits the building of a predictive model for assessing the relative importance of different factors. They concluded that emphasis on technology tended to lead to organisations becoming excessively concerned about the storage and accessing of knowledge. As a consequence organisations may give unnecessary priority to the data management issues. When key knowledge was in a tacit form, firms need to ensure that structures exist which permit easy data access, which in turn leads to high levels of employee dialogue. Even for those firms in which data are in an explicit form, the research suggests structure is more critical than technology. The study also suggests that tacit information is the most critical form of knowledge in terms of supporting innovation. Thus firms which worry less about technology and instead focus on effective structures and tacit knowledge management systems are more likely to achieve the objective of new knowledge being used to enhance the organisation's added value activities.

In their study of the strategies most appropriate for the survival of firms in an increasingly competitive and turbulent world, Murray and Greenes (2006, p. 232) concluded that the exploitation of knowledge was the most important organisational core competence. In their view it is only through new knowledge that organisations can continue to learn, adapt and if necessary transform themselves into totally different entities in order to sustain their long-term performance. The authors have proposed that this type of organisation should be considered as the 'enterprise of the future' (or EOF). Their definition of an EOF is an entity which is a 'self-organising adaptive learning network in which employees seek to fulfil individual and organisational objectives.'

Murray and Greenes have proposed that underpinning the creation and operation of an EOF are the four pillars of leadership, organisation, technology and learning. In relation to leadership the aim is to guide the organisation to rapidly sense, anticipate and respond to changes in the external environment. Leaders must also have the capability to rapidly formulate new strategies in the face of fundamental environmental change. To achieve this outcome, leaders need to have a detailed understanding of their organisation's strengths and weaknesses and recognise the critical role of leveraging the knowledge assets which exist within the organisation.

In terms of the organisation pillar, the authors echo the views of others concerning the importance of moving away from traditional hierarchical structures and placing greater reliance on informal social networks existing within the firm, as this can ensure rapid access to new knowledge. This structural change is even more critical in those organisations where much of the key new knowledge exists in a tacit form. To optimise knowledge transfer, they propose organisations should encourage employees to participate in social networks outside the organisation, such as those which exist within the supply chain of which the organisation is a member.

Although technology is consider a critical pillar, Murray and Greenes concluded that in many cases an organisation's technological infrastructure is built on outmoded, data-centric models. Knowledge may exist but it is often locked away in numerous different databases dispersed throughout the organisation. As a consequence accessing and integrating knowledge are extremely difficult tasks. The outcome is existing systems create a barrier to rapidly developing solutions to newly identified problems which may suddenly confront the organisation. In their view some of the key issues associated with the effective exploitation of technology to assist knowledge management activities include:

1. Technology should exist to enable and enhance problem solving.
2. Utilised technology should have the capability to rapidly handle large volumes of unstructured data accompanied by support tools which permit exploitation of these data sets to rapidly reach decisions.
3. A balance should be achieved between data localisation and centralisation such that all systems are seamlessly connected in order to offer users a totally informed, rapid response system.

The pillars of leadership, organisation and technology are critical in relation to supporting the fourth critical pillar of learning occurring within the organisation. The key features of this learning environment include (Haeckel 1999):

1. All employees are capable of rapid learning in order to respond to changing situations.
2. The focus of learning is upon optimising innovation across the entire organisation.
3. Learning activities lead to the creation, flow and retention of new knowledge both inside the organisation and within the external learning networks of which the organisation is a member.
4. The working environment is conducive to stimulating and supporting active learning among all employees.

RETHINKING RESPONSE

Case aims: To illustrate how adopting a different approach can counter the activities of more innovation-orientated competitors based in emerging economies.

Incumbent global leaders are facing intense competition on a scale never before experienced. Emergent nation companies are now also using knowledge to identify and exploit opportunities. Chinese firms, which used to be reliant upon low-cost labour, are now drawing upon knowledge management to increase efficiency, offer customised products, manufacture a wider range of products and rapidly develop new products which replicate the features of next-generation products only recently launched by Western firms.

In assessing how Western firms can remain leaders in their respective markets, Sirkin at al. (2008) recommend that these organisations implement a number of actions. These include:

1. Think globally in seeking new knowledge from people inside the organisation across all markets where the organisation does business.
2. Seek new knowledge to support new approaches to innovation that does not involve long or extensive periods of development, testing and evaluation. Avoid recriminations over failure but instead focus upon learning from mistakes.
3. Create a culture of continuously seeking to improve intellectual assets while concurrently challenging every convention that currently determines the nature of operations in existing markets, serving customers and managing supply chains. Develop new external partnerships to support the process of challenging current operational conventions.

LEARNING ISSUES

Senge (1990) proposed that a clear relationship exists between poor organisational performance and the failure of organisations to learn from experience. Hamel and Prahalad (1993) have extended this perspective by proposing the learning process must be translated into the acquisition of new knowledge that can be used to upgrade those areas of competence which permit organisations to remain more effective than their competitors. They concluded that learning from understanding the nature of changes in market or customer behaviour is important in ensuring the successful ongoing implementation of new or revised strategic actions. These authors have concluded that market-orientated organisations are more likely to exhibit the behavioural characteristic of continually seeking to exploit new sources of knowledge.

Drawing upon concepts concerning alternative learning styles proposed by theorists such as Senge, Chaston (2004) proposed that non-innovative organisations tend to exhibit a 'single-loop' or lower-level learning style. The consequence is that virtually no new learning occurs because of a tendency by management to place reliance upon utilising existing knowledge in the problem-solution process. This style can be contrasted with 'double-loop' learning or 'higher-level' learning commonly encountered in more entrepreneurial organisations. This latter behaviour trait permits these entities to be more versatile, flexible and adaptive than single-loop learners. Double-loop learning is effective only if the activity results in understanding how to configure new sets of competences and also how these new competences can be acquired. This requirement has caused some authors to propose that where there is a dynamic capability to translate new knowledge management into new competences this should be classified as 'triple-loop' learning (Flood and Romm 1996).

Triple-loop learning relates directly to dynamic capability. It requires understanding of not just how to configure sets of competences, but also the way new competences can be acquired. The significant requirement for dynamic capability is to exploit new knowledge that can enhance long-term organisational performance. Nevertheless the preference for a specific learning style has no real benefit to the organisation unless appropriate internal structures, policies and processes exist to exploit the knowledge available to the organisation. To gain an understanding of the nature of learning systems in conventional versus entrepreneurial firms, Chaston et al. (1999) undertook a survey of knowledge management practices within UK manufacturing companies. This study revealed there are very distinctive differences between the learning systems used in conventional, conservative companies when compared to their entrepreneurial counterparts. The study provided the basis for proposing that the factors leading to the operation of an effective learning system permit the implementation of innovative, proactive strategic actions.

In relation to *knowledge sources*, conventional firms are biased towards drawing upon existing information from within their organisation. This contrasts with entrepreneurial firms, who are biased towards exploiting knowledge sources external to the organisation. Conventional firms usually seek ways of using existing knowledge to further upgrade internal organisational processes. Bias in entrepreneurial firms is towards using new knowledge to support ongoing development of products or customer services. On the issue of *documentation mode*, entrepreneurial firms adopt a somewhat informal approach to knowledge storage, whereas conventional firms tend to create a formalised, central record system to act as a repository of key information critical to the effective operation of the organisation's memory system. In the case of *dissemination mode* entrepreneurial firms seek to ensure that information is shared between all employees. In contrast, conventional firms appear to adopt a somewhat informal orientation, apparently assuming individuals will share knowledge with each other on an 'as needed' basis.

The *learning focus* of the conventional firms is orientated towards single-loop learning, whereas in the entrepreneurial manufacturing firms the focus is biased towards double-loop learning, seeking to draw in new knowledge as the basis for enhancing the effectiveness of their problem-solving activities. In relation to *value-chain focus*, conventional firms' attention is on activities associated with further improving the efficiencies of internal organisational processes. Entrepreneurial firms appear to be biased towards seeking to add value to those dimensions of the value chain concerned with offering enhanced value to customers. Management of *skills development* in entrepreneurial firms is centred upon improving the competencies of work teams. This is contrasted with the conventional firms, where training is directed towards upgrading the capabilities of individuals within the workforce.

SINGLE-LOOP LEARNERS

Case Aims: To illustrate how failing to utilise new knowledge can be a barrier to implementing successful strategies to sustain ongoing performance.

Early into the emergence of the modern market entertainment industry in the 20th century, America managed to dominate both the film and popular music sectors. Its strategic model was to build large organisations and then to use this quasi-monopoly power to gain control over their respective market distribution channels. In the case of the film industry, prior to World War II, Hollywood invested in film distributors and cinema chains across the world. The record industry's approach was to create a small stable of 'recording stars,' expend vast sums of money on promotion, influence radio stations to frequently feature their artists when broadcasting music and to build close commercial relationships with retail chains and music stores. These models served both industries extremely well until the advent of digital technology and the arrival of the Internet.

Hollywood rapidly appreciated that digital technology would lead to their audiences buying or renting videos and staying at home. The major studios could have sought to blunt this trend by refusing to permit their films to be converted to a video format. Instead, by applying double-loop learning, they recognised the need to participate in the digital revolution (Bhatia et al. 2003). Through contractual, collaborative and acquisition activity the studios became major players in the video, CD and DVD markets. Over time, in part to defeat film pirating, the studios shifted from a strategy of delaying digital releases until a film had been in cinemas for many months to a simultaneous release of a new film into different terrestrial and on-line distribution channels. In addition the major studios recognised that innovation and creativity can easily be stifled if there are only a few producers of a product. Hence over the last 20 years, the major studios have provided funds to independent film companies, directors and producers in return for the distribution rights to those films which they perceive have significant potential as mass appeal products.

(continued)

SINGLE-LOOP LEARNERS (continued)

In contrast, the music industry's response to change brought about by digital convergence was very different. Its primary focus has been to seek to retain control and to exhibit a preference for a single-loop thinking style (Edmondson 2008). This orientation was reflected in ongoing consolidation of the record industry's quasi-monopoly status through a series of M&As. By the beginning of the 21st century the major players in the industry had been reduced to just four. These were Universal Music Group (a merger of Polygram and MCA that owns Interscope, Motown and Island Def Jam), Sony BMG Music Entertainment (merger of Sony and BMG and owns Arista, RCA, Columbia, Zomba and Epic), EMI Group (owners of Capitol and Virgin) and Warner Music (owners of Atlantic and Elektra). Although there was some recognition of the reduced creativity within large, hierarchical organisations, the only real attempts to overcome this lack of innovation was to fund certain independent record producers to undertake projects such as recording lesser-known groups. In most cases, however, the strategy for innovation was to wait until a new group or singer managed to achieve a market following without having a major recording contract and then to recruit them to their label by outbidding the other recording studios.

The advent of the Internet and pop groups such as UK's Arctic Monkeys creating their own website to build links with fans and to promote their forthcoming first record should have demonstrated that this new technology was going to change the structure and nature of the music industry. Early indications of the Internet's capability to reduce the record industry's power were followed by a real 'body blow.' This was the launch of Napster, which allowed users to upload and download music files via the Internet at little or no cost (Channel 2004). The response of the record industry, via its trade association, the Recording Industry Association of America (RIAA), was to sue Napster on the grounds that the company was infringing the copyrights of the music industry and encouraging consumers to also ignore the copyright laws. The courts eventually found for the plaintiffs—namely, that Napster was in breach of the copyright laws. Having scored what appeared to be a complete victory in the Napster case, which resulted in Napster being shut down, the RIAA became confident that it was now able to stop any use of the Internet for downloading music without the permission of the relevant copyright holder. Hence the RIA next sought to obtain similar rulings for two more file-sharing websites, Grokster and Morpheus, which had appeared in the market (Randall 2004).

The courts examined the structure of the services at issue and recognised that the Grokster and Morpheus systems relied on non-centralised software, which meant the companies could not have actual knowledge of the files that people were sharing with each other. This was because these systems, unlike Napster, permitted users to search from one website visitor's computer to another until they found the file that they wish to download. The RIAA lost both cases. Unable to shut down the commercial file-sharing industry, the organisation has continued to pursue the difficult and image-damaging route of suing individual consumers who are downloading files from the Internet.

(continued)

SINGLE-LOOP LEARNERS (continued)

By retaining a single-loop orientation based upon preserving its existing business model, the music industry missed the opportunities available to revise its distribution strategies in a digital world and thereby retain a dominant control over the market. As a consequence it failed to learn from Hollywood, which having recognised the power conferred as the owners of creative materials, moved to gain control of newly emerging distribution channels. The outcome of the record firms' myopia and dependence on using the copyright laws to defend themselves resulted in new, more entrepreneurial players such as Apple with the iTunes and iPod products entering the music market and capturing a huge share of the available revenue.

3   Strategic Planning

The purpose of this chapter is to cover issues pertaining to:

1. Knowledge being the most important asset in Western organisations seeking to compete in increasingly volatile and turbulent markets.
2. The start point in planning future strategies is to undertake a complete assessment of the nature and quality of the organisation's knowledge assets.
3. Determining the relationship between knowledge assets and the value added capabilities of the organisation.
4. Utilising network analysis theory to determine the relationships between knowledge and value added outcomes within the organisation.
5. Assessment of knowledge and value added outcomes being enhanced by including the supply chains of which the organisation is a member.
6. Benefits in adopting a zero-based planning approach to provide a more realistic assessment of capabilities and future performance.
7. The conventional sequential linear strategic planning model may result in merely extrapolating past performance as the basis for defining future achievements.
8. Zero-based planning may be enhanced by adopting a more entrepreneurial approach to planning involving a 'spider's web' orientation.

KNOWLEDGE ASSETS

Recognition of the importance of new knowledge providing the basis for Western firms to sustain a competitive advantage over new competitors located in emerging economy nations is evidenced by the fact that expenditure on intellectual assets in the Organisation for Economic and Co-operative Development (OECD) area has grown faster than expenditure on tangible fixed assets in recent years (Tojo 2006). In 2002, total expenditure on research and development (R&D), software creation and higher education was larger than spending on machinery and equipment. The US Federal Reserve estimated that in the United States alone, corporations invest approximately $1 trillion annually in intangible assets associated with exploiting knowledge (Nakamura 2003). Research on the benefits of spending on intellectual assets indicates that these assets make a larger contribution to economic growth than funding the purchase of new machinery and equipment. One of the key benefits of R&D spending is an increase in productivity, with estimated gross rates of return on this type of spending ranging from 10 to 20 percent.

Tojo proposed that the creation of increased added value from intellectual assets is highly contingent on management capabilities within individual firms and the implementation of appropriate business strategies. The added value potential of many intellectual assets is highly skewed. A small number of patents, for example, can account for most of the total value of firms' patent portfolios. The role of management is to direct investment into areas of higher than average return and to develop internal processes that ensure these returns are realised. Well-managed firms which recognise the critical importance of new knowledge providing the basis for greater added value usually achiever higher productivity, profitability and sales growth than their counterparts which continue to focus on the acquisition of tangible assets or seeking growth via M&A activity.

Adams (2008) suggests that as knowledge becomes more important to organisations, new concepts are emerging to help managers deal with the unique challenges of leveraging and profiting from intangible knowledge assets. In her view knowledge actually is embedded in an organisation in the following different forms:

1. *Human capital*: People are the source of ideas and innovation. Their knowledge, competences and experience become part of the organisation once this is shared by the rest of the organisation.
2. *Structural capital*: Shared knowledge becomes internal structural capital. The highest form of structural capital is intellectual property (IP) such as patents.
3. *Relationship capital*: External knowledge links provide the basis for relationship capital. This type of capital exists within three categories: customer relationships, external network and branding.

In terms of understanding and being able to exploit knowledge, Adams proposes that management need to create an inventory of knowledge assets. She suggests assets include:

1. *Human capital*: Who are the key people? What are the experiences, knowledge and competences that they provide the organisation?
2. *Structural capital*: What are the key added value processes and to what degree are these constituted upon unique or superior knowledge?
3 *Relationship capital*: What are the key external knowledge relationships (e.g. suppliers, intermediaries, customers) and what is their relative importance in the provision of important knowledge?

RETURN TO PROFITABILITY THROUGH KNOWLEDGE

Case Aims: To illustrate how exploitation of knowledge can permit a long-established company to again become successful.

Despite Germany's global reputation for excellence in engineering and manufacturing, the country's largest heavy industry company, Siemens, has faced problems in recent years due to big infrastructure contracts going wrong and project overspends. An added burden between 2006 and 2008 was the company being found guilty of obtaining contracts by bribing officials and politicians. This resulted in Siemens being fined $1.6 billion and facing massive legal costs in attempting to defend itself over this matter (Anon. 2010a).

With senior executives tainted by the bribery affair, for the first time in the company's history Siemens appointed an outsider as the new CEO, Peter Loscher. He is an Austrian who has spent most of his life working in the pharmaceuticals industry. Loscher perceived that one of Siemens' fundamental problems was a lack of a competitive advantage that would permit the company to succeed against other heavy engineering companies based in countries such as China, which are able to exploit the benefits of significantly lower operating costs. His solution has been to focus on identifying market sectors where the company can exploit knowledge as the basis for rebuilding competitive advantage. Key areas selected for implementation of this strategy are the energy and transportation sectors, with specific focus on contracts involving investment in technically advanced infrastructure projects. The company is winning contracts even in very mature market sectors, such as building heavy turbines for power stations. Success in this latter case is due to Siemens' focus on exploiting new knowledge to create a new generation of turbines that offers customers significantly lower operating costs. This is because these turbines are more energy-efficient than products available from competition. The company has also taken the unusual step of offering capital financing assistance to customers linked to guarantees that claimed energy savings will be achieved.

The company has also been highly successful in the increasingly competitive global wind energy market. In this case the company has avoided head-to-head confrontations with the leading competitors. This has been achieved by exploiting new and existing knowledge to develop wind turbines that can be anchored off-shore where winds are stronger but operating conditions are more extreme.

Siemens in the past has been criticised for having an excessively diversified product line. This diversity is now providing the basis for offering a range of complementary products when bidding for 'green' power generation contracts. High-voltage direct current (HVDC) provides an example of the company exploiting product diversity and new knowledge to achieve market leadership. The appeal of this technology is it permits large amounts of electricity to be distributed using much thinner cables, thereby leading to much lower losses of energy during energy transmission across a country's power grids.

(continued)

RETURN TO PROFITABILITY THROUGH KNOWLEDGE (continued)

The company is also becoming more involved in the medical diagnostic market through both acquisitions and increased research spending. In recent years the company had been losing market share in key markets for x-ray machines where at one time it was a world leader. Although Siemens produces high-quality machines, prices had become uncompetitive. In recognition of the growing demand for more rugged and lower-cost machines for the healthcare industry in the developing world, the company has invested in new knowledge to provide the basis for developing products that are best suited for use in these nations. This strategy has involved relocating manufacturing of this new generation of x-ray machines inside key markets such as India and China. To support entry into new areas of medical technology, the company has purchased Dade Behring, a leading edge medical-diagnostics company, for $11.4 billion.

Another European firm which has exploited new knowledge in order to improve performance is Nokia, the Finnish telecommunications and mobile telephone company. Similar to many Finnish companies which have performed well in global markets, Nokia's heritage is based upon the investment in R&D to generate the new knowledge upon which to base the creation of new products. This philosophy permitted an early entry into the mobile phone market, and for a number of years the company enjoyed market leadership in this sector. Although until mid-2011 the company remained the highest-volume producer of mobile phones, in recent years, as the knowledge upon which mobile phone base technology has become more widely available, Nokia has been losing sales to Asian producers exploiting lower operating costs as the basis for supplying much cheaper products.

Finding ways of combating this threat have highlighted Nokia's apparent failure to sustain its investment in new technology to avoid losing market leadership. The benefits of investing in new knowledge are demonstrated by the success of Apple's iPhone. This is a more expensive product than the conventional mobile phone, but the product represents the application of new knowledge to evolve a multi-faceted mobile telecommunications device.

In September 2010, Nokia announced that the current CEO, Olli-Pekka Kallasvuo, had been replaced by Stephen Elsop. This individual was previously the head of Microsoft's business division and also worked for Adobe Systems. Elsop was closely involved in last year's negotiations to create a new software knowledge exchange alliance between Microsoft and Nokia. His appointment is perceived by the business press as Nokia's recognition that it needs to respond to an industry knowledge shift, with firms such as Apple and Google (producers of the Android phone operating system) demonstrating that smart phones represent the direction of future success within this sector (Ward 2010).

VALUE CONVERSION

Knowledge has real benefit only when converted into a tangible entity through which to generate added value for the organisation. In areas such as the provision of specialist consultancy or financial advisory services, new knowledge may offer almost immediate monetary gain due to an ability to offer new services to clients. For most organisations, however, the conversion of new knowledge into measurable financial benefit will usually be a much longer-term process. This is because of the long time lag between new knowledge creation and the production of a new product or installation of process capabilities coming on-stream (Allee 2008).

An in-depth assessment is usually necessary when seeking to determine how knowledge can provide the basis of a competitive advantage which can provide the basis for an organisation's long-term strategy. This is necessary in order to determine how the conversion of knowledge into a tangible form can enhance added value activities. In relation to this assessment there are three issues to be considered—namely, (i) adding value to inputs, (ii) adding value to outputs and (iii) determining whether other value conversion opportunities inside an organisation are being overlooked (Lev 2001). In relation to the capability to translate knowledge into competitive advantage, Adams and Lamont (2003) propose that two forms of capacity are required. Firstly is ownership of an 'absorptive capacity.' This involves recognising the value of new knowledge and applying this to the development of new products or services. The other trait is a 'transformative capacity,' which involves the processes of gathering, organising, assimilating and translating new knowledge into a form that provides the basis for supporting successful innovation.

In relation to understanding how knowledge is converted into outcomes that create additional added value, Nohria and Eccles (1992) have utilised social network analysis (SNA) and organisational network analysis (ONA). This methodology, although in use within the social sciences since the 1930s, has not been used in management research until relatively recently. Allee (2002) concluded that, although the approach provides powerful insights into knowledge exchange, it has the possible weakness that the methodology may result in excessive focus upon the exchange process without the analysis also encompassing the need for a link to ensure the aim of enhanced added value is achieved. In her view a more effective approach is to use value network analysis (VNA). This methodology is specifically designed to identify whether links exist between knowledge generation and achieving added value. Allee suggests that VNA permits the user to acquire understanding of value creating roles and exchange relationships both within and outside the organisation. The technique has the added benefit of providing a framework for the systematic analysis of all of the operational processes associated with value conversion inside the organisation.

From their review of the literature, Biem and Caswel (2008) concluded there are a number of different approaches for undertaking VNA analysis. These include the e3-value framework, the c3-value framework and Allee's (2002) relationship framework approach. A common feature of these different methodologies is that the process involves 'actors,' a 'value port,' a 'value object' and a 'value exchange.' The actors are economic independent entities who are contributors to the exchange process. Actors can be an individual or groups of individuals within an organisation or based in other entities external to the organisation. The value port is the connection point between actors through which knowledge exchange can occur. To be a value object, whatever is exchanged must have economic value to one or more of the participating actors. The nature of the value object is somewhat variable and can include items such as pure knowledge, a performed service or goods which offer some form of tangible benefit.

Biem and Caswel consider that the c3-value framework is merely an extension of e3 models but offers the added advantage of providing the basis for strategic analysis of the organisation. The entry point in the c3 framework is to utilise Barney's (1991) proposal that the RBV of the firm is based upon competitive advantage being achieved by ownership of strategic resources that are valuable, rare, inimitable and non-substitutable. This permits an analysis of strategy in relation to the three dimensions of customer, capabilities and competition. Particular emphasis is placed on ways of using knowledge to achieve a superior competitive advantage. The authors posit this approach is superior to Allee's framework, which focuses on participants, transactions, deliverables and exchanges. The analysis within Allee's framework is mostly visual, consisting of detecting patterns of exchanges between participants without necessarily providing the basis from which strategic planning processes can be evolved. Biem and Caswel suggest this potential drawback can be overcome by focusing upon the economics associated with the interactions in a knowledge exchange. Their perspective is the actor represents the legal entity endowed with the business intent and functional capability required to initiate actions that lead to added value. The value proposition is the benefits that the customer receives from the product or service supplied. This value proposition is contextual, dependent on the type of business and the nature of the market. It can take various forms, such as just-in-time delivery, enhanced convenience or customisation.

ASSESSING KNOWLEDGE CONTRIBUTION

Possibly the most widely utilised framework for determining the source of value added activities is Porter's (1980) value chain model. This model envisages the organisation as being engaged in five core activities—namely, inbound logistics, operations, marketing, outbound logistics and customer services. Underlying these core processes are support contributions involving technology, procurement, general management, finance and administration, and HRM. The scale of the added value outcomes is determined by the key knowledge competences which exist within the organisation. The fundamental role of knowledge when incorporated into the value chain model is that it can provide useful insights concerning the macro view of the organisation's exchange activities. This is achieved by considering how knowledge can enhance inter-organisational processes, from raw materials acquisition through to the delivery of outputs to customers (Biem and Caswel 2008).

Although Allee's (2008) technique for mapping the relationship between knowledge and value added processes was originally proposed in relation to inter-organisational activities, the same concepts are applicable to constructing internal organisational maps. In developing such maps the following issues will require assessment:

1. Is there a coherent logic in the way knowledge flows through the organisation leading to enhanced added value?
2. Do the organisational systems ensure there is an effective interchange of knowledge such that employees are receiving appropriate support when seeking to exploit new knowledge while fulfilling their assigned responsibilities?
3. Are there forms of knowledge exchange which are more dominant than others and do these dominant exchanges result in optimisation of added value activities?
4. Are there weak or ineffective internal organisational links that are reducing the benefits associated with knowledge exchange?
5. What patterns of knowledge exchange ensure implementation of strategic actions?
6. Is knowledge exchange supportive of ensuring an adequate level of innovation and creativity inside the organisation?
7. What are the key roles of staff involved in knowledge exchange and are these enhancing the scale of added value achievements?
8. Are there opportunities for leveraging knowledge exchange to further enhance added value outcomes?
9. What are the immediate and visible outcomes from knowledge exchange activities?
10. What are the resource demands created by the provision of new knowledge in different areas of the organisation?
11. How could changes in processes and policies contribute to increasing the benefits achieved from knowledge exchange activities?
12. What are the critical areas of knowledge exchange which should receive priority in terms of allocating scarce resources?

Recognition of the benefits of enhancing the performance of firms within a supply chain through a full and open interchange of knowledge can help organisations acquire greater understanding of how to evolve new strategies more capable of meeting customer needs. This outcome is especially important in more rapidly evolving or changing markets. Knowledge acquisition across entire supply chains can act as a catalyst leading a fundamental rethink about the most appropriate future strategy for optimising customer satisfaction. To illustrate the benefits of this approach, Andrews and Hahn (1998) point to the examples of Nike and Xerox, which have changed their roles from traditional manufacturing companies to become, respectively, brand-orientated and service-based companies.

The advent of the Internet and on-line purchasing has acted as another catalyst in relation to exploiting new knowledge from external sources to enhance the strategic planning process. On-line selling activities by a company or by a partner member within the supply chain has resulted in a huge increase in information flow, which, by being available on a real-time basis, can help planners obtain faster and more immediate indications of potential changes in customer needs. Andrews and Hahn have described this process of exploiting real-time data from various points along a supply chain as value web management (VWM).

VWM requires the creation of more sophisticated data acquisition, storage and analysis systems in order to make sense of the huge volume of data being generated by the operation of on-line supply chains. The benefit is that by continuously retrieving and sharing, acquired information can be translated into new knowledge that permits the evolution of strategies to help organisations more rapidly respond to volatile and turbulent external environments. Recognition of the opportunities offered by on-line transactions to generate new knowledge in real time has led to some software development companies developing new products which are collectively being labelled as customer requirements planning (CRP) systems.

LESSONS FROM KNOWLEDGE SHARING

Case Aims: To illustrate how a large multi-site organisation can ensure effective knowledge exchange.

Proctor & Gamble is one of the world's most successful branded goods companies. The firm has sought to sustain market leadership through the utilisation of knowledge as the basis for supporting product improvements and the development of new products. As a global corporation, one of the essential elements of using knowledge to enhance added value activities is to ensure that knowledge exchange occurs between the company's 8,000 research staff, 40 percent of whom work outside of North America. To achieve this goal, P&G has established a 'connect and develop' strategy based around a corporate intranet and 'smart' reporting systems for knowledge sharing, communities of practice, supporting technology entrepreneurs and exploiting joint venture projects (Sakkab 2002).

(continued)

LESSONS FROM KNOWLEDGE SHARING (continued)

P&G's intranet website is named 'InnovationNet.' Through using this system researchers can trade information and make connections across the entire company. The system has a user audience of 18,000 innovators across R&D, engineering, market research, purchasing, and patent divisions, hosts 600 websites for global project teams and 20 communities of practice teams. InnovationNet has been upgraded to include 'Smart Learning Reports.' These allow researchers to capture business-building insights from each other's experimental work, which are typically posted in the form of monthly on-line reports. Staff can now mine the insights contained within these reports via standard search engines and text analysis software that identify potential concepts of interest in assisting their own project development activities. The Smart Learning Reports system operates on a 24/7 basis, providing access to knowledge covering individual researchers' interests, identifying 'virtual neighbours' with similar interests and providing an automated e-mailing system for distributing relevant reports to all interested parties.

A critical learning experience for P&G is that despite the availability of today's electronic communications technologies, the barriers to effective knowledge exchange and exploitation remain substantial. This has led to these conclusions:

1. Both the owner of relevant knowledge and the individual searching for a solution must be proactive and persistent in their mutual search for connections.
2. Non-obvious connections require more energy to establish than obvious connections.
3. Non-obvious connections occur more easily where there is a large community of participants involved.
4. Connections in general, and less obvious ones in particular, occur more frequently when the language of 'what's needed' and 'what's possible' becomes more universal. This conclusion is based upon the fact that when two highly experienced scientists from the same field talk to each other their technical language can become a barrier to creating new connections outside their field.

ZERO-BASED PLANNING

One of the potential obstacles with the conventional strategic linear planning model described in many management texts is the tendency for the process to direct management attention towards analysing the organisation's past activities. This can result in decisions being based on extrapolating current internal process activities on the assumption these provide the basis for sustaining future performance. This approach was described by Wetherbe and Montanari (1981) as 'traditional incremental budgeting' (TIB). Concerns exist that the approach does not generate a sufficiently insightful analysis. As a consequence organisations may rely on perpetuating existing strategies unless there is a very dramatic change in environmental conditions which forces a fundamental rethink about future operations.

Criticisms of the TIB philosophy led to the emergence of zero-based budgeting (ZBB). The initial form of the concept centred upon accurately determining the real actual financial expenditure requirements of the organisation instead of merely assuming that future budgets could be based upon current spending, adjusted for influence such as market growth, investment plans or inflation (Pyhrr 1973). Emphasis on the financial planning aspects of ZBB caused the technique to be perceived as especially effective in public sector organisations. This is because planning in these organisations is often driven by expectations of next year's financial budget being closely related to the current year's actual expenditure.

Dirsmith and Jablonsky (1979) proposed that ZBB could be extended beyond financial forecasting and provide the basis for a complete re-examination of organisational strategy. Their proposal was that by undertaking an evaluation of the fundamental validity of sustaining an existing strategy this permits both qualitative and quantitative assessments of the ongoing validity of prevailing organisational beliefs and values. Observation of real-world application of ZBB to strategic planning in organisations revealed the drawback that many managers tend to prefer specific, well-defined rich data sets which can provide the basis for justifying conclusions. Dirsmith and Jablonsky, by observing effective application of ZBB in companies such as Texas Instruments, concluded that to overcome this behaviour trait there was a need to adopt a 'helicopter perspective.' This approach involves observing the company from the outside, often by obtaining third-party perspectives from sources such as customers and suppliers, as the basis for defining perspectives which can identify the most appropriate response to future fundamental changes in the external environment. Dirsmith and Jablonsky concluded the approach will be effective, however, only if the organisational culture is orientated towards innovation, creativity and a preparedness to be highly adaptive in the face of environmental change.

By the early 1990s, ZBB had fallen out of favour in most organisations and ceased to receive any significant coverage in academic texts on business planning. This was due in part to the difficulties associated with ensuring managers were adopting a helicopter perspective. Additionally other theories such as the resource-based view (RBV) of the firm were seen as being more effective. The decline in the appeal of the concept led to ZBB becoming perceived merely as a useful tool for re-assessing current operations in terms of making changes in organisational structure or internal processes in the face of minor performance problems. Ewaldz (1990), for example, proposed ZBB was an effective technique for creating leaner firms during a recession. In applying the technique he proposed it could assist actions such as identifying marginal products that should be discontinued, deciding actions about withdrawing support to smaller, non-profitable customers and implementing actions to protect cash flow.

The demise of the ZBB is somewhat unfortunate because the basic principles are useful when seeking solutions for sustaining future performance by exploiting a unique, knowledge-based competitive advantage. This is because the start point in defining and determining how to utilise new knowledge requires that consideration of other aspects of the organisation's activities should be put to one side. By temporarily sidelining the question of 'where are we now?' this permits issues such as tangible assets, channels of distribution and supply chains being seen as relevant only after a decision has been made concerning how unique knowledge provides the basis upon which to base future strategies and plans (Chaston 2004).

NON-LINEAR ZERO-BASED PLANNING

In terms of adopting a conventional linear planning approach when defining strategy through utilisation of a zero-based approach, as summarised in Figure 3.1, the organisation will need to decide which areas of knowledge are a key strategic resource, what are the knowledge capabilities of competitors and how might key sectoral knowledge requirements undergo change in the future. This analysis permits identification of the gap which may exist between what an organisation currently knows and what knowledge will be needed in the future. Knowledge gap identification provides the basis for a strengths, weaknesses, opportunities and threats (SWOT) analysis.

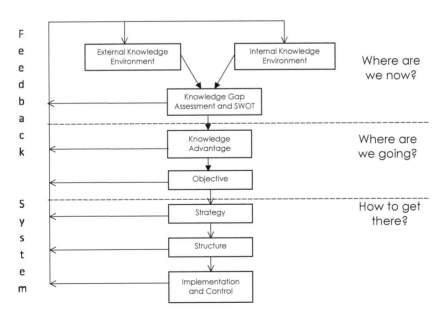

Figure 3.1 Sequential zero-based strategy planning model.

An understanding of existing gaps between the knowledge capabilities of the organisation and competitors provides the basis defining external opportunities and threats and the organisation's internal strengths and weaknesses. Upon completion the SWOT provides the basis guiding identification of the organisation's future objectives(s) and strategy in relation to exploiting knowledge as the basis for sustaining a long-term competitive advantage. Only once this key decision has been reached should any consideration be given to issues such as organisational structure, investment in tangible assets and internal processes most suited to marketing the organisation's products or services (Zack 2003).

An area of strategic management theory where there have been differences in opinion is the effectiveness of linear strategic planning process models. A key factor influencing this debate is some researchers, when seeking to validate the effectiveness and applicability of the linear, sequential strategic planning model of the type shown in Figure 3.1, have encountered real-world management practices that are often at variance with espoused theories.

One the most vocal critics of the linear sequential process model is the Canadian academic Professor Henry Mintzberg. In reviewing the different typologies of strategic planning which are presented in the academic literature, he described the linear sequential planning process as belonging to the 'Design School' approach to management (Mintzberg 1990). Two other typologies which he feels share the same philosophy of using detailed analysis leading to the prescriptive definition of an optimal strategic solution are the 'Planning School' and the 'Positioning School.'

Mintzberg believes that validation of management theories should always involve an assessment of the degree to which a concept provides real-world organisations with effective decision tools. He concluded that in many organisations, strategy actually evolves gradually over time as managers make sense of what influences performance and acquire a deeper understanding of the factors influencing success. Mintzberg's (1999) typology for this type of strategic behaviour is the 'Learning School.' He believes the typology shares a number of common traits with other views on strategic process management, such as the 'Power School,' the 'Cultural School' and the 'Environmental School.' In comparing these approaches with the Design School philosophy, he feels these all validate the perspective that strategies emerge through experience and cannot be defined on an *a priori* basis through the analysis of prior trading activities.

Mintzberg's fundamental concern with the Design School is the specification of a deliberate, detailed strategy cannot be achieved with any real degree of absolute certainty in today's increasingly uncertain and turbulent world. The reaction by some academics has been to question the validity of Mintzberg's viewpoint. Ansoff (1991) posited that a drawback of the Learning School and other related typologies is their approach is essentially descriptive. This means the manager is not offered any guidance about how to acquire a quantitative understanding of the external environment confronting the organisation. He also rejects Mintzberg's view that Design School models are static. In Ansoff's opinion this approach to strategic modelling has evolved over time and is able to accommodate the influence on business performance of increasingly uncertain futures.

The debate over the validity of prescriptive versus descriptive management models can be extremely confusing for both students and management practioners seeking guidance upon the most effective process model through which to develop a strategic plan. Ultimately the choice is down to the individual. The majority of students and management practioners in the Western world tend to be rational, logical thinkers who prefer to reach a conclusion based upon quantitative analysis of the variables impacting organisational performance. As a consequence these individuals, despite articulated criticisms of process weakness, still tend to favour systems which are reflective of the Design School approach to strategy formulation. Hence these individuals may be more comfortable utilising the version of the model shown in Figure 3.1. One justification for the ongoing validity of the approach has been provided by Liedtka (2000, p. 29) who suggested that:

> Design offers a different approach and would suggest processes that are more widely participative, more dialogue-based, issue driven, conflict-using rather than conflict avoiding, all aimed at invention and learning, rather than control . . . Finally and perhaps most importantly, we should recognize that good designs succeed by persuading, and great designs by inspiring.

One of the causes of Mintzberg's reconsideration of the relevance of linear planning models was his research on the behaviour of entrepreneurial organisations. This caused him to conclude that the leaders in these organisations tend to adopt a less structured approach when considering issues which they perceive as critical to reaching an appropriate strategic decision (Mintzberg and Waters 1982). Other researchers such as Kets de Vries (1990) have reach similar conclusions—namely, that entrepreneurial organisations tend not to engage in formalised, long-term planning using formal, logical sequential models of business process.

In view of the contradictory evidence concerning the benefits of formalised planning in entrepreneurial firms, possibly the preferred option is to accept a contingency approach—namely, for certain firms in certain industries managed by certain individuals facing certain circumstances, the use of a formalised, strategic plan will contribute towards improving business performance. It also appears reasonable to conclude that individuals engaged in managing an entrepreneurially orientated business in a complex and changing environment may find that the business planning process is not an advantageous method through which to reach key business decisions.

Beaver (2007, p. 18) presented a very thoughtful review about the issues associated with the debate about the use of strategic planning in entrepreneurial firms and the advantages this may confer. In presenting his conclusions he made the following observation that:

> It is easy to state the obvious—that thinking and managing strategically is an essential pre-requisite of business success and superior performance for all firms, whatever their size, sector or complexion. To do so is to court naïveté and ignore the role and meaning of strategy and its effect on enterprise prosperity. This is not to deny the value and importance of corporate strategy and business planning but rather to appreciate the complexity of the subject matter and its relationship with organisational achievement in the face of possible difficulties in the operating environment.

Where the entrepreneurial organisation does engage in some form of strategic planning, the process utilised will probably rarely mirror that shown in Figure 3.1. Instead entrepreneurial organisations tend to exhibit a wide range of different approaches (Chaston 2009). A common trait which exists among entrepreneurs is variation in their preferred entry point into the planning process and the degree to which the components in the conventional sequential process are actually analysed as the basis for selecting future actions. As shown in Figure 3.2, one way to summarise this situation is to consider an alternative model in which zero-based strategy planning process is seen as somewhat analogous to a spider's web. At the centre is the major issue of most concern—namely, determining future use of knowledge to achieve competitive advantage. In deciding whether future objectives are both feasible and realistic, different organisations will opt for reviewing few, some or all of the key topics summarised in Figure 3.2. Furthermore one can also expect significant variation in the order in which entrepreneurs will review these variables.

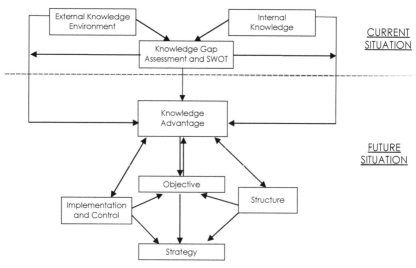

Figure 3.2   Alternative approach to zero-based strategy planning.

KNOWLEDGE-BASED STRATEGIC RECOVERY

Case Aims: To demonstrate how knowledge can be exploited to deliver a strategy based upon superior quality even in a mature service sector industry.

There is a tendency for knowledge management theory to assume knowledge exploitation is most effective in knowledge-intensive industries. As a consequence there is the risk that managers in more mature industrial sectors may perceive the introduction of new knowledge as less relevant as an aspect of the strategic planning process.

An example of how knowledge management can benefit a firm in a mature sector is provided by Fortune Motors in Taiwan. In Taiwan one of the most highly competitive sectors is the car servicing and repair industry. Fortune Motors firm has over 3,500 employees, and is one of the largest car dealership networks in Taiwan, with about 90 franchises nationwide and approximately 1 million customers. In 2002 the senior management recognised there was a growing problem with sustaining long-term customer loyalty. This was creating a barrier to the company strategy of delivering maximum lifelong value to customers. Although Fortune had abundant experience in the maintenance and repair services business, implementation of an integrated service process was not being achieved. This was due to diseconomies of resource usage and internal inefficiencies within the operational process. Another factor was the uneven quality of work by technicians due to the fact that technicians were responsible for overall maintenance rather than a specific part of the maintenance job. Furthermore the company had not established any standard policies and procedures which would permit junior technicians to develop higher-level skills. As a consequence Fortune Motors was encountering a high-rework level in all of its outlets (Shang et al. 2009).

In an attempt to overcome these problems, in 2003 the company established a service innovation strategy based upon the exploitation of new knowledge. This new approach was entitled the eCare system. This system is based upon the three processes of knowledge acquisition, integration and transformation. To gain a detailed understanding of the process problems confronting the company, an integrated database was created which contained customer profiles, car maintenance and repair records and data on the skill levels of technicians in all of the franchises. These data provided the basis for generating new knowledge that permitted identification of patterns to match customer service demands with available employee skills. These data also revealed that a single technician could not carry out all repair processes on an entire car and achieve a high-quality outcome. This new understanding led to a restructuring of organisational processes whereby maintenance specialties were matched with different skill levels and distributed across all service centres. Different tasks in the maintenance and repair processes were handled by technicians who had appropriate specialist capabilities. Fortune Motors generated new knowledge concerning all of the employee capabilities within the organisation. This provided the basis for the co-ordination of different skills to support enhancement of service quality and more accurately predict the time required to complete a specific service task.

(continued)

KNOWLEDGE-BASED STRATEGIC RECOVERY (continued)

In order to offer customers the most professional services and fault diagnoses, Fortune exploited knowledge generated from analysing cases of both employee successes and failures. The company used this new understanding to expand and deepen internal knowledge of how to optimise customer satisfaction. This was accompanied by focusing upon building stronger customer relationships as the basis for acquiring greater understanding of how best to deliver customer satisfaction. Accumulated internal knowledge and understanding of customer needs were used to create a learning platform for achieving superior service provision relative to competition.

The next stage in achieving strategic aims was to enhance the process provision system by creating a differentiated service system. This involved classifying customer service requirements into the provision of professional or convenience services. The start point in this new service delivery system is that where a car problem is diagnosed as severely damaged, the central shops are then responsible for repairing the vehicle. The central shops are equipped with the most up-to-date technology, equipment and employees who have a high-level car maintenance certificate. When a car needs just a minor repair or maintenance, the vehicle is assigned to the firm's small or medium-sized satellite shops. These small and medium-sized shops have no expensive equipment but are able to rapidly and cost-effectively undertake simple maintenance services. The company's eCare system utilises knowledge acquired to integrate and coordinate overall operational flows, product flows, customer knowledge flows and professional knowledge flows from all of the organisation's outlets. The system is specifically designed to ensure ongoing sharing and transfer of new knowledge.

Implementation of the eCare system created three benefits. Firstly, customer satisfaction was increased because customer return rates rose from 85 to 90 percent. Secondly, operational efficiency was increased as evidenced by workload productivity rising from 232,000 to 260,000 vehicles per month. Thirdly corporate capability was increased because the utilisation of outlet capacity reached 85 percent and labour hour utilisation rose to 95 percent. These achievements, coupled with effective management systems for generating additional knowledge, significantly upgraded Fortune's competitiveness in Taiwan's automobile market.

4 Assessing External Environments

The purpose of this chapter is to cover issues pertaining to:

1. Determining the leading sources of productivity within supply chains.
2. Factors influencing the relative productivity of nations.
3. The issue of supply chain dominance and the benefits this confers on organisations.
4. The increasing use of collaboration in place of traditional transactional, often adversarial, organisational relationships.
5. The risks of organisational collaboration in relation to how this can lead to a loss of key knowledge critical to the organisation's ongoing success.
6. Alternative approaches to acquiring new knowledge without reliance upon collaboration.

VALUE CHAINS

In terms of understanding the external environment and determining which organisations are achieving the highest added value within a market system, one approach is to extend the Porterian value chain model to encompass other members of the supply chain of which the organisation is a component element (Fisher 1997). As noted by Quinn (1993, p. 15), 'companies that take their value chains apart can determine what functions they do best and concentrate their resources on those parts of the chain.' The typical members of a value chain may include suppliers, competition and intermediaries. The existence of intermediaries is more prevalent in B2C markets where distributors and retailers assume the role of contributing to outbound logistics by purchasing goods from various companies and undertaking distribution and merchandising roles. In contrast, in many B2B markets, where the percentage of total sales to each individual end user is high or the product is extremely bulky, most companies will distribute goods direct to the final customer without the involvement of intermediaries.

In the private sector an assessment of the relative added value activities of supply chain members is usually based upon profitability. Given there is typically size variation between organisations, one approach for achieving a standardised measurement of added value is to examine relative productivity. This is calculated by dividing total profits by the number of employees. Examination of added value within the public sector is complicated by the lack of a profit generation role. In these cases some other form of assessment will have to be made. This can be based on dividing total costs by the number of employees or by dividing the total level of service provision by the number of employees, calculating a standardised output per organisation.

There are very few supply chains in which all of the members achieve the same level of productivity. This reflects the fact that within such systems, there are the following sources of advantage that will permit some organisations to achieve a higher than average profit per employee (Dobson 2005; Watson 2001):

1. *Scale power*: Larger organisations usually enjoy economies of scale in relation to factors such as (a) the size of purchases ensuring suppliers offer price discounts or (b) ownership of a large manufacturing facility permits the organisation to exploit operating efficiencies not available to its smaller competitors.

2. *Position power*: In some supply chains a small number of organisations are able to control the flow of goods through the system by refusing to do business with suppliers who do not accept these organisations' procurement demands. A common example of this situation occurs in consumer goods markets in those cases where there are only 3–4 major supermarket chains who dominate the sale of grocery products within a country.

3. *Supplier power*: In some supply chains a key input resource may be available from only a small number of suppliers. Under these circumstances these suppliers are able to limit the availability of their output as the basis for achieving their desired price.

4. *Knowledge power*: In some supply chains there may be a limited source of key knowledge that is required by other supply chain members in order to deliver their product or service. This will permit the holders of important knowledge to demand a high price in return for permitting the supply chain to access this knowledge. Examples of this situation can be the service sector (e.g. merchant bankers managing their clients' M&A activities) or contained within the goods supplied to the market (e.g. a customised, highly advanced computer system).

Macro-environmental factors exist which should also be evaluated. This is because these factors may influence future value added activities of one or more members of the supply chain. During an economic upturn, for example, end user expenditure tends to increase and customers are more likely to seek new, more innovative products or services. Hence during an upturn organisations will need to determine whether there is a greater opportunity to sell new products or services and whether this opportunity can be made more rapidly available by sharing proprietary knowledge with other supply chain members.

Within the macro-environment one of the most important factors influencing future added value performance is technology. Under those circumstances where a significant technology shift is likely to occur, then firms will need to decide whether the most effective response is to focus on acquiring total ownership of the technology or to enter into alliances that permit knowledge sharing. This latter scenario is evidenced by the action of Western car companies seeking to respond to the success of Toyota's hybrid vehicle, the Prius. Having recognised the threat that the new technology represents, the major Western car manufacturers have entered into collaborative agreements with research institutes and component suppliers in order to more rapidly acquire knowledge concerning the development and production of electrically powered vehicles. For example, Chrysler has formed an alliance with the American electric sports car firm Tesla to exploit the latter's knowledge of using lithium cell batteries as a vehicle power source.

PRODUCTIVITY

The World Economic Forum (2010, p. 4), in its relative assessment of nations' economies across the world, proposes that:

> The level of productivity . . . sets the sustainable level of prosperity that can be earned by an economy . . . more competitive economies tend to be able to produce higher levels of income for their citizens. The productivity level also determines the rates of return obtained by investments. Because the rates of return are the fundamental drivers of the growth rates of the economy, a more competitive economy is one that is likely to grow faster in the medium to long run.

In their assessment of the productivity of nations, the World Economic Forum researchers have developed a model which evaluates the relative importance of what they consider the twelve key variables (or 'pillars') that permit them to rank a nation's performance. These 12 pillars are:

1. *Institutions*, which constitute the legal and administrative framework within which individuals, firms and governments interact to generate income and wealth in the economy.
2. *Infrastructure*, which provides the physical structures that permit the integration of the national market, connecting different regions within a nation and linking the nation's companies to overseas sources of supply and revenue.
3. *The macro-economic environment*, which determines the economic stability of a nation without which adequate levels of commercial

investment will not occur. Stability also ensures that the government can provide services effectively, efficiently and economically.

4. *Health services*, which are critical because workers who are ill cannot function to their full potential and thereby optimise organisational productivity.

5. *Higher education and training services* are required in order to ensure the existence of a pool of well-educated workers able to adapt rapidly to changing environments or utilise the latest advances in technology.

6. *Efficient markets*, without which the supply of reasonably priced goods cannot be made available to a nation's population. Market efficiency also has a critical role in creating a healthy level of competition, which ensures only the most productive organisations survive over the longer term.

7. *Labour market efficiency*, which is critical for ensuring that workers are allocated to their most productive roles in the economy. There is also the requirement that labour markets are sufficiently flexible to support the rapid move of workers from areas of low productivity to areas of higher productivity.

8. *Developed financial markets*, which ensure the savings of a nation's citizens are directed to the most productive areas of an economy. These markets also require sufficient sophistication that capital is made available for private-sector investments by corporate investors through mechanisms such as loans and equity.

9. *Technological capability*, which has become critically important because in today's highly competitive world, because technology is a critical element for sustaining innovation.

10. *Market size*, because the greater the number of customers the higher is the probability that firms can exploit economies of scale.

11. *Business sophistication*, which is concerned with the quality of a country's overall business networks and the quality of individual firms' operations and strategies. This is particularly important for countries at an advanced stage of development, when the more basic sources of productivity improvements have often been exhausted or are no longer accessible.

12. *Innovation*, which in developed economies is the only way in which firms can sustain long-term success through the exploitation of a strategy which seeks to extend the frontiers of knowledge as the basis for developing new-to-the-world products and services.

The conclusion of the World Economic Forum researchers is that the most fundamental requirements determining productivity are the four pillars of institutions, infrastructure, macro-economic environment and health services. In relation to seeking to further enhance productivity, six more critical pillars are higher education and training, market efficiency, labour market efficiency, developed financial markets, technology and market size.

Only once these are in place will the achievement of even higher levels of productivity be influenced by the two remaining pillars—namely, innovation and business sophistication.

Analysis of productivity based upon this multivariate model for 2010 resulted in Switzerland achieving first-place position in the world. This was due to an excellent capacity for innovation and a very sophisticated business culture. Sweden is ranked number two, caused by a unique combination of efficient public institutions, highly ethical behaviour in the private sector, high levels of education and training, rapid adoption of new technology and a commitment to innovation. Singapore's third-place ranking reflects this nation's labour market efficiency, financial market sophistication, superior infrastructure and a highly trained workforce. The United States is ranked number four on the basis of the highly sophisticated and innovative nature of private sector organisations, supported by an excellent university system that collaborates strongly with the business sector in R&D. Other key factors influencing the United States' ranking are the scale opportunities afforded by the being the world's largest single market. Germany's ranking of fifth is reflective of excellent infrastructure, highly efficient markets leading to intense local competition, sophisticated businesses and an aggressive orientation for adopting the latest technologies.

POWER LOSS AND DECLINE

Case Aims: To illustrate the long-term risks of relinquishing power to another member within a supply chain.

Ultimately one of the most dangerous strategic decisions is to be prepared to relinquish power within a supply chain in return for a short-term gain such as increased sales. During the first half of the 20th century manufacturing firms sought to retain as much control as possible over the sale and distribution of their products by exercising power over downstream value chain activities. Producers developed their own distribution capabilities, including sales, installation, service, the provision of credit and other post-purchase support services.

By the 1960s many large companies, in seeking to sustain sales growth in the face of rising inflation impacting profitability in their domestic markets and fighting to counteract overseas competition from the emerging Asian Tiger nations, began to listen to the advice of certain academics and consultants. As pointed out by Thomas and Wilkinson (2006), these experts advised firms to focus on their core competences and reduce involvement in activity which could reduce operating costs. Unfortunately, although these actions may have provided a temporary improvement in operating costs, companies that followed this advice also shed those activities associated with retaining control over downstream supply chains.

(continued)

POWER LOSS AND DECLINE (continued)

For example, in the late 1980s, Goodyear Tire & Rubber Company, then the largest tire company in the world, in part due to a perspective that survival depended upon copying the Japanese, adopted a company-wide total quality management (TQM philosophy). This led to an inward orientation in which sales and distribution management were considered non-critical competences. Resources to support Goodyear's highly successful existing US dealer network were reduced or re-allocated to the manufacturing operation. This loss of downstream market management resources led to multiple sales outlets appearing in towns where in the past there had only been exclusive Goodyear dealerships. As downstream supply chain loyalty declined, the company sought to sustain revenue by authorising Sears, Roebuck and Co. and Wal-Mart Stores, Inc. to stock their products. These dominant retailers exerted their purchasing power to demand both new brand names and discounted prices. Consumers were offered brand names such as Wrangler or American Eagle tires. Independent tire retailers and garages that needed to respond to this new source of competition put new brands on their shelves alongside Goodyear tires. Having lost downstream control and facing rising pressures to reduce prices, Goodyear closed its manufacturing operations in the United States and moved these operations overseas to lower-labour-cost countries.

The Goodyear story is not unique. Many other manufacturers, in their desire to sustain short-term sales growth, have become dependent upon selling their products through retail chains that have acquired dominant control over numerous different supply chains. Few seem to appreciate that once a significant percentage of total sales are through value-orientated retail chains, these retailers will insist on these manufacturers maintaining the same high standards of quality and service but also demand year-on-year price reductions if they wish to avoid being delisted. Wal-Mart, for example, has a 30 percent share of the US market for household staples such as toothpaste, shampoo and paper products and 20 percent of all CD, DVD and video sales. This means suppliers who sell the majority of their products through this retailer have no choice over agreeing to demands for lower prices. One consumer products manufacturer, Newell Rubbermaid, Inc., acceded to pressure from Wal-Mart as the company's biggest customer to drastically reduce prices. To meet this demand Rubbermaid's Wooster, Ohio plant was closed and manufacturing operations were relocated to China. The question which Rubbermaid should have considered before transferring manufacturing knowledge overseas is how long before a Chinese company develops the expertise to outbid the company and become the replacement supplier to Wal-Mart?

As noted by Thomas and Wilkinson (2006), not all manufacturers have sought to chase the elusive dream of sustained growth by reducing their level of power within their market systems. The authors point to examples of companies that have retained control over their distribution strategies by focusing on sustaining product and/or service quality, such as Avon, Dell, Harley-Davidson, Starbucks, Sherwin-Williams and Caterpillar.

(continued)

POWER LOSS AND DECLINE (continued)

In many consumer goods markets, attempting to retain power in sectors dominated by retail chains is no easy process. Companies such as Kellogg's and Heinz have achieve this outcome by developing and exploiting their knowledge over how to create and retain brand leadership, thereby ensuring that consumer demand will ensure in-store retention by the major retailers. For smaller companies where this is not a feasible option, then possibly actions might be implemented to create new distribution channels. In recent years achieving this goal has been made much easier by the advent of the Internet, permitting organisations to leap over retailers and sell directly to the consumer.

SUPPLY CHAIN DOMINANCE

For the organisation involved in a supply chain where one or more other members have exerted power to achieve higher productivity through system domination, the issue arises of what opportunities exist to alter this situation. Resolving this problem is important because the solution may lead to an improved added value outcome for the organisation. One approach for identifying the nature of customer-supplier relationships within a supply chain is proposed by Cox (2001). He suggests that the start point in the process is to understand whether within the supply chain suppliers or buyers are the dominant party. As summarised in Figure 4.1, the three possible outcomes are (i) customers are in a dominant position, (ii) neither customer nor supplier has achieved dominance or (iii) suppliers hold a dominant position.

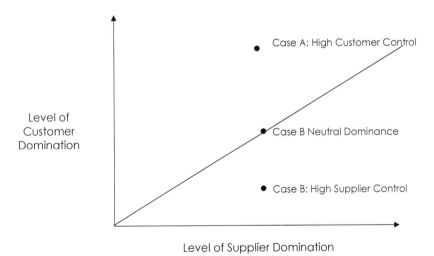

Figure 4.1 Customer-buyer power relationship.

Where an organisation has achieved dominance, it is usually able to exert pressure on the other party in the customer-supplier relationship to demand special terms such as significant price discounts. This will typically result in the dominant party then being able to achieve a higher than average level of added value for its role within the supply chain. Different sectors of industry appear to lend themselves to different forms of dominance. For example, customer dominance is more likely to be evident in sectors such as food retailing, aerospace and the car industry. Sectors where supplier dominance is more likely to occur include large-scale IT systems integration, pharmaceuticals and global-scale professional services (Womack and Jones 1966).

For organisations facing reduced profitability due to their weak position within the supply chain, there are a number of possible strategic options that might be considered in order to remedy this situation. These include:

1. Breaking the semi-monopoly of the dominant parties by finding other additional organisations with whom to do business.
2. Circumventing the scale of dominance by revising the nature of the distribution processes within the supply chain or seeking to construct new relationships that permit the creation of an alternative supply chain.
3. Acquiring greater negotiating power by engaging in M&A activities to consolidate organisations at the same level within the supply chain with the aim of moving towards a semi-monopoly status.

A KNOWLEDGE OWNERSHIP BATTLE

Case Aims: To illustrate how knowledge can change power balances with a service industry supply chain.

For many years the UK car insurance industry was dominated by independent local brokers who, by being close to the consumer, were able to strongly influence end user decisions over which insurer with whom to take out a policy. Although the larger insurers attempted to counter this downstream domination by having their own branch offices in larger towns and cities, this solution was expensive. Furthermore the insurers typically had less knowledge of consumers in an immediate area than the independent brokers. The advent of declining telephone and computer-based client management systems led Direct Line to launch a centralised call centre approach to selling car insurance. The cost savings that permitted lower-priced insurance policies, accompanied by a massive advertising campaign, led to Direct Line moving into a market leadership position. Furthermore, because the company now had immediate access to customers, this new approach to supply chain management broke the downstream customer knowledge dominance previously held by the local brokers (Watson 2001).

(continued)

A KNOWLEDGE OWNERSHIP BATTLE (continued)

The loss of market share to Direct Line caused most of the other major UK insurers to adopt this model. However, later entry into the call centre–based approach did mean they struggled to replicate the same scale of customer base held by Direct Line. In recent years the advent of the Internet has created another powerful competitor in the knowledge ownership stakes—namely, the independent price comparison websites. By acquiring and then making available to consumers knowledge about the cost of insurance premiums being charged by the different insurance companies, this has led to the emergence of a new source of downstream knowledge-based domination in this industry. In an attempt to counter this move, some insurers such as Direct Line refuse to be featured on the price comparison sites. However, in order to sustain this independence, Direct Line has been forced to significantly increase its promotional expenditure in order to communicate that interested customers cannot purchase an insurance from the company via any of the UK's price comparison websites.

KNOWLEDGE SHARING

Research by the Nordic business schools on the behaviour of firms in B2B markets and the requirement of firms in some service sectors to focus on building long-term customer relationships have led to the conventional view of buyers and sellers being engaged solely in some form of 'arms-length' transactional exchange being challenged (Morgan and Hunt 1994; Gronroos 1994). The alternative view that has emerged is that in some cases the buyer and seller perceive there are mutual benefits in building a relationship based upon collaboration and co-operation.

Initially researchers focused on single buyer-seller scenarios to propose that there are were now two types of marketing—namely, transactional and relationship marketing. This new dimension within marketing theory is best viewed by perceiving that relationships between customer and supplier exist on a continuum. At one end are transactional, competitive, short-term relationships, and at the other end, long-term relationships based upon collaboration and co-operation (Jarillo 1988; Webster 1992).

As a wider understanding about relationship marketing has developed, this has resulted in researchers beginning to examine the validity of the concept in relation to achieving sustainable competitiveness across entire supply chains (Dyer and Singh 1998; Jap 1999). The conclusions reached are that collaboration within supply chains may increase levels of added value and decrease costs. This is because the sharing of knowledge permits stronger inter-organisational alignment of processes and more effective exploitation of compatible competences between supply chain members (Kalling 2003). Mohr et al. (1996) identified that collaborative orientation based upon non-coercive knowledge exchange was of critical importance in terms of aligning interests, fostering shared values and achieving mutual support. Ford et al. (2003) posited that in order for effective knowledge exchange to occur without any member using power to abuse the effective operation of a relationship-based supply chain there is the need for trust, commitment, dependence, certainty, reciprocity and shared cultures. Polo-Redondo and Cambra-Fierro (2008) concluded that once these conditions exist within a supply chain this will accelerate standardisation of organisational processes that can support achievement of significant cost reductions for all of the members. Im and Rai (2008) believe that even more important than any improvement in supply chain efficiency is that knowledge exchange generates learning which can assist in supporting new, more innovative approaches in the development of new products and operational processes.

ACCESSING KNOWLEDGE VIA NETWORKS

Case Aims: To illustrate how network-based collaboration can assist in enhancing innovation within an industrial sector.

Océ is a leading Dutch manufacturer of copiers and printers, and it determined that in order to respond to low-cost imports there was a need to re-design the company's innovation strategy. The firm decided to focus on the initial stages of the R&D process while concurrently forming collaborative relationships with suppliers in order that these members of the supply chain could play a much stronger role in the engineering phase of new product development. To achieve this aim Océ launched its own 'knowledge industry clustering' (KIC) by acting as the hub organisation orchestrating collaboration between strategic suppliers to exchange, create and accumulate their knowledge (Batenburg and Rutten 2003).

Océ employs nearly 21,000 people, 1,600 of whom work in R&D services. The company headquarters in Venlo in the Netherlands employs 3,500 people, including 1,100 in R&D. For some years Océ has been working more closely with suppliers in an 'early supplier involvement' (ESI) scheme. However, suppliers were not involved in the engineering process development activity prior to the completion of a prototype. They were asked to start from the blueprints made by Océ and then suggest modifications and changes to the design that would enable a more efficient manufacturing of each of the parts. Océ undertook all assembly activities. The suppliers' role was confined to process engineering without being asked to propose changes to the subassembly.

At the beginning of the 1990s, Océ changed its product development strategy by focusing upon core competences in the areas developing new technologies, concepts and products. This new model was based upon Océ outsourcing all product engineering to key suppliers. The weakness of this strategy, however, was that Océ had to rely on technically advanced suppliers who had the skills needed to practice product engineering at a time when few suppliers had these capabilities. Océ's new emphasis on collaborating with suppliers exhibiting innovation and design competences led to key suppliers being willing to strengthen their skills to support Océ's product development efforts by committing to becoming actively involved in inter-firm collaboration.

(continued)

ACCESSING KNOWLEDGE VIA NETWORKS (continued)

To create this new network Océ actively supported the creation of layered supplier networks by bringing suppliers into the KIC project. In a typical KIC cluster, firms are brought together into a network constituted of members with different specialisations and engineering capabilities. One of the suppliers is appointed lead partner, responsible for managing a specific project by co-ordinating the activities between network members and Océ. The company's selection of network participants is based upon the criteria of (i) having past experience with the supplier before KIC, (ii) an evaluation of the supplier's technical performance, and (iii) the involvement of external advisors to identify potential candidates. Two-thirds of the KIC suppliers appeared to be a new partner for Océ, reflecting importance placed upon the supplier's technical capabilities.

Batenburg and Rutten's evaluation of the KIC initiative involved an assessment of how inter-organisational relationships were managed within the networks. Key factors identified as critical were the willingness of members to jointly share risks, total openness in knowledge exchange activities, reciprocity in data exchange and evidence of total trust among network members. Another identified key factor was the separation of the formal and technical management within the KIC clusters. The formal side, such as contracts, budgets and schedules, was handled at the management level. This left the engineers free to concentrate on the technical content of the project. Lines of communication were short because the engineers from the various firms communicated directly with each other without requiring prior permission for knowledge interchange from their respective senior line managers. Where possible Océ stood back from the network. This behaviour was designed to promote a maximum level of knowledge exchange between network members. The researchers concluded that the existence of the networks permitted members to draw upon each other's assets in a mutual adaptation process that optimised asset utilisation and exploitation of available knowledge. In their view this was an especially critical outcome. This is because the leading-edge nature of the innovation being undertaken was heavily reliant upon the use of tacit knowledge which would not have been accessed in the more conventional transactional buyer-seller relationship.

KNOWLEDGE PROTECTION

In reviewing the enthusiasm within the literature concerning the benefits of becoming involved in knowledge sharing collaborative networks, Cox (2001) points out that the priority of any firm within a supply chain is about appropriating as much added value for themselves as is feasible. Sharing knowledge that assists other firms to enhance their added value activities is of little benefit unless this is the only strategy through which an organisation can survive. In his view the presentation of a perfect world based upon collaboration and trust exists only because (Cox 1999, p. 168):

Most writers operate with a theoretical understanding of the causes of sustainable business success, and focus their analysis on the description of what companies do, rather than have a theoretical understanding of what it is that allows companies to be successful in the first place.

This author posits that companies can remain successful only if they possess some form of advantage or power over other members of a supply chain. This situation can lead to conflicts of interest between other supply chain participants because everyone in the chain is seeking to appropriate greater added value for themselves. Cox believes acceptance of this perspective is critical for academics attempting to guide organisations on how to effectively manage supply chain strategies and processes.

Ownership of the assets that are the necessary components within a supply chain will be protected by those who own these and will be contested by other organisations seeking access to these assets at the lowest possible cost. As a consequence the organisation which has access to the knowledge that will support supply chain innovation will need to continually guard against the release of any unique knowledge that can eventually lead to new competitive threats from either upstream or downstream sources. Furthermore the innovator would be unwise to release unique knowledge unless this leads to greater access being granted to other areas of superior added value capability which exists elsewhere within the supply chain.

This scenario is a very apparent risk of companies who outsource key aspects of the operations to firms based in emerging economies. This is because companies such as Apple that use Chinese companies to manufacture their products, such as the iPhone and iPad, are helping Chinese firms acquire an adequate understanding of the relevant technologies, thereby possibly placing them in a position at some later date to enter world markets by manufacturing duplicate products under their own brand names. The adverse impact of such outcomes has long been evident in the case of the American car and electronic consumer goods industries. In the 1970s and 1980s, in the face of inflation and rising operating costs in the United States, companies moved their operations off-shore, opening factories and forming alliances with firms in countries such as Korea and Japan. Within only a few years these overseas partners moved from manufacturing products for American original equipment manufacturers (OEMs) to developing their own, often superior designs which provided the basis for successful entry into the US firms' home markets.

In order to comprehend the opportunities and threats associated with knowledge or competence sharing, Cox proposes that the organisation should undertake a review of the nature of the existing supply chain in order to identify the properties of power which exist within the system. Issues which should be examined include:

1. The physical resources that are required within a supply chain to create and deliver a finished product or service to a customer.

2. The nature of the exchange relationships which exist between particular supply chain resources and the flow of revenue in the value chain.
3. The ownership and control of particular supply chain resources that allow certain resources to command a greater share of total system added value than others.

Acceptance of Cox's alternative perspective will tend to indicate that organisations should take great care in deciding whether involvement in a collaborative supply network is the most effective strategy through which to achieve superior added value performance over the long term. Adoption of a collaborative operational philosophy is of benefit only when the company can optimise its share of the added value available within a market system. Evidence of the benefits of adopting this approach to innovation and knowledge sharing is provided by cases of supply chains in which companies have been able to retain dominant control over particular supply chain resources and added value opportunities. Examples of companies which have achieved this outcome include Microsoft, Cisco and Intel in the IT industry, and in the retail sector major supermarket chains such as Wal-Mart and Tesco.

Helper (1991), as a supporter of the benefits of vertical, integrated, collaborative supply chains, quite correctly pointed to how these have been a critical factor influencing the success of the world's most profitable car manufacturers, Honda and Toyota. He contrasted this orientation with American car companies, such as GM and Chrysler, which have continued to exhibit a more transactional orientation towards their suppliers. The American companies' approach reflects the cost-reduction opportunities associated with switching suppliers as the basis for supporting predatory purchasing practices. This behaviour does not indicate that the American automakers do not perceive the advantages of collaborating over engineering during the design and development phase for a new vehicle. It reflects an embedded attitude that leads these firms to seek annual re-bids from suppliers in an effort to lower input costs.. This only occurs , however, because of the power dominance these firms have achieved over the years. The downside is that suppliers do not trust their customers. This in turn has resulted in no relational linkages emerging which might have assisted the US car industry to sustain market leadership through innovation. The other drawback is suppliers are often expected to recover the cost of design services as part of winning the initial contract, and these high design costs are rarely ever totally recovered due to car makers' predatory pricing policies (Sturgeon et al. 2008).

When justifying the superiority of a collaborative versus an adversarial supply chain orientation, it is necessary to recognise that American and Japanese car companies in recent years have been following different strategies, even though both groups operate within an industry sector where profit margins are extremely low.

Toyota and Honda's strategy has been that of remaining ahead of competition through innovation. As car manufacturing has become increasingly technologically complex, industrial sector successful implementation of this approach is highly dependent upon collaborative knowledge exchange. In contrast the US car firms' strategy has been to generate profits by focusing upon maximising sales volume to achieve economies of scale and to exploit their location inside the world's largest car market. The problem soon to confront both these supply chain models will be how to counter the Chinese, as this country's car industry, now the largest in the world, starts to aggressively fight for share in world markets. This can be expected to lead to a further erosion in the industry's profit margins because Chinese manufacturers can exploit lower production costs, have a large domestic market providing the basis for achieving huge economies of scale, have few concerns over infringing intellectual property (IP) rights and have a willingness to adopt adversarial procurement attitudes, often overtly supported by their own government, where this is deemed to be a beneficial behaviour trait.

Another frequently quoted example of collaborative supply chain networks is the success enjoyed by firms based in Silicon Valley, California. In fact when Japanese competition forced the US semiconductor industry into crisis during the 1980s, most observers predicted the demise of Silicon Valley. Instead the area continued to flourish due to activities of early PC developers such as Apple and the subsequent exploitation of the Internet by firms such as Google and Yahoo. In reviewing the early phase of the post-1980 recovery, Saxenian (1990) concluded success was strongly influenced by the existence of strong social relationships that led to collaboration and reciprocal innovation among networks of specialist producers. These events have caused some academics to conclude that the only successful model for a post-industrial society is for firms in high technology sectors to participate in collaborative groups (or 'clusters') to optimise the added value outputs that exist within any supply chain (Bresnahan et al. 2001).

TO CLUSTER OR NOT TO CLUSTER

Case Aims: To illustrate some of the potential problems associated with accepting the perspective that clusters will always assist economic growth initiatives.

In the early 1990s academics' strongly articulated view that business networks are the most effective post-modern industrial structure led to governments funding network formation programmes. Unfortunately few of these initiatives ever achieved a long-term positive cost/benefit outcome. This led academics to switch their support to the role of clusters influencing economic performance. These views caused governments in countries such as New Zealand and UK to fund initiatives to support the creation of clusters as a strategy stimulating economic growth.

(continued)

TO CLUSTER OR NOT TO CLUSTER (continued)

Similar to the outcome of the previous public sector initiatives to create business networks, once government funds began to be expended it became apparent that attempting to create new clusters is not a guaranteed panacea for achieving economic growth. On the basis of his analysis of government-funded initiatives in the UK, Perry (1999) concluded that a number of factors must be taken into consideration at the planning stage. This is because certain key variables can determine the success or failure of cluster formation projects. In an industrial sector where a few large dominant firms tend to retain control of proprietary knowledge and where knowledge leakage is minimal, attempts to create clusters may be frustrated. In contrast, where there is rapid diffusion of knowledge about a new technology, this may lead to numerous new business start-ups that co-locate to access knowledge and to share scarce resources. Even where there is an opportunity for these new start-ups, however, should the prevailing business culture of owner/managers be that of operational autonomy, this behaviour trait may frustrate external facilitation attempts to promote the creation of knowledge interchange clusters.

In subsequent research on cluster formation in the New Zealand timber industry, Perry (2007) identified other additional factors that may frustrate cluster formation. One factor is resistance to collaboration between firms at different levels of a supply chain. The prior existence of other forms of collaboration can also impact cluster formation. In those cases where a trade association effectively represents members' interests, this may cause firms to perceive little benefit in creating a cluster. Alternatively, where firms have previously experienced problems caused by activities of a trade association, this may result in a high level of resistance to any new attempts to stimulate co-operation through clustering.

Another factor is the nature of the power relationships within a cluster. In the case of a cluster constituted of numerous small firms, the size of the cluster may be a barrier to achieving consensus over strategy. Furthermore, because small firms have limited capabilities, members are unable to contribute sufficient resources to the cluster to permit this entity to make any real contribution towards assisting business growth. The alternative model of a large firm acting as the core of the cluster can overcome the resource constraint problem. Then, however, there is the risk that the large firm will use the acquired power to mandate adoption of a strategy which is beneficial to the organisation but is detrimental to the growth prospects of other members of the cluster.

BENEFIT ASSESSMENT

The activities of major US firms exhibiting a less adversarial orientation and instead engaging in active collaboration in the IT industry in recent years do appear to support the view that greater benefits may accrue from exchanging versus competing for access to new knowledge (Kenney and

Von Burg 1999). For example, this approach was utilised by Apple in the development of the iPhone, which involved collaboration with the UK company Arm, which designed a much-needed microchip which has high data processing capability but low energy usage requirements.

The IT industry also provides examples that not all performance aims can be met through involvement in networked supply chains. In some cases it is apparent that even major firms may identify knowledge which cannot be accessed through collaboration and is critical to future added value activities. Under these circumstances the firm is likely to engage in M&A activity to gain ownership of the required knowledge. This outcome is illustrated by Google's desire to become involved in social networking, and to achieve this aim it purchased YouTube for $1.6 billion. More recently some of the industry's major players have clearly decided that they lack the necessary internal knowledge to succeed in the rapidly growing technology storage sector. IBM purchased Netezza Corporation for £1.7 billion. This latter organisation supplies products that integrate databases, servers and storage hardware into an easy-to-install, low-operating-cost, single system. IBM's rational for the deal is the acquisition would 'help its business information and analytics offerings' (Nuttall 2010, p. 25). Hewlett-Packard outbid Dell to purchase 3Par for $2.4 billion and in 2011 Microsoft paid $8.5 billion to acquire the creators of the world's first free on-line telephony operation, Skype.

In the face of apparent scenarios which contradict the view that collaboration via networks or clusters is always the optimal solution, it would appear advisable that firms should adopt a contingency approach when assessing their supply chain interaction strategy. One approach for use in contingency planning is summarised in Figure 4.2, where the two dimensions are 'mutual benefit from collaboration' and 'knowledge-based added value opportunities.' This leads to the following decision outcomes:

1. *Transactional strategy* is applicable in fragmented markets where profit margins are low and there are numerous buyers and sellers. Under these circumstances both buyers and sellers would be advised to adopt an arm's-length approach to relationships in order to maximise choice and profitability.

2. *Mutual dependence strategy* is applicable in fragmented markets where profit margins are low but the formation of alliances may permit buyers or sellers to strengthen their negotiating positions and thereby enhance profitability.

3. *Dominance strategy* is applicable when there is opportunity to achieve high profitability by retaining control over areas of key knowledge and not being prepared to share this knowledge with other members of the supply chain.

4. *Network strategy* is applicable when there is an opportunity for members of a supply chain to enhance added value outcomes by sharing knowledge with one or more members of the supply chain.

Mutual Benefit from Collaboration

		Low	High
Knowledge-Based Added Value Opportunities	High	Leadership Dominance Strategy	Networking Strategy
	Low	Transactional Strategy	Mutual Dependence Strategy

Figure 4.2   Contingency relationship matrix.

5 Internal Competence

The purpose of this chapter is to cover issues pertaining to:

1. The resource-based view (RBV) of the firm, which proposes internal competence is the key to acquiring and sustaining competitive advantage.
2. The importance of knowledge as the key competence for sustaining the survival of Western organisations.
3. The role of entrepreneurial competence to ensure the ongoing creation of new or improved products and internal operational processes.
4. The importance of exploiting superior competence of the workforce to differentiate the organisation from competition.
5. The opportunities for using CRM to support superior competence in understanding and responding to customer needs.

RESOURCE-BASED VIEW

The strategic philosophy concerning market success based upon exploiting superior internal capability is known as the 'resource-based view' of the firm (or RBV). Edith Penrose was one of the first academics to identify the importance of the relationship between strategy, business growth and internal capabilities of the organisation (Augier and Teece 2007). She perceived key internal capabilities as the productive services available to a firm from internal resources, especially those based upon exploiting the organisation's managerial experience. Her research was concerned with managerial behaviour in general. In relation to entrepreneurial activities, she merely identified that certain leaders are more able to exploit new opportunities because they exhibit a greater level of 'dynamic capability.'

The RBV literature stresses the importance of an organisation's ability to organise resources to produce goods and services that will permit creation of a competitive advantage. The philosophy can be contrasted with the alternative 'environmentalist perspective,' which is based upon on the competitive positioning of products within a market. Competence is the ability to co-ordinate the deployment of available assets to permit an organisation to achieve specified strategic goals. Sanchez (1993) suggests that for any activity to be recognised as a competence it must meet the three conditions of organisation, intention and goal attainment. Competence building is any process which leads to changes in existing assets and capabilities or the emergence of new capabilities to improve organisational performance.

Savory (2006) noted that ownership of specific resources does not guarantee attainment of a sustainable competitive advantage. In his opinion, to achieve a sustainable advantage, the resources must be effectively configured to meet some form of unique market need. He suggests that the successful configuration of resources depends upon three abilities:

1. *Competence*, which is the ability to use the resource to an acceptable level of performance.
2. *Capability*, which is the ability to co-ordinate the use of a specific combination of an organisation's resources.
3. *Dynamic capability*, which is the ability to re-configure both the use and co-ordination of a specific resources according to changes in the organisation's external environment or strategic direction.

Barney (2001) concluded that RBV helps managers understand how different internal resources can generate a strategic advantage. The logic also assists identification of the most critical resources which are owned by the organisation. Mahoney and Pandian (1992) note that a core competence can sustain the firm's competitive advantage by acting as an isolating mechanism creating entry barriers at the level of individual organisations and mobility barriers at the sector level.

RBV theory has been criticised by Priem and Butler (2001). They perceive there is a problem of the firm's strategic advantage being based on causally ambiguous resources. In their view this can occur because managers encounter difficulties determining which combination of capabilities provides the actual basis for achieving strategic advantage. Sveiby (1997) also argues that resource advantages are highly context-dependent and that what may be valuable in one industry may not valuable in another.

COMPETENCE TRAP 1

Case Aims: To illustrate that core competences may need to be revised in response to changing market circumstances.

Application of RBV theory is dependent upon the organisation's ability to continue to succeed in turbulent environments that require the firm to update existing competence or develop a new core capability. Leonard-Barton (1992) proposed that capabilities can become 'core rigidities.' This outcome can inhibit innovation by placing the organisation in a 'competence trap.' Prahalad and Hamel (1994) describe this situation as the 'tyranny of the served market' in which dominant prevailing management thinking blocks new or unconventional actions to identify business opportunities. Sadly this type of rigidity in strategic thinking can cause historically successful organisations to eventually go into decline (O'Driscoll et al. 2001).

(continued)

COMPETENCE TRAP 1 (continued)

Novotel is an international hotel chain founded by two French entrepreneurs in 1967. Steady expansion in the 1970s and 1980s owed much to the distinctive competence in the areas of reliability, systems management and control procedures (Haberberg and Rieple 2001). The chain developed a standard format for hotel room designs, furnishings and service quality standards which enabled offering guests, especially business travellers, a uniform standard of comfort throughout Europe and later in other parts of the world. In the late 1980s, Novotel continued to deepen internal competences in relation to its hospitality control systems. A rigid set of rules and procedures, the '95 Bolts,' was established. This governed every aspect of the worldwide operations in minute detail, from how guests should be greeted to room charge discount discretion by frontline staff. Unfortunately the new systems created difficulties among staff wishing to exhibit personal warmth towards their guests and react spontaneously to their requests. This situation created an image of Novotel seemingly to have become less hospitable. New competitors emerged but rigid control procedures prevented managers in the field from matching lower price offerings or offering service prioritisation for regular guests. Novotel lost business and recorded a sharp decline in profits. By ignoring changing market and competitive dynamics, Novotel transformed a core competence into a core rigidity (Haberberg and Rieple 2001).

Waterford Crystal is a highly renowned name in the international tabletop industry and is one of the world's leading brands in the premium crystal market. During the late 1980s and early 1990s, the company was faced with a major recession in its principal market, the United States. As prevailing economic conditions worsened, the company's high-income target consumers started to trade down, buying lower-priced crystal and modifying their tastes. The company responded with the launch of a new brand, Marquis, designed in a more contemporary way and positioned in a lower price tier of the premium crystal market. Furthermore, for the first time in the company's history, production of this new product was outsourced to Slovenia and Germany. The new brand achieved great success without cannibalising sales of the primary brand. Nevertheless the company did not learn from this experience and failed to recognise that existing competences and reliance on traditional designs could not sustain the business over the longer term. By the new millennium, even with the introduction of new designs, the company strategy did not provide an adequate response to the worldwide trend of more casual dining. The final blow was the 2008 recession, in which, similarly to other many other luxury brands, the company faced a massive decline in sales. Debt rose to almost 500 million euros and the Irish government, by then facing a rising public sector deficit, was in no position to act as a guarantor for new bank loans. As a result the company went into administration (Nolan 2009).

KNOWLEDGE COMPETENCE

A key driving force since the beginning of the Industrial Revolution has been the activities of entrepreneurs discovering and exploiting new knowledge as the basis for innovation in existing industries and in the creation of totally new industries. In the 20th century there was an exponential increase in the rate of new scientific and technological breakthroughs. Current evidence would suggest this pace of new knowledge creation will be sustained in the 21st century. The implication of this scenario is that the exploitation of new knowledge will remain a critical competence within organisations seeking to sustain long-term growth (Sheehan 2005). Prahalad and Hamel (1990) perceive competence in terms of an ability to innovate as being the collective learning in the organisation which permits co-ordination of a diverse range of production skills and permits integration of a multiple stream of technologies.

Knowledge is possibly best used to enhance added value activities by creating a superior product or service capability which is of benefit to customers. Kaplan and Norton (2001) introduced the concept of 'strategy maps' to provide a useful framework for linking strategy, activities and knowledge resources. The purpose of these maps is to help organisations more effectively develop strategies in a knowledge-based economy. A key component of strategy maps is 'strategic themes,' which Kaplan and Norton describe as 'the drivers of knowledge-based strategy.' Themes become relevant when the organisation is able to combine the ingredients of skills, technologies and organisational culture to create internal processes that deliver tangible outcomes such as customer satisfaction, customer loyalty, growth or increased profitability. The relative importance of these themes will vary between organisations. As noted by Massingham (2004), themes provide only a starting point for identifying the knowledge activities that can lead to acquiring a sustainable competitive advantage. Significant additional work, often involving further R&D, is usually demanded before themes can be converted into effective strategies or improved operational processes.

A key issue facing senior managers is the degree to which their organisations can continue to rely on exploiting existing knowledge versus the importation of new knowledge to support innovation. Existing knowledge tends to be widely available within an industrial sector and thus rarely able to support really radical, innovative new ideas. As a consequence entrepreneurial organisations which seek to sustain growth through proactive activities have long understood the critical importance of sustaining their competence through the exploitation of new knowledge. The implications of existing versus new knowledge as sources of opportunity are summarised in Figure 5.1.

Scale of Business Opportunities

		Low	High
Exploitation of New Knowledge	Low	Conventional Business Operations	Conventional Product/Market Diversification
	High	Entrepreneurial Alternative Opportunity Search	Entrepreneurial Diversification

Figure 5.1   Opportunity/knowledge matrix.

Reliance on the exploitation of existing knowledge usually only permits the organisation to sustain current business strategies and in some cases, identify opportunities to utilise existing knowledge as the basis for product or market diversification. This does not mean, however, that organisations orientated towards implementing entrepreneurial strategies should ignore existing knowledge. In most cases, existing knowledge can provide a much lower risk source of future business revenue than is available from relying solely on new knowledge. Hence even entrepreneurial firms should seek to achieve an appropriate balance over which sources of knowledge are to be utilised in relation to deciding about launching low- versus higher-risk business propositions.

In some cases when new knowledge first emerges, there may be no obvious commercial application. For example, when first invented, the laser was described as a 'solution looking for a problem.' The important action when an immediate application for new knowledge is not apparent is for the organisation to permit a certain proportion of resources to be applied to looking for new application opportunities. One company which has excelled at applying this philosophy is 3M Corporation. Within this organisation scientists and managers from different departments are encouraged to exchange information. This is because such interchanges can often lead to new opportunities being identified which may lie outside of the experiences of the individual(s) who initially identified an area of new knowledge. Such was the case with the Post-it note, in which a new glue formulation was developed which exhibited poor adhesive properties. Subsequently another 3M innovator sought just these qualities to develop a system for temporarily attaching a piece of paper to another surface without causing any damage to that surface.

Although cases such as the Post-it note make entertaining reading, reliance upon being successful based upon a random search for new knowledge is usually much less effective than the alternative of focusing upon a new technology which immediately offers the organisation a new source of entrepreneurial opportunity. Firms which base their strategies on exploiting new technology tend to be attracted to the leading-edge core technology. This is technology which can provide the basis for above-average business performance through the creation of new products and, in some cases, entirely new industries. Hence, in terms of analysing future opportunities and threats, it is necessary to assess how new knowledge can best be exploited by combining new knowledge with the current leading-edge technology (Ohmura and Watanabe 2006).

At the beginning of the 20th century, the two leading-edge technologies were electricity and the internal combustion engine. These were then overtaken by electronics. This new technology generated solid state devices and provided the foundations for IT to become the current leading-edge core technology. The degree to which firms exploit new knowledge in relation to advances in IT will vary by industry sector.

Organisations need to be aware that the interaction between new knowledge and a leading-edge core technology is a dynamic process. For example, it can be the case that firms engaged in the provision of professional services need to seek ways of replacing extremely expensive individual staff with machine-based solutions. An example of this scenario is provided in the healthcare sector, where surgeons having evolved a new surgical technique may then develop computer-based systems to deliver part or all of their new medical solution. As the understanding of new IT-based advanced manufacturing and service solutions becomes more widespread, the technology will increasingly be incorporated into conventional manufacturing and service process activities. The possible outcome is that a new knowledge/IT solution may cease to be an ongoing source of competitive advantage. This situation means the entrepreneurial organisation must continually strive to identify and exploit new approaches for exploiting the latest advances in knowledge and IT to sustain organisational performance.

DEFINING CORE COMPETENCE

Case Aims: To illustrate that in high-technology industries an effective strategy requires an emphasis on knowledge generation competence.

Eli Lilly and Company is an American, global, high-technology company which uses both internal R&D and external research partnerships worldwide to develop solutions for many of the world's most urgent, unmet medical needs. The company philosophy is to adopt a core competence approach to strategy formulation by understanding how to manage the relationship between resources, capabilities and processes in order to achieve a sustainable competitive advantage. To achieve this goal, Lilly's identified core competences are the exploitation of knowledge in execution of both research and market management activities. Research and development facilities are located in Australia, Belgium, Canada, England, Germany, Japan, Singapore, Spain and the United States. The key R&D objective is to reduce the time needed to identify a lead compound and introduce an innovative product from five years down to 500 days (Kak 2004).

(continued)

DEFINING CORE COMPETENCE (continued)

The pharmaceutical industry is a sector where increasingly no single organisation has the research competence to produce the medical innovations that the customers want. Hence Eli Lilly has entered into a number of research alliances worldwide to gain access to new research competences in relation to identifying additional high-potential drug candidates. An alliance with Logan Pharmaceuticals, for example, gives the company exclusive rights not only to several potential oral therapies for diabetes but also to a proprietary technology that may help its scientists to make additional discoveries in the treatment of diabetes, obesity and certain cardiovascular diseases.

Eli Lilly was the first large pharmaceutical company to collaborate with Millennium Bio Therapeutics, which has a unique technology to help identify proteins that may be useful as medicines. Lilly has also entered into agreements with other companies, e.g. Thera Tech, Inhale and Emisphere, that are working on drug delivery approaches which one day may change treatments associated with protein products. A dedicated centre has been created to accelerate and integrate biotech activities from initial discovery through manufacturing a commercially viable product. Alliances are also being pursued in the area of revolutionary advances in the life sciences that can lead to the discovery of novel therapies.

Since the early 1990s, Lilly Research Laboratories have thoroughly reengineered the company's competence in relation to the discovery, development and acquisition of high-potential new products. The company strives to create an environment that enables individuals to optimise their contribution by reducing barriers to productivity. Within the pharmaceutical industry, potential demand for medicines can go unrealised due to a variety of problems within the industry supply chain associated with the delivery of treatments to patients. For example, patients may suffer symptoms but not seek treatment. Others may receive the wrong diagnosis, representing unfilled potential. In order to overcome this problem Lilly has focused on developing enhanced competence in relation to information management. This has been accompanied by the company adapting to new distribution channels, new media and new applications of information technology, such as creating on-line medical education sites for the medical profession and the general public.

To ensure optimal exploitation of core competence the company has created various new systems in the areas of the new product development involving enhanced levels of creative suggestions by employees and establishing cross-functional teams. This team-based approach linked to emphasis on flexibility of response is seen as critical for supporting organisational effectiveness in relation to reducing the time taken to identify new discoveries, develop new medicines and undertake product testing and subsequent market launch. This flexibility competence is also important in emphasising to employees that there is no single strategy that fits all eventualities, which necessitates the organisation having the ability to evolve and respond to changing and increasingly turbulent environments.

ENTREPRENEURIAL COMPETENCE

Droege and Dong (2008) suggested that a unique ability of managers within entrepreneurial firms is their ability to acquire new, often as yet unrecognised, competences. This is because these individuals are more able to recognise new opportunities either through intuitive assessment or by drawing upon their personal accumulated experiences. Individuals and organisations that exhibit an entrepreneurial orientation are more willing to act independently of prevailing industry conventions, explore new ideas and seek to discover new markets. Covin and Slevin (1989) have proposed that this orientation, which provides the basis for exhibiting unique competences, consists of five dimensions: autonomy, innovativeness, proactiveness, risk taking and competitive aggressiveness.

The attribute of autonomy refers to the ability to implement independent actions in the identification and exploitation of a new idea. Sustaining autonomy in larger, more hierarchical organisations is often difficult. This is a key reason that smaller entrepreneurial firms are often first to identify new market opportunities. Innovativeness describes the degree with which a firm utilises a strategy of exploiting new ideas that can provide the basis for developing new products, services and processes. Even when the specific actions needed to pursue an opportunity are not yet clear to the organisation, inaction is to be avoided. This is because even in uncertain environments, implementing some form of action offers the greatest opportunity for staying ahead of competition. As identified by Covin et al. (2006), firms exhibiting an emergent, less structured approach to defining strategy usually achieve higher sales growth than those which follow a more structured, planned approach to strategic management.

Proactiveness is distinct from both innovativeness and competitive aggressiveness. It is a critical core dimension of entrepreneurial competence because it reflects a willingness to seize opportunities well before these become apparent to other organisations. The proactiveness dimension can shape the firm's competitive environment, influence trends and, in some situations, create demand (Lumpkin and Dess 1996). Proactive strategies focus on anticipating and acting upon market opportunities. Proactive firms are frequently the first to market, thereby causing other firms to revise their strategies and to belatedly engage in acquiring equivalent organisational capabilities.

Virtually all strategic decisions involve uncertain outcomes. Some decisions, however, involve greater risk than others. This is because management may not yet fully understand the nature of an identified new opportunity or the scale of resources necessary to ensure a successful outcome for an innovation project. Entrepreneurial organisations are thought to be more prepared to take strategic risks. This is because of a willingness to accept greater levels of uncertainty about the outcome of their actions.

Competitive aggressiveness describes a firm's response to competitors' actions. Unlike proactiveness, competitive aggressiveness differs from the former by usually involving a reaction to an identified change. Additionally, competitive aggressiveness can be present in both conventional and entrepreneurial organisations. Hence there is some dispute among academics about whether this organisational competence is necessary for a firm engaged in implementing an entrepreneurial strategy.

As organisations grow, evolve and diversify, this is usually accompanied by formalisation of structure, job roles, control systems and a hierarchical approach to defining the nature of permitted decision-making. In stable markets or in industries where technology remains virtually unchanged, it is very probable that this type of organisational evolution will deliver higher efficiency and productivity. As firms located in emerging economies such as China and India, competing on the basis of lower-cost or competitive pricing, continue to grow, it is usually beneficial to adopt highly formalised structures and policies. In contrast, in Western companies, in which ongoing success is dependent upon innovation to support a differentiation positioning, there is a need to recognise that as the level of organisational formality increases this is usually accompanied by a decline in entrepreneurial activity (Madsen 2007). Hence a vital leadership competence in these Western organisations is to ensure that structures and systems remain suited to sustaining a strong entrepreneurial orientation.

One of the reasons that some firms fail to sustain entrepreneurial orientation can be explained in terms of the existence of 'resource stickiness' (Mishina et al. 2004). The most common forms of resource stickiness are to be found in an organisation's human and financial assets. Stickiness can arise for two reasons. In some cases the organisation lacks sufficient organisational capacity to re-allocate resources away from existing business activities in order to re-assign these to more entrepreneurial endeavours. In order to overcome this obstacle, companies wishing to sustain long-term growth through innovation need to invest in the creation of a certain degree of 'organisational slack.' This can be used to support the implementation of new activities when emerging entrepreneurial opportunities become apparent. The other cause of resource stickiness is that although slack resources do exist within the organisation, senior managers exhibit an inadequate level of 'entrepreneurial ambition.' As a consequence available spare capacity is not allocated to pursue innovation. Instead senior managers allocate slack resources to less risky activities, such as improving the efficiency of existing organisational processes.

PERFORMANCE COMPETENCE

Many of the published articles about the influence of internal capabilities on the strategic success of highly successful entrepreneurial firms tend to be based upon anecdotal, usually qualitative evidence, concerning observations about a very limited number of organisations. The risks associated with using such findings are the data may not be of sufficient validity to provide the basis for generalisations that are applicable to defining which competences are fundamental key factors, critical to implementing an entrepreneurial strategy. To overcome this potential problem Chaston and Mangles (1997) used a number of a published studies on competences associated with business growth to evolve a composite qualitative model summarising which key competences were found to be common across various research studies. The model shown in Figure 5.2 provided the basis for a large-scale quantitative study of UK firms in both the manufacturing and services sectors. Discriminant function analysis was applied to the survey data. This permitted the creation of a quantitative model describing how variations in capability can be expected to influence business growth rates. This model demonstrated that there are certain important internal generic competences of a strategic or operational nature that strongly influence business performance.

The entry point of the model in Figure 5.2 is the critical capability of the organisation to be able to identify emerging opportunities and to evolve an effective strategic response. This competence will exist only if the leadership has articulated a clear vision for the future and embedded a commitment towards sustained entrepreneurial activity throughout the organisation. Dulewicz and Higgs (2003) have described this leadership competence as

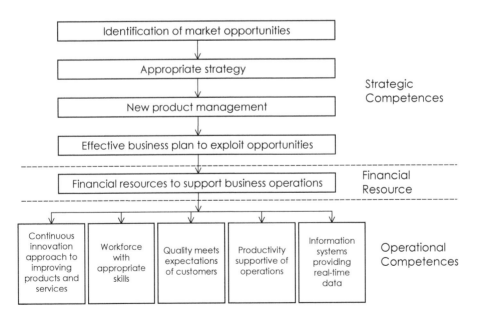

Figure 5.2   A qualitative model of organisational competences to support long-term business performance.

'emotional intelligence.' In their view this competence requires that the leadership is able to:

1. Define the case for strategic or organisational change.
2. Effectively engage employees in accepting the need for change.
3. Ensure change can occur because employees have an adequate understanding of the relevant issues.
4. Ensure the existence of effective plans and appropriate performance review practices.
5. Ensure employees have the resources, tools and processes to implement change.
6. Continue to engage with employees throughout the entire change process, resolving problems and sustaining commitment.
7. Facilitate the ongoing development of employees' competences through emphasis on organisational learning.

Day and Schoemaker (2005) have suggested that visionary leaders also require an ability to identify weak signals in the external environment. In commenting on weak signal identification, MacKay and McKiernan (2004) posit that conventional strategic planning tools are somewhat ineffective in permitting organisations to recognise the emergent phases of a new opportunity. Furthermore they feel that individuals who exhibit the skill of recognising weak signals also seem to have an unusually highly developed intuitive ability to identify new opportunities and to evolve entrepreneurial responses well ahead of competition.

Exploiting a newly identified opportunity involves developing a strategic concept to exploit the new opportunity in a way which will be superior to any existing offerings in the market. Figure 5.2 also indicates planning activity is necessary to assess the validity of a business proposition in terms of actions to successfully exploit the identified opportunity. The importance of this competence has been validated by Khan and Manopichetwattan (1989). Through a large-scale study of manufacturing firms, they determined that non-innovative firms exhibit a limited understanding of strategy, have poor planning skills and lack the ability to implement an integrated response to changing environments.

There is a common adage used by bankers and venture capitalist that 'actual plans take twice as long to implement and actual costs will be twice as high as forecasted.' Parks' (1977) research supports this perspective. He found that a common scenario among entrepreneurial firms is new product projects frequently encounter cost overruns, generate lower than forecasted sales revenue and take longer than expected to progress from idea identification through to market launch. Given the high probability that such situations will emerge, there is a critical need for entrepreneurial firms to have sufficient financial resources to be able to survive any unforeseen problems which may arise during the development of a new product (Hogarty 1993). The source of funds to support innovation can come from various sources, including retained profits, cash inflows from trading, external borrowing or issuing new equity. The fact that very successful entrepreneurial ventures tend to fund much of their innovation activities by relying upon retained profits is confirmed by venture capitalists. These individuals consistently find that the most successful firms achieving growth through innovation typically have strong, healthy balance sheets (Hellman and Puri 2000).

The degree to which product performance is enhanced by innovation can range from a new, improved product which is essentially only marginally different from the existing product (e.g. Max Factor announcing a new, more effective eyeliner brush) through to the development of a highly significant new proposition (e.g. the iPad). The scale of change and the frequency with which improved or new products are launched into markets vary by companies and industrial sector (Biggadike 1979). In mature, low-technology consumer goods markets such as soaps or detergents, product change may be quite minimal, with minor improvements to existing products occurring every two to three years. This situation reflects that the fact that there are few opportunities to radically alter the sector's base technology. This can be contrasted with rapidly growing, high-technology markets such as telecommunications and electronics, in which ongoing advances in technology provide the basis for the frequent introduction of new, next-generation products (Montoya-Weiss and Calantone 1994).

TECHNOLOGICAL COMPETENCE

Case Aims: To illustrate how technological competence has sustained one of the world's most successful engineering companies for over 100 years.

Rolls-Royce is one of the oldest engineering companies in the world. From the very beginning the firm has outperformed competitors through a commitment to R&D as the basis for achieving and sustaining engineering excellence. The company has a vision of 'being trusted to deliver excellence, being only as good as the last success and always trying to produce the best, then strive to improve it.'

Henry Royce built his first motorcar in 1904 and in May of that year met Charles Rolls, whose company sold up-market cars in London. In December 1906, Rolls-Royce made its first public share offering to finance a new factory and to purchase additional machine tools. The city of Derby made an unsolicited proposal during the final stages of negotiations and was selected on merit as the location for the new factory. Work began in the autumn of 1907, with the official opening following in 1908. It was during World War I that the company began to focus on producing aircraft engines. After World War I, Rolls-Royce resumed car production, introducing the new Phantom I and II. During the 1920s and 1930s, when the UK government cut back on military spending, the company self-funded the development of new-generation aircraft engines. Its engines powered the UK aircraft that successfully competed in the Schneider Trophy races. Its most famous engine was the Merlin, which powered aircraft such as the Spitfire and the Mustang fighters and the Lancaster bomber in World War II. After the war the company became a leader in the development of advanced jet engines.

(continued)

TECHNOLOGICAL COMPETENCE (continued)

Unfortunately technological problems, a changing UK government defence policy and the more general managerial problems facing Western manufacturing firms led in 1971 to Rolls-Royce going into receivership. The UK government recognised the critical role the company played in the country's aerospace industry and funded the reconstruction of the business. During the reconstruction phase, the company was divided into two separate companies, aerospace/engines and motorcars. Another British company, Vickers, bought the car division, and continued to produce Rolls-Royce and Bentley cars until 1998, when the operation was sold to Volkswagen.

Currently the company's engines are powering the new Eurofighter and will be used in the US/UK Joint Strike Fighter (JSF). In civilian aviation, the company has led the world in new developments. The world's first supersonic passenger jet, Concorde, which was powered by four Rolls-Royce Olympus engines, was capable of travelling at twice the speed of sound. The company's engines powered all UK passenger jets before the UK civilian aircraft construction industry went into terminal decline. The advent of the jumbo jet was a major threat because of the preference of the US airlines to have American power plants. Rolls-Royce again used technological leadership to successfully compete with GE and Pratt & Whitney in world markets. In 2007 the company launched the Trent 900, which is the world's cleanest high-thrust engine, with emissions well below all current and proposed legislations, generating only 40 percent of the CO_2 per passenger kilometer of an average family car. The company has also been deeply involved in the marine defence industry, providing both gas turbine and nuclear power plants for naval and civilian vessels for numerous countries across the world. The company's commitment to retaining technological leadership is evidenced by its announcement in 2009, the middle of the worst recession since the 1930s, of plans to build a new wide-chord fan blade (WCFB) factory in Singapore. This was rapidly followed by the announcement of plans to invest in four new factories and two advanced research programmes in the UK.

OPERATIONAL COMPETENCES

Chaganti and Chaganti (1983) determined that the highest level of profitability in manufacturing firms is among those organisations which utilise a strategy of offering a broad range of products and use innovation to frequently update their product lines. These firms are also prepared to respond positively to market demands for product customisation. The researchers noted, however, that innovation has an equally important role in being used to implement improved process changes inside the organisation that can result in higher productivity. The usual focus of process innovation will be to achieve one or more of the three key strategic aims of reducing costs, improving quality and saving time.

Laforet and Tann (2006) concluded that in relation to sustaining business growth in entrepreneurial UK manufacturing companies, there was much greater reliance on process rather than new product innovation within these organisations. Innovation activities they identified included the utilisation of new computer-based technologies and the automation of production lines. The conclusion about the dominant role of process innovation in this one sector, however, should not be considered as a generalisation that can necessarily be applied to other sectors of industry. For example, in the case of the US timber industry, Wagner and Hansen (2005) determined that process innovation was more important among large firms and that product innovation was a more certain path for achieving business growth among smaller companies.

The importance of organisations achieving a productivity competence is reflected by the fact that many governments consider data on the productivity of firms in their countries as a key indicator of the competitive capabilities of their respective economies (Mayhew and Neely 2006). In most firms, labour costs are often the highest single area of expenditure. For firms seeking to achieve higher productivity, there are a number of capability enhancement options available which can save time or reduce direct costs. Gunasekaran et al. (2000) have proposed that in many cases, firms can make very cost-effective productivity gains by continuously seeking new ways of improving work flows. This can involve simple actions such as revising procurement practices, identifying and removing bottlenecks on the production line, introducing a more structured approach to switching between items being manufactured and investing in upgrading workforce skills. The researchers also reviewed the alternative solution of replacing employees with machines. Similar to Aris et al. (2000), they concluded this can be an extremely effective strategy through which to improve productivity. Certainly in terms of Western companies seeking to defeat overseas competitors from emerging nations, sustained investment in the latest machines is probably the only way to effectively combat the lower labour costs enjoyed by these competitors.

PROCESS COMPETENCE

Case Aims: To illustrate that a new process technology can offer a significant entrepreneurial opportunity.

In the 1950s and 1960s, the US steel industry was dominated by eight major American companies that operated large, integrated plants using economies of scale as the basis of achieving a competitive advantage (Slywotzky 1996). In the mid-1960s, however, the Japanese steel industry entered world markets, offering lower-priced steel produced from more modern, vertically integrated steel plants coupled with the exploitation of lower labour costs. Concurrently US manufacturers in sectors such as the car and drinks industries were switching to aluminium and plastics as a lower-cost raw material. The reaction of the US steel industry was not to re-examine its future process technology or be concerned about responding to substitutes for steel. Instead the industry focused upon attempting to persuade the US government to introduce tariff barriers to limit steel imports.

(continued)

PROCESS COMPETENCE (continued)

One entrepreneur who recognised the need to introduce an alternative process technology into the US steel industry was Ken Iverson at Nucor. He focused on the use of small production units, or mini-mills, located near to customers, which used scrap steel instead of iron ore as their raw material. By 1985, Nucor's success was reflected in the company's stock market value of $1 billion, almost equalling the market value of one of America's largest steel companies, Bethlehem Steel. Iverson was an entrepreneur who realised that standing still in a price-sensitive, commodity-orientated industry is not a viable option. In the early 1980s, the price of scrap steel, the raw material used in mini-mills, was rising dramatically. Additionally expansion by competitors was causing mini-mill sector capacity to begin to approach total market demand. Iverson's response was to avoid price competition by moving up-market, offering a higher-grade product at a higher price. To achieve this goal Nucor built a thin-strip, continuous casting plant in Indiana to produce flat-rolled steel for use in manufacturing sectors such as domestic appliances and the car industry. In order to reduce reliance upon scrap, the company also built an iron carbide plant in Trinidad, which processed low-cost iron from Brazil. The iron carbide, which provided an alternative to scrap, was shipped to Nucor's US mini-mills on barges which were routed via the port of New Orleans. The outcome of this second process innovation was that other American mini-mills could not compete with Nucor's new business model. Furthermore, not even the large integrated Japanese steel producers could match the low cost of production for flat-rolled steel which had been achieved within Nucor's re-designed operation.

PEOPLE

Large firms frequently claim their employees are the company's most valuable asset. This perspective relies upon the view that in an increasingly competitive world, where most companies have access to the same knowledge about customer needs and exploitable technologies, the only key difference may often be the superior intellect, work skills and commitment of an organisation's workforce (Hoffman 2000). Superior employee competence is considered an especially valid perspective in service sector markets. This is because in many service markets, such as consumer banking, there are minimal differences between the propositions offered by different suppliers. Consequently exploiting the skills of employees is often the only way to ensure customers receive a service experience superior to that available from a competitor (Fuchs et al. 2000). An example of this approach to people-based differentiation is provided by Singapore Airlines, whose capability of its staff has permitted the airline to regularly be rated by passengers as one of the world's best international carriers.

Another influencing factor in relation to greater reliance upon superior employee competence is that this is a critical philosophy in those organisations which have adopted relationship marketing (Gupta and Singhal 1993). The recognised importance of closer relationships initially emerged in B2B markets. This occurred because factors such as shorter product life cycles, increasingly complex technologies, rapidly changing customer buying patterns and increasingly sophisticated customers have necessitated that to survive many organisations need to work in closer partnerships with both key suppliers and customers (Webster 1992). Within only a short time, however, more competitive and turbulent consumer markets caused companies to recognise that the lifetime value of each customer in terms of total purchases over his or her lifetime means there is a need to maximise customer retention. This approach involves an orientation based upon achieving stronger customer loyalty. To achieve this goal employees have needed to re-direct their efforts away from generating the next sale from any source in order to focus on building long-term relationships with existing customers (Gronroos 1990).

PEOPLE COMPETENCE AND STRATEGY

Case Aims: To illustrate the key role people can play in a service industry where product differentiation is rarely an achievable strategic option.

The success of one world's first budget airlines, Southwest Airlines in the United States, can be attributed in large part to its people, who consistently deliver excellent service quality. Examples of service quality include national awards for lowest customer complaints, most on-time arrivals and the high quality of baggage handling services. In terms of overall industry ratings, Southwest is the only US airline to consistently offer below-market prices and above-average service quality (Czaplewski et al. 2001).

A fundamental component in the implementation of the company's business strategy is its treatment of employees. The airline emphasises putting employees first, even before customers. In fact the company has adopted the unusual mantra of 'customers come second . . . and still get great service.' This attitude is reflective of the company's core vision that the better employees are treated, the better they perform. A key managerial philosophy is that by providing purpose and meaning in the workplace, competing aggressively for the most talented people and preparing employees with the skills and knowledge they need to perform will ensure that everybody understands both their external and internal customers. Southwest makes extensive efforts to attract the very best people. However, it defines talent differently than most other companies. The airline prefers to employ new staff on the basis of personal attitudes and then train these people in specific skill sets. This perspective is based upon the belief that peoples' inherent attitudes and behaviour cannot be changed. To assess appropriate attitude, Southwest's interview process includes group interviews, placing applicants in a variety of situations to demonstrate their attitude to working in a team and their capacity to act spontaneously. The company also considers employee training to be a continuous process rather than a single event at the beginning of their employment. Throughout their time with the airlines, employees are cross-trained on multiple jobs to enrich their work experience and to prepare them to perform flexibly in different positions as needed.

QUALITY AND INFORMATION

During the 1970s, many Western manufacturers were fighting to sustain profitability in the face of both inflation and refusal by militant unions to accept revisions in working practices. As a consequence these firms passively allowed the topic of quality to disappear from the organisational radar screens. Countries such as Japan, quick to realise the vulnerability that this situation created, moved into world markets offering higher-quality, reliable products at reasonable prices. One of the critical competences developed within leading Japanese companies was the exploitation of the concept known as total quality management (TQM). The essential basis of this competence was to reject the conventional perspective of the retrofit resolution of quality problems once these have become apparent in the finished product. Instead TQM is based upon a commitment to identifying and resolving the source of any problems that might impact quality standards, not just across the entire producer organisation, but also within the component supply organisations upstream in the supply chain (Anderson and Sohal 1999). It was only after inflation began to decline and unions began to adopt a more co-operative attitude that European and American firms recognised the critical importance of product and service quality and became more able to match the level of quality achieved in Japanese corporations.

Kotzab et al. (2006) concluded that information management is especially critical to firms in seeking to exploit innovation as a strategy for enhancing added value outcomes within the supply chain of which they are a part. Tanabe and Watanabe (2005) reached similar conclusions about the critical importance of managing information as the basis for optimising the performance of entrepreneurial service firms. The potential importance of effective information management is that this competence can provide the basis for achieving a competitive advantage. Exploiting information has been greatly assisted by the advent of lower-cost hardware and software systems that permit the high-speed analysis of large quantities of data. In recent years this technology has led to the emergence of integrated customer relationship management (CRM) and enterprise resource planning (ERP) applications (e.g. SAP and Oracle) to facilitate both faster understanding of customer needs and optimising the efficiency of internal processes across the entire organisation (Coltman 2007). One sector which has greatly benefitted from exploiting CRM systems is banking. This is because those banks which have used CRM to compile data on customer expectations versus actual experience have been able to develop marketing programmes capable of building stronger long-term customer loyalty than their less IT-orientated competitors.

The core function of a successful CRM strategy is to create a sustainable competitive advantage by a using a better understanding of customers to deliver greater added value services to existing customers and for attracting new customers. Organisations which have possibly benefitted most from a key competence in exploiting CRM technology are those which utilise automated information management systems to warehouse and then analyse real-time data generated by the activities of their on-line customers (Thompson et al. 2003). Using segmentation tools these firms can analyse acquired data in relation to dimensions such as socio-demographics, variation in demand for products or services and customer pricing sensitivity as the basis for evolving more innovative approaches to presenting new, customised on-line offerings. Additionally by analysing changing real-time purchasing patterns these organisations are able to develop more accurate forecasts of future demand. Improved forecasting accuracy will reduce operating costs. This is because the level of lost sales due to 'out-of-stock' scenarios can be avoided and indications of a decline in a product's sales can immediately permit a downward reduction in inventory levels.

Amazon.com is a leading example of how CRM competence has helped the company build a globally successful on-line brand (Javalgi et al. 2005). To enhance the value and breadth of the company's offerings, Amazon has introduced an affiliation strategy. This has resulted in other suppliers contributing to the creation of a huge on-line product catalogue. Amazon achieves an additional sense of community with consumers by providing shared buyer experiences in the form of customer feedback and recommendations based on analysing individual customers' purchase behaviour. Furthermore by website customisation, such as Amazon's 1-Click service, the customer is provided access to faster order processing based upon retention of credit card and delivery information records from prior purchases.

6 Gap Assessment

The purpose of this chapter is to cover issues pertaining to:

1. Identifying strategic gaps that may represent opportunities or threats.
2. Assessing the market positioning of organisations relative to customer needs and competition.
3. The influence of scale on business performance.
4. Sustaining performance in mature markets and industries.
5. Supply chain power and the management of risk.
6. Strategies appropriate for different stages on the product life cycle (PLC) curve.

GAP IDENTIFICATION

The resource-based (RBV) and knowledge-based views of the firm provide ways to identify what strategies should be utilised to achieve the aim of maximising long-term added value. Managers need to make choices about which competences and knowledge resources can support organisational heterogeneity within a market. One method for generating understanding to assist this process is 'gap analysis' (Harrison 1996). Where an assessment of organisational competence and external environment reveals internal capability sufficient to ensure successful market performance, this indicates the organisation is in a 'positive strategic gap' position. This places the organisation in the position of being able to exploit any opportunity or cope with any threat. In contrast a 'negative strategic gap' will exist where internal capabilities are inadequate in relation to the external environment. This situation will mean the organisation is unlikely to be successful when responding to identified opportunities or attempting to overcome potential threats.

The iteration whereby the organisation is able to determine the nature of current gaps and determine how effective management of internal capabilities can permit achievement of the goal of optimising future added value is as follows:

1. Identify the resources and knowledge associated with delivering customer satisfaction.

2. Use gap analysis to identify the relative capabilities of market participants to deliver customer satisfaction.
3. Identify the resources and knowledge required to deliver higher satisfaction than competition.
4. Identify the internal competences required to optimise internal processes that can optimise achievement of long-term added value.
5. Use gap analysis to determine how internal competences may require enhancement to deliver long-term added value.

MARKET ASSESSMENT

In the private sector added value is realised only once the organisation sells output to customers. The magnitude of sales will be influenced by the degree to which output satisfies customer needs relative to competition. One technique for acquiring this knowledge is to construct a product space map of the type shown in Figure 6.1. In the illustrated example it is proposed that the two key customer satisfaction parameters are the level of services required by the customer and the price customers are willing to pay for such services.

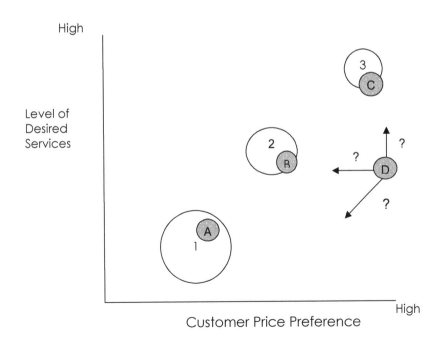

Figure 6.1 Product space map.

In many markets there will be variations in customer need. The example in Figure 6.1 proposes three different customer groups. These are Group 1, customers seeking low price/low service, Group 2, seeking average price/ average service, and Group 3, seeking a high-service/high-price proposition. This scenario exists, for example, in the airline industry, with Group 1 being those who use the 'no frills' airlines, Group 2 being economy class passengers flying on the larger international airlines and Group 3 being business and first-class travellers. Once understanding of customer requirements has been established by plotting the service/price proposition offered by the various suppliers to the market, the organisation can identify the effectiveness of different providers to meet customer needs. In Figure 6.1, company A is effective in serving Group 1, company B in relation to Group 2 and company C in terms of Group 3. The company facing the strategic dilemma is company D, which has a service/price offering which is of little appeal to any customer group within the market. Assuming company D wishes to remain in this market, a strategic decision will have to be made in terms of what customer group is of interest and hence the revisions in service and price offering required to achieve this aim.

The example in Figure 6.1 has only one company capable of fulfilling the needs of customers in each segment in the market. This is a somewhat rare outcome because in most markets there will be a number of firms seeking to attract customers within a specific segment. Where this occurs, there is a need for the firm to also undertake an assessment of the competence relative to these competitors. One approach is to examine relative competence in relation to competition and to meeting customer preferences. As summarised in Figure 6.2 this approach leads to four possible outcomes. Where the company is failing to meet customer needs and has low competences, this represents the worst possible scenario. The outcome probably demands

Capability to Fulfil Customer Needs

		Low	High
Competence Relative to Competition	Low	Strategic Failure	Competition Competence Gap
	High	Customer Need Competence Gap	Zero Gap Scenario

Figure 6.2   Market performance assessment.

a complete reconsideration of the organisation's future existence. In the case of low competence versus competition, there is a need to determine whether this competence gap can be closed. The same requirement exists in relation to a low ability to fulfil customer needs. Where no gaps are identified this means the firm is in a strong position to sustain the existing strategy relative to the prevailing external environment.

MOVING BETWEEN MARKETS

Case Aims: To illustrate the benefits of using an entrepreneurial strategy focusing on operating across a number of different market sectors.

An examination of the behaviour of firms over a business cycle led Connell (2007) to conclude that overall profitability tends to be higher among firms which exhibit an entrepreneurial orientation and have adopted a strategy of always offering a range of alternative product or service propositions. Connell posited that this decision rule increases the probability of the firm being able to compensate for a profitability decline in one area of operations being offset by ongoing success in another sector of the market.

One example provided by Connell to illustrate the strategic philosophy of having a diversified business portfolio is Bombardier, a Canadian firm founded in 1942 as a snow/winter equipment manufacturer. In the 1960s Bombardier launched its highly successful Ski-Doo snowmobile range. When the energy crisis of 1973 led to reduced sales of Ski-Doo, CEO Laurent Beaudoin moved into new areas of engineering such as trams and subway cars. In the 1980s Bombardier entered the aerospace industry with its purchase of Canadair. Manufacturing regional and business jets, Bombardier became the number three commercial aircraft manufacturer after the acquisition of Short Brothers, Learjet and de Havilland. Since 1988 the company operations have been divided into Group 1, involved in transportation, motorised consumer products and aerospace, Group 2, a financing and leasing business, and Group 3, a service business engaged in the repair, maintenance and overhaul of regional aircraft.

From 1996 to 2004, Bombardier's revenue grew by14.7 percent. During the economic downturn over the period 2000–2001, Bombardier's revenue growth averaged 18 percent and there was no apparent evidence of a potential decrease in future growth rate. Between 2002 and 2005, however, Bombardier's regional jet business suffered because of weakening in the market for airlines purchasing smaller jets. Compensation came from increased sales in the business jet market fuelled by corporate transportation cost-cutting and security issues.

The company's rail business also grew, driven by rising demand in Europe and China. Bombardier's financing of finished goods inventories for products supplied to customers remained strong, while aircraft financing performance declined to the point of becoming a potential candidate for discontinuation. Rail maintenance services business grew, which compensated for a slowdown in aircraft services activities caused by the underlying market contraction problems in the world's airline industry.

SCALE

From the early days of the Industrial Revolution it was apparent that as a firm becomes a dominant player in an industrial sector, certain fundamental advantages begin to emerge such as the ability to negotiate better prices from suppliers and to achieve lower unit production costs than its smaller counterparts. Subsequently economists labelled this effect as achieving 'economies of scale.' The operational advantages of market leadership have been empirically validated across a diverse range of industries from mining through to IT. In commenting on the importance of achieving economies of scale, Rich (1999, p. 27) concluded that:

> The economics of corporate life and death lead to one inescapable conclusion: In the long run, it's grow or die. Growth is imperative not only for companies in growth industries, but also for those in mature markets. If the market for a company's goods and services is growing and that company doesn't grow, then the company begins to lose market share. Ultimately, share loss means the firm won't be able to achieve economies of scale in R&D, advertising, product development, and production.

Although striving to sustain business growth may be seen as essential by the strategist in order to maximise achieved total added value organisation, this goal is not a simple task. For example, Rich's (1999) study on 'unbroken growth' companies examined the performance of 3,700 companies with annual sales in excess of half a billion US$. Of these 3,700 companies, only 21 companies (less than 1 percent) had sustained year-on-year sales or profit growth over the 20-year period from 1977 to 1997. This researcher concluded that a characteristic shared by members of this small group of consistently successful companies is a willingness to encourage risk taking and to support innovation without being too quick to punish managers for the occasional failed idea or mistake.

Another added benefit of greater size, which was first identified in the Boeing plants building B29 bombers during World War II, is that over time as a workforce gains experience from undertaking the same tasks, the production cost per unit will decline. Known as the 'experience curve,' this describes the phenomenon that firms which produce the largest proportion of output usually enjoy a cost per output lower than their smaller counterparts. As a result, assuming a similar prevailing price across an industrial sector, larger producers will enjoy a much higher level of added value per unit than the lower-volume producers.

Although the original emphasis on becoming a larger firm originated in manufacturing industries, over recent years the concept has spread into the service sector. This is despite the fact that the high labour content within the service provision process means fewer opportunities exist to achieve economies of scale and, furthermore, experience curves tend to be much flatter. In commenting upon the more limited operating cost savings associated with creating larger business entities within the financial service sector, Koguchi (1993) proposed that the emergence of excess capacity in the industry is why financial institutions have been forced to seek new ways of improving their utilisation of resources. This has led to some major banks expanding the size of their operations through M&A activity. However, the validity of seeking to achieve scale advantages in the financial services sector has yet to be unequivocally demonstrated. Koguchi's OECD-sponsored analysis of 108 separate studies was unable to identify firm evidence of the existence of substantial economies of scale or scope in the financial services industry. He suggests that an alternative to M&As in the financial service sector is to use existing resource capabilities to support diversification into new areas of service provision, thereby achieving 'economies of scope.'

GROWTH IS NOT ALWAYS GOOD

Case Aims: To illustrate that not all strategies based on sustaining business growth are actually beneficial to an organisation.

Deans and Larsen (2008) concluded that not all growth is good for business. They support their view with an analysis of the burger chain McDonald's, which through the late 20th century focused on a strategy of sustaining growth by opening new outlets. As new stores cannibalised the market for older ones, franchisees could not make any profit, average revenues per restaurant fell from $1.3 million in 1993 to $900,000 in 2002. Franchisees started cutting corners, food quality suffered, bathrooms got dirty and service quality declined. In 2002, for the first time ever, McDonald's posted a quarterly loss. With share prices dropping to $16, the company terminated this strategic focus on growth through adding outlets. Instead the new CEO, Jim Cantalupo, announced that McDonald's was retrenching. In 2003, McDonald's launched its 'Plan to Win' strategy, which focused on renovating existing stores, improving menus and slowing international growth.

Deans and Larsen posit that successful growth strategies are those which focus on delivering greater customer satisfaction and where possible rely heavily on innovation to offer a superior portfolio of products or services. In their view an excellent example of this scenario is the renaissance achieved by Apple, which has been reflected in the share price rising from $7 in December 2002 to $200 by December 2007. This share price recovery reflects the stock market's positive response to events such as 100 million iPods sold since 2001, three billion iTunes downloads as of August 2007 and the launch of the iPhone.

MATURE INDUSTRY OPPORTUNITIES

It is all too easy for managers within an industry to apply 20/20 hindsight vision to explain the failure of their firms or, in some cases, the disappearance of entire industrial sector. In the years preceding such failures, however, such clarity of insight by managers is usually somewhat rarer. One of the reasons for this situation is that senior management thinking is often influenced by the cultural heritage of the firm, which in the past led to outstanding market performance. Middle- and sometimes even lower-level managers may also be resistant to any suggestions concerning the need to consider a fundamental shift in future strategy. The probability that any one individual will be able to achieve a major shift in strategy in a large company, especially in a mature, long-established industry sector, will be heavily influenced by the 'softer' aspects of senior management behaviour, such as their attitudes towards structure, co-ordination and control (Hearne 1982). Some of the differences that exist between inflexible versus responsive firms which influence the degree to which the organisation is open to the idea of strategic change are summarised in Table 6.1.

Table 6.1   Comparing Attributes of Firms in a Mature Industry

Attribute	Inflexible Firm	Flexible Firm
Top management	Fixed ideas	Open-minded
Key values	Order, stability	Importance of responding to changing customer needs
Structure	Tight, formalised, hierarchical	Designed to best meet circumstances; may be tight or flexible
Leadership style	Directive, autocratic	Flexible depending upon circumstances, which may range from need for autocracy to broad freedom for self-decision
Planning process	Very detailed, heavy emphasis on financial data	Flexible and reliant upon an appropriate fit-for-for purpose approach
Control systems	Very detailed, reliant upon frequent preparation of extensive analysis of data	Flexible with the aim of identifying and diagnosing causes of any problems

Most firms operate in mature markets. Hence there is a critical need for the strategist in these organisations to identify the probable nature of future market conditions in order to determine what opportunities exist in order to avoid a major decline in financial performance or, in some cases, overcome threats that could lead to a total demise of the entire operation. In those cases where firms retain the same, unchanging product portfolio, the imbalance in capacity versus market demand prevalent in mature industries will inevitably lead to price wars as companies strive to sustain current sales levels. Under these circumstances, it will usually be those firms with some form of resource advantage, such as being located in a low labour-cost economy or having access to low-cost raw materials, that will emerge the winners. This outcome is a virtual certainty for those Western firms whose current or future competitors are located in emerging economies such as China and India. Hence the strategists in Western firms will usually need to identify how emerging trends in key areas such as customer behaviour or new technology might offer the potential framework for a revised strategy based upon innovation. This solution may offer the hope that the organisation can avoid participation in a price war, which is very likely to severely damage profitability.

MAJOR PLAYER BEHAVIOUR

Case Aims: To illustrate the organisational behaviour utilised by major Western firms seeking to sustain entrepreneurial behaviour.

For Western firms to continue to remain successful in mature markets it is usually a necessity that they continue to engage in entrepreneurial activity. The dilemma facing these organisations is how to retain an entrepreneurial environment while retaining a level of policies, procedures, systems and processes in order to manage and control their complex and often diversified business activities. To provide further understanding of how this goal can be achieved, Zimmerman (2010) has provided an analysis of managerial process within two global leaders, GE Company and Intel.

GE utilises a strategic business unit (SBU) concept which involves the creation of relatively autonomous organisations that are free from bureaucratic influences that could restrict their freedom to pursue innovation. To ensure visibility, attention and recognition, most of these SBUs report directly to GE's CEO. In the case of chip manufacturer Intel, a corporate culture exists which values initiative, risk taking and confrontation of ideas. These values include an ability to express disagreement, present alternative solutions and gain agreement for action on the basis of demonstrated superior knowledge, not position power.

(continued)

MAJOR PLAYER BEHAVIOUR (continued)

It should be recognised that such systems do not avoid strategic errors being made. For example, in the early years of the 21st century, GE's Finance Group was enjoying the benefits of the huge profits that were being made participating in the financial services sector. However, like many of its counterparts in this industry, the 2007 global banking crisis left GE Finance with a balance sheet containing toxic assets, the write-downs on which severely damaged the profitability of the entire GE Company. In the case of Intel, this company appeared to have not recognised the potential growth in demand for low-energy consumption microchips required for powering netbooks, iPads and smart phones. The launch of Intel's new generation of chips using 3D transistors, which use less than half the power of 2D transistors yet are 37 percent faster than the company's current 32nm chips, does provide a partial solution to becoming a player in the low-energy chip market. Nevertheless industry observers doubt the new product will permit Intel to overcome the lead achieved by Arm Holdings Ltd., which is the current leader in this sector of the microelectronics industry.

STRATEGIC OPTIONS

In developing guidance for how firms should identify opportunities for innovation, Hearne (1982) proposes the idea of implementing a 'strategic dissection' of the organisation with the aim of understanding the following issues:

1. *Customers*: This should cover issues such as current customer needs, how these are met by the company and competition, what indicators suggest emerging shift in customer need, and how shifts in the macro-environment might influence future customer behaviour.
2. *Competition*: This should cover issues such as key players, their cost structures, what vulnerabilities exist in the current strategy and how capable these firms are of reacting to change within the sector.
3. *Technology*: This should cover issues such as the base technology, how dominant this technology will remain in the future, what indications exist of new or emerging technologies and how these might impact the sector in the future.

In seeking to validate the idea that emphasis on innovation was a critical determinant of profitability, Hambrick (1983) utilised the PIMS database to examine the average ROI over a four-year period in relation to 400 large B2B firms operating in mature industries. His conclusion was that there are a number of different strategic paths through which firms can sustain high added value. One group was constituted of firms which are highly innovative, are able to protect innovations through patents and are very efficient users of available manufacturing capacity. This ability to exploit patents to protect the business is a relatively rare feature in many industrial sectors. In those sectors where such protection is not available, the highest ROI is usually achieved by firms which offer superior products or services, rely on innovation to retain this superiority leadership and are efficient users of available capacity. Another group which achieves high profits is those which exist in an industrial sector where technology is highly stable, and through emphasis on productivity and efficient asset utilisation, firms are able compete because declining costs support the capability to sustain profits, even when it is necessary to offer lower prices. Although this latter group enjoys high profits, the intensity of competition usually will mean that unit profit margins are low. This situation can lead these firms to achieve an ROI somewhat lower than firms which compete on the basis of innovation and offering superior-quality goods.

Another aspect of performance in relation to strategy revealed in Hambrick's study was that firms which have a broad base of customers seem to enjoy a more stable ROI than firms which specialise in serving a very narrow customer segment. This generalisation appears valid for firms which compete on the basis of quality and also for those which offer low prices. It seems probable that higher ROI stability is achieved in those firms whose business is spread across a number of markets because these organisations are less impacted by a slowdown in sales to any one single customer group. The other conclusion in this study is no matter which strategy is utilised, the success of firms in mature industries is critically influenced by the effective utilisation of capital assets. This means that firms which match investment with capacity optimisation needs are more likely to survive than firms which do not carefully assess supply and demand. These latter firms usually face a major decline in ROI because they are the owners of extremely expensive but under-utilised production capacity.

SURVIVING IN VERY MATURE INDUSTRIES

Case Aims: To illustrate strategies Western firms can adopt in mature markets facing price competition from overseas suppliers.

Western firms in high-technology industries can usually rely upon the launch of next-generation products to defend themselves from the threat of competitors based in lower-labour-cost, overseas locations. This solution, however, is less often available to highly mature industries engaged in long-standing traditional manufacturing processes such as those in the clothing and apparel industries. As a consequence many Western firms in the face of intense price competition from lower-cost imports are often forced to downsize and at the extreme may be forced into bankruptcy.

(continued)

SURVIVING IN VERY MATURE INDUSTRIES (continued)

It has long been known by small firms that an effective strategy for avoiding competition from larger companies, especially in relation to avoiding price wars, is to occupy a market niche meeting the specialist needs of a small number of customers. As well offering protection, a niche positioning may permit the firm to command a premium price for the products or services supplied (Chaston 2009). In seeking to determine whether a market niche strategy is an alternative option for larger Western firms in highly mature industries facing competition from overseas suppliers, Parrish et al. (2006) examined the strategies of the domestic clothing and apparel firms in the United States.

The study revealed that downstream US companies such as sewn-goods producers tended to adopt a niche strategy in terms of targeting specific consumer groups. Upstream companies such as yarn producers and mill producers usually focus on the product based upon the importance of innovation to offer technically superior goods. One factor contributing to this trend is that sewn-goods producers and auxiliary companies are closer to the consumer. These companies are more easily able to monitor spending and consumption patterns, and thereby have greater insight into market characteristics. Another factor is that upstream companies invest more capital in research and development, reflecting the technologically intensive nature of the fibre/yarn/fabric industry. Market size, socio-demographics and relatively high per-capita incomes mean there are a multitude of market niche opportunities available in the United States. The competitive advantage of domestic firms is their nearness to consumers and deeper understanding of the nation's culture. Nearness to markets also helps these firms react rapidly to identified changes in consumer behaviour, such as the emergence of a new fashion trend. This permits the offering of a specific service such as customer service, quick returns or short lead times, which permits differentiation from overseas firms, whose location creates logistics problems in relation to achieving a rapid response to changing consumer spending patterns.

For most firms, growth beyond being a medium-size business is often limited by the total size of their domestic market. One strategy to permit further growth is to become a multi-niche operation. Another solution is available in those cases where similar specialist niches exist elsewhere in the world. It is this strategy which has proved effective for some German firms that have expanded and become global leaders by focusing upon a specific niche where customers demand superior quality or advanced technology solutions.

SUPPLY CHAIN POWER

A market system contains all of the organisations engaged in the production and delivery of goods to the end user. In many B2B markets, where the product is large and the unit purchase value high (e.g. capital goods), distribution is usually direct from the producer and no intermediaries are involved. Systems which exist have tended to evolve over time with the primary influence being the ability of system members to optimise the costs and added value achievement associated with the creation and the distribution of the products or services involved. Thus, for example, in many developed economies major national supermarket chains have added procurement and distribution process to their retail activities, leading to a significant decline in the number of wholesalers and small, independent shops.

Typically very large organisations have the greatest power to exert control over the behaviour of the system of which they are a part (Hingley 2005). This is because their buying power permits them to demand the lowest possible prices from suppliers. As noted by Galbraith and Curtis (1983) there is a tendency for strategists to focus on the lateral behaviour of competitors at the same level with a market system, while concurrently ignoring the implications of power shifts occurring as either upstream or downstream organisations grow in size and acquire greater power to negotiate new terms and conditions with suppliers.

Fortunately for many planners, most power shifts tend to occur over a period of time sufficient to permit their other members of the supply chain to develop modified strategies for coping with systems change. Thus, for example, as supermarkets began to emerge as an increasingly dominant power within the consumer goods industry, major branded goods companies such as Nestlé and General Foods were able to implement marketing activities usually based upon increased promotional expenditure to strengthen brand loyalties, thereby justifying their claim with the major supermarket chains that consumers will expect to find their products on the retailers' shelves. Where there is evidence of growing downstream power, even large suppliers should assume that over the longer term there will probably be an erosion in profitability as power shifts permit intermediaries to acquire greater ability to demand lower prices or up-weighted sales promotion activity from suppliers. Under such circumstances, one effective strategic response for the supplier is to add value to its product proposition. This move can be used as a defence against demands for price reductions or increased promotional expenditure from major customers. An example of this latter scenario is provided by Procter & Gamble, which has added value to its relationship with the retailer Wal-Mart by accepting greater responsibility for stock management and in-store product line performance activities within the latter's outlets. Wal-Mart has benefitted from reduced operating costs and out-of-stocks, which in turn have reduced the pressure on Procter & Gamble to offer this retailer more competitively priced goods or increased levels of sales promotions.

SUPPLY CHAIN RISK

Case Aims: To illustrate that competence acquisition which increases power can ultimately prove non-productive.

Supply chains offer firms the opportunity to engage in vertical integration through M&A activity. Downstream integration allows manufacturing firms to move closer to the consumer or lower down the supply chain. In the early 1990s, the pharmaceutical firms in the United States perceived that supply chain downstream M&As and formal alliances offered two major benefits—namely, greater control over intermediaries' purchasing behaviour and the capacity to gain detailed information concerning patient care and treatment outcomes. Of the two benefits it was probably the drug firms' primary aim to achieve greater control over healthcare markets. The validity of this latter perspective is supported by the fact that a major focus of vertical integration was the acquisition of organisations known as pharmacy benefit managers (PBMs), which control the prescription drugs pharmacists can purchase which are acceptable to the private healthcare insurers (Simonet 2007).

The potential risk of certain firms gaining sufficient power over a supply chain is this may result in these organisations implementing actions that may be detrimental to either other supply chain members or the end user. In the case of the drug industry by downstream acquisitions the major firms had the potential of freeing themselves from prevailing competitive pressures by exerting control over prescriptions among organisations which had been acquired or with which formal alliances had been agreed.

By the late 1990s the rising cost of healthcare and the need to reduce public sector spending caused both governments and patients to question the drug industry's claims of acting in a responsible and caring way. Pressure from government agencies such as the Federal Trade Commission (FTC) in the United States forced the pharmaceutical firms to avoid situations which evidence an abuse of power. Furthermore intense competition between PBMs drove down margins. This caused the drug firms' to dismantle their PBM integration relationships within their supply chains. In commenting upon this outcome, Simonet (2007, p. 157) concluded that 'vertical integration offered no major gains, and worse, sacrificed innovation opportunities.'

NEW VALUE CHAIN OPPORTUNITIES

Size is of little benefit unless greater scale is accompanied by an adequate level of profitability. This is because the larger the organisation, the greater are the profits required to fund activities such as defending against competitive threats, investing in innovation or modernising ageing capital assets. Hence the other key issue in reviewing potential trends within the market system is to identify at which point within the system other organisations are engaged in activities which will permit them to capture a greater proportion of the sector's added value, and to assess whether this represents a threat that could negate an organisation's ability to sustain current profitability (Mudambi 2008).

A classic example of an ability to exploit the potential in added value creation within a market system is provided by the case of Microsoft. At the time Bill Gates founded his company, the conventional view in the computer industry for achieving market leadership was to manufacture and sell PCs. Gates, however, recognised that as knowledge of how to manufacture PCs became more widely available within the industry, there would be increasing pressure on firms to cut prices and spend huge sums on promotional activity in order to sustain market share. Over time this pressure to focus on 'shifting more boxes' would drastically reduce profitability. His alternative strategy was to focus on the creation of software, which would optimise the performance of PCs. This led to the development of operating systems such as MS-DOS and software applications such as Word and Excel, which were subsequently adopted as the standard by the majority of the world's PC manufacturers. This shift in added value within the supply chain permitted Microsoft to become a highly profitable global participant in the computer industry. Other previously dominant players in the computer industry such as IBM were eventually forced to withdraw from involvement in the manufacture of PCs because of an inability to generate any profit from this area of their business.

From his analysis of trends within value chains, Mudambi (2008) concluded that scenarios such as Microsoft's success are increasingly common in any knowledge-intensive industry. In his opinion the reason for this trend is that within these industries widespread understanding of production technology has resulted in the outcome of intense competition between companies engaged in the manufacture of high-volume, standard goods. As a consequence very few of these organisations will be able to sustain an adequate level of profitability. Mudambi posits that profit erosion is usually accompanied by a migration of higher-level value added activities towards some other point within the market system. Usually this shift is towards knowledge-based R&D activities that can lead to the commercialisation of new technology and superior, knowledge-based, innovative marketing management capabilities.

ORGANISATIONAL PROCESSES

In many markets, products or services rarely survive unchallenged for an extensive period of time. This is because changing customer needs or the advent of new technology rendering current products obsolete are ever-present threats. A very useful analytical tool for identifying such trends is the product life cycle curve (or PLC) (Venkatraman and Prescott

1990). The standard representation of the PLC is to show sales revenue over time passing through the four phases of introduction, growth, maturity and decline.

Academics such as Hofer (1975) have proposed that the PLC concept is a very effective tool for assessing market conditions and changing added value outcomes as the basis for determining whether there is a need to revise strategy as an organisation's various products enter a new phase on their respective life cycle curves. The introduction phase on the PLC is concerned with the launch of a completely new product, with the emphasis on R&D to develop a marketable product, accompanied by promotional activities to persuade customers to try the new item. As sales tend to be low relative to operating expenses, during the early part of the introduction phase, the product will usually generate negative added value. The growth phase is when new customers are entering the market and existing customers are becoming repeat users. The strategic focus will be on increased marketing activity coupled with expenditure and the development of competences to support capacity expansion. During this phase, with sales rising faster than expenses, total added value will rise. Eventually all of the potential customers will have been attracted into the market and hence sales will plateau as the product moves into the maturity phase. With the only source of growth coming from stealing sales from competition, marketing expenses will tend to rise and average prices will tend to fall. The outcome is that as the product progresses through the maturity phase, total added value will decline. Eventually customers will decide that another, usually newer or different product is of more interest and the existing product will enter the decline phase. Companies will tend use price to sustain sales, and hence during the last phase of the PLC total added value will usually fall dramatically.

There has been some criticism of using the PLC concept in business planning on the grounds that in the real world, sales curves rarely follow the precise four-phase pattern of the type presented in management texts. In an attempt to determine the validity of these criticisms, Thietart and Vivas (1984) undertook a study of strategy management during different phases of the PLC. This research involved a cross-sectional study of over 1,000 firms within the US Profit In Marketing Strategy (PIMS) database by selecting firms in the growth, maturity and decline phase on the PLC curve in various consumer and B2B sectors of industry. In their examination of internal organisational processes, Thietart and Vivas noted that variation in strategic behaviour was apparent between firms operating in different industrial sectors or at different levels within their respective supply chain. Firms in high-growth, technology-driven industries tended to focus on an RBV strategy to achieve product performance and service quality superiority. Leading firms in mass markets all exhibit similar competences in relation to their ability to manufacture relatively standardised, low-technology products. This situation requires a RBV strategy which focuses upon superior marketing skills, thereby permitting first entry into markets, highly effective promotional campaigns and distribution channel domination to protect market share.

The results of their study caused Thietart and Vivas (1984, p. 1405) to conclude that:

> The PLC approach can be used prescriptively for allocating effort and resources among different activities of the firm. It can also be useful for choosing and implementing strategic actions dealing with the financial, marketing, production and R&D aspects of the firm as the product moves from one stage to another.

SYSTEMS SHIFT

Of concern to the strategist when assessing internal organisational process gaps is that a scientific or technological advance may emerge that has the potential to create a fundamental shift in the competences required of organisations. Such scenarios have emerged on a number of occasions since the early days of the Industrial Revolution. The application of steam power to create railways and steamships transformed agriculture from a sector constrained by geographic distance to a sector involved in multi-national business operations (e.g. the beef industry in Argentina; the wheat belt of North America). Concurrently steam power led to the demise of the stagecoach for transporting people and canals for moving most industrial materials.

Where an analytical approach to identify a fundamental shift in technology may prove ineffective is in relation to the occurrence of unexpected or 'wildcard' events. Such events usually occur because there is a shift in customer behaviour which has not been recognised by existing firms. In the case of the Internet, for example, the wildcard event was the huge untapped consumer demand for participating in on-line social networks. Even highly experienced firms such as Google and Yahoo failed to appreciate the major commercial potential opportunities which social networks offered. This was despite the fact that by late 1990s, there were already futurists suggesting social networks were the next new opportunity. For example, Oliva (1998, p. 52) had noted that 'another quickly emerging wild card is the virtual community phenomenon: online networks of members who communicate regularly and develop relationships around a shared special interest.' The failure of existing firms to recognise the validity of this perspective meant that it was left to entrepreneurial newcomers such as Myspace and the even more successful Facebook to exploit the massive global demand for on-line social networking.

PROCESS MORPHING

Case Aims: To illustrate entrepreneurial outcomes are dependent upon respective strategies in relation to the management of competences.

Rindova and Kotha (2001) have used the phrase 'managing by morphing' to describe the process whereby entrepreneurial firms when confronted with rapidly changing market systems respond dynamically by revising or re-directing their resources to develop competences capable of supporting an effective strategic response. To demonstrate the application of their morphing concept, the researchers undertook a comparative analysis of two of the leading US firms that were early entrants into the world of Internet search engines, Yahoo and Excite.

In 1993–1994 a team of students at Stanford University in California set themselves the goal of developing software which used a computer programme to search and index websites. Their technology included some very advanced features such concept extraction, which involves searching for families of words instead of just single words. The students formed a company called Architext, subsequently renamed Excite. Meanwhile two other Stanford students, Jerry Yang and David Filo, were creating their own list of favourite websites, which they organised into a hierarchical directory of categories. Encouragement from other techies at Stanford was the stimulus for these two individuals to start visiting and categorising in the region of a 1,000 new sites/day. The sense of humour that is a characteristic of these two individuals led them to describe their site as 'Yet Another Hierarchic Officious Oracle,' which was the origin of their very memorable business name, Yahoo.

The organisational structure of these two operations was very different. At Yahoo, the directory which formed the basis of their search engine was maintained and expanded by a large team of 'web surfers,' who identified, visited and then classified new websites. The Californian lifestyle and orientation of the Yahoo operation business was reflected in the names on the two navigational buttons on the website—namely, 'new' and 'cool.' In contrast, Excite's operation was software-driven, using a search technology known as 'spiders' to scan the Internet and automatically develop an index listing new websites as these were identified. The company employed fewer staff and instead ran the operation using row upon row of computer servers linked to very powerful workstations. Initially Excite's computerised search engine generated results faster and in greater quantity than Yahoo. The latter's search engine, however, was seen by users as providing more relevant information. By licensing spider technology from third-party suppliers, Yahoo was soon able to match Excite's search speed. In response to this situation, Excite developed an in-house editorial staff to review and categorise new websites. Both companies needed external financing to fund their expansion. Excite negotiated funding from a Silicon Valley venture capital firm, Kleiner, Perkins, Claufield and Byer, in December 1994. Yahoo, having declined takeover offers from Netscape and AOL, in April 1995 obtained funding from another Silicon Valley venture capital company, Sequoia. Only two years later, both companies made their stock market debut through IPOs. On April 4, 1996, Excite raised $31 million in new capital.

(continued)

PROCESS MORPHING (continued)

This was then exceeded by Yahoo, which on April 12 raised $85 million. By 1996 new competitors such as Google and HotBot were entering the market and the ability to operate fast search engines as the basis for sustaining a competitive advantage began to decline in importance. Yahoo's response was to seek to build awareness for the brand by exploiting the firm's reputation as being the really switched-on, coolest company on the World Wide Web. This identity was extremely useful in generating revenue from other Internet firms. For example, Yahoo was adopted as the default engine by the then leading browser company, Netscape. In 1996 Yahoo launched a $5 million television advertising campaign. This was the first time a major Internet company had used an off-line, terrestrial medium to build brand share. Excite responded by launching its own $8 million television campaign, built around Jimmy Hendrix's classic rock song, 'Are You Experienced?' Despite this higher level of spending, Yahoo still remained a more highly recognised brand name than Excite. The key reason for Yahoo's success was the strategic decision in 1996 to start offering new content such as stock market quotes, maps, news, weather, sports, classified advertising and 'chat rooms.' Content differentiation was achieved by creating specifically labelled sections such as Yahoo Finance. The company then moved to strengthen regional and international brand identity by creating ten regional sites in the United States and seven sites overseas. To execute these activities Yahoo exploited its existing relationships with companies such as the Reuters News Service and the Japanese media conglomerate Softbank. Lacking such well-developed market contacts, Excite was forced to rely on reaching agreements with companies such as AOL and MSN-Europe to provide content and to expand the distribution of its search engine's services. Excite's attempts to match Yahoo's success had by the end of 1997 caused the company to virtually run out of cash. To overcome this problem, the company fired about 50 percent of its in-house editorial team. The cost-cutting exercises failed to solve the cash problem. To survive the company was forced to accept a takeover offer from @Home, a US provider of high-speed, on-line access services.

Meanwhile Yahoo, instead of expanding the technology of its search engine and focusing exclusively upon dominating the search business, attempted to evolve into an all-purpose portal for Internet users. In contrast, a then much less known private company, Google, run by Sergei Brin and Larry Page, was focusing upon developing an even more effective search engine. When Google launched its own search engine in 1999, Yahoo outsourced Google's product and allowed its tens of millions of users to become intimately familiar with a superior technology from a rival company. Meanwhile, having failed in its portal strategy, Yahoo decided to become a media and entertainment company. In 2001 it hired Terry Semel, the former chairman of Warner Brothers, as CEO. He apparently failed to grasp the benefits of search engines providing the basis for generating revenue from on-line advertising. In 2007, in the face of declining revenue, Yahoo re-appointed Jerry Jang to replace Semel as CEO. Yang's return in no way mirrored the impact of Steve Jobs' return to Apple. Yang seemed unable to set out a fundamentally new strategic direction for his company (Keen 2008). The company then appointed Carol Bartz as the new CEO.

(continued)

PROCESS MORPHING (continued)

Her evaluation of the company caused her to conclude that Yahoo was unlikely to regain the market share lost to Google and hence would be unable to survive by remaining an independent operation. Hence in 2009 she negotiated an alliance with Microsoft. Under the terms of this alliance, Microsoft would run the technology behind both its own Bing search engine and Yahoo's search results, while Yahoo would handle the direct sales of sponsored advertising.

7 Issues, Objectives and Stakeholders

The purpose of this chapter is to cover issues pertaining to:

1. Avoiding personal bias in the categorisation of opportunities, threats, strengths or weaknesses.
2. The prioritisation of strategic issues.
3. Techniques for assessing performance gaps.
4. Defining the organisation's strategic objective(s).
5. The benefits of adopting single versus multiple objectives.
6. The role of key stakeholders and their influence on objective setting and fulfilling desired performance criteria.
7. The emergence of corporate social responsibility (CSR) strategies to meet the wider societal demands which may be placed on the organisation.

KEY ISSUES

Managers' classification of a variable as an opportunity or threat and strength or weakness will influence how these individuals subsequently interpret the nature of the identified variable and the actions to be implemented. This effect is an important aspect of 'categorisation theory' in that an incorrect classification of a variable can lead to errors in the way the factor is handled in any subsequent business plan (Dutton and Jackson 1987).

Categorisation of a variable as an opportunity or a strength may be perceived as implying a positive situation over which the individual or organisation has a significant degree of control. In contrast a threat or a weakness may be perceived as a negative situation over which the organisation has less control. Once a variable has been labelled but further information is seen as being required to enhance decision-making, the nature of the information sought might also be biased towards acquiring data which is of a positive nature in relation to an opportunity or strength and of a negative nature in relation to a threat or weakness.

Managers also need to be aware that a number of interpersonal factors can influence acceptance of strategic objectives, plans and strategy implementation as these are being proposed (Graham 1997). Where the proposer of an idea or objective perceives themselves to be an important or powerful individual, then this person will believe his or her suggestions should be given priority over alternative ideas tabled by others whom this individual considers less important members of staff. Where one department is perceived as more important relative to other departments, then this department's proposals are likely to gain greater acceptance than ideas from sources elsewhere within the organisation. Other factors of less influence are experience and formal education, with more experienced staff and those with a degree being more able to garner support for their ideas from others. Furthermore the quantity of information can also influence acceptance of proposals because most managers tend to give greater credence to proposals which are lengthy or highly detailed.

Very few organisations enjoy a dominant market position or have access to a scale of resources such that an appropriate planned response can be allocated to every variable identified in a SWOT analysis. During the implementation of the SWOT it is rare that clear-cut conclusions can immediately be reached. More usually there is a need to undertake a re-iteration of the SWOT to generate fuller understanding of the situation facing an organisation. Once a SWOT analysis has been finalised, managers will need to prioritise variables to decide which should be classified as 'key issues' requiring urgent attention in any subsequent business plan. The issue of prioritisation will also be influenced by the orientation of the analysts. Individuals who are strong advocates of RBV will tend to identify internal competences as key issues. In contrast marketing-orientated individuals will probably determine that aspects of the external environmental should be selected as the most important key issues that require significant attention when drafting the strategic plan.

ENERGY COST ISSUE

Case Aims: To illustrate how a wider perspective may lead to recognition of an opportunity to lower sustainable electricity generation costs.

One of the fundamental dilemmas facing organisations in the sustainable energy generation industries is their inability to match the lower costs associated with power generation using hydrocarbon fuels. Even though sustainable energy has gained from more governments committing to a sustainable energy policy to reduce greenhouse gas emissions, companies engaged in exploiting energy sources such as wind or wave power may face major operating cost problems unless they can attract government subsidies. Without such subsidies many of these companies are unable to generate a profit from exploiting sustainable energy technologies. Recent cutbacks in government subsidies means the sustainable energy sector in many Western nations is now confronted by the strategic requirement to overcome the cost gap between their proposed technology and continuing to use hydrocarbons to generate electricity.

(continued)

ENERGY COST ISSUE (continued)

The tendency of most sustainable energy firms is to locate their operations in the country where they are based. However, when one adopts a broader perspective over the location of operations, then in the case of solar power a more viable scenario is to base generation facilities in a higher than average level of sunlight. Further cost reduction can occur by moving away from just relying on solar panels and instead to using a technology known as concentrated solar power (CSP). This involves using directive mirrors to generate heat that is used to run steam turbines that produce electricity (Jansen 2009). Added efficiency is achieved by storing spare heat in tanks containing melted salts that can continue to power the turbines at night. A concept known as Desertec is already being promoted by a European network of scientists and is beginning to attract serious interest from both European financial institutions and large engineering companies. In theory one single system based in the Sahara could meet the EU's entire demand for electricity and a massively up-scaled version could deliver the world's entire supply for electricity. Currently the estimated costs of CSP are about 0.15 euros per kilowatt compared to 0.06 euros for coal or nuclear stations. However, Desertec members believe this cost gap could be reduced, assuming funding can be made available to support commercialisation of the technology and the construction of power lines to distribute the electricity generated in the Sahara to customers in Europe and/ or elsewhere in the world.

ISSUE PRIORITISATION

There are organisations for which a greater focus on internal versus external key issues is an appropriate orientation. In most cases, however, it is possibly better for an organisation to allocate attention to both external events and the internal competence issues in order to effectively optimise overall future added value performance. One technique whereby this can be achieved is through the use of a modified version of the GE-McKinsey Matrix to develop 'Opportunity' and 'Threat' Response Matrices (Hatten and Rosenthal 1999; Rowe et al. 1994).

The shared aspect of both these matrices is to assess the relative importance of different scenarios in the external environment in relation to the organisation's level of relevant competences. In order to classify the scale of identified opportunities and threats, it is necessary for the organisation to determine which key variables are critical contributors to outcomes in the external environment. These variables will usually exhibit a certain degree of both sectoral and organisational specificity. In many cases, however, key influencers found in most scenarios are variables such as market size, market growth, customer loyalty, customer price sensitivity, intensity of competition, complexity of technology, rate of technological change, sustainability, environmental protection and economics. Each variable is assigned a score on a simple 1–10 scale, where the higher the score the greater the contributive influence. The scores are summed and the total divided by the number of variables to convert the overall measurement back to a number between 1 and 10. Scores of 0–3, >3–7 and >7–10 are considered to respectively indicate a scenario is of low, average or high importance.

A similar analysis is undertaken in relation to relevant internal competences to support achievement of the desired level of added value. Again some variables will usually exhibit a certain degree of sectoral and organisational specificity whereas others key influencers will be common to most scenarios. Examples of this latter type of variable might include workforce skills, age of assets, production capacity, financial resources, R&D capability, market management ability, access to key raw materials/components, information management ability, service quality and logistics management. The same scoring and analysis system as used for the external environment analysis permits competences to be assessed in relation to providing the organisation with a low, average or high capability. The scores when combined with the relevant scores in relation to the external environment for each scenario are then entered onto the respective matrices of the type shown in Figures 7.1 and 7.2.

As shown in Figure 7.1, the location of a specific scenario on an Opportunity Response Matrix will determine priorities in relation to the future allocation of organisational resources to exploit identified opportunities. Specifically the nine different actions are:

Market Determined Future Added Value

		Low	Average	High
Level of Relevant Internal Competences in Relation to Delivering Added Value	Low	No future	Limited future	High-risk
	Average	Limited future	Ongoing stable future	Internal competence upgrade future
	High	Withdraw resources to create cash	Future diversification	Entrepreneurial emphasis to sustain future leadership

Figure 7.1 Opportunity response matrix.

1. Low Opportunity/Low Competence: This scenario indicates there is no future for this area of activity and hence no ongoing activity should occur in this area.

2. Average Opportunity/Low Competence: The organisation lacks the competences to exploit this situation and hence there is a limited future in relation to exploiting this opportunity.

3. High Opportunity/Low Competence: This is an area of critical concern and high risk. This is because examples of high added value opportunities are extremely rare but, unfortunately in this case, the organisation lacks the required competences. A priority action is to determine the viability and scale of investment required to acquire the required level of enhanced internal competence. This will be followed by an assessment of whether the level of associated risk justifies such an investment.

4. Low Opportunity/Average Competence: The organisation lacks the competences to exploit this situation and hence there is a limited future in relation to exploiting this opportunity.

5. Average Opportunity/Average Competence: In most cases this scenario is likely to be an important contributor to the organisation's primary core source of added value. Hence the opportunity should continue to be seen as sufficiently important that the existing allocation of resources will be sustained in the future to ensure there is ongoing development of internal competences appropriate for any changes in external environmental circumstances.

6. High Opportunity/Average Competence: Given the high level of opportunity this means the scenario can make a very important contribution to the organisation's future overall added value performance. Hence priority should be given to upgrading the organisation's level of competence in this area of activity.

7. Low Opportunity/High Competence: Relative to the scale of opportunity, the organisation is over-resourcing this area of activity. Resources should be allocated elsewhere, which will then permit this scenario to evolve into a cash cow situation.

8. Average Opportunity/High Competence: The organisation has achieved a level of competence greater than is required by the identified opportunity. Hence a diversification of resources should be implemented whereby some resources are transferred to support the development of competence in other similar types of external opportunity.

9. High Opportunity/High Competence: This is likely to represent one or more areas of opportunity where acquired competences have permitted the organisation to achieve a leadership position. In order to sustain leadership in the future, priority should be given to ensuring the organisation continues to exploit innovation as a path by which to stay ahead of competition.

Future Threats to Targeted Added Value

		Low	Average	High
Level of Relevant Internal Competences in Relation to Delivering Added Value	Low	Ignore	Monitor	Crisis scenario demanding immediate containment
	Average	Monitor	Implement appropriate actions utilising current	Transfer of resources to upgrade competence
	High	Transfer most resources to other areas of activity	Release some resources to other areas of activity	Immediate action to implement viable solution

Figure 7.2   Threat response matrix.

As shown in Figure 7.2, the location of a specific scenario on a Threat Response Matrix will determine priorities in relation to the future allocation of organisational resources. Specifically the nine different actions to respond to identified threats are:

1. Low Threat/Low Competence: This scenario can be ignored for the foreseeable future. This is because the analysis reveals a minimal threat accompanied by an absence of the competences required to respond effectively.
2. Average Threat/Low Competence: The organisation lacks the competences to effectively respond to this threat. However, given that the scale of the threat is assessed as average, ongoing action should be to monitor the scenario to ensure no deepening of the threat level goes unnoticed.
3. High Threat /Low Competence: This is an area of critical concern and high risk. This because in relation to the scale of the threat the organisation lacks the required competences to be able to respond to the situation. An immediate priority is to put a threat containment plan in place while the organisation examines how appropriate competences might be developed that can eventually diminish the scale of this threat.
4. Low Threat/Average Competence: The organisation has the compe tences necessary to handle this threat. However, the low threat level suggests that the only action should be to monitor the situation to ensure no increase in the threat level emerges.
5. Average Threat/Average Competence: This scenario is likely to have a reasonably significant potential impact on future operations. However, the organisation has the necessary competences to handle the situation. Hence a threat management plan should be implemented which draws

upon the organisation's existing capabilities without additional resources being needed to be allocated to upgrade existing relevant competences.

6. High Threat/Average Competence: Given the high threat level this scenario represents in relation to the organisation's average level of competence, priority should be given to investing in the additional resources required to achieve an upgrade of the organisation's level of competence.

7. Low Threat/High Competence: Relative to the scale of threat, the organisation is over-resourcing this area of activity. Resources should be allocated elsewhere which are in greater need of competence upgrading.

8. Average Threat/High Competence: The organisation has a level of competence greater than is required to manage the identified threat. Hence resources should be transferred to other more important threat scenarios which could benefit from enhanced competence.

9. High Threat/High Competence: This level of threat is of concern and priority should be given to overcome the identified problems. Fortunately this is an area where the organisation has already developed the necessary level of competence to ensure an effective response to the situation.

STRATEGIC THREAT RESPONSE

Case Aims: To illustrate how recognition of potential threats can be countered by focusing upon sustaining a unique competitive advantage.

The problem facing Western manufacturers is that over time they can expect entry into their markets by increasingly sophisticated Chinese companies which have acquired the competences to compete on the basis of equal product quality and lower prices. In order to counter this threat Western manufacturers need to identify opportunities for developing and sustaining competences that provide the basis of a unique competitive advantage. One such company in the UK is John Guest Ltd, one of Europe's biggest suppliers of plastic fittings in the intensively competitive plumbing and engineering sectors (Marsh 2010b).

The company was founded by John Guest in 1961, a self-taught engineer who invented a series of 'snap-fit' components. The philosophy of the company has been to focus on innovation in both new product development and manufacturing processes. To remain ahead of competition the company also spends heavily on advanced capital equipment. The company site in West Drayton has 153 of the world's latest plastic injection moulding machines supplied by the German producer Arburg. These are supported by 150 automated assembly machines which have been predominantly developed by the company's own engineers. These systems are in operation on 24-hour-a-day basis but have been designed to achieve a level of process flexibility to permit the company to make short runs across more than 3,000 products. Many of these products are protected by patents. John Guest's sons now run the business but continue to sustain the philosophy of focusing upon ensuring the operation has the necessary competences to sustain ongoing innovation. Currently the company is examining new opportunities in emerging markets such as solar energy.

(continued)

STRATEGIC THREAT RESPONSE (continued)

Another strategic response available to Western companies is to focus on a specialist sector of an industry and to exploit leading edge technology to supply unique products. An example of this approach is provided by the UK firm Fandstan Electric, which is a world leader in two narrow sectors of the rail industry—namely, the supply of esoteric third-rail systems that use composite track structures to enhance the transfer of power from the rail to the locomotive, and pantographs that are sited on top of trains to connect them to overhead power line gantries. Although the company has factories in China and the United States, the core operation is the Chard factory in Somerset, where the focus is on exploiting technology to develop specialist welding systems that are capable of joining extremely thin pieces of aluminium and steel. The company managing director, Michael Bostelmann, describes the firm's approach to sustaining a competitive advantage as 'gentle innovation' which involves ongoing R&D in those areas of technology which are central to the business. Once new approaches to welding which are difficult for competitors to duplicate have been developed in Chard, these competences are then transferred across to the company's other factories elsewhere in the world. In 2009 at the peak of the recession, pre-tax profits were £11.5 million, which at 10 percent of sales is extremely high for the intensively price-competitive rail industry. Company earnings have grown four-fold over the past 15 years, and future growth is likely to be even higher due to increasing demand for the construction of new metropolitan railway networks, especially in developing economies.

PERFORMANCE ASSESSMENT

In addition to identifying the key issues which will need to be managed to ensure ongoing organisational success, it is usually beneficial to determine whether the organisation's forecasted financial performance will meet expectations. Where adequate information is readily available, one approach to assessing performance outcomes is to implement a 'financial gap analysis.' This involves plotting planned and probable performance over a medium-term period such as the next five years (Guo 2002). The difference between probable and planned performance provides the organisation with an understanding of the scale of the problem concerning inadequate future performance. The usual focus in financial gap analysis is on revenue and profits. It is often beneficial, however, to also undertake a similar analysis for ROI.

The advent of increasingly sophisticated data analysis and statistical software packages provides the forecaster with a wider range of different tools for examining future trends. It is extremely rare for any of these forecasting techniques to provide a certain, totally accurate estimate of future performance. This is because future performance can be influenced by a multitude of variables, many of which cannot be accurately interpreted for inclusion in forecast equations. However, experienced executives can often make reasonably accurate guess-estimates of probable performance in relation to different scenarios. This capability can be exploited by using managers' perspectives on the probability of alternative scenarios as the basis for constructing a decision tree.

Although a financial gap or decision tree analysis will provide data on the scale of any expected shortfall in performance, the analysis techniques have the drawback of not providing any information which diagnoses the reason(s) for any shortfall in forecasted versus required performance. As a consequence some organisations will need to identify which factors are key influencers of performance and then implement further qualitative analysis to gain understanding of how these are contributing to performance shortfalls. This additional knowledge when combined with the prioritised opportunities and threat analysis can then add further clarity to the future actions required to deliver the organisation's desired financial objectives (Carpinetti and De Melo 2002).

Terwiersch and Ulrich (2008) have proposed that a common cause of a financial gap is poor market performance of one or more items in the organisation's product portfolio. They suggest the nature of this gap can be identified in one of two ways. One approach is to evaluate these products in relation to (a) customer attitudes over desired product performance or (b) the performance of similar products offered by major competitors. An alternative approach to identifying product performance relative to competition is to evaluate the effectiveness with which the organisation exploits technology to deliver the specified performance of a product relative to the technological capabilities of competitors. Terwiersch and Ulrich recommend that an evaluation be undertaken in relation to the position of products on the product life cycle. At the introduction stage the company needs to determine the probable dominant technology which will emerge in an industrial sector and the ability of the organisation, relative to competition, to exploit this technology. In the growth stage the dominant technology will have become obvious and again the organisation needs to determine whether there is a difference between itself and competition in the exploitation of this technology. At the maturity and decline stage, the critical focus will shift to process efficiency and capacity utilisation. Hence assessment for these types of products will need to switch to reviewing organisational operational process competences relative to key competitors.

The aim of any organisation is to ensure that expectations about any key area of performance are matched by actual achievements. Where it becomes apparent that one or more areas of the organisation's operations are facing performance gaps, there is a need to determine why this is occurring. Any evaluation will need to be extended beyond just the issue of inadequate forecasts. This is because as there are a number of different factors that can result in expectations not matching actual outcomes, including some such as economic conditions or new legislation which are beyond the control of the organisation.

INTERNAL GAP IDENTIFICATION

Case Aims: To illustrate how competence gaps can arise from lack of understanding of customer priorities inside an organisation.

GEC-Marconi Aerospace (GECMAe) is a UK manufacturer of pumping systems, pneumatic systems, electro-mechanical actuators, actuator subsystems, and fuel handling and metering equipment for bulk fuel distribution. GECMAe is committed to investing in the latest manufacturing technology. The company has an integrated suite of computer-aided design (CAS) tools to enable tasks, such as design analysis, computer numerically controlled (CNC) planning and rapid prototyping using 3D design software. Further efficiencies were achieved from also introducing concurrent engineering and electronic data interchange into the organisation.

In highly competitive advanced engineering systems it is necessary to respond rapidly and effectively to the changing patterns of customers who are demanding high-quality, low-cost products relevant to their specific operations. The company also faces the need to utilise the latest technological advances to achieve greater product differentiation, particularly in the company's mature and declining markets. Following an assessment of recent performance it was apparent to management that a competence gap existed between what is demanded by customers and the current agility level of the GACMAe manufacturing operation to meet this market demand. This situation was adversely impacting the company's ability to compete successfully in a global market.

Senior management recognised that the cause of a declining ability to meet changing customer needs was that an internal competence gap existed between what the marketing group needed in relation to fulfilling market requirements and the operational capabilities to respond to market need within the manufacturing group. Discussions and data exchange between the two groups revealed that gaps existed in relation to the key competence of translating demand needs into products being supplied. GECMAe identified discrepancies between the marketing and production functions in relation to issues such as enquiry lead-time, manufacturing lead-time, delivery reliability, design flexibility and delivery flexibility. The problems were highlighted by research on customer satisfaction, which revealed the greatest area of complaint was 'slow turnaround time/late delivery.' Analysis of the reasons for new contracts not being won revealed that high price, delivery performance and technical matters were the key factors for poor performance. A key obstacle in achieving cost reductions was that this had to be accompanied by concurrent improvements in technical performance and speed of delivery. In order to close these organisational competence gaps, there was the requirement for the introduction of new manufacturing processes, re-definition of production/logistic systems, greater reliance on IT-based decision systems and investing in upgrading the technical skills of the workforce.

STRATEGIC OBJECTIVE

The purpose of defining a strategic objective is to provide the organisation with a specification of future performance which can be used to guide the selection of an appropriate strategy and permit assessment of actual performance versus forecast upon implementation of the strategic plan. There is some debate in the academic literature concerning the nature of the objective to be specified and whether there is a need to utilise multiple objectives (Denton 2006). In terms of the nature of any objective, given the requirement to assist assessment of progress during implementation, then any aim must meet the parameter of being measurable. In most cases the measurability criteria will mean a preference for a quantitative expression of performance.

Other key requirements of a strategic objective include achievability, sustainability and universality. The purpose of achievability is necessary because there is no purpose in setting a performance target which employees or the financial markets perceive as being impossible. The former will become demotivated and the latter sceptical about making funds available to the organisation. Sustainability is an essential dimension for management seeking to construct an enduring organisation. This is because there is a critical requirement that the organisation continues to perform well over a long period of time. Universality refers to the need for the strategic objective to be perceived as applicable across the entire organisation. This is because all employees must be able to relate to the organisation's strategic objective in order that this overall umbrella aim assists in assessing their personal effectiveness in fulfilling their own job roles or the task role of the department in which they are located.

In relation to the use of a single strategic objective, one possible generic statement of aims is for the organisation to 'achieve and sustain an above-average, long-term added value performance which is greater than the average performance of other organisations operating in the same sector(s) of activity.' In view of the necessary intent for management to focus on constructing an enduring organisation, the phrase long-term performance is a critical aspect of an organisation's strategic objective. This is because managers can usually find a way of achieving short-term increases in added value. They can implement actions such as reducing expenditure on equipment maintenance, not updating key capital equipment or cancelling all new product development projects. The subsequent reduction in organisational costs will be reflected in an improved financial performance for a short period of time such as 12–36 months. Beyond this point, however, these actions will lead to outcomes such as increasing customer dissatisfaction, lower sales and eventually an irreversible downturn in added value performance relative to other organisations that had rejected the concept of managerial short-termism.

The fundamental purpose of a private sector organisation is to achieve an adequate return on investment from the assets utilised in the business.

Not-for-profit organisations such as public sector bodies or charities usually have a somewhat different fundamental purpose. This is because many exist to deliver services which cannot be provided by the private sector. Not-for-profit organisations can therefore usually be expected to specify a strategic objective concerned with the long-term provision of an appropriate quality of services to a maximum number of clients within the target group(s) in which the sector(s) where the organisation operates. In those cases where there are a number of organisations engaged in the provision of such services, then the strategic objective of any single entity should probably be the goal of undertaking the acquisition and utilisation of inputs that can achieve a higher level of added value outcomes relative to these other organisations during the provision of an appropriate quality of client services.

MULTIPLE OBJECTIVES

A key reason for a reliance on a single strategic objective concerned with financial performance is that in most organisations financial measurement systems are more accurate than other systems in generating accurate real-time data. The ability of accounting systems to generate real-time data has evolved and developed over hundreds of years in order to meet the demands of agencies such as the financial regulatory bodies and governments that wish to be provided with highly current information on sales or profits, which can then be used to calculate tax liabilities.

The 2008/9 crisis in many of the world's leading financial institutions has re-enforced existing concerns which have been expressed by both academics and management practioners that commitment to financial performance objectives can cause managers to focus only on 'hitting the numbers.' This in turn may lead to short-term strategic thinking (Mailliard 1997). One issue which is emerging in this debate is whether organisations should continue to base their strategic objective on simple financial performance targets. The alternative perspective that is gaining support is the use of multiple objectives whereby other aims such as customer satisfaction, productivity and product/service quality should be used in defining future aims during the planning process and monitoring performance upon plan implementation.

One of the most widely accepted multiple objective systems is the 'balanced scorecard' concept developed by Kaplan and Norton (1996). Their idea was to combine financial and non-financial issues into a systematic approach that covers four different areas of an organisation's operation—namely, financial, customer, internal business and innovation. The purpose of the scorecard is to translate the organisation strategic intent into measurable units of information, which can be evaluated and compared. As well as defining financial aims such as ROI, non-financial data such as the customers' perspectives and process productivity are included in the specification of long-term strategic objectives.

In those organisations where multiple strategic objectives are utilised, Dwyer (1998) has proposed these should fulfil following requirements:

1. *Relevance*: To ensure decisions reflect the primary objectives of the organisation.
2. *Utility*: To ensure that organisational management can use the framework to explain its policies, programs and initiatives.
3. *Shared ownership*: Decisions taken with the active involvement of organisational managers ensure that information needs of managers as well as formal organisational accountability requirements are met.
4. *Transparency*: To ensure that all employees understand what results are expected as well as how and when these are to be measured.
5. *Time relevant*: To ensure that information needed by all is available when required.
6. *Flexibility*: To respond to the ever-changing environment and the context in which organisational policies, programmes and initiatives take place.

In commenting upon the benefits of multiple performance objectives, Dwyer noted these are of little benefit unless accompanied by an effective framework for both assessing actual performance versus plan and supporting longer-term evaluations of selected strategies. He proposed the framework should incorporate the principles of performance measurement and accountability at all levels within the organisation. In his view the accountability framework should contain the following components:

1. *Profile*: Generating an accurate description of the organisation's policy, programmes and initiatives, including justification for the allocation of resources and intended outcomes from the resources being utilised.
2. *Logic model*: Illustrating how results across the organisation are expected to contribute to the achievement of overall strategic aims.
3. *Evaluation system*: Providing a diagnostic evaluation of performance, thereby permitting identification of issues, data requirements and data analysis processes.
4. *Reporting strategy*: Ensuring that performance evaluation is impact-relevant and can be utilised at all levels within the organisation.

STAKEHOLDERS

Organisations do not exist in a vacuum. Each entity is a member of a market system and the socio-political system of each country in which the organisation has operations. As a consequence each organisation is involved in the management of a complex web of relationships with individuals and other organisations which have a vested interest (or 'stake') in current and future performance. The participants in these relationships, which exist both inside and outside of the organisation, are usually known as 'stakeholders.' It is crucial that the organisation recognise the importance of stakeholders because they often have the ability to influence the future existence of the organisation. Consequently in determining strategic objectives, the organisation does need to ensure that where possible these aims will be acceptable to the majority of stakeholders (Atkinson et al. 1997).

Environmental stakeholders include customers, other members of the organisation's supply chain, investors, the financial community and society in general. Internal stakeholders are all of the current and retired employees, plus their families, who rely upon the organisation to provide an ongoing source of income and financial security. It was proposed earlier that the primary strategic objective of the organisation could be 'to achieve and sustain an above-average, long-term added value performance which is greater than the average performance of other organisations operating in the same sector(s) of activity.' Where the organisation seeks to reflect meeting the broader needs of society in general, then a secondary objective might need to be defined, namely that of 'concurrently seeking to meet the performance expectations of the organisation's key stakeholders.' Some performance expectations of stakeholders are defined in formal contractual terms (e.g. the salary scales agreed with the workforce; percentage interest to be paid to debenture holders). However, the majority of stakeholder expectations are implicit promises which have been defined by the organisation as necessary in order to retain the support of specific stakeholders (e.g. customers being provided with service quality superior to that of competition; supporting local communities in locations where the organisation is based).

The debate may arise when defining objectives to satisfy stakeholder needs in relation to whether any one group should be given priority over others. Harari (1992) expressed the view that commercial organisations must identify the customer as the priority stakeholder. This is because priority given to other groups such as managers or the financial community will result in excessive emphasis being placed on short-term profits. His concern is this latter orientation will usually be detrimental to product performance or service quality. An alternative perspective to Harari's view of giving priority to customers in the setting of objectives is that the organisation should seek to achieve, wherever possible, equality of treatment for all key stakeholders. Such a philosophy will be feasible for any organisation which plans to achieve the long-term outcome of above-average added value. This is because above-average performance will require customers being supplied with superior, high-value products or services, generate high dividend and/or share prices for shareholders, maximise employee job security and generate high corporation taxes to support government funding of welfare services.

To gain further understanding of meeting key stakeholder demands, Greenley et al. (2004) surveyed UK firms in relation to their attitudes towards their primary stakeholders. They determined that the response of firms to stakeholder demands permitted these organisations to be classed into four types of behaviour—namely:

1. Group 1, where shareholder interests are given the highest priority by companies in this cluster, and second are competitors and employees. Customers are seen as having the lowest priority.
2. Group 2, where customers and competitors are the priority, employees come second and shareholders are seen as the least important stakeholders.
3. Group 3, companies that are not too concerned about stakeholders although they do exhibit some concern about fulfilling the needs of their employees.
4. Group 4, companies that do not perceive that any primary stakeholders are of real importance when determining strategies or defining performance goals.

Greenley et al.'s analysis of corporate behaviour indicated that higher awareness of the need to respond to stakeholder demands is present in those firms which exhibit an orientation towards using organisational learning as a key component for developing new or revised strategies. Furthermore those firms which are actively engaged in the use of innovation to enhance market positioning also have a much greater awareness of the need to respond to stakeholder concerns of their customers. The researchers concluded that these variations in behaviour provide evidence of how organisational culture will influence the actions of firms in determining their response to stakeholder demands.

There will be times when long-term survival of an organisation may require hard decisions being made that are to the detriment of one or more of the organisation's stakeholder groups. For example, a company may have to close a factory because the product line is obsolete, or the factory is not suited to being refurbished for the production of a new product or for environmental safety reasons. In this instance equality of treatment does not apply. This because one group of the company's internal stakeholders, i.e. those employed at the factory scheduled for closure, is being disadvantaged. Hence when attempting to resolve the dilemma of stakeholder inequality, it is perhaps best to assess any major decision in relation to the organisation's overarching primary objective of seeking to achieve and sustain an above-average added value performance. In terms of the factory closure, then regretfully although some of these internal stakeholders will be disadvantaged, nevertheless making these employees redundant is necessary in order to sustain the long-term organisational performance, thereby benefitting the rest of the organisation's stakeholders.

STAKEHOLDER IMPACT

Case Aims: To illustrate the variable capability of stakeholders to influence organisational behaviour.

In a recent attempt to determine the degree of influence stakeholders have over organisational behaviour, Spitzeck and Hansen (2010) examined documented cases involving over 50 different major corporations. They concluded that in 17 cases stakeholders had no power to influence corporate behaviour. In 25 cases there was evidence of limited impact related to stakeholder influence. Only 14 cases were identified where companies showed evidence of really listening to the concerns of stakeholders. In another 13 cases a clear link was identified between stakeholder engagement and the adoption of new policies as a result of the dialogue. An example of this latter outcome is provided by a UK retailer that, following expressions of concern by stakeholders, introduced a new policy in relation to the use of palm oil as a product ingredient and the objective of phasing out all supplies of oil from unsustainable sources. Only seven cases could be identified in which stakeholders were granted significant influence on corporate decisions and strategies. These cases tended to be related to companies granting customers extensive options and influence concerning the design of products and services.

In terms of how stakeholders can influence companies' behaviour, Frooman (1999) proposes there are two main options—namely, the withholding strategy and the usage strategy. To demonstrate their impact, he examined the case of the activities of an environmental group, EII, and its actions to persuade the StarKist company in America to alter its behaviour over the sourcing of tuna. Withholding strategies are those where the stakeholder ceases providing a resource to a firm with the intention of making the firm change certain behaviour(s). Employees can withhold labour by striking and financial institutions can refuse to renew loans. In the case of the StarKist-EII example, the environmental group persuaded consumers to boycott the company, thereby influencing StarKist's decision to confront the foreign tuna fishing industry over its practices.

Usage strategies may be those in which the stakeholder continues to supply a resource but applies certain constraints or activity caveats. In the StarKist-EII example, the company implemented a usage strategy against the foreign tuna fishing industry of purchasing tuna only from producers who no longer fished with purse-sein nets and moved to adopt alternative catching methods. In terms of approach, a stakeholder that employs a withholding strategy is prepared to shut off the flow of resources to a firm, whereas a stakeholder that employs a usage strategy is not. The credibility of the withholding threat is determined by the ability of the stakeholder to simply walk away from the relationship with no harm to itself. This will occur when the firm is unilaterally dependent on the stakeholder, which is the case of the consumer refusing to purchase goods. When the stakeholder and firm are mutually dependent, the stakeholder will not be in a position to walk away from the relationship. Both stakeholders will benefit by seeking to meet the concerns of the other. In the StarKist-EII scenario the sales of the foreign tuna fishing industry were linked to the sales of StarKist. The fishermen knew that should a consumer boycott affect StarKist's sales, then eventually their sales to StarKist would be adversely impacted. Thus the industry needed to accede to StarKist's demands regarding choice of how tuna are caught.

(continued)

STAKEHOLDER IMPACT (continued)

Frooman noted that the StarKist case illustrates how outcomes are influenced by the degree to which a firm is dependent upon the stakeholder. Where there is a low level of dependence of a firm on a stakeholder, the firm does not have to be responsive to the stakeholder. The firm is somewhat impervious to stakeholder influence. In those cases where a resource dependency exists, the future of the firm is linked to those who are providing key resources. In those cases where there is a high level of dependence of the stakeholder on the firm, this means that future performance of the stakeholder is closely tied to the ongoing existence of the firm. The foreign tuna fishing industry and StarKist were in this latter category. Their relationship was a mixture of mutual dependence and conflict. This was because they were partners in the same venture and hence both stood to suffer in the face of a consumer boycott.

SOCIETAL STAKEHOLDERS

A long-established concept known as 'agency theory' concerns the role of managers in professionally managed and publicly owned companies being required to act in the best interests of the shareholders. Associated with agency theory is the perspective that where senior executives have minimal equity holdings, the number of non-executive board members should be higher in order to ensure the executives are fulfilling their obligations to meet the best interests of the shareholders (Johnson et al. 1993). The converse of this decision-rule is where top management have a significant equity stake, there is less need for the involvement of non-executive board members in the company's decision-making. The sub-prime mortgage debacle, the collapse of major financial institutions and the huge bonuses being paid within the financial community would seem to raise questions, however, about the validity of agency theory in relation to the effectiveness of non-executive board members protecting the long-term interest of shareholders (Anon. 2009c). It seems reasonable to suggest that these events are reflective of a prevailing attitude among senior managers, who may or may not be owners of significant equity, of implementing strategies orientated towards short-termism and being prepared to put personal wealth ahead of either shareholders or other stakeholders and ignoring the views of non-executive directors. This conclusion would seem to suggest that the presence of non-executive directors on the boards of major financial institutions may do little to prevent senior executives ignoring their responsibility in relation to acting in the best interest of shareholders. In fact one might suspect that in certain situations, some non-executive board members were supportive of short-termism and questionable lending practices. This outcome may reflect the fact that some non-executive directors seek to use their knowledge of corporate intentions to greatly increase their own personal wealth.

Recent vocal criticisms over the questionable managerial behaviour in the banking industry are neither new nor unique. Down through the ages there have been numerous examples of individuals whose desire for profit and low personal moral values have led them to abuse their workforce, mistreat customers or be prepared to pollute the environment or commit fraud. However, over the last 50 years factors such as the emergence of a consumer society, citizens' use of the legal system to challenge the behaviour of large organisations and an increasingly borderless world have all contributed to major organisations facing greater pressure to exhibit a higher level of social responsibility. As a consequence major corporations need to give much greater priority to the views of society in general when defining the performance objectives acceptable to their different stakeholder groups. Furthermore in many Western nations, consumers tend to include the issue of social responsibility of major companies as being a major factor influencing their purchase decisions. An example is provided by consumers who ceased to purchase products from the sporting goods company Nike because of their concerns about the company's use of child labour in some of its overseas suppliers' factories.

The increasing willingness of consumers, organisations and governments to expect certain standards of behaviour from major corporations means external stakeholders may influence the development of an organisation's mission and goals. In theory this can result in companies being required to act in the best interests and the greater good of society. Managers have the task of balancing the competing demands of external stakeholders with the concurrent requirement to protect the best interests of the company's internal stakeholders. In seeking to balance what may be competing demands, organisations are developing a corporate social responsibility (CSR) strategy. Implementation of the CSR strategy has the potential to deliver benefits such as increased community goodwill, improved company image, being supported by social responsibility–oriented investors and avoiding new government regulations.

RESPONDING TO CRITICS

Case Aims: To examine strategic responses to challenges by societal stakeholders.

Primary stakeholders include customers, suppliers, employees, shareholders and creditors. Lawrence (2010) contrasts these with 'societal stakeholders,' who are those which although not engaged in receiving direct economic benefit are nevertheless impacted by the activities of corporations (e.g. the general public, local communities and NGOs). In recent years growing awareness following events such as the Enron collapse or the problems created by the earthquake at the Fukushima atomic energy plant in Japan has led to a rise in the number of individuals and organisations prepared to challenge the proposed actions by both private and public sector organisations.

(continued)

RESPONDING TO CRITICS (continued)

In analysing the increasing importance of nonmarket stakeholders, Lawrence proposes there are four possible response strategies:

1. Wage war on objectors through actions such as filing lawsuits, requesting injunctions, gaining support from politicians or attempting to mobilise public opinion.
2. Withdraw from the confrontation by pursuing a different course of action such as relocating the proposed activity or cancelling the entire project.
3. Wait until circumstances change (e.g. there is subsequent legislation change, the scale of objections declines or one of the involved parties gains the upper hand).
4. Find an acceptable solution by negotiating with the objectors and identifying common ground upon which agreement by all parties can be reached. This process is known as 'stakeholder engagement.'

Lawrence notes that none of these strategies is mutually exclusive. In her view managers can be expected to use a mix of strategies depending upon their perceptions over which action is most likely to lead to problem resolution. Managers' behaviour is also influenced by external variables. One factor is where one party has more resources than another (e.g. ability to fund a long legal battle). A second factor is the degree of relative power held by one party over the other (e.g. a company may be prepared to fight an environmental group but would avoid confrontation with a nation's government). Firms must be aware that relative power positions can shift over time. For example, it might be safe to ignore objections from a local community but the balance of power could change if the national media or an international environment group also becomes involved in the fight. A third factor is the degree of urgency in resolving differences (e.g. where a firm is facing time pressures to launch a product ahead of competition, it may be more amenable to reaching a compromise about the best location for a new production facility).

CSR AND THE DRUGS INDUSTRY

Case Aims: To illustrate how CSR trends can influence strategy in two major corporations.

In recent years the pharmaceutical industry has come under greater scrutiny as consumers, insurance companies and governments have sought to identify ways of trying to halt the apparently relentless rise in the cost of modern medicines. As a consequence major firms are increasingly aware of the need to exhibit an apparent strong sense of corporate social responsibility (CSR) as a way of deflecting criticism over the influence on healthcare economics.

(continued)

CSR AND THE DRUGS INDUSTRY (continued)

Over the past decade, for example, a heated controversy has developed in the UK between the pharmaceutical industry and the European Commission (EC) involving direct-to-consumer advertising of prescription and over-the-counter medications. The EC's stated opposition is that advertising of pharmaceuticals and drug-related products and services is merely expenditure to increase sales and does nothing in terms of educating the general public about reaching medically responsible decisions (Smith 2008).

In his review of CSR trends in the drugs industry in recent years, Smith presents a review of two major corporations, GlaxoSmithKline (GSK) and Bayer Corporation. GSK is a global company located in the UK which operates in 117 countries, has 92 manufacturing facilities, 20 research and development facilities and annual sales in the region of £40 billion. Senior management enforces a CSR culture to ensure that everyone—their employees and their suppliers—adhere to GSK's ethical standards within the laws in the countries in which it operates. Effective CSR is perceived as a critical issue because the healthcare industry is a highly regulated sector. The company website states that 'as a science-based company GSK believes that the rights, dignity and safety of people using our products, both during and after their development, are paramount' (www.gsk.com). An aspect of corporate culture is the belief that humanity should share in the benefits of science. The company philosophy includes the view that better healthcare in developing countries is vital, and it will not supply medicines in countries where it is not feasible to follow GSK's value and ethical standards.

An area where the pharmaceutical industry has faced pressure from external stakeholders is the ongoing need for animal testing, which is used develop further understanding of diseases and in evaluating the potency and safety of new medicines. Some companies do conduct research without using animals. These methods consist of computer modelling and using isolated cells and tissues to identify harmful side effects. GSK believed that using these latter methods did not fully evaluate the potency and safety of its potential drugs. In continuing to use animals, the company is committed to ensuring the humane care and treatment of all laboratory animals and the organisation's own code of practice is based upon higher standards than those specified in any current laws.

Bayer Corporation is another multi-national pharmaceutical which incorporates a philosophy of corporate social responsibility into its long-term objectives. Bayer's stated goal is to grow the value of the company and generate value to the stockholders, employees and society in all countries of operation. One dimension of Bayer's CSR strategy is in the area of improving healthcare in developing nations. An example of this strategy is the partnership with the World Health Organisation (WHO) to develop a new malaria drug with the ingredient artemisone, for which Bayer holds patent rights. Bayer is developing and supplying the product, with WHO being granted sole distribution rights. The price for the product will be set at a level that will allow malaria sufferers in developing countries such as Uganda and Zambia to afford the drug.

8 Strategy

The purpose of this chapter is to cover issues pertaining to:

1. Examining alternative perspectives about 'what is a strategy?'
2. Selecting a competitive advantage to sustain long-term performance.
3. Determining strategic positioning to sustain long-term performance.
4. Relying on RBV versus a competence/environment-based strategy.
5. Creating an effective strategic defence.
6. The critical importance of retaining strategic flexibility.
7. Allocating and prioritising resources.

DEFINITION

A review of management texts and journal articles will reveal that there are significant differences of opinion among academics about precisely what is a strategy. In commenting upon this situation, Markides (2004, p. 6) noted that:

> The confusion is not restricted to academics. If asked, most practising executives would define strategy as how I could achieve my company's objectives. Although this definition is technically correct, it is so general that it is practically meaningless.

The debate over defining 'what is a strategy' is not a new issue. Almost 20 years ago, the editors of *Planning Review* explained that 'nobody seems to know what is strategy anymore.' In an attempt to clarify the situation, the journal asked the MIT Professor Arnolodo Hax to present his perspective in this matter. Hax (1990) posited that a strategy embraces all of the key activities of the organisation and hence should be required to be constituted of the following six specific elements:

1. Provides a coherent unifying and integrative pattern of behaviour.
2. Determines organisational purpose in terms of long-term objectives, actions and resource allocation priorities.
3. Selects the businesses the organisation is in or is considering entering.

4. Attempts to achieve a long-term sustainable advantage by responding to the opportunities, threats, strengths and weaknesses of the organisation.
5. Engages all the hierarchical levels of the firm.
6. Defines the economic and non-economic contributions the firm intends to make to the stakeholders.

Some standard management texts contain similar expositions when defining strategy such as those proposed by Hax. The length and complexity of this type of definition are possibly one reason for the confusion which exists in the minds of both students and management practioners about exactly what is the nature and purpose of an organisational strategy. To overcome this problem, perhaps a simpler definition is hereby proposed. The approach seeks to draw a lesson from a UK advertising claim for Ronseal's range of wood treatment products—namely, 'it does what it says on the tin.' Assuming one is prepared to accept the benefits of simplicity, then a possible definition is:

Strategy is a statement which specifies the nature of the entrepreneurial competitive advantage to be utilised to achieve an organisation's added value objectives.

A key reason for the definition of strategy being 'a statement which specifies the nature of the entrepreneurial competitive advantage' is to communicate there is a fundamental need for the retention of organisational flexibility in the face of flattening demand in many Western markets and increasing success enjoyed by Indian and Chinese firms in global markets. By adopting an entrepreneurial approach to competitive advantage, this will ensure the organisation is able to recognise early signs of environmental change and has the competences and internal culture to respond by using innovation as the basis for evolving a competitive advantage more suited to future trading conditions.

It might be argued that this definition, by inclusion of the concept of competitive advantage, is not applicable to public sector or not-for-profit organisations. However, consideration of the activities of organisations in these sectors will usually lead to the conclusion that competition is an element of their external environments. Charities, for example, compete with other charities for donations. Different areas within the public sector such as education, social services and healthcare compete for resources both between different service provision sectors and between the various agencies charged with delivering the same specific aspect of welfare state provision.

COMPETITIVE ADVANTAGE

A potential risk with the Porterian model of competitive advantage based upon cost versus differentiation and mass versus focused market coverage is some users may adopt a literalist view of the concept. As a consequence some organisations may not realise it is possible to adopt a combined competitive advantage approach (Reitsperger et al. 1993). In the United States and Western Europe a standard response to the emergence of price competition from lower-cost Asian suppliers in the 1980s was to assume that survival could be achieved only by adopting the competitive advantage of superior product performance. To achieve and sustain superior performance usually requires expensive R&D and investment in new technology. Unfortunately it is not always the case that these higher costs can be recovered. This is because customers may be unwilling to pay a premium price in return for superior performance.

One nation which recognised the fallacy associated with a literalist interpretation of the Porterian model was Japan. Entrepreneurial manufacturers recognised that an even stronger competitive advantage can be achieved by offering a superior product, but through the application of appropriate process technologies, making the product available at a lower price. One of the first examples of this 'blended advantage' concept was Toyota, which launched its range of luxury vehicles under the Lexus brand name. These cars were hugely successful because they offered consumers the same standard of quality as the world's leading brands, such as Mercedes and Cadillac, but at prices approximately 25 percent lower than these competitors.

In part in order to overcome some of the criticisms of the Porterian model, Treacy and Wiersema (1995) proposed that the changing nature of markets meant that Porter's two dimensions of market coverage and product performance were no longer adequate in providing the basis for the determination of a successful strategy. In their view the key issue which requires recognition is the growing importance of relationship marketing which causes some firms, in seeking to build long-term customer loyalty, to move away from the more traditional philosophy of transactional marketing. Chaston (2009) expanded the original Treacy and Wiersema model on the grounds that there was insufficient attention to the option of competing on the basis of superior value/lower price. This led to the proposal of a model to cover the four dimensions of transaction, relationship, product performance and superior value. The features associated with a strategy associated with these dimensions are:

1. *Transactional excellence*:

   - Price/quality/value product combination superior to that of competition.
   - Standardised products.
   - Excellence in managing conventional production and distribution logistics processes.
   - Information system designed to rapidly identify manufacturing and/or
   - logistic errors.

2. *Relationship excellence*:

- Product/service combination which delivers complete customer-specific solutions.
- Product solution based on conventional specifications appropriate for the industrial sector.
- Employee obsession with finding even more effective conventional solutions to customer problems.
- Information systems which rapidly identify errors in solution provision.
- Culture of all employees committed to working closely with counterparts within the customer organisation.

3. *Product performance excellence*:

- Product offering outstanding superior performance versus competition.
- Orientation towards always seeking to extend the performance boundaries of existing products.
- Excellence across the entire workforce in understanding how the latest advances in technology might be incorporated into products and/or production processes.
- Culture of employees always striving to apply conventional approaches to finding new market opportunities for exploiting identified product performance improvements.

4. *Superior value excellence*:

- Product value significantly higher than rest of market.
- Skilled in the production of 'no frills' products.
- Excellence in acquiring prior-generation technology and capital equipment at either zero or low cost.
- Information system designed to rapidly identify adverse cost variance trends across the areas of procurement, manufacturing and distribution.
- Culture of employees always striving to find ways of applying conventional thinking to further reducing operating and/or overhead costs.

Most organisations, having analysed market need and the behaviour of competition, will probably determine that it is feasible to exploit internal competences to develop a strategy which represents a combination of two of the four dimensions available. In the application of the revised model, this decision will then result in the selection of one of the strategic positions shown in Figure 8.1.

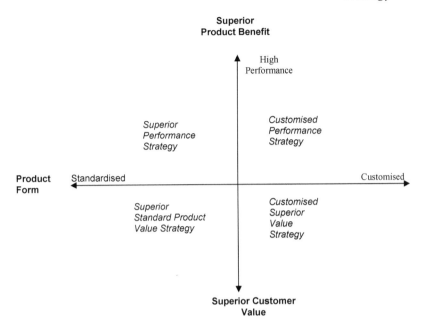

Figure 8.1 Strategic options.

In seeking to define appropriate managerial processes to permit organisations to understand the nature of changing market opportunities leading to the need to revise strategic position, Raynor (2008) proposed senior managers must accept responsibility for managing strategic uncertainty. This will involve attempting to ensure to improve the level of certainty over future performance by implementing actions that can support a selected strategic option. The recommended process in responding to turbulent or increasingly competitive markets is as follows:

1. Anticipate that change is probably inevitable and hence develop an organisational mindset which assumes there is, or soon will be, a need to revise the organisation's strategies.
2. Having gained a clearer understanding of the nature of change, define alternative market scenarios and formulate optimal strategies for each of these scenarios in relation to the constituent elements of technologies, capabilities and resource requirements.
3. Begin to accumulate the assets and resources that will be needed to support the new or revised strategies that will have to be adopted in response to identified probable scenarios. Acquisition of core elements can be pursued without excessive risk because there is minimal

chance these will not be required to support whatever strategies are actually adopted.

4. Closely monitor market trends and when changing environmental conditions validate the accuracy of one or more of the proposed scenarios, begin to develop the new product or service portfolios which will be required to deliver the appropriate strategies which are to be implemented.

TAKE CARE WHEN REACHING CONCLUSIONS

Case Aims: To illustrate that even apparently highly successful companies can make inappropriate strategic decisions.

Higgins (1995) posited that the long-term survival of existing major corporations in the 21st century is critically reliant upon a strategy based upon exploiting entrepreneurship to sustain long-term, competitive advantage. However, it is often dangerous for academic researchers to reach conclusions about firms which they perceive as global exemplars of innovative behaviour. This is because even some of the world's most successful firms do seem to encounter periods when senior management appears forget the importance of innovation.

Even over just the last 20 years, there are many examples of companies identified as excellent which subsequently exhibited a downturn in performance, thereby contradicting the claim of being named as innovative organisations. Examples of subsequent decline in reputation are provided by Higgins (1995). He identified GE Corporation, which has filed more patents than almost any other firm in the United States, and the American computer company Hewlett-Packard as exemplars of innovative excellence. In recent years, however, both companies have encountered their fair share of problems. During the late 1990s with growth slowing for many of the company's older product lines, via its GE Capital division, the company massively expanded involvement in the financial services industry by expanding its provision of loan and leasing facilities to customers (Anon. 2009e). Initially this expansion was hailed by industry observers as an outstanding strategic move by the company. However, as GE became obsessed with always hitting quarterly profit forecasts, GE Capital was increasingly utilised to implement last-minute financial activities such as the sale of assets to close any emerging profit gap. Not surprisingly this behaviour trait led to the same bad habits that existed in the wider US financial community developing with the GE Capital operation. By 2007, GE Capital was equal in size to some of the world's largest banks, providing 67 percent of GE's total sales revenue and 55 percent of total profits. When the global financial meltdown commenced, GE Capital was found to own some extremely high-risk, toxic debt in sectors such as property, credit cards and loans to emerging economies in Eastern Europe. To recover from this highly dangerous position, GE was forced to implement actions such as reducing annual dividends by over 65 percent, raising $15 billion in new capital and drawing upon low-cost loans being offered by the US government.

(continued)

TAKE CARE WHEN REACHING CONCLUSIONS (continued)

In the case of Hewlett Packard, Higgins (1995, p. 97) stated the company 'continues to dazzle the industrial world because it continues to grow at a staggering pace, launching successful new products at a rate few competitors can match.' Unfortunately, again in the face of slowing sales for existing products, the company decided de-emphasise innovation and instead decided to acquire Compaq, a major manufacturer of IBM PC clones. The strategic rationale was this would provide a new platform for growth by helping Hewlett Packard gain entry into new market sectors. As was obvious to many people in the computer industry, at the time of the Compaq acquisition, US manufacturers of PCs were already rapidly losing market share to lower-priced Asian-based producers. Hence it soon emerged that the price of the acquisition was much higher than the business was worth and, as a consequence, Hewlett Packard struggled to remain a healthy company. Eventually recovery was achieved only by a return to the company's prior long-standing strategy, originally defined by the organisation's founders, of exploiting expertise in innovation to deliver better solutions to customers by exploiting new technology.

SUSTAINABLE SURVIVAL

For most organisations, a critical objective should be to ensure long-term survival. This is because the risk exists that a poorly defined strategy may provide only a temporary market advantage. In relation to the issue of time, Mintzberg (1994, p. 15) concluded when commenting about the Design School approach to strategic planning that there is 'the danger that the strategy will be outdated within 3 months. If you go back to that strategy you may be focusing your attention on the wrong areas in the business.' To overcome this criticism and thereby avoid the risk of short-term organisational thinking, then perhaps a slightly expanded version of the previously proposed simple definition is required. Hence an alternative suggestion is:

> Strategy is a statement which specifies the nature of the entrepreneurial competitive advantage to be utilised to deliver long-term added value objectives.

Failure to recognise the importance of entrepreneurship as a key element of strategy can eventually lead to the demise of the organisation or leave the organisation as a shadow of its former greatness. The world of business is littered with such examples (e.g. in the United States the airlines Pan Am and TWA; in the UK the car companies Rover and Morris and Triumph motorcycles). Responsibility for such outcomes must rest with the leadership, often across a number of generations, who decided that life would be much easier by the company totally ignoring innovation and instead focusing on short-term activities to maximise sales and profits available from the existing product portfolio.

In the face of emerging market threats such as the potential impact on Western firms of Chinese firms entering global markets, Shimizu and Hitt (2004) proposed a number of barriers exist which can obstruct actions such as the need to revise strategy, reposition the firm or develop a more effective competitive advantage. These include:

1. Previous successful experiences continue to determine future actions even when this is inappropriate due to success having created a mind-set that prevents managers from perceiving the need for change.
2. Managers exhibiting behaviour traits such as being over-confident about their own abilities, excessive complacency and an unwillingness to admit mistakes.
3. Managers pursuing their own personal goals (e.g. financial wealth) at the expense of the organisation's goals.

During the early phases of failing to recognise the strategic importance of sustaining an entrepreneurial orientation, a failure to invest in innovation can actually lead to a short-term increase in profitability. This outcome may cause the organisation's leader to be held in high esteem by his or her peers, the business press and the financial community. What such individuals are apparently prepared to ignore is the more important task of sustaining the performance of the organisation over the longer-term. By ignoring this responsibility the outcome can be a failure to fulfil the responsibilities associated with (a) sustaining the existence of other members of the supply chain, (b) creating employment opportunities in the communities where the operations are based and (c) generating the corporate taxes needed by governments to meet the social welfare needs of future generations of less advantaged citizens in the countries where the organisations are based.

DEMAND DECLINE

Case Aims: To illustrate how an inability to respond to changing demand can lead to industry decline.

Strategies typically fail because the organisation resists or is slow to understand and adopt its new initiatives. To illustrate how this can occur, Lewis and Loebbaka (2008) examined how the aerospace aluminium industry originally evolved in the defence during World War II. The three largest firms were Alcoa, Kaiser and International Light Metals (ILM), which created barriers to new entry through (i) massive plant capital investments, (ii) geographic proximity to the customer base and (iii) intensive industry certification and quality systems requirements.

(continued)

DEMAND DECLINE (continued)

Strategic decay began to erode the aluminium supply chain's competitive posture as the global economy slowed in 1992. As airline industry profitability stalled, deliveries were cancelled. Alcoa, Kaiser and ILM faced an excess-inventory crisis, deteriorating pricing and a market where capacity dramatically outpaced demand. The North American aerospace aluminium industry had not strategically prepared for the 1992 downturn or the subsequent geographic shift in supply as the European Airbus entered the market share.

Universal Alloy Corporation (UAC) entered the aerospace aluminium extrusions market during the 1992 and Boeing, faced with a reduced vendor base after multiple facility closures, engaged UAC as a new supplier. This strategic discontinuity eroded Alcoa, Kaiser and ILM's strategic distinctiveness and competitive posture as new competition appeared from focused extruders (UAC). Weak signals of demand change emerged in the aerospace industry during 1999 and 2000, suggesting a slowdown in commercial aircraft sales. The 9/11 terrorist attack on the Twin Towers in New York accelerated this demand downturn. UAC's strategic response cycle included deploying personnel across non-aerospace markets to develop new customers and to reorganise internal support staffs around the operating and sales structure. Post-9/11 UAC developed new markets and made plans to acquire complementary press assets to enhance its future aerospace competitiveness. The company has also focused on 'boutique metals' to fit into new airframe structures. In response to increasing boutique aluminium prices as a result of supplier consolidation, Boeing moved into carbon fibre composites as an alternative material for future airframe structures. The advantage of composites is they are lighter than aluminium and thereby can enhance aircraft fuel efficiency. The continued rise in fuel prices and the need for the airlines to reduce emissions mean composites can be expected to dramatically reduce demand for aluminium in the aerospace industry. The problem for UAC is that carbon fibre technology is outside of the company's experience and manufacturing competences. Hence this demand for new, lighter, non-metallic materials in the aerospace industry may again lead to stagnancy and decline for specialist aluminium suppliers in the world aerospace industry.

THE COMPETENCE DEBATE

In part due to some academics' enduring desire to challenge established ideas, Porterian theory has been criticised by adopting an excessively market-orientated approach to defining competitive advantage. Some of the leading critics, such as Prahalad and Hamel (1990), are strong supporters of the RBV concept. They present the perspective that RBV theory is a more realistic rationale for explaining success. This is because exploitation of a superior key competence provides the basis for the competitive advantage which permits the organisation to outperform other firms in the same market sector. Prahalad and Hamel substantiate their view about the critical importance of acquiring a core competence by drawing upon examples such as Honda. They posit that this company's superior engineering capability in the field of designing and manufacturing vehicle drive chains is the reason why the company has achieved a leadership position in the global car industry.

Examples such as Honda do appear to provide a valid reason for supporting the RBV concept in the case of firms operating in highly stable, mature, usually relatively low-technology markets. In these environments companies may face huge difficulties in achieving any form of significant tangible difference in product benefit that can be offered to the market. Thus identifying a core competence that might provide the basis for a competitive advantage that differentiates the company from competition is a possible feasible strategic philosophy (Hayes and Upton 1998). Service industry markets are probably the most difficult in which to achieve the aim of providing a tangible, perceivable difference in the benefits made available to customers. One potentially successful alternative strategy in this sector to identify a set of organisational competences which permit the organisation to defeat competitors by offering greater value, in the form of better value or higher service quality.

Hamel and Prahalad (1994) expressed the view that RBV theory is also validated by examples from high-technology industries where the key competence is contained within an organisation's ability to assemble a bundle of skills and technologies which permit the organisation to develop a unique new technology platform. These authors suggest an example of this perspective is provided by the case of Microsoft. The company's core competences in the development of new platforms provided the basis for a competitive advantage which has permitted the company to become the dominant provider of software installed in both business and home PC markets. Once a firm has achieved market dominance for a specific business platform, this greatly increases the probability that acquired internal competences will provide the basis for further market growth and the launch of new products (Wonglimpiyarat 2004). In the case of Microsoft, its platform dominance with its Windows operating system provided the springboard from which to launch a whole series of new products, such as Windows 95, 97, 98, 2000 and NT and its Internet Explorer web browser. Additionally, in order to acquire the technical competence to enter new areas of the software industry, Microsoft has pursued a strategy of acquiring other software firms, such as Forethought, Fox Software, Visio Corp and most recently Skype.

A more balanced approach to the issue of the importance of internal key competences is proposed by Kay (1993). He posited that distinctive competences are a potential source of competitive advantage, but only when applied to appropriate market scenarios. This perspective exhibits certain similarities with the views expressed by Porter. This is because Kay proposes that strategy is a way of relating the business operation to opportunities in the external environment. He emphasises that to be successful, a competitive advantage must be sustainable and, where feasible, also be unique. Kay posits that there are four major sources of strength available to the organisation—namely, reputation, innovation, internal and external relationships and organisational assets. He also proposed that the importance of these sources of strength will vary from industry to industry and from organisation to organisation. Thus, for example, it can be argued that in the case of Microsoft, the company's competitive advantage was a combination of internal competences that led to the creation of its MS:DOS and Windows platform linked to its external relationship with IBM, whereby this company adopted Microsoft technology as the core software to drive its new generation of PCs. It seems reasonable to suggest that without this very unusual mechanism through which to gain access to the IT market, Microsoft would have faced a much harder battle to become the global leader in the software industry.

Sushil (2002) noted that in existing long-established markets, organisations may rely heavily on superior competence to sustain a competitive advantage. She notes, however, that as markets change, new competences may become more critical. Hence companies need to identify future opportunities by monitoring markets to detect early warnings of potential change that may require a fundamental shift in competence in order to develop a new competitive advantage. This perspective supports the view that linking competence to external relationships leads to delivery of greater customer satisfaction. Hence this approach is probably a more secure strategic philosophy than reliance solely upon an internal competence source as the basis for achieving a competitive advantage.

Clark and Scott (2000) have suggested that one approach to combining internal and external values is to recognise the critical influence of four key elements. These four elements are:

1. *Industry foresight*, which involves creating a view of the future based upon insights provided from a broad range of sources such as customers, intermediaries, suppliers and university scientists.
2. *Core competences*, which are the bundle of internal capabilities that are unique and provide the basis for delivering a specific competitive advantage.
3. *Strategic architecture*, which is the map defining the challenges facing the organisation and describing the actions required to develop needed functional capabilities and competences.
4. *Strategic intent*, which describes the direction of future actions and the optimal strategic position for achieving the added value objectives of the organisation.

Reliance on a market-orientated strategy without regard to creating the internal competences to support delivery of superior products or services can risk the organisation being overtaken by a competitor which has developed more advanced internal competences and thereby is able to offer an upgraded benefit proposition. An analysis based upon the two variables of core competence and market understanding can reveal the potential implications of failing to develop a more balanced view of how to achieve and sustain an effective strategy. A lack of ability for both core competence and market understanding will typically eventually lead to failure. However, a weakness along even one dimension suggests the organisation has a questionable long-term future. Greater certainty over future performance is more likely to be achieved by combining both market understanding and ownership of appropriate key competences in the creation of a sustainable competitive advantage.

MULTIPLE COMPETENCE STRATEGIES

Case Aims: To illustrate the importance of adopting a multiple competence approach in determining future strategies.

Loewe and Chen (2007) have expressed the view that innovations which are differentiating and sustainable usually involve more than one element of the organisation's business activities. They refer to the example of the US Commerce Bank, which has outperformed larger institutions by focusing upon innovation along the dimensions of:

1. Focusing on customer segments more concerned with service and experience than with low price.
2. Providing a different customer experience by creating a 'retailtainment' atmosphere in the bank's outlets.
3. Remaining open for much longer than competition in the evenings and at weekends.
4. Focusing upon added value generation based upon savings deposits rather than loans, resulting in a much lower loan-to-deposit ratio, which provided protection for the bank during the global banking crisis.
5. Hiring based upon attitude, training for skills, empowering front-line employees and seeking to make every employee an owner.

The authors also make the point that merely relying upon the competences contained within an R&D department operation is a myopic approach to strategic analysis and planning. They point to the example of Cemex, the Mexican cement and building-solutions company. More than 3,500 employees have submitted in excess of 6,000 proposals to its web-enabled databank. Inputs from employees have resulted in initiatives such as the installation of GPS systems in trucks that allow the company to fulfil orders in 20 minutes rather than the customary 3 hours, and Mexicans living in the United States can arrange for the direct delivery of building materials to the site where they want to build a home for their families in Mexico. These and similar strategic actions have transformed Cemex from a commodity material supplier to a value added solution provider, generating growth rates, gross margins and returns on equity that are unparalleled in the cement business worldwide.

(continued)

MULTIPLE COMPETENCE STRATEGIES (continued)

Loewe and Chen have proposed a three-phase strategic action model. This involves a discovery phase to explore ways of developing a wealth of new insights about the world and the company. The focus phase aims at selecting those concepts that are the most compelling and the most likely to be of help in generating new added value. This involves the generation of new ideas about what the company might do in the future. The third phase is concerned with selecting the most compelling ideas that can provide the basis for a new business model for actually going to market that can eventually scale up the entity into a fully fledged, new business. The authors illustrate this latter approach using Whirlpool as an example. The company engages in establishing formal discovery, opportunity elaboration and innovation activities. This involves deploying hundreds of trained 'i-mentors' to coach potential innovators and setting up new management processes to review and guide promising new concepts.

The authors also believe that market experiments are vital in assessing whether an original concept might need to be modified. For example, McDonald's examined setting up self-service vending machines offering a variety of goods similar to the ones found in a typical convenience store. The company learned that among the 150 offered, ranging from batteries to razor blades and milk, DVDs really drove sales. So, McDonald's morphed the concept from a general-purpose convenience store to a DVD rental kiosk. It was also realised the concept could be expanded beyond the physical locations of the company restaurants. This led to over 3,000 Redbox DVD rental kiosks being opened in supermarkets and other non-McDonald's properties, making its Redbox operations the second largest operator of DVD rental kiosks in the United States.

Loewe and Chen do caution that occasionally an apparently powerful new technology may be beaten by a more effective business model. An example is provided by Boeing's announcement in 2001 of its Sonic Cruiser. This new aircraft was designed to cut transatlantic flight time from 7 hours to 5.5 hours. To save this hour and a half of flying time, Sonic Cruiser passengers would have had to pay an estimated $10,000 versus $5,000 for a first-class ticket on another aircraft. However, due to the time taken to travel from a city centre to an airport the Boeing solution could offer only to reduce total centre-to-centre travel time from 12 to 10.5 hours. A new competitor then entered the market—namely, semi-private time-share jets, which instead cut flight time through investing in technology designed to reduce 'on-the-ground time' by flying from London's Northolt airport to Teterboro in New Jersey. This solution avoids the delays associated with commercial flights using big airports and enables the company to cut total travel time to nine hours, at a per passenger cost of just $7,500. In the face of this alternative proposition any further expenditure on the Boeing Sonic project was deemed to be a non-viable investment.

STRATEGIC DEFENCE

For a company which is reliant upon revenues generated by sales from products which have entered the maturity phase on the product life cycle curve, possibly one of the greatest sources of potential threat is the entry of a firm, usually from a developing nation, offering the same benefit proposition at a much lower price. Unless the existing incumbent firm has a new range of products in the growth phase on the PLC curve, senior management will be under extreme pressure to respond to the new threat by also reducing prices. Although such a move may be perceived as a tactical necessity, in reality the company is often being forced to discard the business strategy which has been the basis of past success. As a consequence management may be guilty of repositioning the company in such a way as to destroy all ability to sustain the long-term strategic aim of building an enduring organisation.

For an incumbent, established firm whose market position is not already based upon offering low prices, one possible response to the emergence of a lower-cost competitor is to identify a way of dealing with this threat without making a fundamental adjustment to the organisation's existing long-term strategy. In support of this perspective, Morehouse et al. (2008) proposed that affected organisations should examine short-term tactics to minimise the impact of price competition while concurrently determining how changes in products or markets served can permit retention of the firm's existing long-term strategy. In relation to being prepared to implement an effective tactical response to price competition, the authors recommend the firm should carefully monitor new potential sources of low-cost competition. This is because the sooner a potential new threat is recognised, the greater is the time available to the firm to evolve an effective response.

Once the threat has been identified, further analysis is advisable to determine how the competitor has achieved its cost advantage. Potential sources can include access to lower-cost labour, cheaper raw materials, a different production technology or an alternative channel management strategy. In some cases the incumbent firm may be able to duplicate the same technique as a way of also being able to reduce operating costs. More usually, however, the incumbent firm will not be able to duplicate the competitor's operational processes. Hence research will be necessary to identify other potential pathways through which to reduce costs. This activity may indicate that past market success has caused the company to have become somewhat complacent. As a consequence management has failed to update competences, correct identified operational inefficiencies or permit the emergence slack internals business processes. In this situation, cost savings might be achieved through actions to upgrade competences, tighten operational procedures or make the workforce aware of the need to focus on implementing efficiency upgrades.

Should it become apparent that the level of price competition will be very intense, the firm will probably need to introduce more drastic actions in order to introduce new economies into its operations. These could include relocating manufacturing to a new country where labour or raw material costs are lower, sub-contracting, outsourcing certain areas of the business or introducing new, more advanced technology that can reduce operational costs. In those cases where no significant cost savings can be found to permit profits to be sustained following a reduction in prices, the alternate option is for the firm to seek to strengthen customer satisfaction over their perceptions of the superior value offered by the existing product or service portfolio. This might be achieved by increasing the level of advertising expenditure, leading to heightened customer awareness of the product benefits being offered. Other opportunities may exist by upgrading the range and quality of complementary services offered alongside the core product proposition (e.g. a machine tool manufacturer offering a free production line design and machinery installation service accompanied by an ongoing 24/7 repair service).

Assuming a company is able to mount an adequate defence in the face of increased price competition, this outcome will provide the 'window of time' needed such that innovation can be utilised to develop higher added value solutions involving new products or entry into new markets. Where possible these new solutions should be compatible with the organisation's existing long-term strategy. Occasions may emerge, however, when retention of the old strategy will not provide the basis for the ongoing achievement of desired financial performance. In these circumstances the organisation will be forced to implement a fundamental review of the organisation's long-term future to identify the viable strategic options which remain available.

STAYING AHEAD

Case Aims: To illustrate how a firm must rely on innovation to survive in the face of commoditisation.

In seeking a new direction most organisations would be wise to examine which internal competences will provide the basis for successfully re-directing future actions. An example of the effectiveness of this approach is provided by the Taiwanese microchip manufacturer MediaTek (Anon. 2009f). The company was founded in 1997 as a 'fabless' chipmaker. The business model was that of designing specialist microchips and sub-contracting the actual manufacturing of products to other firms. The company strategy was to utilise in-house technological skills to develop premium-priced, high-quality components. The company's first generation of products was microchips for CD-ROM drives. Expertise acquired from this activity permitted a move into designing microchips which are core elements in other consumer electronic products. For example, the company has become the global market leader in the supply of microchips for DVD players.

(continued)

STAYING AHEAD (continued)

The pace of technological progressin the electronic components industry is such that within only a few years, MediaTek faced intense price competition from companies based in countries such as mainland China. The commoditisation of the firm's core business required the identification and implementation of a new generation of microchip products. In 2004 the company moved into the higher-margin market of making 'chipsets.' These are bundles of microchips which provide the basis of the operating system in mobile telephones. As a latecomer into this industry MediaTek focused on the design of microchips which could be pre-programmed, thereby providing the phone manufacturers with a 'total solution' which significantly reduced the development and assembly times for new telephones. This solution has revolutionised the Chinese mobile telephone market. Previously a handset manufacturer required approximately $3 million, 100 engineers and 9 months of development time to bring a new product to market. MediaTek's bundled solution permits firms to develop a new product in three months using only ten engineers and expenditure in the region of $100,000. MediaTek is now the third largest fabless microchip producer in the world. Although the company's entire current generation of products is used in the low-end sector of the telephone market, the firm is already planning to become the market leader in the supply of chipsets for smart phones.

STRATEGIC FLEXIBILITY

Another potential defect with the Porterian model is the assumption that once a company has determined the best source of competitive advantage, this advantage can be sustained indefinitely. Examination of case materials of highly successful firms that have retained high market share over long periods of time will reveal the fallacy of this managerial concept. These materials typically reveal that in response to changes in market environments, successful organisations retain the ability exhibit flexibility over their choice of competitive advantage. This ability is necessary in order that the organisation sustains an appropriate fit between what the market needs and what a firm is capable of supplying (Markides 2004).

Strategic flexibility should be accompanied by organisational consistency. This is because consistency permits avoidance of reactions to short-term changes in market conditions that might divert the company away from focusing on entrepreneurial developments designed to ensure fulfilment of long-term organisational goals (Hax 1990). In seeking to ensure consistency, the organisation must also avoid becoming so rigid in its thinking that fundamental shifts in market opportunity are ignored. By avoiding fixed pattern thinking this will ensure actions are taken in response to fundamental environmental changes, thereby avoiding a permanent decline in financial performance. To be able to make such a response, the organisation must retain a sufficient level of cognitive flexibility to allow strategies to be modified, which can more effectively equip the organisation's handling of market change.

Hitt et al. (1998) have proposed that an emphasis on strategic consistency occurred in a time when most firms operated in a world of gradual change and the same business strategy could be expected to remain totally relevant over many years. Market boundaries were well defined, appropriate data on market trends were readily available and there were few variations in base technology in use in different areas of the world. Over the last 25 years market environments have become much more volatile. New entrants have emerged, often from developing economies, and new technologies have changed market conditions or spawned entirely new industrial sectors. Furthermore the intensity of competition has increased significantly. In the face of these changes, the more successful organisations have recognised the need to acquire and retain a higher degree of strategic flexibility. Adoption of this philosophy will ensure organisations based in developed nation economies can implement actions such as exploiting the latest leading-edge technological advances to survive in markets which have become much more global in nature.

In reviewing the options of firms seeking to sustain their performance, Hitt et al. (1998, p. 24) posited that 'Strategic flexibility, then, is the capability of the firm to proact or respond quickly to changing competitive conditions and thereby develop and/or maintain competitive advantage.' In their view a critical aspect of achieving flexibility is the existence of a leadership team that has the vision to comprehend how the firm can respond to the opportunities and threats that may emerge in the organisation's markets. A fundamental aspect of this vision is to identify ways to manage the existing businesses while developing new market opportunities or new products compatible with the organisation's long-term strategy. This form of visionary thinking is necessary in order to sustain the company's added value achievement such that generated profits can be reinvested into the new resources required to sustain long-term aims through investment in innovation or the implementation of fundamental organisational change.

An excellent example of a visionary, flexible approach to defining and implementing a strategy to stay ahead of competition is provided by Apple upon the re-appointment of Steve Jobs as CEO. Recognising that it was pointless for the company to seek sustained revenue from the increasingly competitive PC and laptop markets, he decided to exploit the emerging opportunities offered by convergence in the IT and communications industries. To exploit these opportunities he led the development of the iPlayer, the iPhone and then the iPad. The company is aware that staying ahead of competition through the regular launch of the next generation of each of these products offers only partial protection from competition. This understanding is especially relevant as competitors from China seek to gain a significant share in Apple's markets across the globe. Hence in 2011 Apple launched its iCloud. This product is aimed at exploiting cloud computing to achieve greater integration of the multiple computer and communication devices now being used by both business and consumers.

Roberts and Stockport (2009) posit that a company's ability to manage strategic risk is dependent on responding to opportunities and threats through using its internal resources in both a proactive and a reactive way. Achieving this goal requires that the organisation must ensure any revisions in future plans can exploit the core competences upon which the firm has built original success. This outcome does not occur unless the organisation has ensured existing competences are flexible and dynamic, thereby permitting rapid identification and implementation of new, entrepreneurially orientated business activities. Without ensuring that core competences retain a dynamic dimension, there is the risk these competences may become outdated. This will limit the future strategic options available to the organisation. There is also the risk that as competences become inflexible, this will restrict the breadth of potential opportunities that can be considered as viable strategic options by the firm. This is because when core competences are not dynamic they can become internally 'fixed,' which can make change programmes extremely difficult to implement.

Hagen and Tootoonchi (2006) proposed that factors such as insensitivity to negative feedback, self-serving interpretation of negative feedback and managerial resistance to change can prevent firms from exhibiting flexibility sufficient to sustain an appropriate strategic fit in rapidly changing markets. To remove these barriers to flexible strategic thinking, the authors propose the following actions:

1. Create an organisational culture that encourages open communications. This is important because disclosing mistakes and sharing bad information are important in developing the necessary momentum to overcome problems.
2. Create systems that welcome new ideas and permit infusion of new perspectives from outside the firm because this can inject new ideas and external perspectives into the decision-making processes.
3. Limit the tenure of CEOs because bringing in a new outsider CEO provides access to perspectives developed from different experiences and different settings that may re-direct an organisation's strategic intent, policies and assumptions.
4. Regularly appoint new non-executives because this increases the probability of earlier identification of areas of businesses that are performing poorly. These individuals will also bring different experiences and potentially fresh perspectives to the firm.
5. Rotate managers in key positions to reduce continued utilisation of outmoded ideas key positions. This is because rotation can assist in bringing fresh perspectives into different areas of the company's operations.
6. Expand the use of alliances with other organisations to access sources of new ideas.

AN EXAMPLE OF INFLEXIBLE COMPETENCE

Case Aims: To illustrate how declining flexible competence can risk the entire future of a major corporation.

The huge risk associated with permitting rigidity in an organisation's core competence is exemplified by the problems which confronted IBM in recent years. Since World War II, IBM was the exemplar of how to build a globally successful business in the computer industry. IBM's original core competences revolved around helping clients manage and exploit complex data sets. For many years this solution involved the supply and operation of mainframe computers. The company was slow to perceive the data management implications of new trends, such as those offered by microcomputers, replacement of centralised computing systems with free-standing PCs and advances in software becoming more important than hardware. The company became fixated on sustaining hardware sales, and in the case of PCs, the emphasis was on maximising the sale of boxes in the face of growing competition from lower-priced IBM clones. By the mid-1990s this rigidity of thinking was reflected in a massive decline in both sales and profits.

The appointment of an individual from outside the computer industry, Louis Gerstner, injected a visionary understanding of how the company needed to implement fundamental change. He correctly identified that IBM's long-term strategy of helping clients manage and exploit complex data sets was still totally valid, but that the company had become fixated on manufacturing and selling hardware. His solution was to return IBM to its original roots by exploiting the core technological competences of the company to deliver a portfolio of services helping clients to exploit the latest advances in IT to optimise their operations. The outcome was that in only a few years IBM regained the position of being one of the most successful players in the global IT industry.

ALLOCATING RESOURCES

A key aspect of strategic flexibility is the willingness of organisations to monitor their external environments to determine whether existing competences will sustain future performance and to determine whether actions should be implemented to develop new competences. One implication of this perspective is that the long-term viability of the organisation is dependent upon deciding whether resources should be assigned to supporting existing competences or whether there is a need to re-allocate resources to support development of new internal capabilities.

Added understanding of strategic flexibility was generated by research by Miles and Snow in the 1970s. They identified a strategic typology in which firms are classified as prospectors, defenders, analysers and defenders (Miles et al. 1978). These researchers proposed that the changing nature of external environments caused organisations at certain points in their life histories to confront the need to reconsider both future strategy and internal operations. They labelled this activity an 'adaptive cycle' in which the organisation examines the adoption of a more entrepreneurial strategy and revises the two internal domains of process technology and administrative systems.

Within the Miles and Snow typology, prospectors are those firms which are orientated towards identifying new market and product opportunities. Having selected a new opportunity, these organisations have sufficient flexibility in relation to technology and administrative competences to implement appropriate actions to exploit their entrepreneurial orientation. Defenders focus on retaining control over their current business and seek to sustain profitability by exploiting high levels of efficiency in the management of technology and administrative processes. To avoid market confrontations, defenders usually attempt to occupy a small, narrow market domain where their competence permits delivery of a superior product or service offering. Reactors are the least responsive type of organisation. Management is fixated on sustaining the company's existing strategy and internal processes. The usual outcome is that as markets undergo change this rigidity eventually leads to the demise of the organisation. The fourth strategic typology, which lies halfway between prospector and defender, is the analyser. These organisations monitor environmental trends but will not consider development of new products or moves into new markets until there is solid evidence that real opportunities exist. Once the organisation is convinced of the need for entrepreneurial action, adequacy in relation to internal flexibility permits an effective re-allocation of resources to support revisions in competences in areas such as exploiting technology and administrative processes.

Although the Miles and Snow typology provides an effective paradigm through which to classify organisations in relation to their capability to exhibit strategic flexibility, by the late 1990s the model seems to have fallen in popularity among many academics. As a consequence there has been a significant decline in the frequency with which the concept is used as a research model to analyse organisational behaviour. The concept also tends to receive minimal coverage in many of the more recent management texts. To a certain degree this situation reflects the increasing interest among academics about the role of organisational learning and knowledge management in helping organisations evolve new or revised strategies (Chaston 2004).

Another key influence is problems various researchers have encountered in reaching definite conclusions about the relationships which exist between the Miles and Snow typology and the performance of firms in different sectors of industry. Zahra and Pearce (1990) in their review of the research methodology problems associated with the use of the typology noted that a very critical issue was the variation between researchers concerning their approaches to classifying firms and in the application of scales to achieve an empirical basis for determining which fitted into the four different organisational types. Another problem which these authors identified was the tendency of some researchers to examine the nature of the environments confronting firms in a specific industrial sector without engaging in a longitudinal data acquisition process which is needed to identify how the behaviour of firms changes over time.

Sanchez (1997) posited that effective management of strategic change is critically reliant upon the degree to which the organisation is able to transfer resources between different areas of activity. He proposed that resource flexibility will be greater in those cases in which there is a large range of alternative uses to which a resource can be applied. Further enhancement in resource flexibility will occur when switching a resource to an alternative application is a relatively simple activity and does not involve incurring very high costs. The other influence on flexibility is the time required to move a resource from one role to another within the organisation.

The level of strategic flexibility will be reduced where a resource to be transferred is in short supply. Although this situation could be avoided through the ownership of slack resource capacity, this solution is somewhat inefficient and may also be quite costly. The alternative to retaining excess levels of a key resource is to wait until an early indicator of the need for future strategic change is identified. At this juncture the organisation should begin to invest in the acquisition of the additional resources which will soon be required.

In terms of embedding a philosophy of strategic flexibility into an organisation, the issue arises of which approach to planning is more appropriate for achieving this aim. A 'deliberate strategy' is one which is carefully planned and then implemented. An 'emergent strategy' is a strategy that is not deliberately planned but instead develops over time through a series of activities aimed at finding ways for improving future performance. The deliberate approach to strategic planning runs the risk of being excessively rigid and mechanistic. In contrast the emergent process is both informal and flexible. It also offers the advantage of involving employees at all levels of the organisation and permits the strategy to evolve as everybody gains further understanding of changing external opportunities and threats facing the business.

Dibrell et al. (2007) examined planning philosophies within the US timber industry. Through analysis of qualitative and quantitative data they concluded that there were three different approaches to planning within the industry. Rigid firms are those which use a deliberate approach to planning. Exploration firms use an emergent approach. Dynamic firms adopt a blended approach of both deliberate and emergent decision-making. The conclusion from their study was that the dynamic group of firms was the most financially successful. Within these firms the orientation is towards deliberate planning until monitoring of the external environment indicates the possibility of major change. The response is to then draw upon the cognitive flexibility which exists within the organisation to identify a new, more appropriate strategic solution. Within the rigid firms there was much slower reaction to changing events and an unwillingness to move away from the strategy which has proved successful in the past. The exploration firms were likely to recognise signs of external change, but it appeared their informal approach often led to a failure to develop a coherent viable strategy for responding to these different market conditions.

9 Technology Strategies

The purpose of this chapter is to cover issues pertaining to:

1. The nature and role of different types of technology.
2. Managing technological change.
3. Determining an optimal focus in relation to technology selection.
4. Emphasising product versus process technology.
5. Sources of influence in relation to technological change.
6. Planning through the different phases of the S-curve.
7. The role of disruption theory in technological change.

IMPORTANCE

Technological change is possibly one of the most critical of all of the meta-events that can create a future strategic opportunity or threat for any organisation. This is because technology has the potential to offer the basis of totally new industries or permit smaller firms to develop a competitive advantage through which to challenge market leaders. Technology may even allow developing nations to implement faster industrialisation of their economies, which can eventually permit achievement of global market leadership.

Erikson et al. (1990) have proposed that technology can be divided into three types:

1. *Base technologies*, which are fundamental to the production of products or services in an industrial sector.
2. *Key technologies*, which are critical because they provide sources of competitive advantage (e.g. an oil company's capability to undertake successful deep water oil exploration).
3. *Pacer technologies*, which can be expected to evolve into the key technologies of the future. Not every firm has either the skills or resources to be involved in exploiting pacer technologies. However, for those firms which have such capabilities, when linked to investment in R&D this can often provide the basis for achieving a leadership position or sustaining existing market dominance.

The importance of technology varies by industry. In part this is due to the nature of the product offering. Opportunities to utilise new technology are significantly lower in most consumer food products than, for example, in consumer electronics goods. Hence, as illustrated in Figure 9.1, any analysis of future trends should take into account the degree to which technology (a) permits the firm to achieve a higher level of performance relative to competition and (b) provides the basis for generating differences in the scale of added value that is achievable within an industrial sector.

In those cases where technology permits achievement of neither superior performance nor greater value, the market is likely to be very fragmented, containing numerous firms all seeking non-technologically based ways of achieving a competitive advantage. The scenario can be contrasted with situations where specialist firms can identify an opportunity to exploit technology to achieve superiority. In these cases, although technological change will be important, the role of technology will tend to be that of permitting firms to occupy specialised market niches where there are few or no competitors.

Major consumer goods brands tend to exhibit the ability to achieve greater value through superior marketing competence. These firms are also able to exploit technology as a strategic pathway for achieving performance superiority. Success in this latter scenario is usually achieved by an early market entrant that has attracted the majority of the initial customers and then relies upon competences in areas such as marketing or logistics to sustain its leadership position. This strategy is somewhat

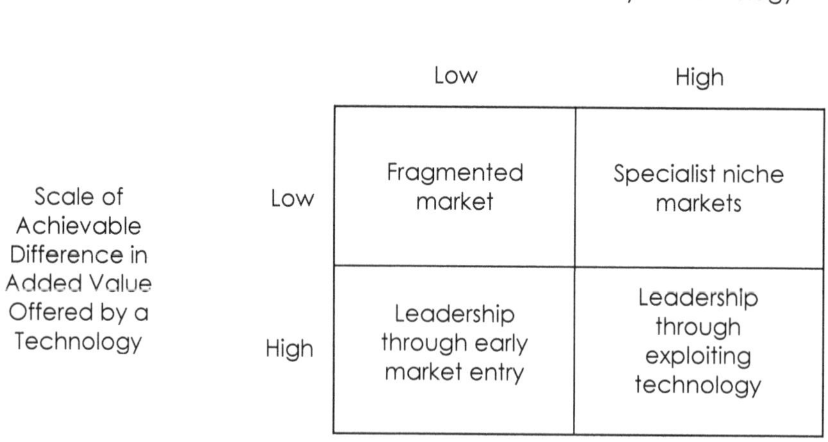

Scale of Achievable Difference in
Performance Offered by a Technology

		Low	High
Scale of Achievable Difference in Added Value Offered by a Technology	Low	Fragmented market	Specialist niche markets
	High	Leadership through early market entry	Leadership through exploiting technology

Figure 9.1   Alternative market opportunities matrix.

different from markets where there are major opportunities for the exploitation of technology to deliver superior performance or greater product value. Although being an early entry is highly advantageous, in order to retain leadership an organisation will have to continue to invest in new or improved technologies in order to effectively block the attempts of competition to also utilise technology as a path through which to match its performance.

POLAROID CORPORATION

Case Aims: To demonstrate how a founding entrepreneur may cause successors to ignore the need for an alternative, more technologically relevant strategy.

Edwin Land was an entrepreneur who had a total commitment to the idea that science is the best instrument through which to develop products that can satisfy deep human needs (Tripsas and Gavetti 2000). He also felt such needs could rarely be understood through market research. Having established his company, the Polaroid Corporation, just before World War II, in 1948 he launched the first ever instant camera. To sustain the company's growth from a small firm to a global player, under Land's ever watchful eye, there was ongoing investment in research to improve picture quality, decrease photograph development time and introduce colour. The company was able to exploit research-based technological leadership in areas such as silver halide chemistry, optics and electronics which permitted the creation of a near-monopoly position in the world of instant photography. Originally manufacturing had been outsourced, but in the 1960s Land brought both camera and film manufacturing in-house. To avoid direct competition with traditional cameras, which were primarily sold through specialist outlets, Polaroid focused its efforts on gaining distribution in mass market retailers such as Kmart and Wal-Mart. Underlying the marketing strategy from the 1960s onwards was a strong corporate belief in the 'razor blade' business model. This involved selling cameras at low prices and making a high profit margin on the sale of film.

From the outset, Land embedded a strategic philosophy into the company that success comes from innovation based upon long-term, large-scale research. In 1972, after eight years of research and half a billion dollars of expenditure, this philosophy led to the launch of the SX-70, a camera which ejected the picture, which then developed as the customer watched. By the mid-1970s, Land decided it was time to delegate some of his responsibilities and appointed Bill McCune as the new president. This individual had been with the company since 1939, was a long-time research colleague of Land and shared his vision of the importance of research-based product development.

(continued)

POLAROID CORPORATION (continued)

In 1985, McCune committed substantial funds to undertake R&D on digital imaging technologies. The aim was to combine digital imaging and instant photography. Ultimately the specified goal was to develop an instant digital camera and printer product (called 'Printer In The Field' or PIF). The other area of research was on a medical system, Helios, which was seen as offering a high-resolution substitute for x-rays. Senior management was initially very supportive of these projects because it mistakenly believed that digital imaging could be made to fit the beloved razor blade business model. Scientists with understanding of digital imaging were recruited. They recognised that neither project would be able to duplicate the instant camera model because digital imaging is a profoundly different market. Furthermore the development team recognised that success required investment in overcoming the firm's basic weaknesses in the areas of low-cost electronics, mass manufacturing and rapid product development. Senior management was highly resistant to recommendations addressing these problems. It also began to become concerned that the products under development did not fit the razor blade model. These individuals also continued to express the view that consumers would always want instant prints, not the ability to take a digital photograph and store the picture on a computer for printing at a later date.

Despite having a created a viable prototype in 1992, Polaroid did not launch its first digital camera until 1996. Although the product received several industry awards for technical achievement, by this time there were over 40 other firms in the market selling digital cameras. The other problem was that the retail price of $1,000 required the product be marketed through specialist retailers. Unfortunately the Polaroid marketing and sales team had experience of gaining distribution only in mass market, price-based retailers. The result was that the product failed to gain market share. Additionally the other major project, Helios, hit a number of problems such as gaining distribution and offering an unacceptable film size to the users, hospital radiologists. Having generated a loss of over $300 million, the entire division was eventually sold to Sterling Diagnostics.

In 1996, Polaroid brought in an outsider by appointing Gary DiCammillo as the new CEO. Although an apparent supporter of the razor blade model, his management background was consumer marketing and he immediately applied this philosophy to the Polaroid operation. Research expenditure was drastically cut and funds diverted into up-weighted spending on advertising. The historic commitment to innovation through research was replaced with a philosophy of developing only new, improved versions of existing products. The dominant players in the world of digital cameras were consumer electronics giants such as Sony, Toshiba, Hitachi and Canon. Polaroid's products were unable to compete against firms that better understood the new technology and had the expertise to produce large volumes of low unit cost output. The final nail in the Polaroid business model occurred because as consumers became familiar with digital cameras, their interest in instant cameras virtually disappeared. On October 12, 2001, Polaroid Corporation filed for bankruptcy.

MANAGING PROCESS

Williams (1992, p. 31) makes the important point that:

Success brings on imitators, who respond with superior features, lower prices, or some new way to draw customers away. Time, the denominator of economic value, eventually renders nearly all advantages obsolete.

In order for a company to determine the speed with which the next generation of products will be required, it needs to recognise that the life cycle of a new product will vary by industry type. Williams identified three classes of industry:

Class 1, Slow-Cycle Resources: Products and services in this class are strongly shielded from competitive pressures by core capabilities that are durable and enduring. Examples of core capabilities behind these products and services include patents, geography, complex buyer/supplier relationships and highly durable brand names, such as Kellogg's Corn Flakes and Ivory soap.

Class 2, Standard-Cycle Resources: Products and services in this class are standardised, high-volume goods. Companies within these industries (e.g. such as (McDonald's) face higher resource-imitation pressures. These organisations tend to protect their existing products by relying upon national or global mass marketing that provides a scale effect, which demands competitors will require significant financial resources to even use innovation as a successful attack strategy.

Class 3, Fast-Cycle Resources: Products and services are 'idea-driven' concepts based upon a concept or technology which creates market uniqueness (e.g. the social networking site Facebook). However, the company must expect soon to be threatened by competitors entering the market with equivalent propositions. Hence survival demands a constant commitment to innovation in order to remain ahead by being the first to introduce the next generation of a product or alternatively develop a new-to-the-world proposition that can create an entirely new market sector.

Stalk (2006) has proposed that in relation to effectively managing innovation in terms of offering guidance in relation to Williams' Class 3-type products, the following guidelines are applicable:

1. Know your product development processes and manage these processes to strict quality goals and deadlines.

2. Do not let support functions impede the main sequence of key development activities.
3. Co-locate critical resources.
4. Organise around tasks at hand.
5. Value experience—manage continuity.
6. Align beliefs, goals, measurements and behaviour to maximise development speed.
7. Have a well-developed and disciplined planning process whose plans are followed by the development team.
8. Improve the product as soon as possible after the initial launch.
9. Ensure capability platforms continue to enable fast product development.
10. Use senior management to facilitate rather than participate in process implementation.

FOCUS

Achieving and sustaining market leadership is usually determined by the scale of superior performance achieved by a firm's new and existing products. In most cases commitment to innovation will be supported by the organisation's ability to exploit key and pacer technologies. Superior technological competence tends to be both a scarce and an expensive resource. Consequently, when determining how internal resources should be allocated across the organisation, there is a need to identify those markets which represent the greatest source of opportunities and threats. In terms of assessing this issue, one approach is to assume there are two dimensions to be considered: markets and product performance. As illustrated in Figure 9.2, this approach results in an assessment based on four different market/product scenarios.

Schmidt and Porteus (2000) proposed that the winner in a technology-based market battle will be influenced by the relative level of competence of organisations in relation to both cost leadership and technological capability. In the case where two organisations have relatively low levels of each competence, the incumbent will probably adopt a retrenchment strategy while the new entrant will invest in the new technology. The former's hope is that the new entrant will fail to commercialise the new technology. Where both firms have relatively high levels of each competence the existing firm is likely to retain dominance for existing products while concurrently pursuing opportunities offered by the new technology. This formidable market position will probably cause the competitor to decide there is no benefit in concurrently investing in the new technology and look elsewhere for an attractive investment opportunity. These authors concluded that this latter scenario is exemplified by Intel, the world's leading developer and

Market

	Existing	New
Existing	Technological change influencing existing product(s) performance or value	Technological change influencing existing product(s) adapted for new markets
New	Technological change leading to a new generation of product(s)	Technological change leading to radical market change and/or diversification

Product

Figure 9.2   Product/market change matrix.

manufacturer of microchips. The company has a history of concurrently investing in the development of next-generation chips while concurrently focusing upon driving down the production costs for its generation of products. This aggressiveness contributes to Intel's cost leadership for the lifetime of most existing products and also signals to would-be competitors the manufacturing cost competences that would be needed to compete over the life of the next generation of products.

Another issue which will usually require assessment is the priority to be given to technological investment in terms of upgrading existing internal organisational processes versus concentrating upon new product development activities (Fox et al. 1998). This decision will require an analysis of alternative scenarios. Where there is confidence that current process technologies are expected to remain appropriate for the foreseeable future, the company can focus on enhancing current market performance (e.g. building market share, entering new market segments). In the case where new technology could permit the creation of the next generation of product(s), actions will be necessary to invest in new product development. This action can be contrasted with the situation where the product technology is perceived as adequate, but opportunities exist to change process technology leading to enhancement of internal organisational processes. Where there is a requirement for concurrent focus on process and product innovation, this more complex situation may demand consideration of a possible fundamental change in strategy.

INTELLECTUAL ASSET-BASED INNOVATION

Case Aims: To examine an innovation strategy based upon exploiting as yet unrecognised or new intellectual assets.

In their analysis of effective innovation strategies, Lindsay and Hopkins (2010) proposed that an organisation's intellectual assets may protect a company from external threats. They suggest that intellectual assets such as proprietary knowledge can be used to support technology-based innovation.

Lindsay and Hopkins have identified the US company Kimberly-Clark as an exemplar of exploiting intellectual assets. Often working in collaboration outside the company, a central team will be assigned the task of acquiring new technology. Low-cost approaches typically focus upon identification of opportunities associated with exploiting innovation in the company's various supply chains. Under the guidance of the company's Intellectual Assets management group, projects have included new ways of managing markets, utilising enterprise software systems to determine new strategies, intelligent manufacturing, and applications of radio-frequency identification (RFID).

The success of this approach to innovation has resulted in Kimberly-Clark adopting a proactive approach to the generation of new appropriate intellectual assets from sources such as patents, publications and knowledge mining as a pathway for further strengthening the company's scale of achieved competitive advantage.

PRODUCT VERSUS PROCESS

In using a decision matrix of the type shown in Figure 9.2, the issue arises over determining which strategy is the most appropriate. It is usually advisable to avoid a 'me too' innovation strategy involving following the path which is already being effectively exploited by major competitors. For Western firms concerned about the growing threat posed by Chinese firms, there is a need to be aware that the two innovation strategies that are providing the basis for competitive advantage are 'production-stage economies of growth and scale' and 'production-stage specialisation' (Brenitz and Murphree 2011). The former involves focusing on a specific stage in the manufacturing process and then using innovation to become a preferred producer. The aim is to reach the point where economies of scale become available to the organisation. For the production-stage specialist, there are two available options. One is to develop a sufficiently differentiated superior product that the company can demand a premium price. The other, not mutually exclusive option is to implement a strategy to achieve market dominance which eventually leads to the emergence of scale benefits.

The reason these innovation pathways have emerged is that China has become the primary manufacturing base for both overseas and domestic firms. As a consequence, as well as enjoying the benefits of lower labour costs, China contains a vast pool of knowledge and expertise that ensures access to the latest technology and advances in manufacturing systems. Additionally Chinese firms have been assisted in those cases where the government deems an industry sector is of national economic importance. This designation results in added benefits such as access to government-funded science and technology centres, being awarded contracts for supplying government departments and banks being instructed to offer advantageous lending terms.

This situation gives rise to the question of whether in response to Chinese manufacturers' success Western firms should allocate more resources towards supporting process innovation. In their assessment of this issue Ettlie and Reza (1992) noted that based upon numerous case examples there is little doubt that process innovation, especially in manufacturing, can have a substantial impact on productivity no matter where in the world a firm is located. Luria (1987), for example, in his study of automobile component manufacturers in the United States, determined that process innovation had contributed a 22 percent overall reduction in total production costs. Llorca (1998) suggested that process innovation can reduce the unit cost of production of the goods, thereby permitting a price reduction or improved profitability. He concluded, however, that the ability to enjoy significant benefits of either of these outcomes is severely limited. This is because in today's world the knowledge to duplicate productions process will usually become accessible to competition in a very short period of time. This situation can be contrasted with product innovation, which typically results in the demand curve shifting upwards and to the right; thereby permitting the firm to charge a higher price. Furthermore the 'first mover' advantage and lag effect before competitors can develop a similar product will usually provide the initiator firm with an ability to exploit its differentiation-based competitive advantage for a relatively long period of time.

TECHNOLOGICAL RISK

Case Aims: To illustrate the potential risks of sharing technology with firms who may later become competitors.

Technology transfer has been a focus of China's economic growth plans for decades. Over the past 30 years, the country's leaders have adopted numerous policies to encourage technology transfer. By exploiting the appeal of gaining access to a huge new market, China's leaders expect overseas companies to make available high-tech products and systems as the price for market entry. This benefits Chinese companies, which can then gain access to advanced technology with relatively little capital expenditure. This outcome can accelerate the growth rate of Chinese firms and enhance profit margins. Although the foreign firm may enjoy short-term financial benefits from access to China's immense marketplace, the longer-term risks associated with technology transfer to a future potential competitor can be extremely high (Jarrett and Wendholt 2010).

(continued)

TECHNOLOGICAL RISK (continued)

For foreign companies once their technology has been successfully transferred to a domestic firm, the risk they may then encounter is to find themselves shut out of the Chinese market. This outcome can occur because some government policies are aimed at increasing domestic industry's share of the high-technology markets as part of a national policy initiative to transform China from a low-technology, manufacturing-based economy to an innovation- and knowledge-based economy. A related issue is the inadequate intellectual property rights (IPR) protection which exists in China. This situation can be hazardous to overseas firms because intellectual property can fall into the hands of a rival company, or an organisation which is an in-country local partner might appropriate the intellectual property and set up a rival business.

Goldwind Science and Technology Company is one of China's largest domestic wind-turbine manufacturers, which actually began life as a research institution. The firm now has a 20 percent domestic market share and is ranked as one of the world's largest wind-turbine producers. Global success has relied on financial and technological support from both foreign and domestic governments and overseas companies. In 1989, Bonus Energy A/S, a Danish wind-turbine manufacturer, partnered with Goldwind and transferred the technology to construct 150 kW wind turbines. In 1996 Germany-based Jacobs Energie GmbH licensed its 600 kW wind-turbine technology to Goldwind, transferring the technology as part of China's National Key Technology and Research Program in 1997. In addition to providing financial support, over the past several years, the Chinese government has enacted policies that give preferential supplier status to domestic wind-turbine manufacturers. From 2005 onwards this policy required 70 percent of the content of all turbines to be produced domestically in order for a company to be considered as a bidder for infrastructure projects.

In 2004, foreign-made wind turbines accounted for 75 percent of the Chinese wind-turbine market. By the end of 2008, China's top three domestic wind-turbine suppliers—Sinovel Wind Co. Ltd., Goldwind and Dongfang Electric Corporation—accounted for nearly 60 percent of domestic market sales, according to China International Capital Corp. estimates. Although China recently eliminated the 70 percent domestic content requirement as part of an agreement reached during the July 2009 US-China Joint Commission on Commerce and Trade, much of the damage to foreign firms had already been inflicted. Despite the supportive role they provided Goldwind in the past, foreign partners now have substantially lower market shares and only a very limited ability to bid for infrastructure projects in China.

SOURCES OF INFLUENCE

New technology has been a critical factor in terms of influencing the world economy during the 20th century. There is no reason to believe that ongoing advances in technology will not provide numerous opportunities for the emergence of new entrepreneurial firms in the 21st century.

This outcome represents a source of threat for those firms that do not invest in developing next-generation products or operational processes. For young entrepreneurs who exhibit competences similar to those of individuals such as Bill Gates, Richard Branson or Steve Jobs, identifying new opportunities or threats will require only an intuitive ability concerning where best to focus their future endeavours. For less gifted individuals living in Western democracies, the task will be more difficult. Hence where insightful intuition is lacking, one approach available is to evaluate potential influence of the factors which might determine whether a new technology will be adopted and thereby deliver greater financial reward (Chaston 2009b). A summary of these key influencing variables are shown in Figure 9.3.

At the core of Figure 9.3 is the customer. As noted by Ibrahim et al. (2008) new technology is usually capable of effectively satisfying existing customer needs. More importantly, however, is whether the new technology can also offer incremental added value opportunities by satisfying as yet unidentified needs of new customers. An example of this requirement is provided by the Internet. This technology was initially perceived as an alternative promotional medium and, subsequently, a system for supporting more convenient customer purchasing. Hence, other than a very small number of highly perceptive futurists, few people could have predicted the Internet would have such widespread impact on numerous industrial processes across various market systems, as well as lead to culture shifts involving completely new forms of social behaviour and buying habits.

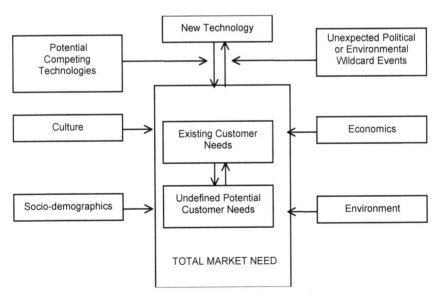

Figure 9.3 Variables influencing the adoption of a new technology.

To survive, any new technology has to out-compete existing technologies (Hoffman 2000). In most cases existing technologies will be utilised by major corporations. These organisations often have a vested interest in avoiding current technology and operational assets rendered obsolete by the emergence of a superior new technology. Hence these firms may utilise their resources and established market position to defeat a new market entrant who is seeking to exploit an alternative technology. An example of this outcome is provided by the major pharmaceutical firms that, at least in the early days of biotechnology, were less than supportive over using this alternative approach in the development of new healthcare treatments.

Another influencing variable is wildcard events. These can occur because a completely unexpected event acts as a catalyst leading to an increase in the market potential for a new technology. One such example was the sudden, very rapid rise in world oil prices in 2007–2008. This acted as a major stimulus for market acceptance of alternative energy sources, such as solar and wind power, and greater consumer interest in switching to hybrid vehicles, such as the Toyota Prius.

In many cases the first generation of products or services based upon a new technology will be expensive to produce and require relatively high prices to be charged at the time of initial launch. During periods of weak economic conditions, potential customers may feel unable to risk purchasing high-price items and market acceptance may be slow. In some cases limited market penetration means profits generated are insufficient to support the R&D activities necessary to drive down production costs. This is a critical outcome because in many cases market expansion involving a new technology can occur only when further advances in the technology lead to production costs declining to the point where products become affordable to a sufficiently large enough number of customers. As demonstrated by consumer goods such as flat screen televisions, the reverse scenario is also possible—namely, during periods of rapid economic growth potential customers are more willing to take the risk of purchasing what currently is a relatively expensive product or service proposition. This outcome will probably hasten the arrival of economies of scale that permit manufacturers to further reduce prices, leading to an increased market share.

Customer acceptance of a new technology will also be influenced by prevailing cultural values. One of the key reasons for the unexpected, very rapid growth in the consumer market for the first generation of mobile phones was the product being perceived as a 'must-have item' among young people. Market penetration rates for subsequent generations of the product were also greatly assisted by the enthusiasm with which young people then moved into texting and sending or downloading visual materials.

Socio-demographic change which can result in the re-shaping of markets will strongly influence the demand for new products and services. In the Western world, the onset of population ageing has led to people aged 50+ becoming the dominant age group within society (Chaston 2009a). Additionally many of these older people are now more financially secure and enjoy a higher standard of living than younger people, especially those who have children. The implications of this scenario are that in the future entrepreneurs would be well advised when assessing the potential for a new technology to give greater attention to the market opportunities among older age groups instead of focusing upon the traditional primary consumer target group of 18–45-year-olds with families.

Over the last 20 years there has been a gradual increase in the scale of the problems associated with population growth, pollution, a finite supply of key natural resources and global warming. Recently citizens in developed economies have become more concerned about the impact of these environmental threats. The consequence is that organisations need to be more aware about eco-protection and attention must be paid to the potential adverse environmental implications of the new technologies being associated with new product and service offerings which are being developed. This is because more governments and more private citizens believe industry should exhibit greater environmental responsibility. This attitude shift has implications in relation to customers exhibiting a purchase preference for those firms which exhibit higher moral and ethical standards.

CHANGING OPPORTURNITIES

Case Aims: To illustrate how declining costs for a new technology result in the emergence of new opportunities.

The electronic calculator provides an excellent illustration of how new opportunities can emerge as the costs of a new technology begin to fall (Brown 1992). An early entrant into this market was Hewlett-Packard, which was able to sell what was perceived as an expensive product to scientists and engineers. However, as the costs of producing calculators began to fall, Texas Instruments (TI), which had extensive experience in high-volume, low-cost manufacturing of electronic products, entered the market with a range of much lower-price products. These appealed to other B2B customers such as accountants and resulted in TI becoming a market leader. For whatever reason, TI decided against pursuing further actions to reduce manufacturing costs. This permitted the Japanese firm Casio, using advances in production technology to support market entry, to offer even lower-priced calculators. This opened up a huge consumer market such as parents and school children. Furthermore, having developed capabilities in the area of full-function, graphic display machines, Casio successfully challenged Hewlett-Packard's dominance of the scientific calculator market at prices which its competitors were unable to match.

S-CURVE

Not all customers or organisations respond at the same speed in terms of adopting a new technology. This behaviour, when analysed in relation to the percentage of customers or organisations adopting a new technology, may result in an S-shaped product adoption curve (Ortt and Schoorman 2004) of the type shown in Figure 9.4. The shape of the curve is influenced by three different phases associated with the adoption process. Firstly there is the 'development phase,' during which the new technology is being identified, developed and evolved into a feasible proposition of appeal to potential users. This is followed by the 'early adoption phase,' during which the more innovative, risk-taking members of the adopting population are prepared to incorporate the new technology into their ongoing purchasing activities. Once the new technology has clearly demonstrated a benefit for the early adopters, the more conservative elements within the adopting population will commence purchasing because they now perceive there are few risks in also becoming users. Ultimately all of the later market entrants will have adopted the new technology and the total number of users will plateau.

In assessing the scale of potential opportunities or threats associated with the expected shape of the S-curve for a new technology, a critical issue is the speed with which the new customers adopt the new technology (Brown 1992). One of the obstacles confronting the introduction of a new technology is the cost of the new product or service relative to the price of goods available from firms using existing technologies. This is because new

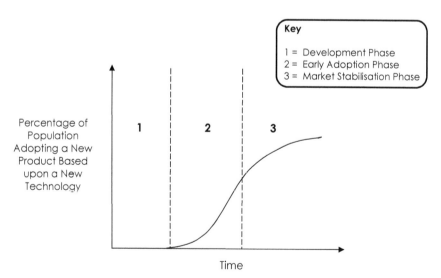

Figure 9.4   The innovation S-curve.

technology is often expensive to develop and it may be feasible to launch the first generation of the new offerings only by charging a relatively high price. As organisations gain experience with a new technology, this usually leads to a decline in production costs, which can then permit a price reduction. As prices fall, new customers may enter the market. This outcome will permit new firms to enter the market by exploiting their capabilities in areas such as managing high-volume production systems or their experience in the marketing of mass market goods. Where a reduction in the cost of a technology is not feasible, product prices will remain high and the probable outcome is the number of customers will remain extremely small.

A concept associated with the marketing of new products is the 'diffusion of innovation' curve. This proposes that potential customers can be divided into five groups—namely, 'innovators,' 'early adopters,' 'the early majority,' 'the late majority' and 'laggards.' The time taken before a potential customer first purchases a product will depend upon which group the individual is a member of. The first purchasers will be innovators, whereas the last individuals to purchase will be the laggards.

Having examined the launch of numerous high-technology products, Moore (1991) concluded that the benefits sought by of each of these five customer groups are somewhat different. Innovators purchase the product because they wish to own the latest technology, being prepared to accept any problems which may exist with the new product. Early adopters will require to be persuaded that the product will work properly and can offer a new way for fulfilling their vision of exploiting a new technology. The early and late majority will postpone purchase until they are persuaded the product offers a functional benefit not provided by existing products. Laggards are price-sensitive and hence wait until the product is virtually obsolete before entering the market.

Moore used case materials from a number of product launches to demonstrate that these different needs will require that the product benefit which is offered to customers will need to change as companies seek to 'cross the chasm' which exists between the five customer types. Moore's chasm theory requires that unless the product benefit is revised to reflect different market needs, then at each phase along the diffusion of innovation curve there is the risk that new products will not attract the next group of customers. This scenario represents both an opportunity and a threat. The threat is a currently successful firm fails to develop an effective new benefit proposition and is unable to cross the next chasm. This outcome is an opportunity for another firm, should this latter organisation become able to deliver the benefit sought by the next customer group.

One of the commonest chasm crossing failures occurs when a small firm is the developer of a new product based upon a new technology. Customers interested in innovator-type products tend to be orientated towards being the 'first to purchase and own' any new technology proposition. They are usually very willing to experiment with the new product to determine how to utilise the new technology. There is acceptance that the new product may exhibit operating faults or not totally fulfil the performance claims made by the supplier. This is not an attitude shared by early adopters or the early majority. They require a product which delivers the performance specification claimed by the supplier and demand that the product does not have any fundamental operating faults. Small firms may lack the R&D, manufacturing or financial resources that can cure the faults present in the early versions of a new product. This provides an opportunity for larger organisations which have these resources to develop a fault-free design which permits them to be the first to cross the chasm from innovation to adoption.

BEWARE OF TECHNOLOGICAL CHANGE

Case Aims: To illustrate the threat posed to long-standing market leaders by a substitute technology.

Throughout the 20th century there have been a number of occasions when an entrepreneurial individual or organisation has developed a new technology or perceived an alternative application of an existing technology which eventually has adversely impacted the performance of the current market leader in an industrial sector. In the majority of these cases highly destructive technological threats tend to originate from outside the current group of companies which constitute the existing industry.

An example of an upstream technological threat is provided by the potential impact of biotechnology being used to manufacture products from agricultural feedstocks instead of using petroleum-based raw materials to produce chemicals, plastics and fuels (Anon. 2010b). The risk is that existing, large packaging producers that are not closely linked with supply chain members pioneering this switch to biotechnology may begin to lose sales to new competitors that are able to offer compostable packaging to branded goods manufacturers. Only by early awareness and taking action to acquire or access the new technology can existing firms protect themselves from such threats. An example of an early response to the need to switch away from using petroleum-based raw materials is the huge US producer of chemicals Du Pont Corporation. The company has linked up with Tate & Lyle, the British sugar company, to start making the chemical propanediol from corn instead of hydrocarbon fuel.

A substitution threat occurs when a new technology offers an alternative to an existing technology. For hundreds of years the core capability of the watch industry was the manufacture of precision clockwork movements, which were the basis of all timepieces. The most successful producers of these movements were the Swiss, who dominated the global watch industry. Following the invention of the microchip it was recognised that this provided a substitute technology for powering watches. Although the Swiss firms were aware of the potential of this alternative technology, they decided against the utilisation of microchips.

(continued)

BEWARE OF TECHNOLOGICAL CHANGE (continued)

The Japanese company Casio recognised that the advantage of the micro-chip is that the technology (a) provided a watch movement at a much lower cost and (b) permitted watches to be manufactured which offered a huge range of different operating features. Hence the company used the micro-chip to develop a complete range of products from low-price, basic mod-els through to premium-price, multi-functional timepieces. Within only a few years, the activities of Casio and other Japanese companies which fol-lowed its lead in the use of the new technology as a substitute solution resulted in the Swiss watch industry losing its dominant global market posi-tion forever.

New technology, if ignored by existing industry incumbents, provides an opportunity for new players to enter the market. This scenario was appli-cable in the case of digital technology being introduced into the world's camera and photography markets. From the invention of photography in the 19th century, the dominant players were organisations such as Eastman Kodak which specialised in the creation of low-cost, high-quality photogra-phy for consumer markets. Concurrently European firms such as Leica util-ised superior product design and engineering skills to improve the quality of cameras through the manufacture of better lenses and developing new inter-nal mechanical systems such as the single- and twin-reflex cameras. By the 1960s developments in the IT industry began to demonstrate that digitalisa-tion and reproduction of visual images offered new opportunities in rela-tion to the future of the camera and photographic reproduction. Although Kodak recognised the threats posed by digitalisation, its strategy seemed oriented towards to protecting its dominance of the photographic film mar-ket, and consequently this contributed to poor performance in exploiting the new digital technologies. This apparent low level of interest exhibited by the leading camera manufacturers permitted Japanese firms such as Sony, Olympus and Canon to launch digital cameras and eventually to achieve a market leadership.

Manufacturers, especially in consumer goods markets, are usually reli-ant upon strong relationships between themselves and intermediaries down-stream in their market to successfully link with the final customer. In the case of the popular music industry, for many years, strategic success was sustained by a small number of large recording companies working closely with retailers and the broadcast industry to achieve market dominance for the singers and groups who they had under contract. The industry was given a clear warning of the potential impact of the Internet on future sales when the Napster company made downloading and file sharing available to the world. Instead of recognising the new world emerging as a result of down-loading, the music industry fought legal battles in order to protect its busi-ness revenues. As a result, it ignored the reality of how the Internet would impact the entertainment and broadcast industries. This myopic response permitted IT companies to enter the music market, as demonstrated by the huge success enjoyed by Apple following its launch of the iTunes and iPod products.

DISRUPTION THEORY

In seeking to explain how apparently well-managed, large organisations permit competitors steal their business by exploiting a new technology, Christensen (1997) used the phrase 'sustained innovation' to
describe the orientation of most large corporations towards focusing
their R&D efforts on introducing incremental improvements in existing products or organisational processes. The potential problem with
this managerial philosophy is the future performance of these firms is
highly vulnerable to a new player entering the market offering a significantly different product or the introduction of a new, significantly
more effective organisational process (e.g. Dell's use of direct marketing of computers to US consumers while existing major computer
manufacturers continued to rely on a direct sales force, distributors or
retail outlets).

Paap and Katz (2004) have questioned the conventional theory of
a large firm's failure being attributed to a lack of recognition of the
scale of the threat posed by a new firm entering its market or the inadequate speed of its strategic response. They support the view posited by
Christensen that market leaders' desire to respond to changing market
circumstances is often constrained by their existing major customers'
insistence on their key suppliers concentrating on further improvements
being made to existing products. As a result large firms may tend to
focus on product or process innovation which can sustain the company's
current market position in terms of staying ahead of other large organisations operating within the same market sector (Demuth 2008). Thus,
for example, IBM did recognise the potential of the mini-computer to
provide smaller organisations with access to more affordable computer
technology. However, demands from the firm's existing large company
clients influenced IBM's decision to continue to develop the next generation of mainframe computers capable of offering even greater, more
powerful data processing capability. This behaviour permitted an MIT-
trained entrepreneur, Ken Olsen, operating from an old textile mill in
Massachusetts, to launch the Digital Equipment Corporation (DEC).
The new firm's success was based upon the strategy of making computers affordable to smaller organisations by supplying them with the first
generation of mini-computers.

The implications of Christensen's theory is that smaller firms seeking
to implement a growth strategy in an existing industry should develop a
very different new product or revise internal organisational processes to
offer a desired customer benefit not yet satisfied by the incumbent, large-
firm market leader. This approach is known as 'disruptive innovation.'
It is applicable to those situations where the new proposition is significantly different from the prevailing business conventions being followed

by large firms. The outcome is either the creation of a very different customer usage pattern or an offering of a product which delivers a radically different benefit proposition.

Christensen's concept of disruptive innovation being the primary cause of a major downturn in financial performance among large firms is widely accepted by the academic world. There are a number of well-documented examples of poor organisational performance that exist which validate Christensen's viewpoint. Nevertheless there is also evidence to suggest his theory is not a universal explanation that can be applied to inappropriate strategic thinking in all industrial sectors (Cravens et al. 2002). For example, a review of case materials in most branded consumer goods sectors would suggest that only a minority of large company performance downturns can be explained by the advent of a disruptive technology. This is because the expertise which exists within these major corporations should permit an immediate response to a newly emerging market trend by utilising their huge internal resources to mount a successful counterattack. Possible responses may involve establishing their own similar operation or acquiring the entrepreneurial new market entrant before the latter organisation can become a threat of sufficient scale to adversely impact future business performance. For example, when Canon first started to make inroads into the photocopier market with its lower-price desktop machine, Xerox clearly had both the technical expertise and dominant market position which would have permitted it to defeat its new enemy. Similarly it seems unexplainable why the major firms in the branded foods and food service industries did not observe McDonald's early success and immediately opened their own chain of fast food outlets. Instead they appear to have not only ignored the threat posed by Ray Kroc, but also just remained on the sidelines as James McLamore and David Edgerton began to expand out from Miami with their Burger King operation.

Some examples of failures by incumbent large firms not explained by disruption theory can be attributed to a loss of strategic flexibility and proactive culture within these organisations (Chaston 2009b). There appears to be no simple explanation of why successful firms morph into totally conventional, passive and non-innovative entities. Senior management may become fixated on believing the strategy which was successful in the past will continue to serve the company well in the future, despite market evidence about the need to shift to a new strategy capable of sustaining high added value performance (Slevin and Covin 1990; Amabile et al. 1996). Thus those leaders whose preference is to avoid implementing strategic change would do well to reflect on Parnell et al.'s (2005) review of corporate failure. These authors concluded that that organisational leaders 'should resist the notion that to-day's source of competitive advantage will be eternal.'

THE TESLA DISRUPTION

Case Aims: To illustrate how an entrepreneurial solution can challenge the conventional technology utilised by existing large corporations.

In deciding to exploit new technology to challenge existing industrial practices, the entrepreneur can expect to face a number of problems. These include the new technology meeting expected performance expectations, delay in development leading to the need for an injection of additional capital and the possibility that incumbent companies, observing and learning from the entrepreneur's mistakes, are able to enter the market with an equivalent product.

Such is the case in the development of the Tesla, the world's first electric sports car (Copeland 2008). The company is named after Nikola Tesla, an eccentric late-19th-century inventor. The Telsa company has developed and commenced manufacturing the first zero-emission sports car, the Tesla Roadster. This is the first production sports car powered by electricity to enter the market. With a range of 220 miles per charge and an ability to accelerate from 0 to 60 mph in 3.9 seconds, some of the innovative technology behind the project came from lessons learned in the computer industry during the development of lighter, more powerful and more efficient batteries for use in mobile devices such as the laptop computer.

The car was conceived by Martin Eberhard, an engineer and serial entrepreneur who was convinced he could create a practical, zero-emission vehicle by fitting numerous lithium laptop batteries into an existing sports car chassis. Earlier in his career, he launched a series of start-ups, including an electronic-book company, which he co-founded, called NuvoMedia. He sold this business to Gemstar for $187 million in 2000. His strategy for minimising the development costs for the project was to build the car by licensing electric drive-train technology from another company (AC Propulsion) and using an existing car-maker to do the manufacturing. During the development phase of the project, Eberhard was responsible for inventing new approaches to battery-cooling, electric motor and power electronics patents used in the vehicle. Unable to persuade any venture capital company to fund his ideas, he met with Elon Musk. This individual is the co-founder of PayPal and was forced out of the on-line-payment company, but still made millions when the company was sold to eBay. Some of his millions are invested in SpaceX, a private rocket company which aims to start taking people to the International Space Station by 2011. Musk agreed to invest $6.3 million into Telsa and was appointed company chairman. The price of his participation, however, was to have major control over strategy. For example, Musk saw the franchise-dealership arrangements in the US car industry as an increasingly expensive, margin-killing business model. His alternative model is that of owning and operating his own network of Tesla dealerships. As the project progressed, with Musk injecting more funds into the project, disagreements between him and Eberhard emerged. In the key area of product design, Musk's viewpoint was influenced by his vision to build the next great American car company. This caused conflict with Eberhard, who had the more humble dream of rapidly developing and marketing a relatively low-cost, zero-emission sports car.

(continued)

THE TESLA DISRUPTION (continued)

By the end of 2006, Musk and other investors such as Google's Larry Page and Sergey Brin, who had become involved in the company, were forced to inject more funds into the project. By then, however, major problems began to emerge over the spiralling estimated costs for manufacturing the vehicle and numerous failures by the development team to meet critical project milestones. To reduce the rate at which the company was burning through cash reserves, plans to build a car plant to produce a zero-emission saloon car in 2010 were mothballed by the board. Eberhard had negotiated with the UK sports car company Lotus to produce the Roadsters. The agreement included financial penalties should production not begin on schedule. When delays occurred, Lotus invoked a $4 million penalty clause and this, plus other problems, caused Musk to have Eberhard removed from the board and to appoint Ze'ev Drori, an operations-focused Silicon Valley veteran, as the new CEO. A technical team led by Hal Straubel re-examined every component with the aim of identifying where savings could be made that would permit manufacturing costs to be lower than the launch price. Having achieved this goal, Tesla started production of the Roadster in March 2008.

Eberhard's response has been to turn to the courts to seek compensation for his removal from the project (Reed 2009). Meanwhile Musk has decided there was a need for him to gain even greater control over the project. Hence he has appointed himself as both chairman and CEO. Media coverage of these events, plus the decision of Darryl Siry to resign as the head of sales and marketing because of his concerns over certain aspects of company strategy, has made life difficult for Tesla. However, the 2008 crisis over rapidly rising world oil prices and the need for the US government to help the US car industry become more involved in new, greener technology have provided a wildcard event for Tesla. This is because the company has been awarded major government funding from the US Department of Energy to progress development of the company's Model S saloon car, and Daimler agreed to purchase a small stake in the company for $50 million. This development will permit Musk to move from a position of being a niche producer of a sports car into the much larger high-volume, saloon car market. The only question which now remains is whether other car manufacturers, having learned from Tesla's use of technology such as lithium batteries, are able to successfully launch their own electric cars.

(*Source*: www.teslamotors.com)

10 Knowledge, Networks and Innovation

The purpose of this chapter is to cover issues pertaining to:

1. The role of knowledge in sustaining organisational performance.
2. The knowledge acquisition process.
3. Exploiting networks to access new knowledge.
4. Enhancing entrepreneurial activities through open innovation.
5. Factors influencing the effectiveness of open innovation.

KNOWLEDGE MANAGEMENT

Murray and Greenes (2006) proposed that gaps in an organisation's essential knowledge represent major threats. Conversely opportunities are valuable knowledge that is available to the organisation, but not yet fully exploited. Hence these authors suggest that all organisations should regularly implement an assessment of their knowledge assets. This permits identification of any weaknesses and may reveal hidden assets that offer a new source of revenue. They quote the example of Texas Instruments, where this operational philosophy permitted the company to realise over $100 billion in additional revenues from licensing, royalties and patents.

When competitors have adopted a strategy based upon aggressive price competition, one counter-strategy to avoid profit margin erosion is to use innovation as the basis of differentiating the firm from others in the same market sector (Roig and Dobon 2008). The increasing complexity of today's markets and rapidly changing technology often mean that successful innovation is critically dependent upon the exploitation of existing knowledge and the concurrent acquisition of new knowledge (Chaston 2004). Given that Western firms will increasingly be required to utilise this approach to defeat threats from emerging nations, there is a need for these organisations to carefully preserve internal resources and to acquire the new knowledge necessary to successfully develop and launch new products (Chaston 2009b). One solution for firms which lack sufficient resources or have an inadequate knowledge base is enter into a collaborative alliance by becoming members of business networks or a joint ventures (Witt et al. 2008).

MANAGING KNOWLEDGE AT ERICSSON

Case Aims: To illustrate how the management of new knowledge acquisition can assist innovation in a high-technology industry environment.

Each phase of the new product development process from idea generation, concept generation/validation, planning, development, testing and launch will involve employees in organisational learning. This activity is necessary to acquire new knowledge to complement existing competences which they have already developed through work on earlier projects. High-technology firms face an unrelenting pressure to create next-generation products in order to stay ahead of competitors seeking to gain market share for products based upon existing technologies. To gain further understanding of the learning process in such situations, Döös et al. (2005) undertook a qualitative study of learning and knowledge management in the Swedish telecoms company Ericsson.

The researchers identified a number of factors that influenced the effectiveness of the learning process and how this impacts new product development. For learning to occur there must exist a corporate culture that emphasises employees' active engagement in learning as an ongoing, continuous activity which assists in the fulfilment of assigned tasks and responsibilities. The complex nature of developing new products involving the use of high technology will mean that rarely will one individual have sufficient knowledge to resolve problems or propose the most optimal solution. As a consequence inside Ericsson there is strong emphasis on the concept of 'co-creation.' This involves allocating new product projects to teams constituted of individuals with an appropriate skills mix. It is frequently the case that when a new problem is encountered, resolution is achieved by the team drawing upon and re-combining the knowledge and prior experience which exists within its knowledge pool. The company also recognises that interaction between teams, often as a result of informal meetings or social events, is critical. This is because access to additional external sources of knowledge can often help teams overcome what appears to be an insurmountable problem.

Ericsson has recognised that the structure of an organisation can either enhance or impede the new product development process. Experience has shown that the most effective structuring is to create small, decentralised operations which have the delegated authority to reach decisions without needing to waste time gaining approval for action from managers at higher levels within the organisation. The company has also recognised that learning in decentralised entities can be enhanced by creating communication systems that support inter-team interaction. This will lead to higher levels of horizontal knowledge exchange.

Ericsson is a multi-location operation and believes horizontal knowledge exchange is important to accelerate problem resolution and to avoid a team in one location struggling with a problem which has already been solved elsewhere within the company. To further assist horizontal knowledge exchange the company has appointed 'trouble shooters.' These individuals interact with teams, provide guidance, suggest solutions and arrange new inter-team links. The trouble shooters also engage in networking with each other and with contacts outside the company as a mechanism for co-resolving problems encountered by teams for which they have been assigned oversight responsibility.

KNOWLEDGE ACQUISITION

Jain and Jain (2003) noted that market research can often be complemented by internal data sources as the basis for gaining a better understanding of customer behaviour. Henning et al. (2003) proposed organisational knowledge can be classified into three categories—namely, (1) knowledge to satisfy customers' needs, (2) knowledge to understand customers' motivations and (3) knowledge of customers' knowledge of markets. Batra (2010) proposed organisations should identify gaps in relation to the knowledge expertise which exist within their organisation. Actions can then be needed to (i) transfer knowledge to new staff, (ii) ensure information/knowledge sharing is a component of organisational culture and (iii) ensure the organisation is able to capture best practices. He also concluded that by involving employees in learning and knowledge management this will lead to new practices and ideas being generated. To build long-term customer relationships, Bose and Sugumaran (2003) proposed that a critical aspect of knowledge management is the ability of the organisation's back-office system to convert raw data into a form which can be utilised by front-office decision-makers.

Those organisations which are committed to exploiting innovation as a path through which to sustain market leadership can rarely expect to be successful unless they have created systems to ensure the effective utilisation of new knowledge which has been acquired (Sharma et al. 2007). These authors posit that effective knowledge management requires finding ways of blending tacic and explicit knowledge. Achievement of this aim (a) leads to enhancement of the knowledge content associated with existing products/services, (b) accelerates the development time for new products/services and (c) expands knowledge proliferation to support entry into new markets. A key factor for meeting these objectives is the creation of systems where both existing and new knowledge is stored and then easily re-accessed by other employees. In their research on professional services, Chen et al. (2006) concluded that within less innovative organisations there is a tendency to prefer an informal approach to knowledge management. This is reflected by staff relying on personal understanding, colleagues' experience and personal networks as their favourite modes of knowledge acquisition.

Taylor and Wright (2004) examined knowledge management practices in the provision of healthcare services. These researchers concluded there are three key variables influencing process—namely, (i) 'organisational climate,' which reflects the organisational culture based upon open leadership and a willingness to learn from mistakes, (ii) 'infrastructure and process,' which is determined by the quality of information and a performance orientation and (iii) 'strategy implementation,' which involves the existence of a strategic vision and workforce satisfaction. An effective organisational climate is usually one where new ideas are welcomed and staff are motivated to engage in organisational improvement. Without appropriate infrastructure and process, the workforce is unable to participate in decision-making, capture new knowledge or undertake reflective learning to ensure the generation of new ideas that can lead to improved performance.

KNOWLEDGE SHARING

Case Aims: To illustrate the benefits of knowledge sharing in the travel industry.

The advent of the Internet and on-line purchasing has generated increasingly large quantities of real-time data about buyer behaviour. Converting these data into valuable knowledge has been greatly assisted by the advent of computer-based, automated, customer relationship management (CRM) systems. The conventional management philosophy is to utilise CRM to isolate proprietary knowledge that can provide the basis of differentiating an offering from that available from competition. More recently, however, an alternative perspective is emerging—namely, by sharing knowledge generated by CRM systems, this can enhance the value added proposition to be made available to customers. In their review of this trend, Warkentin et al. (2001) concluded that increased knowledge sharing is generating benefits such as greater back-office efficiency, greater customer intimacy, improved strategic planning, flexible adaptation to market changes, improved decision-making and more rapid and flexible management of supply chain processes.

The advent of the Internet and on-line buying led some experts to suggest that when the actual supplier offers the same proposition as intermediaries at a lower price, firms in this latter position in the supply chain would find business survival is increasingly difficult. One such group that was seen to be at risk was travel agents. This is because of the ease with which customers can now purchase their tickets directly from the airline websites. Fan and Ku (2010) suggested that an effective response by service organisations facing this threat is to consider using their CRM systems as the basis for entering into knowledge transfer agreements with other members of their supply chain. To examine the benefits of this activity Fan and Ku researched the knowledge exchange practices which are emerging in the travel industry. They concluded that travel agents and actual service providers such as the airlines are increasingly engaging in the exchange of customer knowledge. Real benefits which were identified included improved back office productivity, enhanced service quality and use of customer data to jointly develop new services.

NETWORKS

Networks are a form of collaboration in which organisations with a common interest work together to exchange ideas, knowledge and/or technology (Dean et al. 1997). The motivations for entering into networks are numerous, but firms needing to urgently develop new products or services canaccess to networks and thereby significantly enhanc innovation outcomes (Heracleous and Murray 2001). More intangible factors associated with network membership include the possibility to acquire power, influence, credibility and favours. Successful networks are likely to be characterised by the capacity to adjust member involvement over time in response to changing circumstances (Elmuti and Kathawala 2001). Drawbacks associated with network membership may include loss in organisational flexibility or independence accompanied by a considerable time commitment in order to manage inter-firm relationships (Kosa and Lewin 2000).

The late 1980s saw researchers beginning to question the view that entrepreneurs act in isolation as autonomous entities. As a consequence of further research it has become increasingly accepted that many entrepreneurs are linked with a broad network of different actors (Hoang and Antoncic 2003). Mitra (2000) identified that one of the most effective strategies especially for small firms to enhance company performance is to participate in networks. In the case of the use of networks by marketing-orientated small and medium size enterprises (SMEs), these organisations are more likely to rely on networking to access information than their large firm counterparts.

Camison and Villar-Lopez (2010) consider networks a crucial aspect of influencing the success of entrepreneurial organisations. They confirmed that access to new external knowledge is a key influencer of performance in export markets, and that in the case of small firms, the most successful ones are members of export networks. Wincent and Westerberg (2005) found that SMEs engaged in networking exhibit a higher degree of entrepreneurial behaviour when compared to firms less involved in collaborative activities. Lindsay (2005) proposed the entrepreneurial capability of firms is influenced by their ability to utilise new outside knowledge. This is because organisational learning by employees is enhanced by networking, which often assists in the identification of more effective responses to new opportunities or environmental threats (Morgan 2004; Lim and Chan 2004; Holmqvist 2003; Dawes 2003).

Tolstoy (2010) posited that in high-technology industries, successful entrepreneurial firms recognise the importance of exploiting networks as a strategy for accessing external knowledge sources. Palacios et al. (2009) concluded that collaborative knowledge management is a critical factor influencing the level of entrepreneurial behaviour in both the biotechnology and telecommunications industries. Inter-firm relationships permit network members to share knowledge which can lead to the development of new products and production processes. This view was supported in studies by Elfring and Hulsink (2003) and Ojala and Tyrvained (2009).

OPEN INNOVATION

The traditional approach to innovation in most organisations is to retain ownership and confidentiality of proprietary knowledge by adopting a 'closed innovation' approach. This involves not being willing to collaborate with other organisations in the development of new products. More recently organisations are beginning to change their approach to innovation by adopting 'open innovation' models which are designed to overcome some of the limitations associated with closed systems. Success in open innovation benefits not only the firm which has the original new idea but also those organisations involved in the collaborative processes that eventually lead to the launch of the new product (Chesbrough 2003).

Chesbrough has suggested there are four types of individuals involved in open innovation—namely:

1. *Innovation explorers*, who specialise in undertaking discovery-level research in public sector laboratories, corporate R&D laboratories and spinoffs of laboratories that used to be a part of a larger organisation.
2. *Innovation merchants*, who focus on developing a narrow set of technologies that are codified into intellectual property and brought to market or sold to other organisations.
3. *Innovation missionaries*, who create and seek to advance new technologies, but are not really interested in financial gain. Instead their aim is that of serving the common good of society. This approach often occurs in the software industry.
4. *Innovation marketers*, who perform the functions of bringing new products to market either for their own or for other organisations. Their aim is to exploit their understanding of markets and customers as the basis for generating significant incremental revenue.

Among some of the factors influencing this shift in organisational philosophy, Chesbrough has proposed the most important has been a rise in the number and mobility of knowledge workers. An associated factor is the growing availability of private venture capital which is used to finance the creation of new firms. Huang et al. (2010) posited that open innovation enables an organisation to be more effective in creating new products as well as enhancing existing value added activities. These authors proposed the process also helps create value by leveraging many more ideas from a variety of external concepts and allows greater value capture in the utilisation of the firm's existing assets.

An important factor spurring the process of open innovation is the rising cost of technology development in many industries (Chesbrough 2007). Chesbrough notes that not all companies apply the same approach to openness. In his view the process can best be described as a continuum ranging from a high and to a low degree of openness. Chesbrough (2003) identified different roles that companies can adopt when involved in open innovation—namely, funders, generators or organisations that bring innovation to the market. Christensen et al. (2005) argue that firms manage open innovation in different ways depending on (i) their position in the innovation system, (ii) the stage of product/service maturity and (iii) the scale of the value proposition.

Lichtenthaler (2009) examined radical innovation and concluded the degree of openness seems to rise with the degree of emphasis on radical innovation. This appears especially relevant in relation to projects involving external technology commercialisation. He proposes there are two reasons for this situation. The first is the opportunity to commercialise knowledge which, although being utilised within the organisation, can generate incremental revenue from being shared with others. The second reason is that open innovation is useful when seeking to accelerate the market acceptance for a new technology or to achieve creation of a new market standard. Lichtenthaler found that firms which emphasise radical innovation are not always able to develop all the required knowledge internally. Hence there is a need to rely on complementary external sources to support the creation of a commercially viable new proposition.

Lichtenthaler (2008) concluded that the higher the level of R&D intensity within the firm, the greater is the involvement in seeking to utilise new technology as the basis of exploiting innovation. Lazzarotti et al. (2010) posit that as firms increase their level of R&D, this will be accompanied by expanding their involvement in forming collaborative links with other organisations. In their view open innovators choose an aggressive technology and innovation strategy with the aim of acquiring sufficient technological leadership that this will permit them to become a first mover in existing or new markets. In terms of understanding the nature of open innovation, their study of Italian manufacturers led them to conclude that organisations could be classified into one of the following different groups:

1. *Open innovators*, who collaborate with a wide set of partners in most or all phases of the innovation process.
2. *Specialized collaborators*, who open only a small part of the innovation process to a wide variety of partners.
3. *Integrated collaborators*, who collaborate with only a limited set of partners along the entire innovation process.
4. *Closed innovators*, who open a very small part of the entire innovation process to a very small number of partners.

Slowinski and Sagal (2010) have proposed the following actions that influence process effectiveness. These can provide the basis for guidelines of good practice:

1. Incorporate external thinking into the strategic planning process.
2. Convert planning outcomes into a set of prioritised project briefs.
3. Utilise a structured process for the make/buy/partner decisions.
4. Look inside the company first when seeking new ideas.
5. Treat collaborative idea searches as a mutually beneficial process.
6. As new data are acquired, use this to update and further refine the project brief.
7. Establish and maintain alignment with all internal and external relationships.
8. Use a structured process for planning and negotiations.
9. Negotiate with a focus on 'win-win' outcomes.

A key characteristic of open innovation is the process does not necessarily take place within the boundaries of the firm. Instead innovation may be distributed among a larger number of different actors. This approach is often described as a 'boundary spanning activity.' The outcome is that knowledge flows between partners occur due to the increasingly permeable nature of company boundaries (Elmquist et al. 2009). These authors also note that there are two key dimensions influencing the innovation process—namely, the number of partners involved and the internal versus external focus of the innovation programme.

The risk facing firms, especially in high-technology sectors, is that a company that is internally focused due to reliance upon a closed innovation approach may miss new opportunities. This is because many of these fall outside of the organisation's current business activities or can be exploited only by working with other organisations (Chesbrough 2007). This risk can be avoided when senior management becomes persuaded of the benefits of exploiting ideas that originate from outside the organisation. For this to occur, however, management needs to recognise that the boundary between a firm and the surrounding environment must be porous, thereby enabling the development of a collaborative approach to knowledge exploitation.

In those cases where open innovation involves collaboration with customers, Fang (2008) suggested there are two dimensions of customer participation—namely, acting as a passive information resource or through active involvement as a co-developer. In his view the nature of the role can influence the speed with which the product comes to market and the radical nature of product innovativeness. In many consumer goods markets, supply chain networks constituted of suppliers, retailers and distributors are highly connected. As a consequence there is a high level of inter-organisational knowledge interchange. This can assist the speed of new product development. There is, however, a tendency of the downstream members to be somewhat conservative in response to ideas based upon radical innovation. This reaction may have a detrimental impact on the level of product innovativeness. To overcome this obstacle it is probably better for the supplier to engage in open innovation by also partnering with the actual final customer. Fang validated this perspective through a study of intermediary and customer behaviour in a number of supply chains. The results indicated that high information flows between supply chain members can accelerate the speed of innovation. When the developer is attempting to implement radical solutions, however, it is usually preferable to interact with the final customer.

OPEN INNOVATION IN ACTION

Case Aims: To provide examples of how major companies are using open innovation to enhance performance.

One example of the benefits of open innovation is provided by Nokia's market success in the telecoms industry due to the strong lead which had been achieved in creating the global system for mobile communication (GSM) technology, which became the standard for cellular phones (Häikiö 2002). This outcome required working closely with a number of other companies, as well as the governments in many European countries. To achieve the aim of dominating the global wireless communications industry, Nokia willingly licensed its research to other organisations and partnered with companies, including competitors, to develop the new technology and associated handsets.

Another example of the benefits offered by open innovation is provided by the consumer goods giant Procter & Gamble. In order to survive in the increasingly competitive world of branded consumer goods, the company decided to accelerate the scale of new product development activities by working with external partners in the identification and exploitation of new opportunities. In 2000, the CEO A. G. Lafley announced that the target was to have 50 percent of new ideas coming from outside the company within five years. In support of seeking to achieve this aim by 2005, the company had formed collaborative relationships with 2,000 suppliers and 7,000 other external partners (Huston and Sakkab 2006). In the case of P&G's Pringles Print initiative, the company now offers Pringles with pictures and words printed on each potato chip. This was achieved by locating and adapting an ink jet technology that a bakery in Bologna, Italy was using to print messages on cakes and biscuits. This existing knowledge permitted the creation of the Pringles Print at a fraction of the cost compared to that which would have been incurred should a totally new R&D project have been necessary. Development time was also reduced by 50 percent by P&G avoiding doing the development work without external assistance.

In the semiconductor industry, IBM's semiconductor foundry now shares knowledge and resources with four other companies. In addition IBM established a research alliance with Toshiba and Chartered Corporation, with the aim of sharing the high costs and risks of developing leading-edge semiconductor processes. The company has also revised the corporate philosophy in relation to managing intellectual property rights in areas such as patents and technology. This has involved moving from focusing upon preventing IP leakage to a philosophy of licensing IP to other organisations. This action has created a significant new revenue flow (Chesbrough 2007).

(continued)

OPEN INNOVATION IN ACTION (continued)

In 2004 General Mills determined that to accelerate the pace of the company's innovation activities it would be beneficial to recruit new external partners. To support the process and enhance the transparency of its commitment to open innovation, the company launched its World Wide Innovation Network (G-WIN). This permits employees and external sources such as scientists and food industry researchers to collaborate over the identification and solution of problems, thereby helping General Mills to develop more effective products and production processes. For example, the company formed a partnership with a company in Thailand to assist in the development of a range of frozen Chinese foods under the Wainchee Ferry brand name. This product offered restaurant-level quality in home prepared products. The overseas partner provided knowledge of flavourings and the sourcing of authentic Asian ingredients. A key factor in the success of the company's open innovation projects is the philosophy that successful collaboration demands all participants receive mutual benefits from engaging in the activity (Bellairs 2010).

One of the most well-known exploiters of open innovation is Apple, using the process to establish a new dominance in sectors such as music, mobile phones, electronic books and smart phone apps. The philosophy of the company is to rely upon open innovation to exploit customers' desire for variety in entertainment content and ease of access to desired data. The company firstly came to recognise the benefits of open innovation during the development of the iPhone concept. Development of its smart applications ('apps') concept permitted the company to exploit the fact that the capital requirements to develop new software are relatively low. To maximise the benefits of this product concept, the company provided open access to the iPhone technology, which has permitted numerous external partners to develop thousands of new iPhone apps (Rufat-Latre et al. 2010).

FACTORS OF INFLUENCE

Although open innovation can provide access to a larger pool of ideas, as noted by Birkinshaw et al. (2011), the costs can be considerable, practical problems over intellectual property ownership can arise and lack of trust may frustrate achievement of optimal project outcomes. Van der Meer (2007) reached similar conclusions in his study of open innovation in Dutch industry. He determined that large companies in that country focus primarily on generating incremental income from making their internal obsolete ideas available to other organisations. This leads to outcomes such as patent information licensing, new business start-ups, business spinoffs and new collaborative ventures in overseas markets.

Van der Meer found that even when large Dutch firms have moved from a closed to a more open approach to innovation, the subsequent projects often meet with failure. Primary causes of failure include insufficient commitment, impatience over timescales, inadequate resources and the use of the wrong strategy. In contrast Dutch small and medium-size enterprises (SMEs) appear to be more engaged in the exploitation of new knowledge through involvement in open innovation. A major factor explaining this variance is although the smaller firm may exhibit a strong entrepreneurial orientation, it often lacks the internal resources to develop a new idea through to being a commercially viable new product proposition. To overcome this obstacle many smaller firms enter into a collaborative relationship with a larger company. This action provides access to the necessary resources required to bring the new product to market.

In their analysis of collaborative innovation, Rycroft and Kash (2002) identified different path dependencies which can influence the nature of the behaviour of the core firms within an innovation network. In their view open innovation involves all parties engaging in inter-organisational learning. The nature of this learning is influenced by whether learning involves existing knowledge or the discovery of new knowledge. The related issue is which organisation is responsible for making available its internal learning when defining the key technological parameters to be utilised in a project. Rycroft and Kash provide the example of the American corporation GE in its role within an innovation concerning turbine blades for its jet engines. GE focused on two internal core capabilities, systems integration and the designing the 'hot side' of the jet engine. Other activities are the responsibility of complementary asset suppliers. This can be contrasted with the approach often found in incremental innovation projects involving the use of an existing, widely accepted design. In this latter situation network participants will share responsibilities in executing the project which is aimed at achieving an incremental improvement in an existing product. Rycroft and Kash suggest this latter approach is exemplified in the collaborative approach utilised in the incremental innovation of Intel's range of microchip products.

The nature of network member dependencies is also influenced by national, cultural and geographic factors. In relation to national and institutional cultures there is a tendency for these to be deeply embedded within all organisations. At times this can be an obstacle in effective collaboration. Lundvall (1998) noted that national cultural factors can be sufficiently strong as to influence innovation styles. An example is the distinctions that have been drawn between countries with regard to the time horizons within corporate entities (e.g. short-term in the UK, longer-term in Germany) or the priority placed on team- or group-based innovation (e.g. low team orientation in the United States, high in Japan). It can often be difficult to avoid these cultural influences frustrating the rapid exploitation of new technological opportunities. For example, Kenworthy (1995) believes the cultural norms in the United States which place a high value on individualism and adversarial processes have severely impeded the development of technological collaboration among organisations in numerous sectors of industry.

Cultural resistance to collaboration can persist even when it becomes obvious that network formation is a requisite antecedent to be a successful company in a sector. Lundvall (1998) noted that only very recently has closer co-operation among competitors and between suppliers and users acquired organisational legitimacy in the United States (Lundvall 1998).

Rycroft and Kash determined there is an increasing need for collaboration between organisations based in different countries. This type of collaboration can result in problems caused by countries' different attitudes and values. In their view the factor dominating successful outcomes is the ability of organisations from different countries to develop sufficient trust in each other to permit a genuinely open and effective exchange of knowledge. These researchers suggest that over time both intra- and inter-country learning occurs. This strengthens the innovation network because new knowledge and skills are added to existing core capabilities and associated assets. Rycroft and Kash believe that another influential factor is where geographic concentrations of expertise exist. These can have a strong influence over knowledge sharing and collaboration. They provide the example of Silicon Valley, California, where software engineers exist in dense social and professional communities that can transcend inter-firm rivalries. This is because professional respect, loyalties and friendship are more important than corporate loyalty, and this ensures the rapid diffusion of knowledge between different firms.

In an attempt to determine which factors have the most dominant influence on open innovation, Tellis et al. (2009) undertook a study of organisational performance across 17 different nations. Their conclusion was that the two most critical factors influencing successful open innovation were corporate culture within individual firms and the scale of investment in maximising the expertise of the workforce within these firms. Factors such as national culture, access to capital and national workforce capabilities, although verified as contributory factors, were seen as much less important in determining whether organisations are effective in the collaborative development of new products involving radical innovation.

Trott's (1998) conclusion that firms which focus on innovation are more likely to survive an economic downturn was endorsed in a recent survey of over 1,000 CEOs of major businesses conducted by IBM (2008). These individuals expressed the view that in the face of the worst recession since the 1930s, long-term growth is critically dependent upon entrepreneurial behaviour. Chaston (2009b) and Chesbrough (2003, 2007) posited that in an increasingly complex world, the market performance of firms necessitates the use of open innovation in order to more effectively exploit both existing and new knowledge which is required to successfully exploit entrepreneurial opportunities which can sustain business performance.

MANAGING PROCESS

Case Aims: To illustrate how collaboration can be enhanced by the use of appropriate management systems.

In a review of successful collaborative innovation Owen et al. (2008) concluded the three key factors influencing outcomes are leadership, performance management systems and continuous learning. The role of leaders is to develop and communicate the strategic direction of collaborative innovation throughout the participating organisations. Leaders must accept responsibility for creating the shared cultural values required to remove any barriers to collaboration. Performance management systems are necessary in order to define the standard approaches involved in the assessment, selection, operation and evaluation of the collaborative partnerships. In this way organisations can ensure collaborative relationships are consistent across all projects. The role of continuous learning involves defining and building capabilities for idea generation, relationship management and collaboration. For optimal results, knowledge gained through collaboration should be captured, shared and re-used.

In the mid-1990s, to exploit the benefits of collaborative innovation, the pharmaceutical company Eli Lilly and Company adopted its 'research without walls' philosophy by beginning to cultivate an extensive network of external partners in the biotechnology industry, academia and other centres of innovation (Owen et al. 2008). To further accelerate open innovation, in 2001 the company merged its R&D prospecting and corporate business development groups into a newly created Office of Alliance Management. By 2007, the Office of Alliance Management was handling over 100 R&D partnerships focused on new technology, products and services, with a further 160 projects concerned with developing new manufacturing processes.

Results of Lilly's efforts have been impressive. The company has launched numerous new products, invigorated its innovation pipeline and achieved increased revenue growth. One example of success is provided by the drug Byetta. This was developed by working with Amylin Pharmaceuticals and is now manufactured and co-marketed by Lilly. Launched in June 2005, within 12 months annual revenue reached US$430 million. Other successes include Cialis and Actos, which are new drugs which generate annual revenue of US$971 million and US$448 million respectively.

11 Public Sector Strategies

The purpose of this chapter is to cover issues pertaining to:

1. Public sector reform in the face of declining financial resources.
2. The relevance of strategic planning in public sector organisations.
3. Managing the strategic planning process in the public sector.
4. The purpose and relevance of performance measurement.
5. The nature of public sector entrepreneurship.

PUBLIC SECTOR REFORM

Faced with delivering manifestos of seeking to meet the needs of society in the face of increasingly inadequate public sector funding, in the late 1980s some politicians became enamoured with the idea that reforming public sector practices could close the gap between service supply and demand. Known as the New Public Management (NPM) model, the emphasis was on achievement of the '3 Es' of economy, efficiency and effectiveness. The focus on economy related to minimising the cost of inputs and ensuring their most economic use in the provision of services. Efficiency is concerned with optimising the cost of outputs. Effectiveness involves maximising outputs (Chaston 2011).

As politicians sought to manage the growing problem of funding the welfare state to divert attention away from the electorate blaming governments for anythey claimed huge inefficiencies and ineffectiveness existed due to poor working practices within the public sector (Denhardt et al. 1989). In presenting this perspective, politicians were prepared to imply that public sector employees were the primary obstacle standing in the way of change. They espoused the need to introduce private sector management models on the grounds these would remove the lethargy and resistance to change which they felt they encountered when working with civil servants. The justification for reform was that productivity would increase when public sector organisations (PSOs) were run on more 'business-like lines.' This strategy was claimed to be the most effective way of improving efficiency, levels of service provision and service quality. Unfortunately to date there is little evidence that NPM has led to significant improvements in efficiency or effectiveness. In fact available data suggest that changes made in working practices in the public sector under the banner of modernisation can actually lead to a decline in productivity, morale and organisational loyalty (Osborne 2010).

During the 1990s, although there was a general acceptance of the need for greater austerity in public sector spending, some governments continued to increase the size of their public sector deficits (Harrinvirta and Mattila 2001). During the early 21st century, consumers, business and governments all became enamoured with low interest rates resulting from limited intervention of central banks in support of an economic model based upon higher spending supported through higher borrowing. The first indication of trouble was the emergence of problems in the United States' sub-prime mortgage market. This was followed by banks in both the United States and Europe, due to their involvement in complex financial derivative products, being forced to admit their balance sheets contained high levels of toxic debt. In order to avoid a banking collapse of the scale previously not seen since the 1930s, governments were forced to intervene. This resulted in a massive increase in public sector deficits. The scale of these deficits was further exacerbated in some Mediterranean countries because their governments had been making the mistake of in sustaining economic growth through excessive borrowing. By 2009 the only solution for many Western nation economies was to implement massive cuts in public spending.

PUBLIC SECTOR STRATEGIC PLANNING

The problem now confronting the public sector, given the apparent failure of concepts such as NPM, is what alternative managerial concept can be used to sustain the delivery of services in the face of the funding crisis now facing most PSOs. A key area of emphasis under the banner of NPM was the need for public sector organisations to adopt a more proactive orientation towards the influence of the external environment on the operations and the optimal exploitation of available internal resources. This was deemed necessary in order to achieve an economic, effective and efficient delivery of services. The perspective led to the concept of strategic planning being introduced into the public sector to assist management develop more appropriate plans for managing an increasingly complex world, while learning to cope with a capped, or sometimes declining, resource base. Bryson (1981) posits that providing a new sense of direction is precisely the purpose and philosophy underlying the concept of strategic planning. In terms of defining the purpose of using strategic planning in the public sector, Bryson (1995, p. 11) subsequently proposed the activity is 'a disciplined effort to produce fundamental decisions and actions that shape the organisation, what it is, what it does and why it does it.'

Further support for the benefits of utilising strategic planning in the response to significant change is provided by Pullen (1993). He believed that during periods of discontinuous change in the public sector, such as a major reduction in financial resources, managers need to focus on organisational and managerial processes that can permit reconstitution into new, often significantly different operational entities. In his view managers who spend their time worrying about which boxes on their organisation chart should be shifted around or deleted are liable to become involved in a losing proposition. Pullen believes that strategic planning will provide the basis for an organisational re-creation by focusing on creating, building and hoarding strategic resources that can support a rapid adaptation to sustaining the delivery of core services in increasingly different external environments.

Early attempts at introducing strategic planning into the public sector from the private sector frequently met with failure. Ring and Perry (1985) suggested this outcome was probably because consultants hired to advise public sector agencies frequently failed to understand the nature of the differences which exist between the two sectors. As a consequence insufficient attention was given to how private sector process models needed to be revised to reflect the operational realities confronting the public sector manager. One of the most fundamental differences between the two sectors is the nature of the customer and degree of freedom which exists in the availability and allocation of resources utilised to deliver services that are available to an organisation.

PROGRESS REPORT

Case Aims: To illustrate the degree to which a strategic planning philosophy has been adopted by local government operations in the United States.

In the face of rising inflation and declining tax revenues, municipal authorities in the United States first began to introduce a strategic approach into the planning process in the mid-1980s. To determine the degree to which the subsequent two decades have influenced the ongoing utilisation of this planning philosophy, Poister and Streib (2005) undertook a large-scale survey of CEOs in municipalities across America. They found that 56 percent of respondents still had yet to move towards utilising strategic planning. Of the 44 percent who were utilising this approach, the majority were restricting involvement in the process to senior managers and elected officials. Less than half of these latter organisations were involving their lower-level staff in the activity. In terms of the overall purpose of the planning process, 92 percent utilised the activity to define performance goals, 82 percent to assist in developing a vision for the future and 78 percent for the identification of appropriate action plans. Slightly fewer organisations (72 percent) utilised the activity to identify external stakeholders' needs and concerns. Only 60 percent of respondents used the activity to assess internal capability, 52 percent to identify strengths, weaknesses, opportunities and threats and even fewer (36 percent) to take this opportunity to assess the feasibility of proposed future strategic actions.

(continued)

PROGRESS REPORT (continued)

In relation to nature of the outcomes achieved, the researchers concluded that although 44 percent had reported use of a strategic planning philosophy, only 37 percent had a fully documented strategic plan, only 33 percent linked the plan to budget priorities and only 22 percent had defined performance measures to be utilised to track actual performance versus targets that had been defined by their strategic plan. In those organisations where the budget was linked to the strategic plan, 84 percent reported that there was clear focus on using any new funds and capital expenditure activities to enhance achievement of specified strategic aims. However, only 48 percent reported that the budget was linked to a performance assessment system designed to ensure that the allocation of internal resources was closely linked to achieving service delivery outcomes specified in the strategic plan.

Of those municipalities which had a strategic plan, 95 percent indicated that assessment of performance by senior managers was linked to the plan, but only 64 percent utilised the same approach when undertaking annual assessments of the achievements of department heads within their organisations. Similarly only 50 percent of these respondents indicated that performance measures were in place which permitted a detailed assessment of actual organisational achievements in areas such as service delivery in relation to targets specified in their strategic plan.

In terms of satisfaction over the use of strategic plans to assist effective management of their organisation, of those municipalities which had a plan, over 80 percent were very satisfied/satisfied that the existence of a plan had enhanced their ability to define outputs associated with their role as providing appropriate services to the general public. As far as actually achieving specified goals, only 30 percent reported that between 60–80 percent of aims had been achieved and even less (10 percent) that between 80–100 percent of their service delivery aims had been delivered. The two most important identified benefits of strategic planning were delivery of higher-quality services (89 percent) and clarification of the organisation's future goals and vision (85 percent). Other identified benefits included improved decision-making (83 percent), more efficient management of operations (81 percent), enhanced communications with external stakeholders (79 percent) and providing clearer direction to employees over assigned tasks and responsibilities (61 percent).

Poister and Streib's overall conclusion was that even after 20 years, there still remained a significant need for many more municipalities to adopt a strategic planning approach. Those municipalities with a strategic plan were successful in linking strategic aims to the determination of annual budgets and specifying overall performance output targets for the delivery of services. The researchers were surprised, however, that only a minority of these organisations were linking their strategic plan with a performance measurement system that would assist in identifying the nature of gaps which might exist between planned and actual service delivery outcomes. The positive outcome reported by the study is that those municipalities which adopted a strategic planning philosophy

(continued)

PROGRESS REPORT (continued)

believed the benefits achieved greatly outweighed the costs associated with the creation and operation of this approach to determining future performance aims. Nevertheless, given that only 44 percent respondents reported the utilisation of a strategic plan to manage in a world of declining resources, the authors did feel that there remains an urgent need for more public sector bodies to adopt a philosophy of using strategic planning to define and guide their future operations.

SECTORAL DIFFERENCES

In a private sector organisation, strategic planning can be a fundamentally simple process, in that the organisation having determined the nature of customer need can then determine how best to meet these needs, with the aim of optimising the use of available resources in a way which ensures achievement of delivering long-term value to the stakeholders. This can be contrasted with the public sector, where the public sector provider has to attempt to satisfy the needs of two customer groups—namely, (i) the 'contracting customer,' usually a legislative entity who decides the nature of the services to be delivered and the level of resources available and (b) the 'served customer' to whom the organisation delivers services. In relation to meeting the needs of the served customer, this process is significantly more complex than in the private sector. This is because, although the served customer may have clearly understood needs, the ability of the provider to satisfy the served customer is controlled by factors such as the service role defined by the legislators and the performance indicators which the contracting customer decides should be met in order for the provider to receive the resources which have been promised by the legislators.

In their analysis of strategic planning models, Ring and Perry posited that the five following contextual issues can be expected to complicate the process model in public sector organisations:

1. The specific natures of the policies and desired service outcomes are often ill-defined by the contracting customer, which creates problems for the managers in the provider organisation seeking to interpret specific definitions of their service provision role.
2. A public sector provider plan will be exposed to a much closer examination and scrutiny by legislators, policy makers, the media and the general public.
3. There are more stakeholder interests and influences which need consideration in the creation of an effective plan.
4. The actions of the legislators or policy makers can often lead to the creation of artificial time constraints either (a) by not being prepared

to define resource availability beyond a single financial year or (b) because there has been a decision to introduce new legislation which the provider is required to instantly incorporate into existing service provision activities.

5. Coalitions and alliances that the service provider may have formed to enhance or expand service delivery often prove to be unreliable due to the instability or unpredictable behaviour of the partner organisation(s).

Ring and Perry concluded that given the complexities associated with fulfilling the needs of the contractor customer, artificial time constraints and the instability of collaborative relationships, public sector providers can be characterised as being low on successful implementation of a deliberate strategy. Instead these organisations' actual strategies can be expected to be of an unrealised and emergent nature. The implications of this conclusion is that to be more successful, public sector managers need to be more flexible, willing to accept sudden changes in time schedules by legislators and able to rapidly develop an alternative strategy in the face of sudden changes in the agency's external environment or access to available resources. To fulfil these managerial requirements probably demands a higher level of adaptability than is demanded of the average manager, even in highly successful private sector organisations. This is because the public sector manager will often face scenarios where there is the need to be creative in the development of new solutions following an unexpected, but ill-defined, change in policy by the contractor customer. Furthermore, in order to meet tight timescales that may be associated with new legislation, the manager may be forced to risk implementing new strategies before approval or acceptance has been obtained from all the key stakeholders. In a world where many developed nations are facinggrowing problems over the size of their public sector deficits, for the foreseeable future governments will be forced to instigate major policies based upon significant reductions in financial resources. The pressure on public sector managers to exhibit flexibility and adaptability can be expected to continue to grow.

Reviewing documented evidence concerning early experiences of strategic planning in the public sector led Bunning (1992) to posit that some managers have concluded that planning ahead is impossible, dangerous or a waste of time. Factors influencing this perception include:

1. Strategic planning requires involvement of outside groups such as customers during the environmental scanning process, which can cause these stakeholders to develop heightened expectations which subsequently cannot be fulfilled.
2. With funding often based upon a one-year-only basis, there is little point in adopting a longer-term perspective.

3. Formal, long-term plans can lock the organisation into actions which are difficult to revise should future circumstances undergo change.
4. The existing governments may not be re-elected and plans to respond to their manifesto may become redundant.
5. Planning can create resource allocation dilemmas which lead to unrest within the organisation among those employees whose resources are adversely impacted by a new plan.
6. Once publicised the plan can arouse criticism and dissent among those most adversely affected by re-defined priorities and activities.

While working with public sector managers in the introduction of strategic planning into their public sector organisation, Bunning encountered adverse perceptions concerning the benefits of undertaking the activity. A common perception is that strategic planning is a ritual to be performed essentially to meet the expectation or demands of others, particularly governments or funding agencies. Another common perception is that the focus in the planning process is not so much on what is to be ultimately achieved but rather on the production of a planning document in order for the organisation to be granted next year's budget. As a consequence managers engaged in the planning process tend to exhibit conformity and/or cynicism. There is also a significant decline in attention, interest and energy once the plan has been created and the resource allocation decisions have been made. An additional problem is the focus of attention often centres upon on the technical feasibility of various alternative proposals, rather than to perceive planning as an interactive process requiring consideration of political, social and technical viability issues. The resultant outcome is the setting of rational, impersonal goals which cause problems for staff when implementing actions specified in the plan. There is also the tendency to adopt a consensus approach to decision-making because the aim is to identify a strategy which is not judged as objectionable by any of the internal organisational stakeholders. As a consequence the needs of the clients tend to be subordinated to satisfying internal stakeholders. In Bunning's view this latter behaviour trait means that the underlying dynamic during the strategic planning process is that of internal political bargaining with acceptance that irreconcilable differences will exist between internal and external stakeholders.

Bunning posited that strategic planning in many government agencies has not led to any significant changes or improvement in performance. In his opinion government agencies are typically more reactive than proactive. Innovation and change are to be avoided because established policies and organisational culture will create insurmountable obstacles to the adoption of any really radical new ideas. In most cases this situation means that a prerequisite for successful change is the appointment of new senior managers who are accepting of the concept of identifying and implementing new ways of working inside the organisation. Accompanying the appointment of new senior staff, there may also be the need to overcome entrenched opposition, which can be achieved only by implementing a fundamental restructuring of the organisation or making some existing staff redundant.

The conclusion that can be drawn from such observations is that the probability of strategic planning leading to change in a public sector organisation can be enhanced by actions which include (Chaston 2011):

1. Making strategic planning the responsibility of senior line managers rather than staff experts, with the chief executive officer acting as the leading advocate within the planning process.
2. Communicating the rationale and need for strategic planning and more effectively preparing managers by ensuring they have developed appropriate knowledge, skills and attitudes.
3. Moving beyond vague goals that are acceptable to everybody towards definition of clearly articulated specific strategic actions and performance objectives.
4. Avoiding the creation of lengthy strategic plans containing highly detailed specification of operational activities because this can lead to the key strategic issues becoming obscured.
5. Ensuring that in the development of detailed operational plans these activities are undertaken by teams which include individuals from the lower levels of the organisation.
6. Ensuring all the plans are linked to assigned budgets in order that financial resources are effectively allocated to key areas of intended activity.
7. Ensuring that the plan achieves a clear match between the proposed strategies and organisational culture.
8. Ensuring that where new behaviours are required by staff in the implementation of the new strategic plan, these are clearly specified and acknowledged in the plan.
9. Ensuring an effective control system has been created for monitoring actual versus planned performance objectives and that this system has the capability to diagnose the cause of identified differences between actual versus planned outcomes.

Plant (2009) feels that in the case of PSOs the link between the strategic plan and the organisation's budget tends to emerge only when strategic priorities have been identified and budgeted funds are received. As a result organisations can find themselves facing the situation of having many more strategic service provision responsibilities than the funds available to support all these tasks. When this situation occurs and funding for specific strategic priorities has not been forthcoming, there is a sense in the organisation that the plan will not result in achievement of key performance goals. In Plant's view, PSOs, especially in a world of decreasing financial resources, should not base strategic decisions purely on the amount of funding available at any specific point in time. Instead there is a requirement to adopt a zero-based planning orientation to permit a fundamental re-assessment of the long-term strategic role required by the organisation's clients.

To achieve this aim the strategic planning process should focus not on funding, but upon identifying gaps between strategic goals and actual performance. The objective of the plan is to determine how and to what degree identified gaps can be closed. With defined performance goals at the beginning of the year, actual achievements can be regularly assessed throughout the year and again at the beginning of the next annual planning cycle. By linking the performance management system to a strategic plan this permits:

1. Objectives being defined against which progress can be measured.
2. Tracking input resources, assessing outcomes and determining efficiencies.
3. Service delivery evaluation, which is the primary outcome responsibility of the organisation.

The complex, uncertain and rapidly changing public sector environment demands flexibility, adaptability and the capacity to anticipate and immediately address emerging issues. PSOs are increasingly dependent upon their frontline staff to deal with challenges of sustaining the delivery of high-quality services even when faced with increasingly scarce resources. These staff must be granted the authority to act independently in the delivery of the service goals specified in the strategic plan. Key skills which they require include the authority to make decisions, the expertise to exercise their delegated authority, an understanding of the impact of their decisions on the organisation and a willingness to share in the consequences of their decisions. This outcome cannot occur should senior management undertake the strategic planning process and development of performance management criteria without involving lower-level staff.

Plant suggests that involvement of lower-level staff will actually strengthen the strategic planning process and lead to the identification of more appropriate performance measures. This is because these individuals bring real-time knowledge of the service delivery process and provide useful feedback on the outcomes of implementing the organisation's strategic plan. He also posits that there is a need for different types of performance measures whereby strategic performance variables can be closely linked with systems for assessing operational and performance outcome variables. The purpose of these strategic measures is to provide an overall perspective on the ability of the PSO to attain the strategic goals associated with the provision of a portfolio of services. Operational measures provide an assessment of the efficiency and effectiveness of actual service delivery. Evaluation measures provide data on outcomes or results of services provided in relation to achieving satisfaction among the clients being served.

In the development of an effective measurement system Freeman (2002) stresses that establishing performance measures does not provide the basis for ensuring strategic success. In his view PSOs have a tendency to develop too many measures, and staff rarely understand why information is being collected or how performance measures assist optimisation of the service delivery process. In these situations the performance measures can become an unnecessary administrative burden with scarce resources and time being allocated to the collection of data which have little value in terms of managing the effective implementation of the organisation's strategic plan.

In assessing other problems that can occur in the strategic planning process in the public sector, Popovich (1998) proposed that these can include:

1. A failure by senior management to accept the need for performance measurements that can provide feedback on the efficiency and effectiveness of service delivery when assessing future service provision strategies in relation to available resources.
2. Senior management seeking to avoid exposing internal problems to external stakeholders and hence wishing to severely restrict the release of performance measurement information to the general public.
3. Senior managers using performance measures to retroactively punish failures uncovered by measurements indicating adverse performance instead of creating a culture that rewards identification of mistakes and proposals to improve future service delivery.
4. Senior managers failing to exhibit the leadership skills required to ensure that service strategies are effectively implemented and that one of the organisation's top priorities is to use performance measures to enhance future performance.

A ZERO-BASED APPROACH

A common trait among leaders of public sector organisations when confronted with a budget cut is to identify which service provision activities can be terminated or reduced in scale. This reaction is then followed by making a decision over the number of employees to be made redundant. The drawback is this approach usually results in no fundamental reconsideration of the purpose and role of the PSO. As a consequence, although the organisation continues to exist, no real attempt will have been made to identify strategic actions whereby the entity can become more efficient or effective in the fulfilment of its role in the provision of services. Although this might have been an acceptable outcome when economies were able to support higher public sector spending, this is no longer the case in Western nations struggling to manage the huge public sector deficits created by the world banking crisis.

One solution in what for the foreseeable future will be a period of public sector austerity is for the leaders of PSOs to adopt a zero-based approach to strategic planning as a mechanism whereby much reduced budgets are utilised in the most effective and efficient way. The overall aim will be that of sustaining high added value during delivery of service provision activities. The implementation of a zero-based approach will involve the following sequence of actions:

1. Through both internal analysis and benchmarking against other relevant private and public sector entities, identifying those areas where high added value is being achieved in the service provision process.
2. Determining whether strategy revision could further enhance the effectiveness and efficiency of services which are already achieving high added value.
3. Identifying those activities where poor added value in service delivery is occurring.
4. Examining which of the poorer areas of performance might be upgraded through actions such as exploiting technology, re-structuring, outsourcing, privatisation or the formation of public/private sector partnerships.
5. In those cases where productivity cannot be upgraded but continuation of service is mandated, examining actions that could enhance effectiveness and efficiency by achieving greater economies of scale.
6. In those cases where service productivity cannot be upgraded and retention of service delivery is not mandated by legislation, accepting these areas of activity will have to be terminated.

Introducing new technology is probably the most likely strategic action capable of achieving an increase in value added achievement for poorly performing areas of service provision. The breadth of opportunity for the introduction of new technology can be expected to vary quite significantly across different areas of the public sector. For example, there are probably more opportunities to introduce a diversity of new technologies in sectors such as defence and healthcare when compared with PSOs engaged in managing the provision of welfare services to the unemployed or the elderly. An important exception to this generalisation is the exploitation of ongoing advances in IT which permit more effective and efficient execution of tasks such as automating information acquisition, storage, information processing and decision-making in virtually every area of the public sector.

In relation to other possible strategies for enhancing added value such as outsourcing, privatisation or the formation of public/private sector partnerships, PSOs need to be extremely careful. This is because all of these solutions have over the years demonstrated a highly chequered history in relation to the success or failure of projects. In terms of the factors influencing outcomes, a common factor identified by researchers is whether the decision to adopt the chosen solution for change was carefully assessed and evaluated prior to implementation (Garcia-Zamor and Noll 2009). In the case of outsourcing the probability of project failure is likely to be much higher in those cases where the selection process was inadequate, thereby causing the appointment of an outsourcing partner who lacks the necessary leadership, competences, resources or organisational structure. Poor performance can also occur where it proves impossible for the PSO and the outsource supplier to develop the degree of mutual trust and commitment which is critical in order that an effective working relationship exists between the two parties (Indridason and Wang 2009).

The basis of many private-public sector initiatives (PPIs) is that these allow private companies to build, own and operate public projects such as schools and hospitals on behalf of the public sector. The appeal to the PSO can be either that the relationship provides access to private sector financing in those cases where public sector funds are unavailable or that the private sector is perceived to introduce expertise unavailable within the PSO (Nisar 2007a). PPI contracts usually require the private sector participant to accept responsibility for managing the assets over the long term based upon the assumption that this is the more cost-effective approach. On the basis of an extensive review of actual projects by Nisar (2007b), it appears that in most cases the actual cost of service delivery over the life of the project would probably have been lower had the PSO retained control as the service provider. This author concluded such outcomes could often have been avoided by the PSO undertaking a more strategic assessment of the available opportunity and ensuring there was evidence of the partner's project management expertise instead of just merely relying upon the private sector partner's estimates of the cost savings that could be expected from the PPI contract.

The usual justification for privatisation is that it will expose the existing entity to competitive market forces, which will lead to levels of efficiency and effectiveness which cannot occur while an organisation remains within the public sector. In her assessment of the privatisation of utilities in the UK, Lynk (1993) concluded that, although such aims are feasible, in many cases the forecasted performance improvements will occur only where the capital assets have been correctly valued at the time these are transferred to the private sector and regulations imposed by governments over future operations do not create obstacles that impair actual service delivery. This perspective is shared by Coram and Burnes (2001). These authors also identified that post-privatisation performance will fail in those cases where there is a lack of clarity over the original rationale for the privatisation. This can occur because decisions are not based upon a valid business case, but instead reflect the manifesto of a current government. Another cause of poor post-privatisation performance can be the poor state of the organisation at the time of the transfer to the private sector. As a consequence it is necessary to expend unexpectedly large sums of money to implement fundamental changes in areas such as the management team, organisational structure or service delivery policies and procedures (Letza et al. 2004).

REDUCING THE BODY COUNT

Case Aims: To illustrate how new technology can dramatically reduce public sector employee costs and concurrently enhance service provision.

The largest component of expenditure in most areas of the public sector is on people: paying their salaries, providing physical facilities in which to work and then sustaining them in retirement by providing a pension, which in many cases in the public sector is a final salary, index-linked scheme. Hence a very important focus in technological innovation is to replace people with machines in the public sector. The advent of the Internet has made this possible, as demonstrated by the introduction of e-technology into the tax department in Singapore (Tan and Pan 2003).

In the past, the Singapore tax system was slow, suffering from manual tax processing systems and an accumulation of paper documents. Further problems occurred due to a lack of experienced staff to process the tax returns. These problems, when added to others caused by a highly bureaucratic organisational orientation, created long delays in the country's tax collection operation. The first significant change to the tax filing process was the introduction of an imaging system to reduce the volume of paper files. The digitised images are stored in a centralised database that is accessible to all tax officers. This led to substantial cost savings as productivity was greatly increased. Digitisation also provided a system that could efficiently process most of the country's tax returns without physical intervention. This is because 80 percent of returns are found to be acceptable and do not require the involvement of a tax official to audit the data. A workflow management system was created for channelling unusual tax cases for inspection by a tax official. The system also selected to whom the file should be sent by using a rules-based system to match a case to the appropriate inspector.

Even with the imaging system, physical data entry was still unavoidable and hence a customer phone filing system was introduced. Despite the simplicity of the instructions provided to the caller, most taxpayers found it uncomfortable to use the system. As a result, an Internet e-filing system was launched, initially for salaried employees and subsequently to include all taxpayers. The Internet filing system contains an electronic-filing personal identification number (EF PIN) for authentication purposes. In seeking to make e-filing effortless for taxpayers, the tax department established computer-based links with a number of government agencies and businesses organisations in order to have them transfer relevant information from their employee records directly into the tax department database. Once the information for a particular taxpayer has been uploaded into the system, all the taxpayer has to do is submit a series of zero returns through the e-filing system. By 2003, this auto-inclusion scheme was acquiring data on approximately 550,000 citizens, which represents 46 percent of all employees in the country.

PUBLIC SECTOR ENTREPRENEURSHIP

The problems currently facing the world in the first decade of the 21st century are not new. During the Great Depression of the 1930s banks failed and unemployment rose to almost 25 percent of the total work-force in many nations. These events prompted a number of academics to re-examine the validity of capitalism as a viable economic principle. One group, the 'Austrian School of Economics,' was profoundly concerned by the future of capitalism in the face of widespread acceptance of pro-socialist models such as communism in Russia and the emergence of extreme right-wing, authoritarian regimes in Western Europe. One of the most influential theorists within the Austrian School was Joseph Schumpeter (1950, 1942). He held the view that capitalism can be expected to go through periods of 'creative destruction' caused by nations and both private and public sector organisations becoming too fixed in their ways and unable to implement the changes required to sustain their ongoing survival. Schumpeter posited that the trigger for creative destruction and economic change is innovation. This causes existing, non-effective institutional frameworks to be replaced by a solution offering superiority over existing propositions. He identified that the source of change is the entrepreneur. The activities of the entrepreneur result in the emergence of a new, significant innovation which Schumpeter described as a 'meta-event.'

The American management theorist Peter Drucker shared Schumpeter's view of entrepreneurship being a 'meta-economic event' which causes a major market change. In his assessment of the exploitation of innovation by knowledge-based economies, Drucker (1985) concluded that the most significant potential was vested within public sector organisations. His conclusion was based upon the observation that in Western society these organisations have responsibility for the management of vast resources but tend to adopt an excessively conservative, conventional decision-making orientation when engaged in the determination of how best to utilise these resources. As the world banking crisis can clearly be considered a meta-event, it seems reasonable to propose that public sector organisations will need to rely on entrepreneurial behaviour in seeking to resolve problems which are associated with the aftermath of the banking and sovereign debt crises (Chaston 2011).

Du Gray (2004) posits that entrepreneurship no longer refers just to the creation of an independent business venture or the characteristics of a successful independent business person. Instead entrepreneurship now refers to the ways in which economic, political, social and personal vitality is best achieved by organisations of all types, including non-profits and governmental agencies. Morris and Jones (1999, p. 74) have proposed the following working definition for public sector entre-preneurship: 'The process of creating value for citizens by bringing together unique combinations of public and/or private resources to exploit social opportunities.' In terms of why entrepreneurship occurs in the public sector, factors of influence appear to include uncertain environments, devolution of power or re-allocation of resource owner-ship. Kearney et al. (2009) believe entrepreneurship in the public sector, unlike the private sector, does not rely upon particular attributes of a specific individual but on a group's desire for organisational change. This is because opportunities for innovation in the public sector arise from circumstances peculiar to the public sector and that innovation is much less focused on commercial considerations. Instead the aim is to sustain or enhance service provision in the face of resource constraints. Kearney et al. propose that a set of internal environmental dimensions exists which stimulate or constrain public sector innovation. These vari-ables include structure, decision-making, control, reward/motivation and culture.

Morris and Jones (1999) assert that innovativeness in the public sec-tor will tend to be more concerned with novel process improvements, new services and new organisational forms. The issue of risk is a central component to the study of entrepreneurial behaviour. Hence it can be assumed that innovative public managers must be prepared to take risks and appreciate that they will face bureaucratic and political obstacles from other, more conservatively orientated managers. Proactiveness in the context of the private sector refers to a posture of anticipating and acting on future wants and needs linked to the associated activities of being concerned with implementation and undertaking the appropriate course of action in order to bring an entrepreneurial concept to fruition. This involves a high level of commitment, perseverance, flexibility and adaptability, plus a willingness to take responsibility for possible failure. Morris and Jones believe that public sector proactiveness involves an emphasis on anticipating and preventing public sector problems before they occur. Effective actions will include creative interpretation of rules and leveraging of scarce resources.

In relation to the emergence of entrepreneurial activity in the public sector, a number of factors are perceived as key influencers. One factor is the emergence of new political manifestos created by legislators respond-ing to their perception for the need to implement actions in relation to the ongoing provision of services. A related issue is when political change is accompanied by a significant reduction or re-allocation of public sec-tor budgets. This type of planning review will influence decisions about the allocation of scarce resources across the organisation and can lead to revised financial decisions in relation to the allocation of funding across a diverse range of capital assets (Berry 1998).

**ENTREPRENEURIAL OPPORTUNITIES
TO EXPLOIT TECHNOLOGY**

*Case Aims: To illustrate how technology can be exploited to assist
service provision productivity and identify new service provision
opportunities.*

In commenting upon the role of technology in the public sector, Mitchell
(2001) suggests that with the growing need to 'do more with less' probably
the only viable way of achieving this goal is through radical, usually disruptive innovation. One opportunity is what he refers to as 'individual agility,'
which involves the wisest possible use of time by an organisation's most
expert staff and, where possible, developing new process implementation
activities that can be utilised by less highly skilled employees. An example of
using an expert's time efficiently is to use hand-held devices or digital cameras that collect data from numerous field-level locations, which can then be
transmitted to a central hub, where an expert can assess the nature of information received and determine appropriate next actions. This approach has
very obvious and multiple applications by the police or other emergency services in the fulfilment of their assigned responsibilities. The same approach
in healthcare, known as 'tele-medicine,' permits a less qualified doctor to
examine patients in remote locations and, when a specialist's second opinion
is desired, the patient data can be sent via web-streaming to a consultant at
a major hospital hundreds of miles away. This same technology can also be
used in a reverse sequence, whereby the specialist can provide web-based
interactive training to numerous less qualified staff elsewhere within a public
sector organisation.

Ferguson et al. (2005) believe that the opportunity for all service organisations to identify new opportunities for technology-based innovation has
been greatly enhanced by the advent of the Internet, which permits access
to huge volumes of data concerning new technological solutions from across
the world and detailed breakdowns of customer service search and purchase
behaviour. For public sector organisations to tap into this market does
require an upgrading of the IT systems and staff's ability to utilise these systems to identify and implement new service provision offerings. There are
two dimensions influencing the exploitation of data. One dimension is the
degree to which the organisation has moved from in-house, static database
systems, to which only data from internal operations is added on a batch-
processing basis, to a real-time knowledge management system, which uses
real-time access to multiple external databases to acquire new data. The
other dimension is the degree to which data are used to analyse the past,
review current operations and assess future opportunities. As illustrated in
Figure 11.1 the position of the organisation on these two axes determines
the degree to which highly innovative, possibly radical new service propositions can be identified and made available.

(continued)

ENTREPRENEURIAL OPPORTUNITIES
TO EXPLOIT TECHNOLOGY (continued)

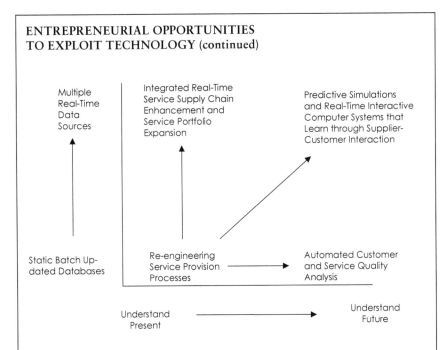

Figure 11.1   Managing service innovation.

Once an effective real-time external data acquisition system is in place, the system can be used to direct questions towards potential and existing customers to determine their service needs and their perceptions of other service requirements. Furthermore by the use of remote sensors within the service provision process, the system can also track service activity in real-time. Subsequent computer-based analysis of these data can provide the basis for determining how the service delivery process might be enhanced (e.g. moving staff resources between areas of low and high service demand; identifying and correcting periods of service delivery downtime).

PRIVATE SECTOR DOWNSIDE

Entire sectors of some industries in B2B markets rely on government and PSOs purchases as their primary source of revenue. As Western democracies struggle to reduce huge national deficits by reducing public sector spending, Western firms within these industries will face a difficult time in finding alternative market opportunities. A traditional solution to a downturn in public sector spending in a domestic market for firms in the civilian capital asset and infrastructure markets, such as construction companies or manufacturers of railway equipment, has been to seek new opportunities in overseas markets. Now, however, these firms can expect to face major competitive pressures from firms in countries such as Brazil and China seeking to expand into these same overseas markets. Furthermore some of the firms, as well as being able to submit highly competitive bids, have a somewhat different cultural attitude to doing business in other countries. They may be prepared, often with the support of their own government, to agree to barter contracts in which they are prepared to accept commodities such as minerals in the place of financial payments. There is also a greater acceptance of local culture which permits them to act in a way which would cause a Western firm to breach their own country's regulations over fraud or face criticisms from key stakeholders over being willing to enter into contracts with governments which have a poor human rights record.

Senior managers in the defence industry face a series of complexities when attempting to identify a viable long-term strategy capable of ensuring survival in the face of Western government spending cutbacks. Some in the aerospace industry may be able to achieve revenue compensation from increased sales from their civilian market products. Others such as those in the somewhat fragmented armoured vehicle industry face the reality that, as well as spending cuts, they can expect Western governments to shift a greater proportion of future military spending into areas such as cyber warfare and robotic products. Unfortunately these tend to be areas where some of the established firms lack the internal competences to succeed in implementing an entrepreneurial strategy based upon moving into these new areas of military technology. In fact in the area of cyber warfare the defence industry faces the dilemma that the likely successful players in this area will probably be firms such as Google or IBM, whose primary business is currently that of supplying civilian markets.

Senior management concerns over government spending cutbacks in Western democracies should also exist in those companies engaged in the sale of consumer products and services. The most obvious impact will be upon the reduction in consumer spending power by those in the public sector who are made redundant.

The impact of this event will vary by country depending upon the proportion of individuals in a nation's workforce who are employed in the public sector. In the United States only 8 percent of individuals are classified as public sector employees. This figure is much higher in Europe, where there is a stronger political ethos towards major service provision via the welfare state. For example, in the UK in 2011 just over 20 percent of the total workforce is employed in the public sector and in Greece, which is facing a massive sovereign debt problem, the figures rises to approximately 35 percent of the entire workforce. Even those public sector employees who retain their jobs will in many Western countries face a reduction in disposable income as governments mandate these employees increase their personal pension contribution in order to reduce the scale of underfunding currently facing most public sector pension funds.

12 Organisational Structure

The purpose of this chapter is to cover issues pertaining to:

1. Chandler's theory that structure follows strategy.
2. Developing appropriate organisational structures for supporting innovation.
3. Factors influencing the selection of an appropriate structure.
4. Adopting a zero-based approach to defining future organisational structure.
5. Applying industrial ecology theory to select organisational structures.
6. Structures for protecting strategic core competences.

STRUCTURE

As one of the earliest academics to focus on the relationship between performance and strategy, Chandler (1977, 1962) posited that initially most firms will utilise a functional, unitary strategy based upon a departmental or 'U-form' organisational structure. Tasks such as production, marketing or finance are allocated to specific departments. In those cases where the organisation eventually enters overseas markets or becomes a more diversified operation, the structure may evolve into a multi-divisional (or 'M-form') entity. Building upon the existing literature concerning strategy and structure, Chandler's (1962) conclusion was that 'structure follows strategy.' He believed that, for example, an effective product-market diversification strategy would be followed by the organisation evolving into a decentralised and divisionalised structure.

The hierarchical relationship between strategy and structure that Chandler proposed has continued to dominate management thinking. He argued that as a firm grows and develops new administrative functions unless a new structure is evolved to meet these new functional requirements, technological, financial and personnel economies of scale cannot be realised. Chandler's perspective was that by structure following strategy this led to improved organisational efficiency. Williamson (1975) used transaction-cost theory to extend Chandler's centralised-decentralised approach concept to cover the existence of a general office staff, the nature of the strategic control systems and the processes associated with reaching resource allocation decisions. He argued that the choice of structural form has implications not only for efficiency, but also for the effectiveness with which strategic goals are met.

Writings in support of the 'structure follows strategy' paradigm have relied upon observations involving qualitative comparisons of different types and sizes of organisations (Mintzberg 1983). This reflects the fact that obtaining empirical evidence on the relationship between strategy and structure requires access to longitudinal information on a large number of firms over a significant time period. Such data are not widely available. One exception to the lack of empirical research is provided by Amburgey and Dacin (1994). These authors used a sample of large US mining and manufacturing firms over the period of 1949 to 1977. The sample contained information on each firm across areas such as products, marketing, administrative structures and the timing of changes in strategy and structure. Amburgey and Dacin's overall conclusion was the data supported the existence of a hierarchical relationship between strategy and structure and that strategy is a more important determinant of structure than structure is of strategy. They also concluded that strategic change has a cumulative effect on the probability of an organisation implementing structural change, whereas only the most recent structural change by an organisation can be related to strategic change. In their view this latter finding suggests that a series of incremental strategic changes cumulatively produce a large effect on efficiency, whereas a series of incremental structural changes will rarely lead to such an outcome.

DIFFERENT STRUCTURE—DIFFERENT OBJECTIVES

Case Aims: To illustrate how different innovation aims are reflected by different approaches to structuring R&D activities.

In reviewing the relationships between structure and the management of innovation, Christensen (2002) proposed that as an organisation moves from a U-form to M-form this will tend to result in decentralisation of the management of innovation. In the case of firms engaged in market or product diversification, Christensen concluded that each operating division will tend to maintain a high level of autonomy in management of innovation. He contrasts this situation with companies engaged in diversification into related market or product areas where a greater degree of central control and emphasis of interdivisional communication occurs. This is because there are common areas of interest in terms of resolving problems that may arise during the product or process innovation process.

A probable outcome of a decentralised approach to managing innovation in an M-form company is incremental innovation will be given priority over more entrepreneurial activities. This can result in the organisation missing the opportunity to significantly enhance performance through exploiting radical innovation. Christensen agrees with other researchers that radical innovation is more likely to occur in a more centralised, corporate U-firm organisation.

(continued)

DIFFERENT STRUCTURE—DIFFERENT OBJECTIVES (continued)

Christensen's perspectives are supported by the results from his case-based study of two Danish companies, Danfoss and Grudfos, both of which are global market leaders in their respective industries and founded by highly entrepreneurial individuals. Danfoss is a company manufacturing a highly diversified range of products within the refrigeration, motion, heating and water controls industries. The company has achieved growth through acquisitions and has an M-form organisational structure. Innovation tends to be of an incremental nature with limited interchange of new knowledge between different divisions. In recent years, however, concerns have emerged over limited inter-divisional co-operation. This has led to the creation of a unit at the corporate level to define overall innovation priorities and to assist the promotion of knowledge sharing about R&D activities across the organisation. Nevertheless the company structure does tend to promote the emphasis given to a low-cost, short-term innovation based upon exploiting improvements in areas of relatively mature technology.

Grundfos is a more focused company operating within the pumps and pump systems market. Growth has been mainly through entrepreneurial, internally driven radical innovation based around a U-form structure. To deliver a strategy based upon being a technological leader in the pump industry, R&D is highly centralised and all major projects are co-located in the Technology Centre and Development Centre. To ensure that radical innovation can be of maximum benefit to the company there is a strong emphasis on maintaining effective inter-functional interfaces between product development, process development and the company's manufacturing operations. In those cases when management decides that entry into a new area of radical innovation is required, but the organisation lacks the necessary technological expertise, the solution is to create a new autonomous R&D unit. This approach was utilised, for example, when Grundfos decided there was a need to move into more sophisticated control electronics to radically improve the energy efficiency of the company's pumps. Once management decided that sufficient new knowledge had been acquired and the new technology was sufficiently mature to be incorporated into other areas of R&D, a cross-functional learning programme was initiated to ensure rapid and effective knowledge transfer.

INNOVATION

The increasingly turbulent nature of global markets has caused some theorists to question whether the Chandler model is possibly a concept which should be challenged in that structure may now influence strategy (Peters 1984). One of the identified examples of this latter perspective is how the nature of structure influences innovation strategies. Bergfors and Larsson (2009) noted that much of the research on structure has been concerned with the link between the scale of innovation and the centralised versus decentralised structure of organisations. The accepted viewpoint is the internal structural characteristics of the organisation can either promote or impair innovation. For example, centralisation may affect employee motivation, initiative, commitment and collaboration. Thus it could be proposed that more organic, more decentralised structures are preferred when seeking to sustain organisational performance based upon innovation.

Bergfors and Larsson suggested RBV theory supports the proposition that R&D activities which are critically important within the firm in relation to building new core capabilities should be under central corporate control. In contrast R&D activities which are not critical for building core capabilities can be decentralised. In those cases where R&D activities are concerned with a narrow range of applications, possibly the activity can be decentralised. Where innovation has the potential to be highly disruptive RBV theory suggests that R&D activities designed to create or defend against disruptive innovation should be centralised. If there is no apparent risk of organisational disruption then R&D that merely builds upon existing research activities can be decentralised.

Similar views have been expressed by Ettlie et al. (1984). They posited that large diversified organisations tend to focus upon incremental innovation with the aim of making ongoing improvements in existing products and processes. Such activities are usually undertaken using the organisation's existing structure and lines of managerial authority. These authors contrast this situation with an entrepreneurial firm seeking to successfully exploit radical innovation. In their view this scenario will require a reconfiguration of organisational structure with the innovators being located in an autonomous unit away from normal day-to-day ongoing business activities. They suggest this alternative structure is necessary to ensure that the project can proceed without interference from other departments within the organisation or face problems when competing for scarce resources. Additionally this approach has the benefit of concentrating all of the technological expertise and capability within a single unit. This permits optimisation of activities such as problem solving and decision-making. A classic example of this philosophy is provided by IBM when the company faced major problems developing its first really successful PC. In recognition of the requirement to provide autonomy and avoid interference from other departments, the company re-located its entire PC R&D programme from White Plains, New York to a small town in Florida.

In an attempt to validate their hypotheses, Ettlie et al. undertook a large-scale survey of manufacturers in the food industry. The results confirmed that respondent firms which were exploiting radical innovation to remain at the leading edge of the industry usually establish autonomous R&D units. In contrast those firms engaged in incremental innovation tend to make no changes in existing organisational structure, continuing to base development projects in existing departments. The research also indicated that as firms become more diversified in terms of operating in different markets and offering a broader range of products, this is usually accompanied by an expanded ability to develop a much larger number of innovative products and internal processes. This observation applied to both incremental and radical innovation activities.

FROM RESTRUCTUCTURING TO RE-STRATEGISING

Case Aims: To illustrate how post-acquisition restructuring can lead to a re-definition in strategy.

As an organisation grows and matures, strategic orientation increasingly turns from exploration to exploitation of resources (March 1991). As a consequence the managerial systems and values of mature companies are better at exploiting areas aligned with existing resources and skills than exploring areas far outside them. Hence when markets begin to exhibit fundamental change, mature firms may turn to M&As as a strategic solution for gaining access to new resources and skills. The issue then confronting management is whether the relationships and dominant organisational philosophy will lead to a strategy shift in the acquired organisation. As noted by Von Krogh et al. (2000) the strategy of acquiring resources through acquisition is accompanied by the risk that the mature organisation is unable to handle a new entrepreneurial subsidiary and an embedded approach to exploiting innovation.

Christensen's (2006) study of the Danish company Telebit provides an example of how innovation and strategic orientation can undergo change. Telebit specialised in the development of leading-edge and network routers and accessories for the computer and telecommunications industry. In 1995 the company was the first in the world to introduce a commercial router based on IPv6 (Internet Protocol version 6) technology. Telebit was positioned as an innovative company possessing competences at the cutting edge of new IP-related technologies. Innovativeness was driven by technological insight, which provided the basis for the company's competitive advantage. The firm focused development activities on IP technology, with the aim of creating prototypes of new routers that demonstrated the possibilities offered by the technology rather than making available a specific product with a clear market position.

As a leading company in the telecommunications industry Ericsson recognised the growing importance of the Internet in mobile telephony. To overcome a lack of expertise in Internet router technology, the company acquired the much smaller Telebit organisation. Immediately after the acquisition Ericsson decided that Telebit needed a fundamental re-organisation and greater focus on fewer areas of R&D. Ericsson required the number of projects to be reduced and resources re-directed to a few large, long-term projects which the company considered strategically important. Telebit's product portfolio reduced to two projects, both of which were directed from Ericsson's head office in Stockholm. These two projects were software for Internet Protocol and Terminal Internet Protocol (TIP).

(continued)

FROM RESTRUCTUCTURING TO RE-STRATEGISING (continued)

Interviews with Telebit staff following the acquisition indicated that the new management structure introduced by Ericsson, leading to a separation of R&D departments from business units, had the advantage of ensuring all research resources were directed towards the commercialisation of two major project technologies. The respondents also identified a major disadvantage—namely, a tendency to discourage more basic R&D activities and termination of any long-term innovation projects which from the outset could not immediately demonstrate a specific market potential. By moving to the role of acting as a supplier of knowledge to Ericsson, this greatly reduced Telebit's open collaboration with a broad base of potential customers. In the past these activities had been critical in the identification of new opportunities and development of new-to-the-world technology. Christensen concluded that Ericsson's restructuring meant Telebit was no longer following the strategy which the company founders had instigated because post-acquisition the entrepreneurial drive created by direct customer contact had been removed.

MULTIPLE FACTORS

In their review of the factors influencing strategy, Nair and Boulton (2008) propose it is necessary to go beyond just the factors of structure or innovation and recognise that other variables also influence strategy. One factor is industry life cycle. As a firm moves through distinct life cycle stages from start-up to maturity this may require reconsideration of future strategy. For example, in the early stage of a life cycle, firms face rapid growth and few competitors. Eventually a dominant product configuration based on end-user requirements will emerge. This will cause competing offerings to become increasingly similar. As the market moves towards maturity total market growth will decline, price competition will increase and profit margins will fall. At this juncture, a firm may need to consider a strategy shift such as product specialisation or seeking to achieve improved cost efficiencies (Lei and Slocum 2005). Life cycle models typically consider strategies based upon incremental product and process innovations. These are characterised by steady evolution and improvement. Adner (2002) suggests that these models may not be applicable during periods of disruptive innovation, during which new unpredictable technologies may completely replace dominant designs and thereby lead to a re-definition of organisational structure within firms operating in an industry sector.

Kassicieh et al. (2002) suggest another key variable influencing strategy is technological change. This is because change can lead to radical or incremental innovations which can have an important role in the formation of new markets and in the development of new products and processes. When a leading firm fails to adopt new technologies this can result in a loss in sales to new market entrants. Boyer (1998) argues that the development of competitive capabilities derives from the strategic choices in organisational architecture and the related infrastructures which are necessary for supporting a firm's competitive position. Leong et al. (1990) consider that determination of strategic position and priorities is accomplished through ensuring the correct structural and infrastructural systems exist. Structural decisions include investments in capacity, facilities, technology and actions regarding sourcing/vertical integration. Infrastructure decisions cover organisational policies and practices relating to the workforce, production and service.

INDUSTRIAL ECOLOGY

Recognition that strategic response involves organisations adapting to external environmental change has led academics to examine the use of the metaphor of biological ecosystems and the role of Darwinian theory concerning the survival of the fittest species as an approach for describing and explaining organisational performance over time. Marten (2001) applied the ecological metaphor to analyse complex industrial systems by comparing these with a biological ecosystem in the electronics manufacturing industry. He proposed that both systems are similar in that they incorporate a selection of parts that together lead to an optimisation of functional performance. In the case of a product this has a large number of electronic components, each precisely suited to each. Nevertheless some important differences do exist between an ecosystem and an electronic product. An ecosystem has a higher level of redundancy than a manufactured product, thereby providing the ecosystem with higher reliability and resilience. This is because cost optimisation in manufactured products results in only one component being used for each specific function. In an ecosystem important tasks such as the generation of oxygen by photosynthesis are normally performed by several different species.

Acceptance of the view that, in an increasingly complex world, various factors can influence the determination of an optimal competitive advantage caused Lei and Slocum (2005) to propose application of industrial ecosystem theory to the strategic management of innovation. He argued that the industrial ecosystem framework is particularly useful in defining a basis through which to integrate corporate and operational strategies while concurrently recognising potential interactions between industry life cycle, technological change and internal RBV factors. One approach to visualising an industrial ecosystem is provided in Figure 12.1. The advantage of this approach is that instead of accepting single factor theories such as structure or technology influencing strategy, the planner is offered a contingency philosophy suggesting that different factors should be considered depending upon the specific circumstances facing the organisation.

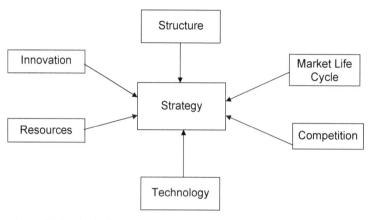

Figure 12.1 An industry ecosystem.

A very early application of the industrial ecosystem concept occurred in research undertaken in Japan in relation to the nation's management of industrial innovation. In this instance the concept was adopted as a new way of analysing and evaluating the complex mutual relations between human activities, industry and the surrounding environment. The definition of relationships provided the basis for determining government policy in relation to the provision of public sector support most likely to stimulate faster economic growth (Watanabe 1972).

One of the more popular applications of the ecosystem metaphor has been in reviewing how interactions between supply chain members can lead to changes in value added achievements of different participant organisations. Industrial ecology has been used by researchers to examine the interactions between organisations in terms of improving supply chain member sustainability by actions such as enhancing energy utilisation, reducing emissions and product recycling strategies (Boons and Berends 2001; Seuring 2004).

More recently Watanabe and Fukuda (2006) have used industrial ecology theory to examine the relative performance of the industrial strategy of Japan and the United States. Their approach involved assessing substitution of alternative factors of production in an industrial system to develop a strategy for achieving the most sustainable form of competitive advantage. Their conclusion was economic stagnation in the 1980s was reversed in the United States by recognising that firms such as Apple and Microsoft, by substituting information technology for traditional manufacturing technology, led to new functionality that re-energised economic growth. This can be contrasted with Japan, which experienced a 'lost decade' due to economic stagnation caused by firms continuing to focus on manufacturing as their strategy for remaining successful in world markets. Although Japan recognised the implications in a shift from manufacturing into IT, the focus was orientated towards using the technology to enhance operational functionality. However, by the beginning of the new millennium firms such as Google and Oracle had recognised that the world was entering a new information age in which competitive advantage required a shift from enhanced functionality to using IT as the core of solution generators centred upon the extraction of knowledge from large, diverse data sets.

In its assessment of what constituted the 21st century National Innovation Ecosystem, the US government's Council on Competitiveness proposed that achieving success in the evolving world of IT included the following key characteristics (21st Century Innovation Working Group 2004):

1. Innovation is much more than just technology because many other complementary resources and services are essential for success.
2. No one single attribute provides an adequate basis for success because modern innovation is dynamic and influenced by a multiplicity of factors.
3. Innovation success and diffusion of innovation is ultimately determined by the demand side, not merely technical capability, providing the basis for new product features.
4. Innovation increasingly depends on working closely with customers, partnering with external sources of innovation, accessing external resources by networking and focusing on exhibiting a global orientation in relation to both market opportunities and the acquisition of new knowledge.

THE ECOLOGY OF CHIPS

Case Aims: To illustrate how an understanding of industrial ecology can assist in the identification of a successful long-term strategy for organisations.

In 1974 the Taiwanese government established a specialist semiconductor and electronics laboratory, ERSO, to assist the country's entry into the electronics industry. The American RCA corporation agreed to transfer obsolete 7-micron IC technology for a royalty charge and to train a group of up to 40 engineers in the design and fabrication of chips. The acquired knowledge was then made available to Taiwanese firms. The early 1980s saw an expansion in the breadth of semiconductor technical capabilities, and the range of products in areas such as design, applications, testing and process technology available from ERSO. By the late 1980s, a number of companies had been established in wafer fabrication with the exception of DRAMs. These were initially seen as too risky for small Taiwanese semiconductor firms when compared with larger companies in Japan and Korea. By the 1990s this latter situation began to change. The computer and electronics firms Acer established a DRAM fabrication plant. This move was followed by the computer scanner firms Umax and Powerchip Semiconductors (Mathews 1997).

(continued)

THE ECOLOGY OF CHIPS (continued)

Virtually every advance in the evolution of Taiwan's electronics industry has been based upon firms adopting a strategy of forming partnerships in order to access the new knowledge required to establish and then remain ahead of competition. All have continued to leverage knowledge through forming partnerships with leading firms as a way of broadening their product base and entering new markets. In the case of the Taiwanese firm UMC, this has been through licensing product technologies and through acquiring equity interests in small, start-up firms in California's Silicon Valley. The Taiwanese firm TSMC moved into microprocessor production by entering into a foundry agreement with the US firm Advanced Micro Devices. Winbond's major product innovations have been achieved through collaboration with firms such as Hewlett-Packard and Toshiba.

In his analysis of how Taiwan's electronics industry has evolved, Mathews used industrial ecology theory to examine how this country avoided the fate of Korean and Japanese firms, whose focus on manufacturing high-volume standardised DRAMs led to the creation of a low-margin, commodity-orientated industry. The ecology of many high-technology industries is for new entrants to develop manufacturing competences to initially act as suppliers to existing original equipment manufacturers (OEMs). Over time the aim is to evolve more complex capabilities to permit the organisation to become an OwnDesign Manufacturer (ODMs). The eventual aim is to evolve into being a fully fledged product developer, manufacturer and marketer of the organisation's own brands (OBMs). The risk, however, is the failure to move beyond being an ODM and to become an OBM can condemn a company to being a low-margin supplier to more successful companies downstream in the supply chain.

Some Taiwanese firms in the electronics industry are members of global commodity chains through having acquired the competences to act only as OEMs or ODMs. However, in the field of advanced semiconductors, firms such as Winbond and Macronix have evolved into successful OBMs. Such achievements reflect that an understanding of the ecology of an industry sector results in an organisation focusing upon an area of specialist knowledge, whereby the firm can develop and sustain a unique competitive advantage. In the case of the semiconductor industry one example of this philosophy is those Taiwanese firms which moved into silicon wafer production but retained their more traditional 'back end' operations associated with the design and assembly of microchips. This has permitted them to become developers and suppliers of specialist microchips used in applications such as high-end mobile phones.

Mathews points out that Taiwan has yet to achieve technological parity with Silicon Valley's level of innovation. Interestingly, however, most of Taiwan's semiconductor firms maintain offices and laboratories in Silicon Valley. This is because they recognise this is a key location of leading-edge innovation in the IT industry. The author also posits that Taiwan's use of technological diffusion and technology leverage which permit small firms to grow into large powerful global operations is an important example of how an understanding of industrial technology can be used to formulate strategies capable of maximising long-term performance.

ZERO-BASED STRUCTURING

The case materials on Taiwan's electronics companies demonstrate the benefits of using industrial ecology theory to determine the strategy and structure most appropriate for optimising long-term value added performance. This observation provides the basis for proposing that when reviewing future strategy the aim is to design an organisational entity which has all of the aspects of structure which are required to maximise added value. Furthermore any aspects of structure which are found to be superfluous to this goal should be removed or shut down.

One approach for undertaking a review of the nature of future structure is summarised in Figure 12.2. The model in Figure 12.2 is based upon an approach which has been evolved within AT&T (Allenby 2000). This company utilised the concept for assessing structure in relation to the management of environmentally sustainable business systems. Nevertheless the process elements are equally applicable to the more generic scenario of utilising industrial ecology as the basis for optimising the structure most likely to support achievement of an organisation's long-term added value objectives.

The first stage in the process described in Figure 12.2 is to assess the impact on the industrial ecological system in which the organisation is involved in relation to influence on strategy and potential future changes in science or technology. This is followed by a review of the current and possible future industry infrastructure. In most cases the industry infrastructure will require a review of the industry supply chain and the added value performance of supply chain members. One approach to determining whether there are benefits in revising the role of the organisation within the future industrial ecology likely to prevail within a specific sector is to construct an added value supply chain assessment matrix of the type shown in Table 12.1.

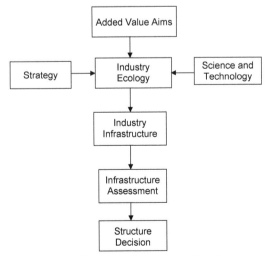

Figure 12.2 Ecology-based structure planning.

Table 12.1   A Value Added Supply Chain Assessment Matrix

	Suppliers	OEMs or Service Providers	Intermediaries
Total Organisation			
Value Chain Elements			
Inbound Logistics			
Process Activities			
Marketing			
Outbound Logistics			
Customer Services			

To generate data for the assessment matrix, the average sector profit margin expressed as a percent of sales is calculated for the organisation's top five competitors. These data are used in the next stage to calculate the percentage of added value performance variance using this formula:

= (company profit margin) x 100/(average competitor profit margin)

The other assessment dimension is that of absolute added value performance. Having calculated the average total profit figure for the top ten companies within the supply, this provides the basis for calculating relative added value performance variance using this formula:

= (company total profit) x 100/(average industry profit of leading ten firms)

Both the calculated variances are then entered into the assessment matrix. Entries greater than 100 percent indicate activities for which added value achievements exceed the competitor and total industry average. These data are used to determine whether any repositioning of the organisation within the supply chain would improve added value performance. The matrix also provides the basis for determining whether the organisation needs to revise strategy in order to achieve increased added value in relation to each of the value chain activities which exceed or at least equal the calculated industry average. Once this assessment has been completed the final decision is to determine what would be the future optimal structure most suited to achieving the organisation's value added aims.

MININIMALIST STRUCTURES

Case Aims: To illustrate how knowledge-based companies have tended to create core structures and avoided diversification into lower added supply chain activities.

Microsoft

The advent of the PC and the arrival of the Internet are meta-events which have permitted knowledge-based firms to adopt simple organisational structures, which by focusing on core activities have permitted added value maximisation. When Bill Gates developed MS:DOS and Windows systems, by persuading IBM to agree to a licence whereby Microsoft software was installed at time of product assembly, this allowed him to avoid involvement in any other aspects of the industry supply chain. This same relationship was then negotiated with other PC manufacturers, permitting Microsoft to retain a minimalist organisational structure.

Subsequently a more complex structure became necessary as the company entered the software upgrade market. This required involvement in the creation of additional structural elements to manage the company's involvement in the distribution of software in the B2B and B2C markets. Even here, however, the advent of the Internet and high-speed broadband has increasingly allowed Microsoft to sell new software direct to customers without involvement in any physical distribution activities.

Amazon

The first major entrepreneurial exploitation of the Internet was achieved by Jeff Bezos when he created Amazon.com. By selling books on-line and using logistics companies such as Fedex, he avoided the need to invest in the creation of physical distribution or the opening of retail outlets. Although the core knowledge of the new business was on-line retailing, the company was required to also invest in an in-bound logistics system and warehouse operation because at the time of business creation this organisational responsibility could not be outsourced.

Dell

An example of an early entrant into the PC industry which was based upon a minimalist structure which was then further enhanced by the advent of the Internet is Dell. The company avoided involvement in either the logistics of supporting intermediaries or opening retail outlets by using mail order and a tele-sales operation. Avoidance of participation in what soon became the low-margin business of manufacturing PCs, the company sub-contracted this responsibility by purchasing products from a range of different manufacturers. The highly integrated nature of the business and the ability to sustain a minimalist structure were further enhanced when Dell commenced selling goods and services via the Internet.

(continued)

MININIMALIST STRUCTURES (continued)

Google

Since the advent of the Internet the more successful firms have tended to focus on exploiting specialist knowledge capabilities and retaining a minimalist structure. For example, Google focused on the creation of the most effective search engine and did not become involved in activities such as becoming an ISP, as did companies such as AOL. Even now Google tends to focus on the sale of knowledge and avoids diversifying into downstream supply chain activities. For example, in the rapidly growing area of smart phones, Google has primarily focused on revenue generation associated with the introduction of its Android operating system. Although the company has launched its own smart phone, the actual product is manufactured by Motorola, and various mobile service operators such as AT&T are licenced to distribute the product.

PROTECTING CORE COMPETENCE

The concept of sub-contracting out an area of business activity because the current area of organisational activity has become uncompetitive is not a new idea. In the 1970s and 1980s, many Western manufacturers in sectors such as consumer electronics developed sub-contract relationships with firms in Asia. This action, now more commonly known as 'outsourcing,' was subsequently criticised by industry observers. This is because in many cases the knowledge acquired by Asia firms such as Panasonic, Goldstar, Daewoo and Sharp permitted these organisations to later successfully enter Western markets offering lower-cost products under their own brand names. Bettis et al. (1992) concluded that outsourcing has often played a prominent part in the decline of Western firms which relied heavily on this approach as the way of remaining competitive in relation to reducing manufacturing costs. Their research revealed that many firms which utilised outsourcing were already performing poorly and that the only survival strategy was to move production offshore to reduce operating costs. Once the outsourcing commenced, corporate logic then prevailed over implementing proportional cutbacks across other activities such as product and process engineering. Eventually firms become less and less able to design new products or to have the capability to take advantage of the latest advances in process technology. Over time this results in design and development skills becoming vested in the supplier to whom the outsourcing contract has been awarded.

Accumulated evidence of the subsequent market performance of many Western firms which moved their production offshore led to the widely accepted view in the 1990s that outsourcing is a bad decision which will inevitably lead to organisational decline. Heikkila and Carlos (2002) proposed that this viewpoint about outsourcing represents a fundamental misunderstanding of the basis of developing effective business strategies in today's more complex world. This is because the basis of strategic success is vested in accumulating skills and competences that permit the firm to remain ahead of competition. Thus without a sustained focus on exploiting new knowledge, then the organisation will be unable to initiate a rapid response to changes in the market, process technology or exploit new technology as the basis for developing its next generation of products or services.

As managers have become more aware of the importance of acquiring and exploiting new knowledge this has led to a more careful consideration of the strategic risks of losing technological competences and skills upon which the sustainability of an organisation's competitive advantage is ultimately based. Hence an important antecedent to reaching an outsourcing decision is to determine (a) the core activities over which the organisation must retain absolute control and (b) which activities are non-core and can be outsourced. In reviewing this aspect of strategic thinking Heikkila and Carlos concluded that the following three types of competence should be retained in-house:

1. *Distinctive competences*, which are the capabilities which are the basis of the organisation's strategic superiority and permit the organisation to remain ahead of competition.
2. *Essential competences*, which are not necessarily unique but are critical in the effective implementation of strategy (e.g. a highly integrated computer-based system for effective management of a complex supply chain).
3. *Protective competences*, which ensure customer needs are always fulfilled. In many cases these are competences associated with ensuring customer quality expectations are always exceeded.

With products and process technologies becoming exponentially more complex, even highly competent organisations are being forced to accept that carefully managed outsourcing is a necessity in order to gain access to new knowledge and to reduce the development cycle for new products. Quinn (2000) concluded even those firms that sustain superior performance through reliance upon leading-edge innovation are increasingly reliant upon outsourcing some aspects of the new product or new process technology development process. Apple, for example, in seeking to bring its iPhone to market was forced to rely upon working closely with the UK electronics development company ARM Holdings in order to acquire a chip capable of processing complex instructions without rapidly draining the limited amount of power stored in the phone's very small batteries.

Quinn posits the view that organisations should consider outsourcing any aspect of the 'innovation chain' which can be undertaken more effectively or at lower cost than retaining the activity in-house. In the pharmaceutical industry basic research is often contracted out to universities. In other sectors firms are willing to outsource early-stage commercialisation and pre-competitive development programmes. Eaton Corporation, a major American equipment manufacturer, uses the Illinois Institute of Technology to undertake early design work on new equipment concepts because this is more effective and successful than retaining this phase of new product development within the company. In the aerospace industry firms such as Boeing often now rely upon key suppliers to develop the technology and sub-systems that will constitute a major proportion of the final product. Where there is close collaboration between organisations, this process is usually known as 'co-development' (Grabher et al. 2008). In some cases co-development is based upon close collaboration between a producer and key customers. GE Medical Devices, for example, works with both scientists at MIT's artificial-intelligence laboratory and surgeons in various hospitals during the development of new medical instruments for use in complex surgical procedures.

Quinn notes that the move towards focusing upon internal exploitation of key core knowledge while expanding outsourcing or co-development activities is usually accompanied by a change in the structure of the lead organisation. Those OEMs which have recognised their primary role is to act as a knowledge centre have delegated a larger proportion of the design and manufacturing of sub-assembly systems to their suppliers. This has resulted in the creation of cascading knowledge networks. Within these networks, the OEM accepts the role for guiding and resourcing the learning process within its market system. This type of network has been created, for example, by the aircraft engine company Pratt & Whitney as a system for upgrading the ability of smaller firms on the eastern seaboard of the United States to act as specialist suppliers to the company (Norman and Ramirez 1993). Another approach to restructuring in order to focus on unique core competences is for the organisation to become a knowledge hub. The primary role of the knowledge hub is that of concentrating upon orchestrating the activities of other organisations that are assigned the responsibility of undertaking tasks which the hub managers do not perceive as being core activities (Chaston 2004).

13 Implementing Strategy

The purpose of this chapter is to cover issues pertaining to:

1. Factors influencing the successful implementation of strategy.
2. The role of leadership in ensuring successful strategy implementation.
3. The influence of organisational culture on strategy implementation.
4. Ensuring internal competences are aligned with strategic actions.
5. Delivering strategic outcomes through customer orientation.
6. Extending strategy to achieve compatibility with other supply chain members.
7. Sustaining performance through entrepreneurial actions.
8. Sustaining performance by maximising idea search activities.

FACTORS OF INFLUENCE

Even the best possible strategy has no real value unless implemented effectively. The process involves ensuring that appropriate organisational practices, actions and tactics as defined in the strategic plan can deliver specified strategic goals (Giles 1991). Wheelen and Hunger (2006) proposed implementation is the sum total of the activities and choices required for the execution of a strategic plan. Even in an organisation merely engaged in the extrapolation of the past strategy, effective orchestration of the implementation process can be a difficult task. Hence for an organisation adopting a radically different strategy, implementation can be one of the most complex set of activities which managers will ever face during their entire careers.

The academic literature has the tendency to treat strategy implementation as a relatively simple process that automatically occurs after strategy formulation is complete. Noble (1999) commented that in many standard texts the activity is treated primarily as a question of organisational design with the aim of ensuring systems and structures are aligned with the organisation's strategic goals. More recently researchers such as Raps (2004) have proposed that strategy implementation is a complex process involving the orchestration of a number of key interacting variables such as structure, people, leadership, culture and control systems.

Zagotta and Robinson (2002) identified a number of factors which need to be considered in seeking to ensure that a selected strategy is effectively implemented. In their view the start point should be that the strategy and proposed actions to be implemented are understood by all employees at all levels within the organisation. To help employees fulfil their assigned tasks, performance indicators should be made available which provide early warning metrics when strategic aims are not being met. This permits employees to take appropriate action to resolve problems before they are unmanageable. Zagotta and Robinson believe many strategic implementation failures are caused because new strategic activities often involve extra work which is just added to employees' existing tasks. Hence management must identify past initiatives no longer to be pursued while specifying which aspects of new strategic implementation should be given priority. This permits these latter actions to be perceived by employees as positive and important actions capable of delivering change and performance transformation.

Strategic success is dependent upon employees having the skills and knowledge necessary to fulfil their assigned responsibilities. Management should attempt to ensure employees are provided with access to the knowledge and resources to achieve alignment between their assigned roles and the strategy implementation. Zagotta and Robinson believe the critical aim is to create a 'virtuous circle' between strategy and strategy implementation. This involves ensuring that during the implementation phase regular reviews are undertaken which incorporate inputs concerning internal and external issues. Internal inputs will include data on outcomes resulting from tactical actions. External assessment will require assessment of factors such as industry trends, competitors and socio-economic change. When variance between planned and actual aims becomes apparent, the organisation can then determine whether the problem is related to poor implementation or the more fundamental issue of whether the selected strategy is still viable.

UNIFIED PURPOSE

Case Aims: To illustrate the importance of organisational actions compatible and supportive of an organisation's long-term strategy.

In the early years following the launch of a successful new business the usual organisational structure created by the founder and sustained by a successor is the 'functional' business model (Miller 1986). This structure is based upon the logical concept of employees fulfilling their assigned common tasks, working together in specific different departments such as marketing, manufacturing or finance. Although this structure can be effective, there can be a tendency for employees to perceive that their primary role is to ensure the optimal performance of their own department, even in those cases where this can be detrimental to the performance of other areas of the organisation. Such behaviour can be massively detrimental to being able to achieve the organisation's long-term added value objective.

(continued)

UNIFIED PURPOSE (continued)

Dell was founded in the mid-1980s by a university student, Michael Dell. The strategy upon which his entrepreneurial start-up idea was based was that the time had come when (a) customer knowledge was sufficient to start marketing PCs directly to the final customer and (b) variable product performance requirements among customers could be met by offering them the ability to customise the specification of a PC to more closely meet their personal needs (Lawton and Michaels 2001). By developing a direct relationship with all of its clients and building computers to order, Dell was able to build a highly efficient, just-in-time process while concurrently reducing on-hand finished good inventory and work-in-progress.

The outcome of this strategy was that Texas-based Dell rapidly became one of the world's largest suppliers of PCs. A key factor in this success was that all areas of the operation were committed to listening to customers, updating PC specifications to meet changing needs, exploiting new technology to continually upgrade product performance and focusing on ensuring that the company supply chain functioned efficiently, thereby ensuring complete customer satisfaction over the order-delivery-customer product usage cycle. Having validated the effectiveness of the strategy, Dell moved into B2B markets and also expanded into the provision of other computer products such as servers and networked systems.

Dell was one of the first companies in the world to recognise that the advent of the Internet provided a new pathway through which to sustain the company strategy. The company created an on-line ordering system which customers could visit on a 24/7 basis to review options, define their personal PC specifications and submit an order. By linking the customer order-entry website direct to suppliers' computer systems, this permitted an even faster response to fulfilling customer needs. At no stage did Dell make the mistake of perceiving its strategy as the basis for moving to a classic arm's-length, adversarial sub-contract manufacturing model. Instead, Dell's relationship with suppliers is that of working in partnership with manufacturers and the company serving as a knowledge hub to ensure both customer and supplier satisfaction.

A critical aspect of Dell's success is that the company has for 20+ years continued to focus on actions that are supportive of the company strategy. As noted by Lawton and Michaels, the Dell strategy has allowed the company 'to devolve all but its core activities, while maintaining effective control over its disparate business functions. This means progress towards an almost virtual structure, secure in the knowledge that their marketing, IT and finance are all designed to support their core competencies and market strategies.'

LEADERSHIP

Rowe and Nejad (2009) posit the most critical factor in successful strategy implementation is the quality of the strategic leadership provided by the organisation's senior management. They perceive strategic leadership as an ability to influence employees' willingness to make day-to-day decisions that underpin the organisation's long-term growth, while concurrently also maintaining the organisation's short-term financial health. To achieve these two goals the leadership must communicate a clear vision of the proposed strategy and gain employee acceptance of common shared values which allow rapid decision-making without the need for complex control mechanisms to monitor every aspect of organisational activity.

Rowe and Nejad concluded that effective strategic leaders ensure there are clear intra-organisational links between short-term and long-term goals. This involves leaders building adequate resources and the staff competences necessary to achieve a sustained competitive advantage. Senior managers who are focusing on achieving short-term goals and neglect ongoing development of core competences are likely to cause the organisation to fail. Effective leaders understand that human capital is an important asset providing the source of innovation and key core competence. While average senior managers focus on the exploitation of current resources and capabilities, strategic leaders combine this focus on immediacy with an ongoing search for new resources, capabilities and core competences. As a consequence strategic leaders exploit actions that maintain current organisational financial stability while concurrently building the necessary foundations for ensuring long-term organisational success. Organisations led by strategic leaders are also extremely effective in the acquisition of new knowledge through ensuring a culture that is supportive of learning at both the individual and group levels.

Wanasika (2009) proposed a key attribute of an effective strategic leader is his or her commitment to ensuring employees understand and are committed to implementing the key organisational plans actions necessary to achieve both short-term and long-term goals. This requires leaders who define strategies which facilitate a contingent fit between the organisation and the external environment. This type of strategic focus necessitates that there is equilibrium between the organisation and external environment variables in order to ensure the organisation is able to establish and sustain a competitive advantage.

Rowe (2001) defined strategic leadership as the ability to influence others to make day-to-day decisions that enhance the long-term viability of the organisation, while maintaining its short-term financial stability. This definition implies the leader can influence others, has a future orientation and the cognitive skills sufficient to provide the organisation with guidance over both short-term and long-term goals. Hitt and Ireland (2005) believe that key attributes exhibited by a strategic leader are a person's ability to anticipate future trends, define a vision, maintain flexibility, think strategically and work with others to initiate changes that create a viable organisation. The ability to work with others involves a high level of skills in relation to communication, planning and implementation. The effective leader will also be able to initiate change which permits the organisation to go in an entirely new direction. Hitt and Ireland also proposed that the effective strategic leader by serving as an exemplar is able to embed into the entire workforce the behaviour traits of integrity and a willingness to earn respect and anticipate environmental change.

Rowe believes strategic leaders who exhibit a 'future orientation' have the audacity to cause internal disruption and take risks in the present in order to sustain the future viability of the organisation. This future orientation is essential in anticipating and proactively predicting future competitive conditions and challenges. In his view strategising is concerned with consolidating available information and using this knowledge to comprehend possible futures. This necessitates that leaders do not dwell on the past or are overly concerned about the present. Instead the strategic leader communicates an inspirational vision of the future based on powerful imagery, values and beliefs.

Boal and Hooijberg (2000) believe another critical capability of strategic leaders is their 'absorptive capacity.' This enables these individuals to learn, synthesise new information and embrace new paradigms. A key determinant of absorptive capacity is the ability to understand how prior knowledge can assist in recognising the value of new information that can further enhance organisational performance. The process of combining existing and new knowledge requires conceptual skills linked with the ability for abstract thinking. Without this latter competence strategic leaders will be unable to reduce complex situations so that they become comprehensible or be able to make sense of complex interactions between factors of influence both inside and outside the organisation.

LEADING STRATEGY IMPLEMENTATION

Case Aims: To illustrate that successful implementation of strategy requires the leader to convince the workforce of the viability of the selected strategy.

Successful implementation of an organisation's strategy demands acceptance and commitment from the organisation's workforce. This is unlikely to occur unless the leader of the organisation is able to convince employees of the validity, benefits and feasibility of the strategy which has been identified as being capable of delivering the organisation's performance goals. The importance of the leadership role is illustrated by the activities of Herb Kelleher, the founder of Southwest Airlines, who fulfilled the role of CEO for almost 30 years (Smith 2004).

From Day 1, Southwest's business strategy was to be America's leading low-cost domestic airline. Many of the ideas developed by Kelleher and his team have subsequently been adopted by the other 'no frills airlines' in other countries across the world. Certain fundamental key components of the model to achieve a high level of added value included selecting less popular routes while avoiding highly congested airports, no assigned passenger seats, selling direct to passengers to avoid paying travel agent commissions, minimal in-flight service, flying a single model of aircraft and a workforce committed to levels of personal productivity that minimise the time which the company's aircraft spend on the ground. Southwest's average trip is less than 500 miles and is 50 percent shorter than its major competitors. Southwest is the only consistently profitable airline in the United States. Southwest is currently the fourth largest airline in the United States in terms of domestic passenger miles flown, serving 59 airports in 30 states. The company has been profitable for every year other than 1971, which was the first year of operations.

(continued)

LEADING STRATEGY IMPLEMENTATION (continued)

Herb Kelleher recognised that to attain and sustain high added value while offering low-price services in the highly competitive US domestic airline industry, he needed the wholehearted commitment and loyalty of the entire workforce. He and his management team established a company culture that provides employees with extensive operational independence, coupled with a relaxed, friendly work environment. Kelleher also established a policy of being completely honest with employees and committing where possible to never making anybody redundant, even during periods of poor sales. In return the company expects employees to be flexible and recognise that part of their job includes helping their colleagues when needed. One example of this orientation is that flight attendants assist in collecting rubbish after landing in order to reduce the time their aircraft is on the ground. Additionally, in the ongoing search for increased productivity to further enhance added value performance, Southwest management actively encourages everybody to propose new ideas to further improve operations.

CULTURE

Organisational culture reflects the internal values which influence interaction between strategy, strategy implementation, structure, systems, style, employee skills and staff behaviour (Muafi 2009). Besanko et al. (2000) posited that corporate culture has a significant effect on an organisation's long-term sustainability and economic performance, thereby determining outcomes such as profitability, staff turnover and employee commitment. These authors proposed that congruence of beliefs among employees will create a unifying force that can enhance organisational performance. Noe et al. (2006) believe key personal attributes of managers and employees who choose to implement an innovative strategy are a long-term orientation, co-operation, a preference for freedom of action to take risks and a high tolerance for ambiguity and uncertainty.

Baker and Feldman (1991) stated that several role behaviours can be assumed to be instrumental in the implementation of competitive strategies. For firms pursuing a competitive strategy based upon innovation, culture should be reflected by employee behaviour which includes creativity, long-term focus, commitment to co-operation, moderate concern over quality and a high tolerance for ambiguity and unpredictability. The authors believe that pursuing a competitive strategy based upon innovation typically requires the organisation to ensure a culture exists which includes selecting highly skilled individuals, giving employees discretion in decision-making, minimal use of rigid control systems, providing resources for experimentation, allowing and even rewarding occasional failure and appraising the long-term implications of actions when assessing employees. The outcome of embedding this type of culture into the organisation is the existence among employees of enhanced personal control and morale plus a strong commitment to achieving the organisation's long-term performance goals.

Riolli-Saltzman and Luthans (2001) suggested that to develop a competitive advantage capable of sustaining performance in the face of newly emerging competition, successful organisations need to exhibit an adaptive, flexible culture. This involves participative decision-making, empowerment, knowledge sharing across boundaries, team sharing of ideas and visionary leadership. In their view this culture is critical in countering the activities of competitors based in emerging nations. This is because to remain successful in such environments, firms require a culture aimed at achieving unprecedented speed in new idea generation and in the launch of next-generation products when there are indications that overseas competitors are beginning to exhibit an ability to duplicate the firm's current products. These authors also believe that a fundamental challenge when creating an organisation capable of operating at high speed is that the internal culture must also ensure the ongoing existence of concern, respect and trust across the workforce. Proposed appropriate cultural values include customer centricity, innovation, knowledge sharing, teamwork, trust and integrity. Riolli-Saltzman and Luthans posit the role of the leader becomes more than merely just being a visionary. There is an added fundamental requirement to be articulate in order to effectively create and shape desired organisational cultural values. This is because only via an appropriate culture can organisations can successfully compete against emerging nation competitors by using a strategy based upon adaptability and flexibility. Effective strategy implementation also demands a culture that emphasises team goals, idea exchange, working as a team to avoid getting locked on a single plan and ensuring the firm avoids simple reactive responses to actions by these competitors.

Trompenaars and Hampden-Turner (1998) proposed an important aspect of organisational culture is the prevailing attitude towards the influence of how differing perceptions of time influence employees' approach to fulfilling assigned tasks. In their view individuals differ in their orientations in relation to past, present and future. These differences may affect motivation. Managers have shared expectations about time, since they are all engaged in organising, planning and controlling. This shared expectation will result in organisations being structured according to these individuals' perceptions. Strategic planning and implementation are activities associated with a future time orientation. Although an organisation may be oriented towards the future, past experiences and present activities may influence perceptions and attitudes towards the future. The critical issue is the degree to which the future of the company can benefit from past and present experiences. This means that long-established firms may have to avoid the past or present from dominating and thereby distorting their preferences when implementing strategies designed to exploit future opportunities.

In those cases where the organisational culture is orientated towards time being perceived as a series of sequential events, which is frequently the case in Western firms operating in mature markets, employees tend to exhibit a preference towards a linear approach engaged in strategy implementation. Tight schedules are planned and changes in the sequence of actions will tend to be avoided as this is seen as a source of uncertainty. The problem is this sequential approach may not be the most effective philosophy in the case of time-critical activities. This is because there is a need for shared and cross-coordinated actions which rarely occur in a sequential time–orientated culture.

STRATEGIC ALIGNMENT

Miller and Warren (1989) suggested that a key reason for the failure of Western manufacturers to compete effectively with new entries from Pacific Rim nations is the common occurrence of senior management failing to ensure strategies are compatible and completely aligned with all of the organisation's operations. These authors contrast this situation with, for example, Japanese multi-location manufacturing firms. In these organisations all departments at each location and management across all locations focus on ensuring their actions underpin and support the organisation's overall strategy.

To achieve a high level of strategic alignment requires all departments within an organisation to fully understand their roles in terms of current operations and have determined what actions are required to contribute towards delivering the organisation's longer-term added value performance goals. This involves inter-departmental interaction in order to orchestrate and co-ordinate activities aimed at achieving optimal outcomes.

The failure of organisations to ensure there is a common focus leading to the implementing of aligned strategic actions is not restricted to the manufacturing sector. Evidence of similar problems is also apparent within the service sector. Inter-departmental variance can in some cases be even more of a problem than in a tangible goods business. This is because of the inability to differentiate intangible services from those offered by competition. As a consequence market performance and customer satisfaction are heavily dependent upon service quality. When departments have different views and priorities this will inevitably lead to the emergence of gaps in the delivery of high-quality services. Khadem (2008) feels the biggest challenge in service organisations is achieving alignment that ensures complete understanding and agreement with the vision, values and strategy across the entire organisation. Employees must share common values and accept the correctness of the leadership's vision and strategy for the organisation. The author also stresses the importance of the prevailing culture being aligned with the core values of the organisation.

MANAGERIAL ALIGNMENT

Case Aims: To review the issues associated with ensuring managers are able to fulfil their assigned strategy implementation responsibilities.

In terms of ensuring that selected strategies are effectively implemented, an organisation's managers must have the competences to fulfil their roles in terms of achieving the strategic goals which they have been assigned. In reviewing this issue, Szilagyo and Schweiger (1984) suggested the probability of managers effectively fulfilling their assigned strategic responsibilities demands that required competences are matched by defined job roles.

In relation to the job role these authors suggested that issues to be assessed include:

1. Importance and extent of environmental scanning.
2. Definition of specialist functional roles.
3. Nature and complexity of problems to be managed.

In relation to required managerial skills and behaviours to fulfil job roles these might include:

1. Specific industry knowledge.
2. Knowledge of particular organisational functions (e.g. marketing, finance).
3. Overall company knowledge.
4. Past performance in related or unrelated assignments.

In relation to required informational factors these might include:

1. Level of intra- and inter-departmental collaboration.
2. Number and importance of internal and external contacts.

Required managerial skills and behaviours in relation to informational tasks might include:

1. Number and quality of relationships with internal and external networks.
2. Level of communication, supervisory and interpersonal skills.
3. Ability to select and motivate colleagues, subordinates and teams.

In relation to the organisational culture variables, these might include:

1. Establishing clear performance goals, standards and priorities.
2. Importance placed on strategic control.
3. Importance placed on innovative activities and decisions.

In relation to supporting organisational culture managerial skills and required behaviours, these might include:

1. Quality of conceptual skills.
2. Control orientation.
3. Innovative behaviour.
4. Flexibility and adaptability in assignments.

INTERNAL ALIGNMENT

The achievement of common purpose has been described by Kim and Mauborgne (1993) as the 'management of due process.' Their perspective is that ultimately the final selection of strategy is usually vested with senior management, whereas implementation activities are the delegated responsibility of an organisation's departments, teams and individuals. There exist a number of factors which can ensure the achievement of common purpose, thereby avoiding differences of opinion leading to organisational dissonance that might disrupt organisational performance. Achievement of organisational alignment is most difficult in a global organisation constituted of a diverse portfolio of different businesses. This is because within these organisations there is the risk that individual business units may be myopic, concerned only about their own unit's performance. This can be detrimental to the overall performance of the total enterprise. To counteract this trait, IBM deploys a management system that includes the following interrelated collaborative management teams (Bramante et al. 2010):

1. *Business technology team*, which concentrates on advanced technology solutions and intellectual property (IP) to infuse into products and services to further differentiate and improve value for clients.
2. *Business strategy team*, which provides longer-term assessment and planning to drive understanding of industry trends, customer dynamics and market opportunities. This strategy team communicates with the technology and performance leaders to help them shape actions in the short term that position IBM in differentiated and defensible segments with a continuously evolving and dynamic offering suite.
3. *Business performance team*, which focuses on period performance and the ability to understand and respond to market realities that are critical in a technology-driven industry with high-velocity innovation and demanding customers. The team primarily focuses on short-term decision-making to drive both current performance and market positioning.
4. *Business finance team*, which advises the teams on the impact of the decisions and investments made in each of the critical business areas.

IMPROVED ORCHESTRATION

Case Aims: To illustrate actions required following recognition of inadequate implementation of strategy.

Unilever is a global business with 40 billion euro turnover, offering a wide range of home, personal care and food products across 400 brands, including well-known global market leaders such as Lipton, Knorr, Dove, Omo and Lux. The company has operations across 100 countries and through distributors operates in a further 50 countries around the world. By 2000, global competition forced Unilever to re-focus on the core competence of marketing fast-moving consumer goods.

(continued)

IMPROVED ORCHESTRATION (continued)

This resulted in a new strategy entitled 'Path to Growth,' aimed at accelerating an evolution from a diverse, fragmented group of local operating companies to a business with regional competitive strengths. A major factor which led to the launch of the Path to Growth initiative was the recognition of the flattening of demand in many of the firm's long-established Western consumer markets.

Path to Growth was the right strategy but implementation proved inadequate. Unilever employs bright, confident, articulate people of many nationalities. As a result, everyone had their own views on how to optimise performance. Coupled with a complex organisational structure, this culture led to what was characterised as an 'over-intellectual, over-presentational and under-actioned' management orientation. Over the last decade, a set of new of methodologies known as 'Strategy into Action' (SIA) has been developed. The SIA approach, based on the principle of Japan's 'hoshin kanri,' has led to policy deployment being modified to reflect different national cultures and incorporation of the best practice techniques from different Unilever operations across the world.

The scale and complexity of the Unilever organisation did require that certain rules and guidelines had to be accepted in all countries. The most critical of these was that there can be only one mission and one set of leadership standards throughout the entire organisation. Although no scope to change or amend the strategic goals is permitted, the management team in each country is free to define its own strategic actions to contribute to Unilever's overall strategic goals.

Performance metrics have been completely revised to match the Strategy into Action methodology. Only the 20 corporate key performance indicators (KPIs) were monitored, whereas previously very different country-level metrics were in use. In some cases these were based upon several hundred variables for assessing actual versus planned performance. The outcome of improving strategy execution is sales have returned to a growth track. The strategic focus on the company's big global brands has led to 75 percent of the revenues now coming from Unilever's 12 'euro billion + brands.' Productivity was enhanced, yielding a total of 800 million euros in cost reductions. Total working capital was reduced from 8.8 percent to 2.1 percent of sales, while operating margin has gone from 8.6 to 16.0 percent of sales.

CUSTOMER FOCUS

In the face of increasing global competition, the tendency of many Western nation firms in the latter part of the 20th century was to implement the strategy of sustaining immediate profitability by reducing costs. These cost savings were usually achieved by actions such as revising internal processes, downsizing and improving workforce productivity through work task automation. The same reaction is now often encountered in Western companies responding to the threat of competition from Indian or Chinese firms.

In the 1990s one of the most popular approaches for achieving cost reductions was business process re-engineering (or BPR). The concept received widespread support and attention following the publication of Hammer and Champy's (1993) bestseller entitled *Re-engineering the Corporation*. Unfortunately there was a tendency of some firms to be so enthusiastic about reducing operating costs that upon introducing techniques such as BPR, strategic focus was concerned only with activities inside the organisation. Little or no thought was given to whether implementing organisational change might be detrimental to the strategic goal of continuing to satisfy the needs of customers (Sehgal et al. 2006). These authors also noted that companies never learned from their strategic errors in the 1990s associated with ignoring customers and focusing solely on reducing costs. This is because the same behaviour is again being repeated by Western firms in the 21st century.

Evidence concerning major firms which thrive and prosper in global markets despite increasing competition from the Asia-Pacific region suggests their ongoing success is closely linked with their emphasis on strategies based upon being highly 'customer-centric' organisations. In his analysis of this trend, Day (2006) concluded that in both B2B and B2C markets, successful Western companies are engaged in a strategic re-alignment and are moving away from being concerned only with optimising internal processes. Instead the new focus is on seeking to identify new entrepreneurial strategies based around working closely with customers.

Effective execution of a customer-centric philosophy will require all departments engaged in the production and the delivery of output to be focused on the priority of meeting customer needs. There is a critical requirement for effective knowledge sharing between key departments. Concurrently all of the organisation's support services such as finance and HRM must also be committed to supporting a strategy which has the primary aim of satisfying customer needs.

Day concluded that some major Western companies have yet to reach the point where strategic re-alignment delivers the goal of totally fulfilling the needs of customers. A key area of failure often involves not proactively revising products or services in response to indications of changing market requirements. He further proposed that the re-alignment process is composed of the following four phases:

1. *Phase 1, Silo Recognition*: This is the point where the organisation recognises that departments are focused upon achieving their own goals such as reducing costs. There is no real attempt to respond to changing market conditions. More importantly, knowledge acquired about changes in the external environment are retained within departments (a process known as 'silo thinking') and not shared with others in the organisation.

2. *Phase 2, Informal Change*: Senior managers and departmental heads primarily remain concerned with internal issues, but certain individuals, usually entrepreneurially orientated sales staff responsible for

managing major customer accounts, begin to work with colleagues across the organisation to develop a more proactive orientation towards serving customer needs.

3. *Phase 3, The Awakening*: Eventually senior management begins to realise that the move to developing closer relationships with key customers is reflected in increased customer loyalty and profitability. In some cases this outcome is brought to their attention by key customers expressing their satisfaction about the level and quality of service they are receiving. At this juncture, senior management recognises that to achieve the strategic aim of sustaining the long-term existence of the organisation there is an urgent need to align internal and external activities such that the primary strategic focus is on becoming a customer-centric organisation.

4. *Phase 4, Achieving Customer Focus*: The final phase in changing the orientation of the organisation involves identifying actions that can ensure closer relationships with customers. Equally importantly senior managers must orchestrate the strategic actions required to ensure that in optimising knowledge exchange activities inside the organisation, all areas of the operation are aligned to meeting the needs of markets served. Alignment actions to achieve this goal will vary between organisations. This variation will reflect differences such as the complexity of the product technology, market structure, the closeness of the relationship demanded by the customer and the location of production sites.

EXTERNALISING STRATEGY

In the 1990s, shorter product life cycles, greater product variety, increased pressure to reduce operating costs by reducing out-of-stocks through speeding up order-delivery cycles and a move towards the globalisation of inputs all combined to require organisations to rethink their way of working with other members of their supply chain. This led to supply chain management becoming an important strategic issue in terms of optimising organisational performance and internal process efficiencies. Firms could no longer merely consider their own strategies when determining future plans. Instead there is a requirement to extend vision outside of the organisation in order to achieve compatibility with the strategies of other key members within the supply chain.

Kopczak and Johnson (2003) concluded that a number of fundamental changes in organisational behaviour are required to exploit the benefits of working more closely with other organisations within a supply chain. These include:

1. *Cross-company integration*: This involves going beyond achieving strategic success by merely ensuring integrated actions inside the organisation and adopting a philosophy of achieving integrated

actions with other members of the supply chain. Achievement of this goal demands that supply chain members discuss strategic objectives and reach consensus on the optimal approach for ensuring convergence in strategic actions across all participating organisations. In many cases achievement of this goal has been greatly aided by organisations agreeing to share information on a real-time basis by creating automated, computer-based data exchange systems.

2. *Mutual cost savings*: In the past most firms concentrated on actions to minimise their own internal costs and gave little concern to whether this created problems or inefficiencies for others with whom they traded. At times this inward-looking attitude can be detrimental to others within the supply chain. Optimisation of a supply chain operation requires members to examine costs across the entire system and to determine what operational changes can be made to achieve a net reduction in overall costs, even though in some cases this can lead to an increase in cost for one or more supply chain members.

3. *Optimal product design*: In the past most firms concentrated on designing and developing products that offered the greatest level of profit. Little consideration was given to whether the product concept added costs to others within the supply chain (e.g. excessively bulky packaging leading to handling and storage problems for intermediaries). In order to optimise product costs for all supply chain operation members, there is a need to examine all aspects of producers' product specifications to determine whether re-designs can be implemented to achieve a net reduction in overall product costs across the entire supply.

4. *Improved demand management*: All members of a supply chain from customer through to raw material suppliers encounter problems due to fluctuations in demand. Unfortunately many of these fluctuations are caused by actions such as a manufacturer announcing sudden price changes, introducing last-minute promotions and sales forecasting errors. The scale of fluctuations can be enhanced by actions such as real-time exchange of sales rate information between supply chain members to improve forecasting accuracy, accompanied by agreement to provide longer lead time over price change announcements to reduce the level/frequency of sales promotion events.

5. *Increasing customer value*: This activity involves members of the supply chain examining how, by collaborating over identifying new innovative approaches to communications and distribution channel management, the final customer receives additional value from the product or service purchased. For example, a manufacturer may develop an on-line product design and product usage advisory system that can be used by the firm's B2B distributors in providing more detailed, customised guidance to end users.

In relation to the growing importance of enhancing supply chain performance in global markets, Morash and Clinton (1998) proposed that integration of purpose between members tends to start with operational co-operation such as sharing information on product movement and stock levels. Having been persuaded of the benefits of working more closely in these areas, this can lead firms to examine other ways in which collaboration over market management tactics can offer greater added value to the final customer. The final stage in the development of the relationship is when members of a supply chain seek to further optimise customer satisfaction by achieving cross-company integration of their individual business strategies.

For those Western firms which have created integrated supply chains, their position near to key customers offers a significant competitive advantage that can be used to combat the entry of overseas suppliers from the emerging nations. This is because data from downstream supply chain members, often provided in real time via computer-based systems, permit rapid identification of changing final customer needs. Once these are identified, lean manufacturing causes supply chains to be much shorter than those of overseas supplies. This permits a rapid logistics response, making available new or different products more suited to newly emerging demand from final customers.

SUSTAINING PERFORMANCE

As evidenced by examples such as Southwest Airlines and Dell, a successful strategy can sustain an organisation for many years without any need for fundamental change. The same conclusion, however, is not applicable to tactical actions associated with the implementation of strategy in response to more immediate changes in the external environments. Markets evolve, customers exhibit new needs and competitors continually seek to steal market share. Under these circumstances to create and sustain an enduring organisation capable of achieving long-term added value targets demands ongoing investment in promoting entrepreneurial behaviour that can provide new, innovative products, services and production processes (Stonich 1990).

Bird (1988) has proposed that sustaining entrepreneurial behaviour to support new, innovative business tactics depends upon the organisation exhibiting an 'entrepreneurial intention.' In support of her perspective she notes that highly successful companies are usually founded by entrepreneurs. It is critical that after their departure for reasons such as retirement or the sale of the business, the entrepreneurial spirit which provided the basis for the creation of the business is sustained by subsequent generations of senior managers. Achievement of this goal requires that the organisation remains focused on responding to the changing needs, habits and beliefs of potential and existing customers. This knowledge provides the basis for strategic actions that fulfil the aim of exploiting innovation as an ongoing pathway through which to achieve success.

The success of entrepreneurs is often related to their ability to respond to newly emerging market opportunities. Bird noted that as organisations become larger and more complex, the speed of response in relation to reaching decisions and implementing actions may decline. This problem seems most common among Western firms operating in their more mature markets. She posits that subsequent generations of senior managers must continue to emphasise retaining a philosophy of being able to make rapid and flexible decisions in response to new opportunities and new ideas. This philosophy should be accompanied by willingness to delegate authority to those managers and employees who are nearest to the market where an emerging new opportunity has appeared.

As most organisations face resource constraints, decisions will often need to be made about implementing entrepreneurial activities. An empirical analysis by Athey and Schmutzler (1995) supported the generalisation that when customer needs are stable and ever greater value is being sought by customers, then process innovation is probably a lower risk and, hence, a more advisable priority. This can be contrasted with relatively new markets where technology is undergoing rapid change and customers tend to revise their benefit demands based upon experiences acquired by exposure to different product concepts. In this latter scenario, the organisation should probably give priority in the allocation of scarce resources to focusing upon developing the next generation of products or services.

Successful innovation is more likely to occur in those organisations where there is a culture which is supportive of identifying and exploiting new ideas as a key mechanism to enhance added value. This is because successful innovation usually depends on horizontal co-operative interactions between departments and vertical interactions with senior management to gain access to required resources. As illustrated in Figure 13.1, the original source of ideas will also influence the most likely primary focus of the innovation activity.

Source of Added Value Idea

		Internal	External
Value Added Idea Focus	Process	Production Flow Added Value Productivity Opportunity	Quality/Service Added Value Improvement Opportunity
	Product	Intuitive Entrepreneurial Added Value Opportunity	Customer-Driven Added Value Entrepreneurial Opportunity

Figure 13.1   Innovation action matrix.

Ettlie and Reza (1992) undertook an empirical study to determine which factors influenced the probability of successful innovation among firms in the US car industry. They concluded the most critical factor was effective interaction between departments in relation to sharing information about identified opportunities and problem/resolution activities while an innovation project was in progress. The study did not reveal a statistically significant correlation between the strength of vertical relationships inside the respondent firms and the impact on the level of successful innovation. Ettlie and Reza concluded that firms which were more internally orientated tend to place greatest priority on actions concerned with improving internal process flows and resolving problems in the 'design through to manufacture phase' in the development of new products. This is contrasted with firms which emphasise sustaining close links with sources external to the firm. These latter firms tend to have a much broader perspective concerning opportunities for innovation, gaining their ideas from sources such as customers, intermediaries and suppliers.

THE SEARCH FOR IDEAS

Multi-national corporations which focus on innovation as the basis for sustaining long-term strategic performance are often at a significant advantage over competitors that operate only in a single domestic market. The advent of the global corporation has further increased the ability of entrepreneurial employees to tap into new overseas sources of ideas. In their review of the entrepreneurial benefits of being a global organisation, Santos et al. (2004) point to the example of Nokia. Although this company was a late entrant into the mobile telephone market, the organisation's broad expertise in global markets permitted identification of new opportunities, which rapidly permitted the company to overtake its US competitor Motorola, which had minimal experience of markets outside the United States. Two key reasons why operating on a global basis enhanced Nokia's entrepreneurial activities were that the organisation had (a) access to a much larger, more diverse pool of knowledge and (b) greater exposure to different factors influencing customers' usage of mobile telephones. More recently, however, Nokia appears to have been less perceptive in its recognition of changing needs and consequently has suffered in the face of other companies being more adept at exploiting the opportunities associated with the arrival of smart phones. It remains uncertain whether the appointment of a new CEO in 2011, who is an ex-Microsoft employee, can result in Nokia re-acquiring past entrepreneurial competences.

In knowledge-intensive industries global firms are able to rapidly identify the geographic location of different pools of knowledge and gain insights into a much broader range of research which is being undertaken across the world. In many cases having identified an especially important knowledge pool, global firms are increasingly opening new R&D facilities at these specific locations. In commenting upon this trend Santos et al. (2004, p. 33) noted that:

> Companies such as Novartis AG and GlaxoSmithKline PLC now realize that the knowledge they require extends far beyond traditional chemistry and therapeutics to include biotechnology and genetics, and the use of advanced computers and robots in drug discovery. Much of this new knowledge has emerged from diverse sources away from the companies' traditional R&D labs in Basel, Bristol or New Jersey. Instead, it is often located far away in California, Tel Aviv, Cuba or Singapore. As a result, these pharmaceutical giants have learned that globalization of their innovation processes is no longer optional; it has become imperative.

For an organisation wishing to exploit new knowledge from an overseas source as the basis for supporting entrepreneurial activities, implementing this strategy involves the two actions of 'prospecting' and 'accessing.' The advent of the Internet has greatly assisted the prospector because an online search will rapidly provide information on topics such as new product launches, new technologies and the latest scientific advances. Some companies have now implemented automated key word and phrase search systems in order to monitor the emergence of potential new opportunities on a 24/7/365 basis. In many cases detailed understanding of new opportunities will require travel to locations which are considered possible sources of new ideas. This may, for example, involve meeting with university researchers or visiting companies which have been identified as being engaged in new development activities of interest to the prospector. Some companies believe that searches are best undertaken by managers engaged in overseas market study programmes. It can also be the case that overseas research is more likely to be successful when the managers embed them into a country's culture and business practices. Where this view is held the company will probably fund selected managers to sabbatical leave lasting several months or arrange their transfers to an appropriate overseas facility.

There is significant risk in successfully accessing new knowledge from another area of the world where the organisation has limited experience or understanding of local culture. This is because the organisation is less able to use industrial contacts and business networks to determine the real capability of overseas developers to produce a commercially viable proposition. One solution for minimising this type of risk is for the company to open its own R&D facility in the country in question. This is, however, an expensive solution. Consequently most companies take this route only where the technology is highly complex and the learning cycle necessitates a fully developed in-country presence. In those cases where the new knowledge is contained within another company, another solution is to acquire the business.

The high costs of business acquisition are a key reason why most firms would prefer to create some form of joint venture or research alliance with overseas organisations. Where the new technology can be acquired as product component or functional service package (e.g. a new software programme) then a lower cost solution may be to negotiate a purchase contract with the supplier. In those cases where the purchased goods are critical to the company sustaining a competitive advantage, then an attempt should be made to negotiate an exclusive supply contract for the item.

Although being global offers the benefit of more easily accessing new technology, there is also the risk that as companies become involved in activities such as overseas manufacturing or sub-contracting, confidential knowledge may leak out of the organisation. This lost knowledge can then be exploited by firms in another country, thereby permitting overseas competitors to more rapidly develop their own capabilities in a new area of technology and eventually evolve into a major new competitive threat. This scenario is one which led to the demise of certain sectors of the American and European consumer electronics industry during the 1980s and 1990s. These companies sought ways to reduce operating costs by opening their own plants in the Pacific Rim or contracting with firms in that area to manufacture their products. Over time many of these activities permitted firms in countries such as Korea to acquire the knowledge to manufacture products which led to them becoming a new source of competition for American and European firms in their own domestic markets.

Currently the problem of knowledge leak is of major concern to leading Western aerospace companies. Potential customers such as the Chinese are insisting that in return for purchasing products such as new civilian jet aircraft, some of the manufacturing activities must be based in their respective countries. These countries have made no secret of their aims to establish their own aerospace industries, initially to supply their domestic markets, but over the longer term to enter international markets. Hence, although being prepared to permit firms in these countries to become involved in co-manufacturing projects, Western firms may be assisting the rate at which overseas companies will become a new competitive threat.

14 Implementation Errors

The purpose of this chapter is to cover issues pertaining to:

1. The strategic risks of focusing upon meeting short-term financial targets.
2. Damaging strategy implementation due to poor leadership.
3. Damaging strategy implementation by retaining outmoded conventions.
4. Strategy implementation impaired by inappropriate structures or systems.
5. The adverse impact on strategy implementation of ineffective top teams.
6. Poor situation analysis impairing assessment of strategic performance.
7. The adverse impact of ineffective strategic control systems.

DRIVEN BY NUMBERS

The purpose of a strategic plan is to define how the organisation intends to achieve the aim of creating and sustaining long-term existence as an enduring organisation. Standard accounting systems are based upon monitoring the performance of the firm over a 12-month period. This time frame can cause managers to focus on meeting the near-term quantitative performance objectives such as annual sales, costs and profits. As a consequence situations may arise in which decisions are made which completely ignore the long-term strategic goals of the organisation. In the face of very poor sales performance, a company strategy based upon innovation and consistently superior products may be ignored. Instead senior management may instruct the marketing department to embark upon actions such as implementing price reductions, up-weighted sales promotion, postponing new product launches and ignoring service quality problems. These actions will probably result in the annual sales forecast being met, but at the cost of failing to introduce new products accompanied by damage to the company's image for no longer delivering superior products and quality of service.

The tendency to emphasise achieving short-term goals is most obvious during economic downturns. The intensity of competition increases as firms seek to sustain current revenue in the face of declining customer spending

(Hall 1980). The majority of firms tend to adopt a survival strategy of seeking to reduce internal operating costs and utilise savings achieved as the basis for offering even lower prices (Bacot et al. 1992). Goodell and Martin (1992) concluded that as well as the intensity of competition increasing during a recession, firms often begin to behave in unpredictable ways, implementing actions such as offering excessive discounts or announcing massive sales promotions. These actions can risk permanently damaging the financial viability of the business. The pressure to respond in this way has been further exacerbated during the economic downturn in Western nations which commenced in 2008 as a result of the banking and sovereign crises, when firms in these countries sought to respond to lower-priced goods entering their markets from countries such as India and China. Although price cuts may help these Western firms sustain an acceptable revenue flow until economic conditions have improved, the strategy will usually be accompanied by a severe reduction in profitability. As profits have fallen many of these Western companies have been forced to cut back on investment in innovation, further reducing their long-term capability to survive in global markets in the face of increasingly intense competition from emerging nations. Furthermore those firms which entered the downturn with limited financial reserves, are servicing high debt levels or are unable to attract new investors can face the possible risk that declining profit margins can ultimately lead to bankruptcy.

One of the key influences of this emphasis on 'making sure we make the numbers' in recent years has been the pressure placed on CEOs by major shareholders, such as the pension funds wanting steady year-on-year increases in dividends and share prices. Another factor is the popularity of paying large bonuses to managers based upon simplistic performance targets such as achieving an agreed level of annual sales. In an article by Guerrera (2009) discussing the excessive emphasis on short-term bonuses in relation to the world banking crisis, she quotes Yale professor Jeffrey Sonnenfeld at Yale University, who commented that 'immediate shareholder value maximisation by itself was always too short term in nature. It created a fleeting illusion of value creation by emphasising immediate goals over long term strategy.' This view was supported by Jack Welch, the previous CEO of the American conglomerate GE Corporation. His apparent hindsight opinion in relation to his leadership role of placing emphasis on always being able to report quarterly profit increases was that it was the dumbest idea in the world. He now believes shareholder value should be a result and not the basis of an organisation's long-term strategy and that companies must remember that their main constituencies are employees, customers and products, not Wall Street or the financial press.

One way of avoiding excessive emphasis on meeting annual performance targets is to create an environment in which managers recognise the importance of adopting a much broader, much longer-term perspective when reviewing corporate performance. This involves assessing the potential impact of proposed actions and the actual outcomes of implemented actions in relation to the latest analysis of current performance. These deliberations provide the basis for assessing the impact of decisions reached in terms of their compatibility with the organisation's long-term strategy. In those cases when the analysis leads to the identification of dissonance between long-term strategy and planned actions to sustain near-term performance aims, this should immediately indicate to senior management that a more careful, insightful assessment of proposed immediate actions should be instigated.

POOR LEADERSHIP

One of the most common reasons to explain failure during strategy implementation is the shortcomings of the organisation's leadership. Harvard professor Barbara Kellerman (2005, 2004) proposed that there is a diverse range of different forms of bad leadership. These include:

1. *Incompetent leader*, who lacks the skills, willingness and ability to make effective decisions.
2. *Rigid leader*, who may be competent but is unable to accept new ideas or proposals to change future activities.
3. *Intemperate leader*, who is unable to control his or her anger or emotions, causing the organisation's working environment to be both unbearable and unpredictable.
4. *Callous leader*, who ignores the needs, wants and wishes of everybody else.
5. *Insular leader*, who ignores the needs, wants and wishes of everybody except the close group with whom he or she works on a day-to-day basis.
6. *Corrupt leader*, who is willing to lie, cheat and steal to achieve any objective.
7. *Evil leader*, who is a psychopath willing to consider any possible action to achieve an objective without any regard to prevailing society values and morals.

Dotlitch and Cairo (2003) posit that even very effective leaders can terminate their run of success and start to exhibit flawed behaviours. These flaws are often closely linked to the same factors that made them successful in their previous managerial roles. These authors concluded that leaders may fail because of who they are and how they act when they are placed under exceptional stress. They identified the following traits in CEOs which can lead to strategic failure within organisations:

Arrogance: Everybody else is wrong.
Melodrama: The need to be the centre of attention.

Volatility: Extreme mood swings.

Excessive caution: Unable or unwilling to afraid make a key decision.

Habitual distrust: A belief that 'others are out to get you.'

Aloofness: Impersonal, cold behaviour.

Childish: Rules are unnecessary and can be ignored.

Eccentricity: Being different just to annoy others.

Passive resistance: Not revealing what one thinks to avoid arguments.

Perfectionism: Excessive emphasis on minor, unimportant details.

Eagerness to please: Putting popularity ahead of the right decision.

Fulmer and Conger (2004) identified the following factors which they feel can result in the failure of a leader to ensure the successful implementation of a strategy:

1. *Failure to deliver results*:

   - Blames others for a failure to achieve promised results.
   - Makes excessively optimistic promises and then fails to deliver.

2. *Betrayal of trust*:

   - Undertakes one thing and then does something completely different.
   - Makes excuses about outcomes accompanied by blaming subordinates.
   - Hides or modifies key information which is damaging to personal reputation or the organisation's market reputation.

3. *Resists change*:

   - Unable to adapt to new ideas, plans or priorities.
   - Excludes consideration of any opinions other than his or her own.
   - Fails to understand or take on board alternative perspectives.
   - Rejects or belittles the opinions of others.
   - Fails to engage in discussions when alternative opinions are presented.

4. *Failure to take a stand*:

   - Indecisive when an urgent or immediate key decision is required.
   - Listens to the last opinion expressed by another individual whom he or she believes has influence over his or her future with the organisation (e.g. the company chairman).

5. *Inability to become involved*:

   - Believes information which contradicts his or her view is unimportant when making a 'big decision.'
   - No interest in being involved in day-to-day activities within the organisation.

Poor performance of an executive in a senior position is often due to the individual happy to abuse the powers that are vested in his or her position and being prepared to force subordinates to execute orders that over time will inflict long-term, lasting damage on the organisation. Vredenburgh and Brender (1998) proposed the primary causes of the abusive exercise of power derive from an individual's personal motives. These can include fast achievement of tasks to impress superiors, a desire for greater control and requiring unquestioning loyalty and obedience from subordinates. Personal motivation is only part of the reason why abuse of power can exist with organisational hierarchies. This is because certain prevailing conditions can also be contributory factors. These conditions include ambiguity or discretion about how decisions are to be made, a lack of openness between managers and excessive pressure by senior managers to improve performance or rapidly resolve problems. The presence of any of these conditions can divert employees away from the organisation's key purpose of endeavouring to sustain long-term performance. In organisations where there is a preference for secrecy such that managers avoid sharing key information with subordinates, this will further increase the risk that abuse of power will occur.

In reviewing the behaviour of leaders who fail, Burke (2006) proposed these individuals could be classified into three basic types—namely, incompetent, ineffective and evil. Incompetent leaders lack the technical competences needed to fulfil the role of visionary and strategist. Ineffective leaders may have the technical skills to analyse complex situations, but limited interpersonal skills mean they will fail to motivate subordinates to implement changes that are necessary to improve organisational performance. In the event individuals exhibiting ineffectiveness or incompetence do not inflict such serious damage as to bankrupt the organisation before being replaced, then a successor will usually be able to reverse the adverse performance trend. Evil leaders are individuals who are unethical and cannot distinguish between right and wrong. As a consequence decisions tend to be made to suit themselves (e.g. firing the finance director who questions illegal accounting practices) or to maximise self-gratification (e.g. awarding themselves huge bonuses). It is often the case that such individuals do so much damage that subsequent efforts to rescue the organisation often fail.

Burke also raises the issue of whether certain leadership deficiencies are more or less important at different stages in an executive's career or when confronted with different managerial challenges. For example, a strength in being willing to make tough unilateral decisions in terms of closing an failing organisational unit could become a weakness when there is a need at some other time to listen to the views of individuals who are more informed about a specific situation. He also proposes that certain flaws such as emotional instability, arrogance or abrasiveness may have greater adverse impact when exhibited by senior managers rather than middle managers. This is because at the upper levels of an organisation, job roles are larger and more complex. Hence the stakes are higher and the costs of failure greater.

Given that a leader in a large organisation is usually surrounded by highly competent subordinates, the question arises about why these individuals do not provide feedback concerning errors of judgement being made by the leader. Unfortunately this lack of feedback is not uncommon in hierarchical organisations in which the prevailing culture centres around decision-making being the preserve of senior managers. The absence of criticism by subordinates is also likely to arise when the leader is known to be arrogant, resistant to criticism or has a reputation for acting vindictively against those who question his or her decisions.

The first major financial scandal of the 21st century, involving the Enron Corporation, a major, diversified US corporation based in Houston, Texas, was in large part due to decisions made by the organisation's leadership (Fernández-Aráoz 2005). Following some years of manipulation and distortion of the firm's financial data to convince the financial markets that the company was profitable when in reality the operation was incurring huge losses, the company was declared bankrupt in December 2001. The ensuing scandal led to the dissolution of the company's auditing firm, Arthur Andersen, which was one of the world's top five accounting firms. The firm was found guilty of obstruction of justice in 2002 for destroying documents related to its annual audit of Enron. The conviction was overturned in the US Supreme Court in 2005 but by then the Andersen name had been irrevocably damaged.

In commenting upon the leadership issues associated with the Enron case, Fernández-Aráoz noted that in many cases such outcomes can be attributed to a failure to undertake an effective search and recruitment process when appointing a new leader. He posits that the 'deck is stacked' against the selectors. This is because there are only a limited number of outstanding individuals available who can actually lead a modern organisation in a rapidly changing, increasingly technologically complex world. Another problem is whether the organisation has correctly defined the skills and attributes required of its next leader. This is because the competences appropriate in the current leader may suddenly be rendered obsolete due to unexpected macroeconomic, political, competitive or technological change.

In today's business world there is frequently pressure from stakeholders, such as major investors, to immediately appoint a new CEO when the organisation is performing poorly. In the face of such time pressures, mistakes can be made and selectors may discount or ignore any negative signals associated with their most favoured candidate. A tendency also exists among most people to base their selection on decision criteria upon those with which they are most familiar. This occurs because factors such as the characteristics exhibited by a popular, previous leader are perceived as offering the safest and least risky basis upon which to make a selection decision. Unfortunately in some cases past behaviour may be inappropriate. This is because there may be a need to appoint an individual with a very different perspective on future strategy in order to reverse poor organisational performance. The impact of an incorrect selection decision can be further amplified when a totally unsuitable leader is accompanied by a management team with whom he or she has worked in the past. This can result in the organisation now being staffed with an even larger number of individuals capable of immediately impeding the definition and implementation of an appropriate new strategy.

BE CAREFUL WHO YOU TRUST

Case Aims: To illustrate that one should never depend upon organisations being successful just because their leaders have a prior track record of success.

Citigroup, Merrill Lynch and Bear Stearns were led by CEOs who had established a reputation of being very successful, providing returns to shareholders and premium yields on bond issues. These organisations were then forced to admit the scale of their losses during the meltdown in the world's financial markets. These disastrous results did not reflect well on their business strategy, which in hindsight was based upon maximising immediate trading profits without too many concerns about the risks which accompanied achievement of this performance. The world was soon to learn that the leadership culture inside these three organisations was that of employees not daring to challenge the decisions of their respective CEOs or communicate any bad news to them. In commenting on this situation, Jennings (2008, p. 43) noted that:

> Fear and silence. It was not that bright people in the companies did not see the problems or risk. The structure, the incentives, and the returns and rewards all contributed to a silence that belied common sense.

Charles Prince at Citigroup was hand-picked by Sandy Weill to succeed him as the new CEO of this huge American financial conglomerate. This nomination ensured that nobody would be likely to question the judgement of the new leader. At Merrill Lynch, Stan O'Neal was known to be a 'numbers guy' who was brought in as the new CEO to streamline operations. He initiated the relationship with Long-Term Capital Management, a hedge fund, taking Merrill Lynch from a safe trading house to a high-risk player in the world's financial markets. As the scale of the sub-prime mortgage disaster began to emerge, O'Neal stated Merrill's exposure was relatively small and under control. Three months later he was forced to announce a $5 billion hit, and just three weeks later he had to increase the liability figure to $8 billion. He could not survive and was forced to tender his resignation. In the case of Bear Stearns, when the scale of the losses became known, it also emerged that the ability of James Cayne as an effective CEO was somewhat questionable. Apparently he spent a lot of time out of the office participating in various recreational and social pursuits. Even more worrying was the fact that nobody in the company who wanted to remain employed would ever dare question his decisions.

(continued)

BE CAREFUL WHO YOU TRUST (continued)

In hindsight it seems that the failings of these CEOs as leaders should have been obvious to financial regulators, investors and the business press, should any of them remembered that simple adage in business that 'it if seems too good to be true, it is too good to be true.' It also seems everybody failed to learn the lessons of history provided by the Great Wall Street Crash of the 1930s. A key factor in the subsequent Great Depression was that leading New York bankers were found to have permitted insider trading, extended excessive levels of credit and taken advantage of investors who had access only to very limited market information.

OBSOLETE CONVENTIONS

In their analysis of why entrepreneurial activity is critical to the ongoing success of organisations, Miller and Friesen (1980) posited that marketing the same product or service proposition over an extended period of time is no longer an option in the world's increasingly competitive markets. Their formula for survival is to re-invest current profits into continuous innovation, accompanied by preparing the organisation for the next shift in environmental conditions. Despite this perspective, it is not unusual to find organisations utilising the same strategies to achieve their performance goals even when environmental trends indicate there is a need to change (Huff 1982). It may be the case that this has occurred because members of the industry have learned through common experience that no other product or service strategy exists which is likely to succeed. A more probable explanation, however, is that many senior managers have a tendency to remain faithful to winning strategies which assisted them in achieving promotion into the upper levels of management in their current organisation. Unfortunately the major risk in this situation is these individuals may continue to support operational conventions which have become obsolete, with the inevitable outcome that continued use is detrimental to organisational performance (Piercy 1991).

One example of this scenario is provided by senior managers who were employed as marketing managers back in the 1980s in Western countries, when profit margins were high and consumer goods markets were still growing. In those days it was possible that by implementing a massively up-weighted promotional campaign, a frontal attack could result in stealing brand share from a competitor. What some of these senior managers fail to comprehend is that frontal assaults in today's branded consumer goods markets are rarely successful. Consumers are less loyal and many have switched to the supermarkets' own label products. During the period of a frontal assault, when the aggressor is offering incentives such as money-off coupons or free products, more consumers will purchase the brand. Prevailing lower profit margins means that sustaining high levels of promotional spending cannot be supported for any significant period of time. Once the marketing spend is reduced back down to a more normal level, virtually all of the newly acquired customers will switch back to their old product. In her article reviewing this situation, Ogilvie (1994, p. 28) quotes the view of Harvard professor John Quelch:

> Brands have become victims of their own success. The big profits they earned led to arrogance—now that profits are drying up, instead of rethinking the overall marketing strategy, brand managers just do more of what isn't working—namely, trade promotions. Product managers are under so much pressure to manage periodic sales promotions that they have little time left for long-term strategic thinking.

Another common view held by many senior managers is the concept that 'big is beautiful.' This perspective can cause them to be supportive of increased promotional spending to achieve higher brand shares for existing products already in the maturity stage on the product life cycle curve. Then when this option is perceived as unsuccessful they implement an aggressive acquisitions policy to continue to grow the company size by purchasing other organisations. Although size can confer certain advantages, such as negotiating lower prices for raw materials and exploiting economies of scale, over 30 years ago, Drucker (1985) stated that: 'absolute size is by itself no indicator of success, let alone evidence of managerial competence.'

Dalton and Kesner (1985) posited that seeking to become an even larger organisation is often detrimental to long-term profitability. In reviewing the available evidence they were unable to identify many mergers aimed at providing scale advantages which over the longer term generated any significant growth in profitability. In most cases the combined profits of these new larger entities either remained flat or declined. This outcome was usually accompanied by a fall in organisations' share prices over time. As a consequence these authors concluded that the only real beneficiaries of growth through acquisition were the senior managers engaged in the activity. This is because their salaries usually rose dramatically following an acquisition, many received extremely valuable stock option packages and they also enjoyed enhanced status within their respective business communities.

In recent years many of the world's largest consumer goods companies such as Unilever and Nestlé have reached the conclusion that the convention of becoming big by continually widening the range of items within a branded goods category is no longer effective (Kahn 1998). This is because pressures in their mature Western markets, such as funding the battle for increased shelf space in retail outlets and the growing popularity among supermarkets for stocking own-label items, mean for many brands total product line profitability has been declining. Concurrently these multinationals are also encountering increasing competition from domestic brands in emerging markets such as India and China. As a consequence some CEOs are demanding their brand managers reduce product variety and in certain cases discontinue the product range entirely. This strategic shift has not been accompanied by these firms reducing their growth through acquisition policies. However, many more companies now require that acquisitions offer the ability to enhance existing product portfolios or provide access to new areas of market opportunity. An example of this latter strategy is provided by Proctor & Gamble's acquisition of Olay, which gave the company a platform through which to expand its activities in the increasingly important market for treatment for ageing skin.

SLOW LEARNERS?

Case Aims: To illustrate that the banking industry continued to pursue strategic actions long after their effectiveness became highly questionable.

By the end of the 1980s the consumer branded goods industry had provided convincing proof of the poor financial returns available from engaging in brand wars involving increased advertising expenditure, higher spending on sales promotions or confrontational price cuts. This lesson, however, seemed lost on bankers in both the United States and the UK, who in the late 1980s and early 1990s engaged in head-to-head confrontations in an attempt to steal market share from each other. The net result was very little change in market share accompanied by a significant decline in profitability in the retail banking sector. Furthermore most of the new consumers attracted to open an account were those whose low loyalty and poor credit records meant their previous banks were pleased to see them depart (Chaston 2000).

A very similar scenario over the last 15 years of apparently ignoring lessons learned in other industries has also applied in relation to banks' desire to use acquisition as a strategy to grow their organisations. In the United States in the late 1980s, two major banks, Citicorp and Bank of America, embarked on an aggressive expansion programme by acquiring various smaller savings & loans in numerous states across the country. The major banks were assisted in their drive for growth by various changes in the federal banking laws. One change, for example, was to permit banks to raise commissions charged on domestic brokerage activities from 10 percent to 25 percent of revenues. This was followed by Bankers Trust acquiring Alex. Brown & Sons, the Baltimore-based regional brokerage, and it prompted other banks to implement similar strategic actions to aggressively enter new areas of business such as underwriting (Geer 1997).

(continued)

SLOW LEARNERS? (continued)

By the early 1990s, bodies such as the OECD were beginning to express concern about the banking industry's apparent insatiable appetite for acquisitions. These concerns seemed to be ignored by bankers, even though they were prepared to admit their ongoing desire for growth was creating significant excess capacity in their industry, which in turn was driving down profitability (Kazuhiko 1993). The apparent solution to the excess capacity problem selected by most banks was to use acquisitions as a path through which to capture economies of scale. A large number of banks, especially in the United States, Japan and some medium-sized and smaller European countries, continued to try to achieve economies of scale by seeking to improve efficiency by increasing the size of their operations through acquisitions. In some cases a further influencing factor was senior managers who appeared to believe that banks have to have a certain size to remain competitive.

In the United States even community banks, observing the activities of their bigger brothers in New York, embarked on expanding out from their own states or regions through a strategy of opening more branches coupled with an aggressive acquisitions policy (Streeter 2006). This was despite the fact that a growing number of well-documented research studies had shown that once a financial institution reaches a moderate size, there is no persuasive evidence that growth will be accompanied by increased efficiency. In fact with conglomeration, as a bank begins to offer a wider range of services, there is a risk that the management cannot control the costs and risks associated with providing an extended range of new or different services.

Recent research on the benefits of M&As in the banking industry, some of it published just before the meltdown in the world's financial markets, has supported earlier conclusions about the questionable benefits of growth through acquisition. Azofra et al.'s (2008) study of European banking concluded that there was little evidence that economies of scale were being realised. This is because following most acquisitions there was rarely any indication of an improvement in overall profitability. Another justification for acquisitions is that they permit banks to achieve economies of scope by diversifying their business into new areas such as insurance, loan securitisation and investor services. Economies of scope may be realised when the cost of producing a given mix of products is lower than the sum of the costs of producing each product independently. However, these types of strategic actions are accompanied by increasing a bank's overall level of business risk. In commenting on this situation, Kazuhiko (1993, p. 22) posited that:

> As large, multi-product institutions enter different segments of the industry, there may be a danger that each market or the industry as a whole may suffer from the concentration of power in the hands of a small number of institutions. They may also manipulate deals to the detriment of customers who have limited information. When a conglomerate operates through a complex and opaque corporate structure, overall assessment of their risk-exposure and business becomes difficult both for the management and regulators, which may result in excessive risk-taking or manipulation of intra-corporate transactions.

(continued)

SLOW LEARNERS? (continued)

In hindsight it seems a pity that neither senior bankers nor banking regulators took note of this warning. Had the banking industry not continued to follow strategies which had been proven over many years to be inappropriate, perhaps the scale of the world recession which started in 2008 would not have been as deep or as prolonged.

STRUCTURE AND CONTROL

Most business start-ups utilise a loosely defined organisational structure in which the founder acts as the locus of control. Typically organisational growth is accompanied by an evolution into a more formalised structure. In most cases this structure will be based upon the allocation of specialist tasks to specific departments. For many organisations this functional (or U-form) remains an appropriate system. Senior management retains the locus of control, but in most cases the specialist knowledge and interaction between directors responsible for each department, plus an effective vertical communication, will ensure the organisational focus remains on implementing actions that support the selected strategy.

The effectiveness of the U-form structure can be downgraded, however, when one department is perceived as more critical to success than others. This is because there can be a tendency of this department to abuse its power in achieving resolution of short-term problems without consideration of the potential impact on overall longer-term corporate goals. Sources of power refer to a specific base of capability to provide some performance or resource considered important to the organisation. Individuals or units possess power to the extent that they are able to address important problems facing the organisation, gain over control resources valued by others, are timely in bringing problems and resources together or have successfully used their power in the past to enhance organisational performance. Yukl and Falbe (1990) established the distinction between sources of power derived from organisational position versus those based on an individual's attributes. This latter source of power usually involves role autonomy, the ability to instil dependence within others or permitting groups or departments to impose their will over those who have less influence inside the organisation.

Situations of dominance during strategy implementation are not unusual in consumer goods companies (Mukhopadhyay and Gupta 1998). They can occur when there is strong top-down pressure to meet quarterly sales forecasts. Another influence is where the marketing department is organised around brand groups in which the successful career path is to initially be appointed to a development brand, progress to a smaller existing brand and eventually becoming a brand manager on one of the company's most important products. The culture created by this brand-focused environment is other departments will defer to largest brand groups even when their requests will disrupt operations, such as production scheduling of out-of-stock smaller brands. Furthermore, because the leading brands are seen as being the most important within the company, managers on development brands often find they are 'at the back of the queue' when requesting resources such as implementing market research projects. This is because the organisational culture supports the perspective that innovation is less important than immediate sales. As a consequence development brands often face delays in the time taken to bring these new products to market.

Hoskinson et al. (1991) proposed that an ability to retain a commitment to management implementation of strategy, especially when an entrepreneurial orientation is deemed critical to achieving long-term performance goals, often begins to diminish as organisations seek to diversify into new markets or focus resources on internal process improvement activities. This occurs because diversification is usually accompanied by the move towards the M-form structure and decentralisation, causing individual divisions to be granted greater managerial autonomy. Unfortunately, because senior managers usually want to remain in touch with key activities for which complexity and information flows are on the increase, decentralisation is usually accompanied by the imposition of tighter financial controls from the centre. This move can cause divisional managers to focus on 'making this year's numbers' and to become averse to making mistakes or taking risks. Emergence of this behaviour trait will probably be accompanied by a decline in entrepreneurial activity because generating revenue from existing products or services is perceived by divisional managers as a much easier and safer proposition. Over time should divisional level performance decline due to a lack of innovation, the usual outcome is for the centre to impose even tighter financial controls and set increasingly non-achievable performance targets. Such actions will further accelerate the downward spiral in organisational performance.

After a sustained period of poor performance in a diversified business, senior management may embark on a strategy of sustaining growth by implementing further diversification through geographic market expansion or making new acquisitions. These actions are usually accompanied by senior managers at the centre being even less able to influence the culture and employee behaviour in both existing and new divisions. Should the centre continue to impose tight financial controls or demand unattainable sales targets, risk aversion at the divisional level will continue to increase. There will be a tendency for divisions to become more insular and inter-divisional interaction and knowledge exchange will disappear. Initially, although the expansion of company operations through diversification may be reflected in increased total sales, over the longer term sales growth will decline. This outcome will often be accompanied by a significant fall in overall profitability.

Worley and Lawler (2006) posited that critical activities such as the implementation of a new strategy will fail in those cases where organisational design and prevailing management practices are inherently against any form of change. In such organisations a lack of genuine strategic intent will be accompanied by an absence of the resources and capabilities required to successfully manage change. Another obstacle is there may be insufficient 'surface area' which is being caused by too few employees interfacing with the external environment. As a consequence there is a failure in the acquisition of the critical information about new trends or emerging new market opportunities. This lack of external focus may cause individuals to become 'ossified' within their current job roles. This will greatly increase the probability of the company being caught totally off guard by unexpected external change. The risk of errors is further amplified when there is a poor working relationship between front office staff interfacing with the environment and the back office staff responsible for the process activities associated with the production and delivery of products or services.

To gain an in-depth understanding of factors that can result in strategy implementation failures, Lesca and Caron-Fasan (2008) utilised action research methodology to study 39 business cases known to have encountered major performance problems. They concluded the following causal factors were highly influential:

1. Absence of a genuine will to succeed among managers and staff to implement proposed actions.
2. Inappropriate or inadequate leadership skills exhibited by managers leading the project.
3. Poorly defined expectations and objectives creating misunderstanding or de-motivation within the project team.
4. Misalignment between the proposed strategy and the actions selected to implement the strategy.
5. A hostile organisational culture leading to lack of support or failure to share critical information within the organisation.
6. An underestimation of the complexity of the actions required to implement the proposed strategy.
7. Weak support, commitment and participation by different departments or work groups for implementation of the proposed strategy.
8. The allocated budget is insufficient to fund the actions that are required.

AUTOCRATIC CONTROL

Case Aims: To illustrate that highly autocratic control over strategic decisions can eventually lead to failure.

An Wang was an archetypal technology entrepreneur who built a hugely successful business by being a first mover in the IT industry. The start of his business success was developing and selling his first technology breakthrough, the magnetic pulse memory core, to IBM in 1956. The next two decades were a period of massive growth for the company. This started with the LOCI electronic scientific calculator in 1965, which provided the basis of the desk calculator market, which Wang dominated for five years.

Wang Laboratories went public in 1967, with Dr. Wang personally retaining control of over 50 percent of the company. The company's first products were the minicomputer, the Wang 2200, and the 1200 BASIC word processing machine. The real lift-off in sales revenue came from the introduction of VS (virtual storage) computers, the Office Information series and Integrated Systems line products, all targeted at the office-automation market. Unfortunately Dr. Wang decided that the word processor was the future of computing and was dismissive about the opportunities offered by the PC. His influence meant that the company ceased to be a leading-edge innovator focusing on creating radically new products. Wang was slow in entering the PC market and the bigger disaster was to continue to use the company's own non-IBM-compatible proprietary operating systems.

In commenting upon the eventual collapse of the company, Finklestein (2005) suggests this is an example of a 'strategy failure caused by a flawed strategist.' The author points out that Dr. Wang served concurrently as president, CEO and director of research, creating a benevolent dictatorship in which he retained ultimate control over every facet of the company. One of the apparent reasons for Wang's behaviour is he always thought that he gave up too much control when the company first went public. He may also have resented that he lost control of exclusive manufacturing rights to his magnetic pulse memory core because IBM exploited gaps in the licensing agreement with the company. Dr. Wang also apparently believed he had been coerced into giving away too much equity when the company went public. Hence he subsequently refused to dilute his holdings to raise additional capital. This resulted in the company relying upon bank borrowing, which eventually led to an accumulated debt in excess of $1 billion. An inability to service this level of debt caused Wang Laboratories to file for Chapter 11 bankruptcy in 1992.

Wang Laboratories died of self-inflicted wounds. What made the company great was an obsessive desire by a benevolent and brilliant dictator to control every aspect of the company. Ultimately this behaviour trait to the company's downfall. Wang Laboratories is a remarkable example of an entrepreneurial start-up that never matured. Driven to control as much of his personal environment as he could, and riding a wave of success that made him a very wealthy man, An Wang made a series of fundamental mistakes that eventually cost his company the longevity and recognition of Wang's contributions in creating the global IT industry.

TOP TEAM PERFORMANCE

Although the business press likes to focus on the abilities of CEOs in articles about organisational success (e.g. Larry Ellison at Oracle; Steve Jobs at Apple) the vast majority of organisations are led by a team of senior managers. Given the expertise and experience which should exist within this group, the issue arises of why top teams fail in their collective responsibility to correct errors when fulfilling their role of overseeing strategy implementation. One explanation is the CEO dominates the decision-making process and the team is either unable or unwilling to question any views expressed by its leader (Miller and Toulose 1986). The other explanation is the team lacks the skills necessary to fulfil its assigned role in guiding future operations (Pearce and Zahra 1991).

In seeking to determine the factors influencing poor performance, Hambrick and D'Aveni (1992) undertook a study of the capabilities of top teams in poorly performing US corporations. They concluded one factor can be the team's inability to establish effective systems whereby key information can be acquired or, alternatively, once acquired can be effectively analysed. As a consequence the top team lacks the ability to either identify the relative importance of different problems as these occur or to recognise the scale of opportunities that might be available due to a change in market conditions or the emergence of a new technology. The authors also noted that as an organisation begins to encounter performance problems which apparently are not being resolved, the more capable senior managers begin to depart the organisation. Their explanation for this trend is these individuals are sensitive to the potential damage to their careers of being associated with the collapse of a major organisation. Hence these individuals seek to leave before the scale of the mounting problems becomes apparent to external stakeholders such as the shareholders or financial institutions.

Dainty and Kakabadse (1992) undertook a similar research project using case materials to identify how poor performance by an organisation's top management team can lead to errors in the implementation of strategy. The focus of their study was on how poor group membership skills can adversely impact the performance of a top team. They labelled their three types of poorly performing teams as 'brittle,' 'blocked' and 'blind.' The identified attributes and weaknesses for each team type are as follows:

1. *A brittle team* exhibits poor focus on the fundamental issues facing the organisation. Members believe expertise, independence and low disclosure are important traits. Group interactions tend to be defensive, with members emphasising their own views and restricting comments to their area of specialist expertise. This type of top team is susceptible to splits, with members departing as a result of internal disagreements, team members becoming disillusioned or external pressures such as adverse market performance. There are serious

interface problems between the centre and departments as a result of inconsistent direction and mixed messages emanating from this type of team located at the top of the organisation.

2. A *blocked team* is constituted of members capable of appreciating and discussing the key business issues confronting them, but they face interaction problems with each other, which can cause poor implementation decisions within the organisation. Group behaviour is characterised by attempting to be open with each other but individuals tend to become defensive when faced with internal management and discipline issues. To avoid dissent the primary focus of the team remains reviewing short-term performance targets and demanding employees increase their commitment to attaining these targets. In effect, the top team is emphasising a sales-driven approach. This orientation often leads to inter-departmental tensions and a lack of meaningful dialogue between different departments. By not adopting a longer-term orientation, often exacerbated by an inability to resolve delivery targets or quality commitments, the market may perceive the organisation as unreliable. This can result in a fundamental crisis that can destroy the organisation.

3. A *blind team* is constituted of members who avoid discussing issues that would upset other team members. Members are respectful towards each other but lack the sense of responsibility to discuss critical external or internal issues that should be addressed. The focus is on the maintenance of present systems. This can lead to strategic blindness in relation to changing circumstances. Colleagues, subordinates and customers are likely to have communicated their concerns to a specific individual who is a member of the top team. To avoid acrimonious discussions this individual does not mention these inputs to the rest of group and hence other team members remain unaware of the identified problem.

INAPPROPRIATE ANALYSIS

Western firms survive adverse trends such as flattening demand in mature markets or new threats from overseas competitors only when they remain able to identify and then respond to adverse market change. The faster the firm recognises that external environmental conditions are impairing successful strategy implementation, the greater is the probability that appropriate new strategies can be defined and introduced.

Wikson (1999) concluded a major barrier in many Western firms is that their environmental scanning and analysis systems have been rendered ineffective by the increased volatility and speed of change now present in many sectors of industry. During the 1980s large firms recognised the advent of the computer permitted the analysis of much larger volumes of data and the more rapid identification of performance variance. Porter and Millar (1985) proposed that modern IT systems permitted in-depth environmental scanning, greater data collection capability and rapid data analysis. This when linked to a decision support system would permit firms to cope with even volatile environments.

One potential problem with such systems is the nature of the data which have been acquired and analysed. In a review of the use of decision support systems used by IBM in the 1980s, Wikson suggests a major drawback was the reliance on financial and production data. Although identifying performance variance from plans, these systems did little to help managers to comprehend the reasons for a failure to achieve specified strategic goals. Even when computerised control systems are re-specified to focus on market data such as customer buying behaviour, the emergence of new customer segments and factors of success among competitors, more informative data are of little benefit when managers ignore the danger signals of environmental change which are becoming increasingly evident. Wikson notes that IBM did recognise the weaknesses in the reliance on internal data in its decision support systems and re-designed its systems to acquire more external information. Unfortunately, although the improved systems provided clear indications of developing market problems, IBM's deeply entrenched corporate culture based upon years of market domination resulted in managers rejecting danger signals that were indicating the current strategy was in need of a drastic overhaul.

In commenting upon the effectiveness of strategic control systems, Wikson (1999, p. 28) concluded that:

> Systems designed according to the organization's existing perception of its strategic environment and within the constraints of acceptability determined by the organization's prevailing culture . . . ran the risk of reproducing (and even legitimizing) the very perceptual limitations against which they were supposed to offer some protection in the future.

In order to avoid the risks associated with incorrectly designed control systems, an organisation should regularly assess whether existing systems are actually providing the information that provides a realistic appreciation of what is actually occurring in external environments. Nevertheless these systems are of little benefit when managers exhibit an entrenched view based upon prior experience and reject data indicating a developing problem incompatible with their understanding and expectations. Consequently an organisation must ensure managers remain open-minded in order to avoid acquired data resulting in misconceived or myopic decisions being reached inside the organisation.

When managers remain open-minded about data which conflict with expectations and prior experience, the problem still remains that many early warning signals are either weak or provide somewhat contradictory evidence about the scale of an emerging threat. Hence the organisation may still fail to react with sufficient speed to implement a new strategy capable of countering the activities of a new competitor. This type of outcome can be avoided by organisations focusing upon developing the entrepreneurial skills of managers. This results in individuals utilising both informal, indistinct external information and data from the formal control systems when assessing performance and determining whether there are potential faults in current strategy implementation activities.

In reviewing the requirement of managers to use both informal and formal data sources, Wikson suggests that the organisation needs to ensure mangers are:

1. Aware of the need to rely on external data as indicators of emerging threats, especially when these data are in the form of weak signals or contradict prevailing views inside the organisation.
2. Able to identify areas of divergence between formal and informal information.
3. Can apply intuition as a component in situation analysis and decision-making as well as accepting qualitative data as an acceptable source of new knowledge.
4. Conducting analysis at several hierarchical levels and in different functional areas across the organisations.
5. Exhibiting a clear understanding of the information provision weaknesses that exist within the organisation's formal data acquisition and decision support systems while retaining an entrepreneurial attitude towards new ideas for knowledge generation.

CONTROL SYSTEMS

The decision model of defining an aim, implementing an appropriate action and then utilising a control system to monitor actual outcomes is a concept which is practiced in most organisations. The simplest and easiest control system is to compare actual performance with forecast performance for variables such sales, costs or profits. These data provide the basis for assessing the degree to which actual results are at variance with planned objectives. Unfortunately it would seem some organisations perceive that this approach, albeit in a possibly more sophisticated form, is an appropriate mechanism through which to monitor overall strategic performance (Preble 1992).

The drawback with these types of financial variance control systems is they merely provide limited knowledge about past events. The purpose of the strategic management process is to guide the organisation along the path of building an enduring organisation. A preference for variance-based monitoring, especially when accompanied by an organisational culture in which managers are orientated towards 'making this year's numbers,' often means that effective strategic control systems are never established. As a result there are no mechanisms to (a) identify weak environmental signals which might indicate a need to review strategy viability or (b) assess emerging environmental data that indicate one or more assumptions made about key issues during the planning process are no longer valid. Preble concluded that without this latter type of knowledge no reviews are ever undertaken concerning of the ongoing relevance of the organisation's strategy.

Where apparently appropriate organisational control systems exist, design faults may exist that cause data being generated to reinforce existing preconceptions. This outcome can cause strategic complacency due to reliance upon what essentially are selective reporting systems which provide only data that mirror existing perspectives, goals and corporate values. As a consequence any indications of new trends such as emerging changes in the external environment are filtered out before data are analysed. This results in managers tending to agree with sustaining current strategic actions while remaining totally unaware of early warnings of future external change (Huber 1991).

Another failure of some control systems is the tendency to generate extremely detailed information about every aspect of the operation. This trend has been accelerated by the advent of computer-based financial and operations management systems. At the 'click of a mouse' managers at all levels can be overwhelmed with data, giving rise to 'analysis paralysis.' In commenting on this scenario, Slater et al. (1997) have proposed that organisations need to focus on a small number of key measurements that are critical to successful implementation of strategy. Their proposal was based upon the three core strategic options model proposed by Treacy and Wiersma (1995) of customer intimacy, product leadership and operational excellence. In relation to customer intimacy, the primary focus should be upon monitoring that the organisation is continuing to develop an even deeper understanding of existing and potential customer needs in relation to providing highly customised products or services. Product leaders' primary focus should be monitoring markets in relation to ensuring innovation continues to deliver an ongoing superiority over competition. Operational excellence is concerned with sustaining internal capabilities that ensure excellence in productivity and efficiency. Hence monitoring in this case should focus on analysing data on key internal performance variables influencing internal operating costs.

LEARNING PROBLEMS

Senge (1990) proposed that a clear relationship exists between poor organisational performance and the failure of organisations to learn from experience. Hamel and Prahalad (1993) extended this perspective by suggesting the learning process must be translated into the acquisition of new knowledge that can be used to upgrade areas of competence, thereby permitting organisations to remain more effective than their competitors. They concluded that learning from understanding the nature of change in markets or customer behaviour is extremely important in ensuring the successful ongoing implementation of new or revised strategic actions. These authors have concluded that market-orientated organisations are likely to exhibit the behavioural characteristic of continually seeking to exploit new sources of knowledge. However, the risk is that organisations which have enjoyed success over an extended period may develop inflexible, non-adaptable behaviour. This is because individuals may become too confident that the current strategy or strategy implementation activities will continue to remain appropriate even when there are clear indications that markets are undergoing change. Leaders who have a strong past history of always defeating the competition can become idolised by subordinates to the point where these leaders' opinions become enshrined as the only acceptable perspective in relation to defining ongoing organisational policies (Miller 1993).

15 Riding the Smart Wave

The purpose of this chapter is to cover issues pertaining to:

1. The application of long wave theory to demonstrate how new technology influences economic cycles.
2. The advent of the 'smart machine' and the 'smart upwave.'
3. Exploitation of smart knowledge to enhance customer service.
4. Exploitation of smart cards to permit real-time processing of customer behaviour.
5. How smart sensors can lower costs and increase data acquisition capabilities.
6. Potential opportunities for reducing healthcare costs by exploiting smart technology.

LONG-WAVE THEORY

In reviewing the factors influencing sustained long-term growth, Reati and Toporowski (2004) point out that neoclassic theories which have dominated economic thinking since World War II have been somewhat dismissive of examining qualitative data such as economic history as an acceptable approach for validating alternative theories. These writers suggest this is despite a number of economic historians having confirmed that long-term economic development of capitalist economies is an uneven phenomenon consisting of periods of sustained growth for about 25 to 30 years, followed by periods of slow growth or economic stagnation.

This cyclical pattern, known as 'long-wave' theory, was first recognised in the 19th century. It was evolved by economists interested in deriving generalised laws concerning the interaction between capitalism and economic trends. Stronger quantitative evidence of the validity of long-wave theory was not available, however, until the Austrian School of Economics led by Joseph Schumpeter (1950, 1942) began to analyse the factors influencing economic downturns such as the 1930s' Great Depression. As Schumpeter and other supporters of long-wave theory have pointed out, the first long wave originated following the introduction of mechanisation and production shifting to factories during the Industrial Revolution in countries such as Britain, France and Belgium.

The second long wave was the era of steam power and railways. Again the technological leaders were the same as in the first long wave, but this time they were joined by Germany and the United States. The third long wave was the era of electrical and heavy engineering. The most success-ful leader nations during the third wave were Germany and the United States. The fourth long wave was the era of mass production, which was led by the United States and permitted this country to become the world's dominant economic power. The fifth long wave, which began in second half of the 20th century, was produced by the combined interac-tion between computers, electronics and communication technologies. The technological leaders which led the generation of this latest wave were the United States and Japan.

The relevance of long-wave theory in relation to the 2008 global reces-sion has been further validated by Perez (2002), who investigated the finan-cial aspects of the theory by combining economic analysis, sociology and history. Her work clarified why at a certain period of the evolution of a new technological paradigm, financial markets progressively abandon the role of providing productive capital and become the dominant influence of outcomes. Perez posits that once this shift occurs, from being the facilitator of new productive asset creation to becoming the dominant influence over economic trends, financial institutions become de-coupled from productive activity and begin to direct the economy according to their own vested interests and criteria.

Drawing upon the long-established theory of the product life cycle curve Perez proposes that at the time of the introduction of the new technology that will provide the basis for a long-term economic upturn, old industries are in decline and unemployment is increasing. Concur-rently entrepreneurs, dissatisfied with existing, old technologies, become extremely active because they perceive there are opportunities to exploit new technologies. To develop and launch a new technology requires sig-nificant financial support. This financial resource is available from prof-its accumulated by firms and their investors who enjoyed success during the previous age of technology.

As a new technology moves into an early growth phase, Perez posits that financial markets become involved, but wealth is concentrated within a very small group of institutions. The scale of funds available exceeds the needs of the owners of the new technology, with the outcome being what she describes as 'casino capitalism.' The key characteristic of financial mar-kets at this point in time is that regulatory frameworks have ceased to be effective, speculation flourishes and asset inflation is apparent in the form of unrealistic, non-sustainable share prices accompanied by increases in the value of other assets such as property. Eventually the financial bubble which is created will burst. The usual outcome is the financial crash pushes even the strongest economies into recession.

Once governments and investors understand the errors in the financial markets which have caused a recession, a more reasoned behaviour pattern begins to emerge. By this stage, the new technologies have demonstrated a capability to support new industries that can generate an above-average return on capital employed. This evidence, when linked with new institutional frameworks being put in place by governments to encourage rational investment behaviour, leads to an increasing flow of funds into the new technologies. This in turn creates a 'golden age' of rising economic output. During this period investors are rewarded by dividends and share price rises that are genuinely reflective of the increasing real wealth being generated by the new technologies. Achieving market success again becomes the driving force within producer organisations, full employment may begin to become a possibility and social cohesiveness will tend to improve.

Eventually, however, the new technologies will move into the final phase on the life cycle curve—namely, maturity. At this juncture, few new product innovation possibilities exist, the technology has diffused across most of the industrial world and few new productivity improvements appear feasible. With markets saturated with output, intense price competition will emerge and profits will decline. This will eventually lead to most nations' economies moving into a long period of stagnation. This is the 'down wave' phase on the long-wave curve. A period of great uncertainty and turbulence will eventually re-emerge. This will remain in place until a new technology has entered the growth phase on the product life cycle curve, leading to the next long-term economic upturn.

THE SMART UPWAVE

The availability of the first commercial computers in the early 1950s has been labelled as the start of the 'Information Age' and some industry experts forecasted the mainframe computer would revolutionise humankind's future way of life. Although these machines permitted large companies to reduce the cost of storing, processing and handling much larger volumes of data, their impact on everyday life was less than suggested by these experts (Wright and Dawood 2009). The next major technology shift in the 1980s was the advent of the low-cost PC and the development of user-friendly software from firms such as Microsoft. These advances were again forecasted to revolutionise the world of business and consumer lifestyles. Smaller organisations and the general public would be able to cost-effectively store, process and analyse data. In their recent review of these 20th century events, Wright and Dawood concluded that even these advances did not permit the Information Age to have either the commercial or social impact that had been forecasted.

Tyson (1998) reached a similar conclusion about the benefits of the computer and related technology, which in his opinion would not be realised until further technological advances permitted the world to enter the 'Intelligence Age.' In his view the Intelligence Age would be based upon building a knowledge base of information about customers, competitors, suppliers and strategic alliances, which permits the rapid identification and exploitation of totally new market opportunities. Kalakota and Whinston (1996) suggested that the probability of this outcome occurring was significantly enhanced by the advent of the Internet.

The initial impact of the Internet on both organisations and society in general was certainly very significant (Soliman and Youssef 2003). The speed of transactions was accelerated and purchasing processes were simplified as paper was replaced by electronic records. Suppliers upgraded their services and customers were provided with the ability to self-manage order placements and transactions. The Internet also led to the creation of new on-line businesses and generated incremental revenue by permitting terrestrial firms to sell existing products or services on-line.

Nevertheless even the Internet did not provide the complete solution required to usher in Tyson's Age of Intelligence. For this to occur there was a requirement for additional technological advances. These include:

1. The convergence of electronic devices such as computers, telephones and televisions to permit all of these to be linked with the Internet.
2. Faster download speeds and the ability to link data acquisition systems such as remote sensors to the Internet without the need for hardwired connections.
3. Access to significantly greater low-cost data storage and analysis capability, which is now available following the arrival of cloud computing.
4. More sophisticated data analysis through access to low-cost advanced statistical analysis software of the type used in automated customer relationship management (CRM) systems.
5. The automation of decision-making within organisations by exploiting advances in artificial intelligence (AI) systems.

All of these advances are now in place and this outcome is seen by some industry experts and futurists as the basis of the next economic upwave. This is being labelled by some futurists as the 'Smart Age' (Anon. 2010c). The new era would appear to offer the world two very significant opportunities. Firstly firms seeking to survive in the face of increased competition in global markets can create organisations in which the core competence is the exploitation of smart age technology based on superior knowledge for sustaining their competitive advantage. Secondly smart technology permits the creation of new solutions to world problems such as the energy crisis, global warming, population ageing, rising healthcare costs and rising costs of delivering welfare state services (Bughin et al. 2010).

ASSESSING OPPORTUNITY

The arrival of a smart world means that organisations as summarised in Figure 15.1 need to determine whether they need to develop new internal competences capable of exploiting the new sources of opportunity which exist. One source of opportunity is the ability to acquire real-time data about customer attitudes, needs and behaviour. This permits more rapid identification of how new or improved products or services can be made available and permits more accurate targeting of customers with specialist needs. The second opportunity which smart products can provide are new services to customers while concurrently keeping the supplier aware of product performance. This offers the ability to more rapidly identify performance problems and in some cases use a supplier-product Internet link to initiate repairs or product upgrades. The third opportunity is organisations are able to access real-time data about all aspects of internal organisational processes. This offers the capability to identify how processes might be improved by actions such as enhancing energy efficiency and also provides early warning of developing performance problems before these can actually impact operations.

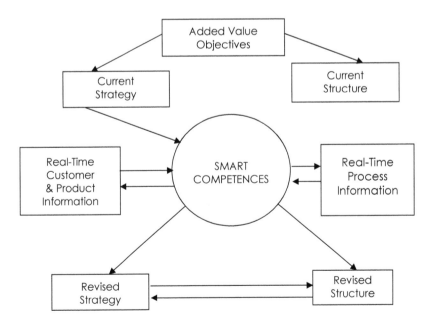

Figure 15.1 Identifying smart strategy and structure.

SMARTER VEHICLES

Case Aims: To illustrate how exploitation of advances in computing can lead to the development of smarter products.

One of the first areas where manufacturers sought to enhance the performance of their products by adding smart capability was the car industry (Sharke 2003). The primary focus was on using smart sensors to increase the safety of the driving experience. A major catalyst in this area was the US Department of Transportation's launch of its 1998 Intelligent Vehicle Initiative, which identified eight areas where intelligent systems could improve road safety. The list included four kinds of collision avoidances (rear end, lane change, road departure and intersection), two types of enhancements (vision and vehicle stability) and two types of monitoring (driver condition and driver distraction). Cars already have the capability of warning drivers when parking and a sensor system that controls the headlights in a bend in the road so that the lights always remain focused on the road. Antilock brake systems (ABS) help to prevent unintentional skidding.

General Motors, in partnership with Delphi Automotive Systems and the US Department of Transportation, is developing an automotive collision avoidance system. This system combines radar, vision, sensors and GPS to look ahead for vehicles and other obstacles. Video cameras watch lane position while the sensors monitor direction, latitudinal and longitudinal acceleration, yaw rate, steering angle and wheel speeds. The global positioning system compares the car's location to map coordinates to inform the system of what lies ahead. An example of the commercialisation of smart sensors is Jaguar. In 2003 the company added the Delphi Automotive Systems' adaptive cruise controls to its new models in North America. The system included a forward alert system that can advise a driver to brake in the presence of slowing traffic ahead. The system can also alert the driver to whether the cruise control is in use.

In addition to reducing the number of collisions, driver assistance systems may eventually improve traffic flows. Highway simulation models indicate motorists tend to overcompensate for slowing traffic ahead of them. With only 10 percent of the cars fitted with driver assistance systems this would reduce excessive braking, and with 20 percent of vehicles using such systems it is theoretically possible this would eliminate traffic jams completely.

The urban setting provides a vast source of visual information. Another opportunity is the use of sensors to improve pedestrian safety. Mercedes-Benz has a trial vehicle equipped with image processing electronics and stereo video and cameras which can detect pedestrians as well as traffic signs and signals, curbs, directional arrows and crossings. Ford Motor Company has developed a pedestrian-safety car that can deploy external airbags during a collision. Just before the moment of impact, a pre-crash sensor senses an impending pedestrian collision and inflates the external bag just above the crash. Two secondary airbags, triggered by a sensor detecting the initial impact, inflate in front of the windshield as the pedestrian is thrown toward it.

(continued)

SMARTER VEHICLES (continued)

It is not just the car manufacturers who are examining the opportunities to exploit smart technology. On the streets of Mountain View, California Google is operating eight driverless cars, seven Toyota Priuses and an Audi. An onboard camera system builds up an image of the car's surroundings. Mounted by the rear-view mirror, a digital camera recognises pedestrians, cyclists and traffic lights in the road ahead. The driverless vehicle uses satellite navigation and motion detectors to determine current position on the road. Bumper-mounted radar emitters scan ahead, triggering the brakes if the car senses cars or objects approaching. An additional rear-facing radar sensor checks for the 'tail-gaters' (Harris 2010).

CUSTOMER KNOWLEDGE

CRM is a process designed to collect data related to customers, to gain additional understanding of customers through analysis of these data and to apply generated added understanding to enhance the customer/supplier relationship. This customer management philosophy began to emerge in the 1990s as organisations acquired information from customers through sources such as UPC product data acquired at point-of-purchase in-store. Cost-effective information analysis was permitted by the rapidly declining cost of hardware and software from companies such as SAP, Oracle, Siebel, Sage and Microsoft to undertake 'data mining.' The advent of the Internet provided a wealth of real-time customer purchase data which further enhanced the knowledge which could be acquired about customer behaviour. Today's CRM systems include on-line order tracking, e-mail and internal knowledge databases that can be used to generate customer profiles and to personalise services. These technologies allow the organisation to gain an insight into the behaviour of individual customers and, in turn, to target and customise marketing communications and messages (Xu and Walton 2005).

The knowledge generated by CRM systems permits the generation of profiles for use in segmenting existing customer buyer behaviour. This can lead to greater understanding about which customers and products have the most impact on the company's revenue flows. Segmentation enables the company to provide more personalised and, therefore, more attractive product and service offerings to individual customer groups. By real-time tracking of purchase data this permits the identification of emerging trends and patterns which provide the basis for predicting possible future purchase decisions by both existing and potential new customers.

In an analysis of the benefits of having access to real-time data concerning customer behaviour, Stone (2009) proposed that this permitted the following ways of exploiting this knowledge:

1. Redefinition of existing views about customers to include not just buying history, but also future intent.

2. Using new and different data analysis techniques that generate additional understanding of customer attitudes, behaviour and relationship between needs and lifestyle.
3. Moving channel management to a higher level by expanding the different media available for communicating to customers.
4. Building responsive information systems that are capable of exploiting data mining to constantly update customer data to develop a proposition that is the right offer to be communicated at the right time through the right channel.

CUSTOMER PERSONALISATION

Case Aims: To illustrate how real-time customer knowledge provides the basis for providing smart services to customers.

With increasing real-time access to market knowledge, this has permitted organisations to personalise their relationships with individual customers by utilising the process of emulating social processes to make recommendations to customers based on an understanding of their preferences. Personalisation is a process that continually adjusts profiles to match targeted content with individuals. In his analysis of the opportunities of personalisation, Jackson (2007) presents the case of UPS, the US-global transportation company which offers personalised services across the entire supply chain. A key part of CRM technology at UPS is the programme called Package Flow Technologies (PFT). Along with productivity improvements and cost reductions inside the organisation, PFT system allows customers to review the status of a delivery and to track the order's current location with an accuracy of three feet.

UPS is one of the top client-pleasing brands in the United States, with the firm achieving a No. 1 ranking for people's 'trust in the company to do the right thing in the event of a product/service problem, excellent customer service, and sincerity of corporate communications among US companies.' To achieve this close customerrelationship, UPS deploys both technology-based services and people-intensive solutions. For example, when a customer needs to reduce cost, UPS might find a solution that involves less shipping activity. The account manager consults a solution developer before meeting with the client, and can view the solution through a CRM application before the client meeting.

Jackson also identifies American Airlines as one of the first companies in the world to recognise the benefits of using computer-based systems for delivering enhanced customer service. The company's first development of a customer-orientated IT management system was its Sabre reservations system, offering travel planning and ticketing services. The first American Airlines website came on-stream in 1995. American Airlines maintains a database of millions people to support the American Advantage (AAdvantage) frequent flyer programme. This system generates a wealth of information about customer travel patterns and purchase behaviour. The start point in exploiting this knowledge was to examine customer travel patterns. American Airlines based personalisation analysis on airport usage and purchasing habits.

(continued)

CUSTOMER PERSONALISATION (continued)

These data permit instant communication of fare discounts by location, presenting only those discounts applicable to the customer's chosen departure location. Another example of personalisation is provided by integration of customers' on-line data by linking this with their mobile phones. The system can then provide passengers with automated event-based information via their phones, such as planes being late and asking whether re-booking an alternative flight is required and also the tracking of delayed bags.

SMART CARDS

One of the earliest examples of smart technology in consumer markets was the introduction of smart debit and credit cards. The card can be read by a smart phone, retailer terminal or a PC. When the connection is established the consumer approves the transaction, which results in a direct billing to his or her account. The advent of the smart card has further assisted the move towards a 'cashless society,' which saves businesses and banks billions each year by no longer having to handle large quantities of cash (Manchester 1997).

Banks are also using the enhanced security of smart cards to help reduce fraud. Government departments and agencies in some countries have introduced smart cards which permit paperless transactions and reduce welfare fraud. Smart cards are also being increasingly utilised as the basis for automatically validating an individual's identity by using the biometric data which are embedded onto the identity card. The most commonly used human characteristic for biometric matching is the fingerprint. Currently there are three different approaches to adding biometric information to smart card systems (Balanoiu 2009):

1. *Template-On-Card (TOC)*, where the identity template is stored on the smart card, but all the biometric procedures are performed outside the smart card by a reader system. This system executes data acquisition, feature extraction and matching, and during this process the reader requests the identifying template from the smart card and matches it with the scanned template.
2. *Match-On-Card (MOC)*, where the original biometric information is stored on the smart card and some of the biometric procedures are performed by a remote reader, such as data acquisition and feature extraction. A new template is constructed for the scanned information; the new template is then sent for validation to the smart card, which performs a matching check with the internally stored template; the final decision is computed by the smart card.

3. *System-On-Card (SOC)*, where the smart card incorporates the original biometric template, the biometric sensor and the biometric processor. All validation procedures are performed on the smart card—namely, data acquisition, feature extraction, template generation and matching.

SMART SENSORS

The advent of smart sensors has significantly enhanced the ability of organisations to monitor events in remote locations, such as products being used by customers or monitoring the performance of equipment at a remote location. Assisting consumers based upon their location has already become a standard component of smart phones, such as Apple's iPhone. Users can use the phone to identify their current location and seek relevant data such as the location of local restaurants or specific retail outlets. Phone users can now download a multiplicity of mobile applications to their computer or their phone, which can assist them while undertaking various daily tasks. Examples of some of the available applications include (Hu et al. 2008):

1. *Map services*, which provide various useful functions when users are driving/walking: directions from the starting location to destination, traditional visual maps and recommended leisure venues and retail outlets.
2. *Travel support*, helping users to locate a desired hotel nearby, purchase tickets and make transportation arrangements.
3. *Decision support*, providing data to help the user reach a decision. One example is price comparison i-applications, which permit consumers to scan the barcode for a product into their smart phone. Users are then provided with information about the price of the same product if purchased from various on-line retailers (Birchall 2010).

Prosser and Schmidt (1999) proposed that the term 'smart element' cannot be applied unless the sensor is able to sense and then actuate an action which permits some form of controlled outcome. An example which meets this specification is a smart sensor used for safety monitoring systems on oil platforms. The sensor measures both platform tilt and sea state and is capable of setting off alarm signals when the sea state exceeds a defined wave amplitude level, while concurrently generating guidance input to the platform's stabilisation system.

The capability of remote sensors in recent years has been advanced by the development of biosensors. These devices incorporate a biological sensing element consisting of a bio-molecule connected to a transducer. The sensor is capable of producing a signal in the presence of a specific chemical or biochemical agent. Biosensors have a number of characteristics, with the most important being their ability to recognise a single compound among numerous other substances within a sample. One example is the glucose oxidase sensor. This has the capability to measure the level of glucose in blood and urine for the diagnosis of diabetes. Other examples are urea and creatinine electrodes, which can be used to control renal functions, the cholesterol electrode used for the detection and prevention of arteriosclerosis and the acetycholine electrode, which can monitor the neurotransmitters related to chemical transmission between nerve synapses.

SMART CLOTHING

Case Aims: To illustrate the emerging opportunities for smart products in the textile and garment industries.

The clothing industry, although somewhat of a late entrant into the world of smart technology, has in recent years begun to exploit the commercial opportunities associated with creating smart textiles. In their review of recent trends in this field, Tang and Stylios (2006) use the term 'smart' to refer to materials that can sense and respond in a controlled or predicted manner to environmental stimuli which have been received in mechanical, thermal, chemical, magnetic or any other form of input. The nature of response can occur in a number of different ways. Visible direct response can include automatic changes in shape, colour, geometry, volume and other visible physical properties. An example of a direct response is to use fabric dyes that are able to change colour with a change in the presence of environmental stimuli such as heat, light, chemical reactions, moisture, pH, pressure and electrical currents. This response can be used to enhance the potential aesthetic appearance of fashion garments or as a detection and response mechanism for garments worn by people in high-risk environment situations. For example, in the medical field, garments are being developed which can detect and warn of the presence of infections, bacteria or viruses. There are also opportunities for garments to change appearance when the wearer exhibits some form of physiological distress. In the fire-fighting sector thermo-chromic dyes have been engineered to change the protective clothing to white under extreme temperatures in order to reflect more heat away from the body.

Indirect smart response may involve changes at a molecular, magnetic or electrical level not apparent to the naked eye, but which are able to trigger controlled reactions or functions. In this latter context the material's response can involve generation of a signal that can be detected by a sensor, analysed and evaluated by a processor, which in turn feeds back to actuators to perform a particular function. The simplest smart electronic garments contain rigid sensors incorporated in the garment structure and connected to other devices through embedded wires. The sensors can continuously measure and monitor various physiological functions such as body temperature, blood pressure, heart beat and perspiration, with the data transmitted by wireless back to a remote central monitoring unit for control and feedback. Early exploitation of this technology is occurring among manufacturers of clothing for sectors such as healthcare, the military and emergency services such as fire-fighting and the rescue services.

(continued)

SMART CLOTHING (continued)

Flexible fabric-based moisture sensors have also been developed. These are multi-layer structures consisting of a top cover layer that receives the moisture, a soaker layer to transmit the moisture to the sensor layer, a sensor layer made of a conductive fibre matrix that allows measurement of the change in resistance, and a final waterproof barrier layer. Although originally developed for incontinence products in the healthcare market and for moisture detection in built environments, the technology is now being used in consumer markets such as high-performance sportswear or protective clothing. Fabric damage can be monitored through plastic optical fibres. These detect broken paths in the fabric and provide information about the degree of damage and location. This technology is applicable for protective clothing, providing information on damage caused by bullet penetration, chemicals, heat and biological agents.

SMARTER OPERATIONS

Although news of smart products make interesting reading, the near-term opportunities to exploit smart technology are more likely to involve enhancement of the management of operational processes inside organisations or to optimise the efficiency of supply chains (Connolly 2007). In terms of managing operational processes, there is now a diversity of sensors in use to help manufacturers create automated systems to identify and rectify production problems. For example, Cognex Corporation has developed a smart imaging sensor which, when used in conjunction with gauging, guidance and inspection tools installed at multiple points on a production line, can inspect for defects, measure parts, monitor colour, and sort and count products. Technology GmbH's Raycon device uses low-level x-rays to inspect for contaminants in packaged goods, checks the weight of individual products and identifies products which are not correctly filled or contain air inclusions. WITT Gas Techniques Ltd. has developed a ceramic sensor which is used to detect leaking carbon dioxide in soft drinks and alcoholic beverages and triggers an alarm.

The objective of optimising the flow of goods through supply chains is greatly assisted by the interchange of information between participant organisations. An early enhancement of supply chains was the use of computer systems to permit the automatic exchange of data between firms. The advent of smart technology has further enhanced automated exploitation of these data in situations such as JIT manufacturing operations where synchronisation of activities is critical through actions such as automatically identifying a potential parts shortage and automatically placing a re-stocking order via the supplier's order-entry system. In the case of organisations which decide agility in meeting rapidly changing needs across a highly diverse customer base is the basis of differentiating the organisation from competition, then implementation of this strategy can usually be achieved only by the creation of smart technology scheduling and logistics systems (Speier et al. 2008).

One of the most critical developments in achieving the goal of enhanced supply chain management has been radio frequency identification (RFID) technology. This is an e-based tagging technology that can be used to provide an electronic identity for any object. By attaching a RFID tag to a product in the initial stages of manufacturing, organisations can then follow the product throughout every stage in the supply chain, even when the actual product is inside in a box or crate. In the case of retail products the RFID tag can be used to support automated pricing of goods at the point-of-purchase by the consumer and provide a way of stopping in-store theft.

RFID tags are microchips that are embedded in the product, pallet or case that store and transmit information about the specific unit. These tags consist of an integrated circuit attached to an antenna. These tags are available in a diversity of forms, with some now as small as a grain of rice. The tags can be passive or active. Passive tags are less expensive because they do not have their own power supply but respond to the radiated energy from a RFID reader to transmit information. Modern supply chain management (SCM) systems are critically reliant upon these tags because they permit the automated planning and coordination of a supply chain from the tracking of unfinished materials and subcomponents, through manufacturing, inventorying, shipment and arrival of the final products at the customer's warehouse. SCM systems enable lower procurement costs, smaller inventories, shorter cycle times, faster response times and a reduction in forecasting errors. The Sara Lee Corporation reported an 18 percent reduction in inventory levels, a 20 percent reduction in replenishment time cycles and 40 percent greater forecast accuracy leading to a 32 percent increase in sales (Attaran 2007). Wal-Mart has concluded that its SCM system led to a $6.7 billion reduction in labour costs as a result of exploiting RFID technology (Attaran 2007).

As the costs of RFID continue to decline this has assisted in accelerating the diverse use of the technology across various sectors. In the agriculture sector increased government regulation about food traceability has resulted in RFID tags being used to meet traceability requirements at a reasonable cost by the farmer attaching a tag to each animal. In the healthcare sector RFID technology is used to track and manage assets, such as medical devices and wheelchairs. Medications and dosages are now being tagged so doctors and nurses can ensure that the right medicine is given in the right amount at the right time to the right patient. These same tags also help drugs manufacturers to reduce drug counterfeiting and theft. Similarly some casinos are now tagging their betting chips to deter counterfeiting, card-counting and other illegal activities. The increasingly important role of RFID tags in defeating criminal acts has in recent years been accelerated in relation to fighting terrorism by the use of these devices to monitor the exact location of objects and packages at any point in their passage through international supply chains.

SMART UTILITIES

Case Aims: To illustrate how smart technology can assist in reducing operating costs.

With the capability to access data from numerous remote locations and to utilise these data sources to undertake complex analysis as the basis for improving decision-making, smart technology is increasingly being utilised to find new solutions to global problems such as optimising energy utilisation, reducing greenhouse gas emissions and environmental monitoring (Anon. 2010d). Scientists from IBM Research Zurich are working on a collaborative project to explore the use of electric vehicles as a storage device for smoothing power fluctuations from renewable resources on the Danish island of Bornholm. Partners in the project include Denmark's largest energy company, DONG Energy, the Technical University of Denmark, Siemens, Eurisco, the Danish Energy Association and Oestkraft. The project is called EDISON, short for Electric Vehicles in a Distributed and Integrated Market Using Sustainable Energy and Open Networks. The small pilot project involves 15 electric vehicles to develop a model for deploying roughly 200,000 wind-powered EVs nationwide by 2020. Denmark already is a leader in wind power, which produces more than 20 percent of the country's energy.

IBM Research China developed "Green Supply Chain," an analytical tool that helps clients optimise their business decisions for lower carbon dioxide emissions, lower cost and improved service levels. The Chinese shipping and logistics firm COSCO used the Green Supply Chain to understand supply chain infrastructure. The system measures carbon dioxide emissions of materials, considers emissions when selecting suppliers and sourcing products, determines emissions associated with manufacturing processes, evaluates the environmental impact of warehousing or storage requirements and analyses emissions for various transportation and distribution modes. COSCO used the data to lower logistics costs by approximately 25 percent and reduced CO_2 emissions by 15 percent. This was achieved while concurrently maintaining service levels for clients and incurring no additional operating costs.

In Boulder, Colorado the local energy company Xcel Energy has installed 20,000 smart meters to track power usage and now offers pricing plans that encourage consumers to shift consumption to off-peak hours. The company has also equipped some homes with a system that informs air conditioners to switch off when demand and therefore the cost of electricity are high. Another utility, NCO, pays industrial customers to shut down non-essential processes during periods of peak demand, thus releasing generating capacity for other users (Anon. 2010a).

Although receiving less publicity than the need to reduce energy consumption, another area which is also becoming a critically constrained resource is water. In the UK Thames Water's most significant problem is the loss of water as a result of leaking pipes. The company is replacing old cast-iron Victorian pipes with plastic ones and installing wireless sensors to provide more rapid understanding of where leaks are occurring. The system has the capability to automatically identify the occurrence of a new leak, schedule a repair crew to visit the site of the problem and automatically text customers about the actions which are being taken.

HEALTHCARE

Commercialisation of scientific discoveries such as sulphonamides and penicillin in the 1930s revolutionised the effectiveness of medical treatments. These breakthroughs also demonstrated the vast sums of money which could be made from inventing new drugs. This led to the emergence of the global pharmaceutical industry at the end of World War II. In the 1950s and 60s, the focus of these drug companies was to discover new anti-bacterial drugs (or antibiotics) that would treat conditions that did not respond to penicillin. In their ongoing search for new drugs which would confer a virtual global monopoly for the treatment of a specific illness, the European and American companies invested vast sums into R&D such that by the late 1980s, annual industry research expenditure was estimated to be in the region of $30–$40 billion. The reward for such expenditure was a whole range of new drugs being introduced, such as serotonin inhibitors to treat depression, beta blockers for heart conditions and blood pressure reduction medications.

The major drug companies claimed the high prices being charged for these drugs were necessary in order to recover their huge investment in research. Meanwhile as the global drugs companies prospered by developing new drugs, surgeons were developing ever more sophisticated techniques which both increased the costs of surgery (e.g. kidney transplants) and created new market opportunities for the pharmaceutical industry (e.g. the need for immune response suppressant drugs for use after organ transplants) (Benner 2004).

The market reality behind the drug industry's success is its sales could be supported only by developed nation economies' employers funding health insurance for employees and the ability of governments to cover a large proportion of their nation's healthcare costs through the creation of the welfare state. Hence over 90 percent of the sales of branded pharmaceutical goods are restricted to the world's top 20 economically successful democracies. The growing inabilities of developed economy nations to fund their welfare programmes and of private sector employers to cover ever-increasing medical insurance premiums have caused governments and the insurance industry to question the ongoing affordability of buying ever more expensive new drugs from the major pharmaceutical firms (Marmor 1998). In America, for example, the annual spend on prescription drugs is in the region of $4,000 per capita and about $2,000 capita in Europe. The huge cost of these drugs bills is why, in both Europe and North America, politicians are being forced to consider legislative actions in order to stop what seems to be an ever-increasing upward trend in the proportion of total healthcare budgets being spent on the purchase of drugs and medicines.

Only to limited degree can governments reduce their expenditure on drugs by refusing to authorise the use of new, more expensive treatments and demanding that doctors prescribe generic drugs, which are older formulations no longer controlled under patent by the originating pharmaceutical company. The importance of this latter solution is evidenced by the fact that by the year 2000, the size of global generic drug market was already in excess of $30 billion. To date the country which probably has most benefitted in economic terms by the trend towards increased use of generics is India (Malhotra and Lofgren 2004). Savings from such actions, however, will in no way close the increasing gap between demand for healthcare services and the public sector funds available to deliver these services. To a certain degree this gap will be reduced as governments impose means testing when determining what services are to be made available either free or at a subsidised price. There will also probably be an expectation by some governments that a larger proportion of the general public will be required to purchase private medical insurance. Nevertheless such moves are at best only a partial solution. Governments will need to find new solutions to overcome this huge fiscal problem, and where these prove unavailable or non-viable, then very difficult choices will have to be made concerning budget cuts in this or in other areas of public sector spending.

Smart technology appears to offer the most viable solution for significantly reducing future healthcare costs. One of the most critical aspects of enhancing healthcare is to utilise the capability of smart technology to manage and exploit the data which are generated during the diagnosis and treatment of patients. Known as 'm-health,' this activity has been greatly enhanced by the advent of mobile technology. It can be expected that effectiveness of m-health will continue to be enhanced as information and telecommunication infrastructures converge to create new mobile health systems. This is because mobile technology can offer benefits in the areas of availability, miniaturisation, speed and communication bandwidth (Simpson 2003).

By utilising wireless-based computing, healthcare providers can access, receive, update and transmit critical patient and treatment information. Computer-based documentation of care will assist in eliminating the human error that can take place in translation in the recording and storage of patient records. Additional benefits will accrue from the use of picture archiving and communication systems (PACS), which permit the computerisation of radiologic film. Users can acquire, store, transmit and display images digitally, which permits, for example, linking the intensive care units in hospitals with the radiology department and medical staff based in other locations.

Computerised provider order entry (CPOE) systems are capable of identifying and thereby preventing potential medical errors at the earliest possible point in the treatment process. The healthcare provider enters proposed action into the computer and the automated system checks for possible causes of error, such as incorrect dosages, wrong drug, drug-allergy interactions and drug-to-drug or drug-food allergies. This technology removes the guesswork from medication administration, reduces staff stress levels, improves clinical effectiveness and enhances productivity by allowing staff to focus on patient care rather than paperwork.

An even greater opportunity for the use of m-health to enhance the effectiveness of healthcare provision is the use of remote telemetry to monitor patients. For example, in the case of patients undergoing treatment for heart conditions, a computer-based system can provide automatic monitoring of major arrhythmia detection though continuous observation and analysis of rhythms. Thus when a patient experiences a potentially life-threatening rhythm change, the monitoring unit concurrently places a phone call and sends a nurse to the patient location (Capuano et al. 1995).

Caring for patients in the United States with chronic illnesses costs in excess of $1 trillion. One way of reducing these costs is to use smart technology to monitor patients in their own homes instead of admitting these individuals to hospital. By the use of remote telemetry, healthcare providers can access a patient's health status, provide patients with appropriate preventive interventions and, by avoiding the need for hospitalisation, improve the patient's quality of care and quality of life. Any remote monitoring system must start with the biomedical devices that generate the person's biomedical data. In commenting upon remote healthcare monitoring systems requirements, researchers at IBM have proposed certain key attributes (Blount et al. 2007):

1. *Patient usability*, because the system should be easy for patients to use. It should require minimal training and minimal maintenance. Where possible the system should be portable so that patients can take the system anywhere they go.
2. *Scalability*, because any system must be able to support large numbers of patients and their associated healthcare providers.
3. *Reliability*, because the system should collect and store patient data even in the face of network failures. The system should store data in downtime situations for later transmission to a central system.
4. *Affordability*, in order that the cost per patient can be covered by existing sources of healthcare funding.

In the past healthcare treatments of conditions such as heart disease relied on early and often continual diagnosis to effectively treat the heart. Recent developments in the miniaturisation of sensors are beginning to now render such approaches obsolete. Sensors have been developed which the patient can wear or have implanted into his or her body which monitor variables such as blood pressure or provide electrocardiograms (ECG). Once these tiny instruments register an irregularity, they automatically contact a diagnosis centre, where doctors are on call on a 24/7 basis (Anon. 2008).

Intelligent implants are a critical aspect of future medical treatments. For instance, the risk when fitting a new hip joint is that the joint could be rejected by the surrounding tissue. Intelligent implants measure how the patient's immune system is reacting and transmit the data via radio signal to the doctor in order that the problem can be localised and treated. Implanted sensors can be also be used to monitor bone healing after prosthetic implant surgery. For example, after a knee or hip replacement the patient is physically restricted in order to provide a stable environment for the bones to grow around the implant. Strain gauges are fixed to the bone to measure the elongation and send data wirelessly to an external monitoring system, permitting the doctor to monitor the progress of the healing process and provide early warning of post-surgical problems that might arise (Connolly 2009).

New technologies are allowing organs and bodily functions to be permanently monitored by doctors when the patient has returned home after surgery. Bio-analytical microsystems can be used to determine blood sugar concentration and provide guidance to the patient over self-treating conditions such as diabetes. An example of current developments in the field of sensor microsystems is provided by the Boston Retinal Implant Project, which aims to restore vision to people affected by degenerative retinal disease. The project is developing an implantable microelectronic prosthetic for patients with diseases such as retinitis pigmentosa and age-related macular degeneration. These diseases cause a loss of rods and cones, the natural photoreceptors, but have little effect on the nerve cells that connect the eye to the brain. The research team has developed a flexible microelectronic device that contains a 30,000-transistor stimulator chip to deliver electrical pulses to the nerves in the retina. The device receives data via wireless from a video camera mounted on the side of a pair of spectacles. It is hoped that over time ongoing advances in technology will permit these signals to be translated into visual images by the brain, thereby restoring the patient's sight.

References

21st Century Innovation Working Group of the Council on Competitiveness (2004), Innovation, The New Reality for National Prosperity, Council on Competitiveness, Washington, DC.

Adams, G. L and Lamont, B. T. (2003), Knowledge management systems and developing sustainable competitive advantage, *Journal of Knowledge Management*, Vol. 7, No. 2, pp. 142–151.

Adams, M. (2008), Management 2.0: Managing the growing intangible side of your business, *Business Strategy Series*, Vol. 9, No. 4, pp. 190–200.

Adner, R. (2002), When are technologies disruptive: A demand-based view of the emergence of competition, *Strategic Management Journal*, Vol. 23, No. 8, pp. 667–688.

Allee, V. (2002), *The Future of Knowledge: Increasing Prosperity through Value Networks*, Butterworth-Heinemann, New York.

Allee, V. (2008), Value network analysis and value conversion of tangible and intangible assets, *Journal of Intellectual Capital*, Vol. 9, No. 1, pp. 5–24.

Allenby, B. R. (2000), Implementing industrial ecology: The AT&T matrix system, *Interfaces*, Vol. 30, No. 3, pp. 42–54.

Allison, C., Chell, E. and Hayes, J. (2000), Intuition and entrepreneurial behaviour, *European Journal of Work and Organisational Psychology*, Vol. 9, pp. 31–42.

Amabile, T. M., Conti, R., Coon, H., Lazenby, J. and Herron, M. (1996), Assessing the work environment for creativity, *Academy of Management Journal*, Vol. 39, No. 5, pp. 1154–1185.

Amburgey, T. L. and Dacin, T. (1994), As the left foot follows the right: The dynamics of strategic planning, *Academy of Management Journal*, Vol. 37, No. 6, pp. 1427–1453.

Anderson, M. and Sohal, A. (1999), A study of the relationship between quality management practices and performance in small business, *The International Journal of Quality & Reliability Management*, Vol. 16, No. 9, pp. 859–872.

Andrews, P. A. and Hahn, J. (1998), Transforming supply chains into value Webs, *Strategy & Leadership*, Vol. 26, No. 3, pp. 6–11.

Anon. (1993), IBM: The axeman, *The Economist,* London, July 31, pp. 59–60.

Anon. (1998), The rebirth of IBM: Blue is the colour, *The Economist,* London, June 6, pp. 65–68.

Anon. (2007), Partnering for survival in pharmaceuticals: The threats facing the industry and the moves to overcome them, *Strategic Direction*, Vol. 23, No. 10, pp. 12–20.

Anon. (2007a), The bank that failed—Britain's bank run, *The Economist*, London, September 22, p. 1.

Anon. (2008), German medical implant technology makes patients more independent, *German Business Review*, January, p. 5.

Anon. (2009a), Fiscal performance and challenges, *OECD Journal on Budgeting*, Paris, Vol. 9, No. 1, pp. 23–43.

Anon. (2009b), Shares in RBS collapse as it faces huge loss, *The Yorkshire Post*, Leeds, January 19, 2009, p. 1.

Anon. (2009c), Friends for life, *The Economist*, London, August 8, pp. 55–56.

Anon. (2009d), The rights of shareholders and the wrongs done to clients, *The Economist*, London, August 8, p. 62.

Anon. (2009e), Losing its magic touch, *The Economist*, London, March 21, pp. 80–82.

Anon. (2009f), Fabless and fearless, *The Economist*, London, August 8, p. 58.

Anon. (2010a), A giant awakes, *The Economist*, London, September 11, pp. 69–71.

Anon. (2010b), Chemistry goes green, *The Economist*, London, July 3, p. 66.

Anon. (2010c), It's a smart world, *The Economist*, London, November 6, pp. 3–24.

Anon. (2010d), Taking research into the world, accessed via www.research.ibm.com.

Ansoff, H. I. (1991), Critique of Henry Mintzberg's 'Design School': Reconsidering the basic premises of strategic management, *Strategic Management Journal*, Vol. 12, No. 6, pp. 449–461.

Appelbaum, S. H., Gandell, J., Yortis, H., Proper, S. and Jobin, F. (2000a), Anatomy of a merger: Behavior of organizational factors and processes throughout the pre- during- post-stages (part 1), *Management Decision*, Vol. 38, No. 9, pp. 649–661.

Appelbaum, S. H., Gandell, J., Yortis, H., Proper, S. and Jobin, F. (2000b), Anatomy of a merger: Behavior of organizational factors and processes throughout the pre- during- post-stages (part 2), *Management Decision*, Vol. 38, No. 10, pp. 674–684.

Aris, S. S., Raghunathan, T. S. and Kunnather, A. (2000), Factors affecting the adoption of advanced manufacturing technology in small firms, S.A.M., *Advanced Management Journal*, Vol. 65, No. 2, pp. 14–23.

Athey, S. and Schmutzler, A. (1995), Product and process flexibility in an innovative environment, *The Rand Journal of Economics*, Vol. 26, No. 4, pp. 557–574.

Atkinson, A. A., Waterhouse, J. H. and Wells, R. B. (1997), A stakeholder approach to strategic performance measurement, *Sloan Management Review*, Vol. 38, No. 3, pp. 25–37.

Attaran, M. (2007), RFID: An enabler of supply chain operations, *Supply Chain Management*, Vol. 12, No. 4, pp. 249–257.

Augier, M. and Teece, D. J. (2007), Dynamic capabilities and multinational enterprise: Penrosean insights and omissions, *Management International Review*, Vol. 47, No. 2, pp. 175–192.

Azofra, S. S., Olalla, M. G. and Olmo, B. T. (2008), Size, target performance and European bank mergers and acquisitions, *American Journal of Business*, Vol. 23, No. 1, pp. 53–63.

Bacot, M. L., Hartman, S. J. and Lundberg, O. H. (1992), Adaptive strategies and survival in an environment dominated by economic decline, *Journal of Applied Business Research*, Vol. 9, No. 1, pp. 34–44.

Baker, H. E. and Feldman, D. C. (1991), Linking organizational socialization tactics with corporate human resources management strategies, *Human Resources Management Review*, Vol. 1, No. 3, pp. 193–202.

Balanoiu, P. (2009), Enhancing privacy for biometric identification cards, *Informatica Economica*, Vol. 13, No. 1, pp. 100–107.

Barney, J. (2001), Is the resource-based 'view' a useful perspective for strategic management research? *Academy of Management Review*, Vol. 26, No. 1, pp. 41–57.

Barney, J. B. (1991), Firm resources and sustained competitive advantage, *Journal of Management*, Vol. 17, pp. 99–120.

Bate, J.D. and Johnston, R.E. (2005), Strategic frontiers: the starting point for innovative growth, *Strategy & Leadership*, Vol. 33, No. 1, pp. 12–19.

Batenburg, R. and Rutten, R. (2003), Managing innovation in regional supply networks: A Dutch case of knowledge industry clustering, *Supply Chain Management*, Vol. 8, No. 3/4, pp. 263–270.

Batra, J. (2010), Knowledge management: Emerging practices in IT industry in NCR, *IUP Journal of Knowledge Management*, Vol. 8, No. 1/2, pp. 57–67.

Beaver, G. (2007), The strategy payoff for smaller enterprises, *The Journal of Business Strategy*, Vol. 28, No. 1, pp. 11–20.

Beaver, G. (2007), The strategy payoff for smaller enterprises, *The Journal of Business Strategy*, Vol. 28, No. 1, pp. 11–20.

Bellairs, J. (2010), Open innovation gaining momentum in the food industry, *Cereal Foods World*, January–February 2010, pp. 4–5.

Benner, M. (2004), Catching up in pharmaceuticals: Government policies and the rise of genomics, *Australian Health Review*, Vol. 28, No. 2, pp. 161–171.

Bergfors, M. A. and Larsson, A. (2009), Product and process innovation in process industry: A new perspective on development, *Journal of Strategy and Management*, Vol. 2, No. 3, pp. 261–276.

Berry, M. (1998), Strategic planning in small, high-tech companies, *Long Range Planning*, Vol. 31, pp. 455–456.

Besanko, D., Dranove, D. and Shanley, M. (2000), *Economics of Strategy* (2nd ed.), John Wiley and Sons, London.

Bettis, R. A., Bradley, S. P. and Hamel, G. (1992), Outsourcing and industrial decline, *The Executive*, Vol. 6, No. 1, pp. 7–23.

Bevens, N. (2007), No bubbly yet—but victory appears certain, *The Scotsman*, Edinburgh, October 6, p. 7.

Bhatia, G. K., Gay, R. C. and Honey, W. S. (2003), Windows into the future: How lessons from Hollywood will shape the music industry, *Journal of Interactive Marketing*, Vol. 17, No. 2, pp. 70–80.

Bhatia, G. K., Gay, R. C. and Honey, W. S. (2003), Windows into the future: How lessons from Hollywood will shape the music industry, *Journal of Interactive Marketing*, Vol. 17, No. 2, pp. 70–80.

Biem, A. and Caswel, N. (2008), A value network model for strategic analysis, Proceedings of the 41st Hawaii International Conference on System Sciences, Honolulu, Hawaii, pp. 1–7.

Biggadike, E. R. (1979), *Corporate Diversification: Entry, Strategy and Performance*, Harvard University Press, Cambridge, MA.

Birchall, J. (2010), Amazon keeps shops in check with app, *Financial Times*, London, November 23, p. 24.

Birchall, J. (2010), P&G woos more brand tie-ups, *Financial Times*, London, November 2, p. 22.

Bird, B. J. (1988), Implementing entrepreneurial ideas: The case for intention, Academy of Management, *The Academy of Management Review*, Vol. 13, No. 3, pp. 442–453.

Birkinshaw, J. and Goddard, J. (2009), What is your management model? *Sloan Management Review*, Winter, pp. 81–90.

Birkinshaw, J. and Goddard, J. (2009), What is your management model? *Sloan Management Review*, Vol. 49, No. 1, pp. 81–90.

Birkinshaw, J., Bouquet, C. and Barsoux, J. L. (2011), The 5 myths of innovation, *Sloan Management Review*, Vol. 52, No. 2, pp. 40–53.

Birley, S. (1985), The role of networks in the entrepreneurial process, *Journal of Business Venturing*, Vol. 1, No. 1, pp. 107–117.

Blount, M., Batra, V. A., Capella, A. N. and Ebling, M. R. (2007), Remote health-care monitoring using Personal Care Connect, *IBM Systems Journal*, Vol. 46, No. 1, pp. 95–113.

Boal, K. and Hooijberg, R. (2000), Strategic leadership research: Moving on, *Leadership Quarterly*, Vol. 11, No. 4, pp. 515–549.

Bogataj, L. K. (2009), Climate change and future adaption, *Economic and Business Review for Central and South—Eastern Europe*, Vol. 11, No. 1, pp. 9–27.

Boons, F. and Berends, M. (2001), Stretching the boundary: The possibilities of flexibility as an organizational process, *Business Strategy and the Environment*, Vol. 10, No. 2, pp. 115–124.

Bose, R and Sugumaran, V. (2003), Application of knowledge management technology in customer relationship management, *Knowledge and Process Management*, Vol. 10, No. 1, pp. 3 -11.

Bower, J. L. (1970), *Managing the Resource Allocation Process: A Study of Corporate Planning and Investment*, Harvard Business School Press, Boston.

Boyer, K. K. (1998), Longitudinal linkages between intended and realized operations strategies, *International Journal of Operations & Production Management*, Vol. 18, No. 4, pp. 356–373.

Boyne, G. A. (2006), Strategies for public sector turnaround: Lessons from the private sector? *Administration & Society*, Vol. 38, No. 3, pp. 365–388.

Bramante, J., Frank, R. and Dolan, J. (2010), IBM 2000 to 2010: Continuously

Bresnahan, T., Gambardella, A. and Saxenian, A. (2001), Old economy inputs for new economy outcomes: Cluster formation in the new Silicon Valleys, *Industrial and Corporate Change*. Vol. 10, No. 4, pp. 835–844.

Bretnotz, D. and Murphree, N. (2011), *Run of the Red Queen*, Yale University Press, New Haven.

Brown, R. (1992), Managing the S curves of innovation, *The Journal of Business & Industrial Marketing*, Vol. 7, No. 3, pp. 41–52.

Brown-Collier, E. K. and Collier, B. E. (1995), What Keynes really said about deficit spending, *Journal of Post Keynesian Economics*, Vol. 17, No. 3, pp. 341–356.

Bryson, J. M. (1995), *Strategic Planning for Public and Non-Profit Organizations*, Jossey-Bass, San Francisco.

Bryson, J. M., Ackermann, F. and Eden, C. (2007), Putting the resource-based view of strategy and distinctive competencies to work in public organizations, *Public Administration Review*, Vol. 67, No. 4, pp. 702–717.

Bryson, J.M. (1981), A perspective on planning and crises in the public sector, *Strategic Management Journal*, Vol. 2, No. 2, pp. 181–198.

Bucknall, K. B. (1997), Why China has done better than Russia since 1989, *International Journal of Social Economics*, Vol. 24, Nos. 7/8/9, pp. 1023–1037.

Bughin, J., Chui, M. and Manyika, J. (2010), Clouds, big data, and smart assets: Ten tech-enabled business trends to watch, *McKinsey Quarterly*, August, pp. 1–11.

Bunning, C. R. (1992), Effective strategic planning in the public sector: Some learnings, *The International Journal of Public Sector Management*, Vol. 5, No. 4, pp. 54–60.

Burke, R. J. (2006), Why leaders fail: Exploring the darkside, *International Journal of Manpower*, Vol. 27, No. 1, pp. 91–100.

Bush, R. J. and Sinclair, S. A. (1992), Changing strategies in mature industries: A case study, *The Journal of Business & Industrial Marketing*, Vol. 7, No. 4, pp. 63–73.

Camison, C. and Villar-Lopez, A. (2010), Knowledge management by external links effect of SMEs' international experience on foreign intensity and economic performance, *Journal of Small Business Management,* Vol. 48, No. 2, pp. 116–142.

Capuano, T. A., Molchany, C., Peters, C., Potylycki, M. J. and Robinson, J. (1995), Remote telemetry, *Nursing Management,* Vol. 26, No. 7, pp. 26–31.

Carpinetti, L. C. R. and De Melo, A. (2002), What to benchmark? *Benchmarking,* Vol. 9, No. 3, pp. 244–255.

Cartwright, S. and Cooper, C. L. (1993), The psychological impact of mergers and acquisitions on the individual: A study of building society mergers, *Human Relations,* Vol. 46, No. 3, pp. 13–24.

Chaffee, E. (1985), Three models of strategy, Academy of Management Review, Vol. 10, No. 1, pp. 88–98.

Chaganti, R. and Chaganti, R. (1983), A profile of profitable and not-so-profitable small businesses, *Journal of Small Business Management,* Vol. 21, No. 3, pp. 43–51.

Chandler, A. (1962), *Strategy and Structure: Chapters in the History of American Industrial Enterprise,* MIT Press, Cambridge, MA.

Chandler, A. D. (1977), *The Visible Hand: The Managerial Revolution in American Business,* Belknap Press, Cambridge, MA.

Channel, C. S. (2004), The twisted path of the music file-sharing litigation: The cases that have shaped the litigation and the RIAA's litigation strategy, *Intellectual Property & Technology Law Journal,* Vol. 16, No. 10, pp. 6–12.

Channel, C. S. (2004), The twisted path of the music file-sharing litigation: The cases that have shaped the litigation and the RIAA's litigation strategy, *Intellectual Property & Technology Law Journal,* Vol. 16, No. 10, pp. 6–12.

Chaston, I. (2000), *Entrepreneurial Marketing,* MacMillan, London.

Chaston, I. (2004), *Knowledge-Based Marketing,* Sage, London.

Chaston, I. (2009a), *Boomer Marketing,* Routledge, London.

Chaston, I. (2009b), Entrepreneurship and Small Firms, Sage, London.

Chaston, I. (2011), *Public Sector Management: Mission Impossible?* Sage, London.

Chaston, I. and Mangles, T. (1997), Competencies for growth in SME sector manufacturing firms, *Journal of Small Business Management,* Vol. 35, No. 1, pp. 23–35.

Chaston, I., Badger B. and Sadler-Smith, E. (1999), Organisational learning systems in relation to innovation management in small UK manufacturing firms, *Journal of New Product Management and Innovation,* Vol. 1, No. 1, pp. 32–43.

Chen, X., Yamauchi, K., Kato, K., Nishimura, A. and Ito, K. (2006), Using the balanced scorecard to measure Chinese and Japanese hospital performance, *International Journal of Health Care Quality Assurance,* Vol. 19, No. 4, pp. 339- 348.

Chesbrough, H. W. (2003), The era of open innovation, *Sloan Management Review,* Vol. 44, No. 3, pp. 35–41.

Chesbrough, H. W. (2007), Why companies should have open business models, *Sloan Management Review,* Vol. 48, No. 2, pp. 22–28.

Child, J. and McGrath, R. G. (2001), Organizations unfettered: Organizational form in an information-intensive economy, *Academy of Management Journal,* Vol. 44, pp. 1135–1148.

Christensen, C. M. (1997), *The Innovator's Dilemma,* Harvard Business School Press, Boston, MA.

Christensen, C. M. (2001), The past and future of competitive advantage, *Sloan Management Review,* Vol. 42, No. 2, pp. 105–109.

Christensen, C. M. (2001), The past and future of competitive advantage, *Sloan Management Review,* Vol. 42, No. 2, pp. 105–109.

Christensen, J. F. (2002), Corporate strategy and the management of innovation and technology, *Industrial and Corporate Change,* Vol. 11, No. 2, pp. 263–288.

Christensen, J.F., Olesen, M.H. & Kjaer, S.J. (2005), 'The industrial dynamics of open innovation—evidence from the transformation of consumer electronics, *Research Policy*, 34(10), 1533–49.

Christensen, K. S. (2006), Losing innovativeness: The challenge of being acquired, *Management Decision*, Vol. 44, No. 9, pp. 1161–1182.

Cirman, A., Domadenik, P., Koman, M. and Redek, T. (2009), *The Kyoto Protocol in a global perspective, Economic and Business Review for Central and South—Eastern Europe*, Vol. 11, No. 1, pp. 29–54.

Clark, D. N. and Scott, D. N. (2000), Core competence strategy making and scientific research: The case of HortResearch, *Strategic Change*, Vol. 9, No. 8, pp. 495–503.

Coltman, T. (2007), Can superior CRM capabilities improve performance in banking, *Journal of Financial Services Marketing*, Vol. 12, No. 2, pp. 102–114.

Connell, C. M. (2007), Pursuing three horizons of growth—three cases: Bombardier (Canada), Disney (US) and Hutchison Whampoa (China), *Business Strategy Series*, Vol. 8, No. 1, pp. 14–25.

Connelly, B. (2008), Origins of the credit crisis, *The International Economy*, Vol. 22, No. 4, pp. 44–48.

Connolly, C. (2007), Sensor trends in processing and packaging of foods and pharmaceuticals, *Sensor Review*, Vol. 27, No. 2, pp. 103.

Connolly, C. (2009), Miniature electronic modules for advanced health care, *Sensor Review*, Vol. 29, No. 2, pp. 98–103.

Copeland, M. V. (2008), Tesla's wild ride, *Fortune*, July, pp. 13–17.

Coram, R. and Burnes, B. (2001), Managing organisational change in the public sector—lessons from the privatisation of the Property Service Agency, *The International Journal of Public Sector Management*, Vol. 14, No. 2, pp. 94–113.

Covin, J. G. and Slevin, D. P. (1989), Strategic management of small firms in hostile and benign environments, *Strategic Management Journal*, Vol. 10, pp. 75–87.

Covin, J. G., Green, K. M. and Slevin, D. P. (2006), Strategic process effects on the entrepreneurial orientation-sales growth rate relationship, *Entrepreneurship Theory & Practice*, January, pp. 57–81.

Cox, A. (1999), Power, value and supply chain management, *Supply Chain Management*, Vol. 4, No. 4, pp. 167–174.

Cox, A. (2001), Managing with power: Strategies for improving value appropriation from supply relationships, *Journal of Supply Chain Management*, Vol. 37, No. 2, pp. 42–51.

Cravens, D. W., Piercy, N. F. and Low, G. S. (2002), The innovation challenges of proactive cannibalisation and discontinuous technology, *European Business Review*, Vol. 14, No. 4, pp. 257–268.

Cunha, P. M. and Da Cunha, J. V. (2006), Towards a complexity theory of strategy, *Management Decision*, Vol. 44, No. 7, pp. 839–850.

Czaplewski, A. J., Ferguson, J. M. and Milliman, J. F. (2001), Southwest Airlines: How internal marketing pilots success, *Marketing Management*, Vol. 10, No. 3, pp. 14–17.

Dainty, P. and Kakabadse, A. (1992), Brittle, blocked, blended and blind: Top team characteristics that lead to business success or failure, *Journal of Managerial Psychology*, Vol. 7, No. 2, pp. 4–18.

Dalton, D. R. and Kesner, I. F. (1985), Organizational growth: Big is beautiful, *Journal of Business Strategy*, Vol. 6, No. 1, pp. 38–48.

Dawes, P. L. (2003), A model of the effects of technical consultants on organizational learning in high-technology purchase situations, *The Journal of High Technology Management Research*, Vol. 14, No. 1, pp. 1–20.

Day, G. (2006), Aligning the organization with the market, *Sloan Management Review*, Vol. 48, No. 1, pp. 41–49.

Day, G. S. and Schoemaker, P. J. H. (2005), Scanning the periphery, *Harvard Business Review,* October/November, pp. 135–146.

Dean, J., Holmes, S. and Smith, S. (1997), Understanding business networks: Evidence from the manufacturing and service sectors in Australia, *Journal of Small Business Management,* Vol. 35, No. 1, pp. 78- 85.

Dean, T., Brown, L. and Bamford, C. E. (1998), Differences in large and small firm responses to environmental context: Strategic implications from a comparative analysis of business formations, *Strategic Management Journal,* Vol. 19, No. 1, pp. 709–723.

Deans, G. and Larsen, M. (2008), Growth for growth's sake: A recipe for a potential disaster, *Ivey Business Journal Online,* Vol. 72, No. 5, pp. 17–32.

Demuth, L. G. (2008), A viewpoint on disruptive innovation, *Journal of the American Academy of Business,* Vol. 13, No. 1, pp. 86–94.

Denhardt, R., Jennings, E. T. and Wildavsky, A. (1989), Image and integrity in the public service, *Public Administration Review,* Vol. 49, No. 1, pp. 74–79.

Denton, D. K. (2006), Performance improvement, *International Society for Performance Improvement,* Vol. 45, No. 3, pp. 33–37.

Dibrell, M. C., Down, J. and Bull, L. (2007), Dynamic strategic planning: Achieving strategic flexibility through formalization, *Journal of Business and Management,* Vol. 13, No. 1, pp. 21–35.

Dirsmith, M. W. and Jablonsky, S. F. (1979), Zero-based budgeting as a management technique and political strategy, *The Academy of Management Review,* Vol. 4, No. 4, pp. 75–84.

Dobson, P. (2005), Exploiting buyer power: Lessons from the British grocery trade, *Antitrust Law Journal,* Vol. 72, No. 2, pp. 529–542.

Döös, M., Wilhelmson, L., Backlund, T. and Dixon, N. (2005), Functioning at the edge of knowledge: A study of learning processes in new product development, *Journal of Workplace Learning,* Vol. 17, No. 7/8, pp. 481–493.

Dotlitch, D. L. and Cairo, P. (2003), *Why CEOs Fail: The 11 Behaviors That Can Derail Your Climb to the Top and How to Manage Them,* Jossey-Bass, San Francisco.

Droege, S. B. and Dong, L. C. (2008), Strategic entrepreneurship: Imitation versus substitution, *Journal of Small Business Strategy,* Vol. 19, No. 1, pp. 51–62.

Drucker, P. F. (1985), *Innovation & Entrepreneurship: Practice and Principles,* Harper & Row, New York.

Drucker, P.F. (1993), The theory of business, *Harvard Business Review,* September/October, pp. 95–104.

Du Gray, P. (2004), Against enterprise (but not against enterprise, for that would make no sense), *Organization,* Vol. 11, No. 1, pp. 37–57.

Dulewicz, V. and Higgs, M. (2003), Leadership at the top: The need for emotional intelligence in organisations, *International Journal of Organizational Analysis,* Vol. 11, No. 3, pp. 193–210.

Dutton, J. E. and Jackson, S. E. (1987), Categorizing strategic issues: Links to organizational action, *The Academy of Management Review,* Vol. 12, No. 1, pp. 76–87.

Dwyer, R. J. (1998), Utilizing simple rules to enhance performance measurement competitiveness and accountability growth, *Business Strategy Series,* Vol. 8, No. 1, pp. 72–77.

Dyer, J. H. and Singh, H. (1998), The relational view: Cooperative strategy and sources of inter-organizational competitive advantage, *The Academy of Management Review,* Vol. 23, No. 4, pp. 660–679.

Edmondson, H. E. and Wheelwright, S. C. (1989), Outstanding manufacturing in the coming decade, *California Management Review,* Vol. 31, No. 4, pp. 70–81.

Edmondson, V. C. (2008), A preliminary review of competitive reactions in the hip-hop music industry: Black American entrepreneurs in a new industry, *Management Research News*, Vol. 31, No. 9, pp. 637–649.

Edmondson, V.C. (2008), A preliminary review of competitive reactions in the hip-hop music industry; Black American entrepreneurs in a new industry, *Management Research News*, Vol. 31, No. 9, pp. 637–646.

Eisenhardt, K. M. (2002), Has strategy changed? *Sloan Management Review*, Winter, pp. 88–91.

Eisenhardt, K. M. and Martin, J. A. (2000), Dynamic capabilities: What are they? *Strategic Management Journal*, Vol. 21, pp. 1105–1121.

Elfring, T. and Hulsink, W. (2003), Networks in entrepreneurship: The case of high-technology firms, *Small Business Economics*, Vol. 21, No. 4, pp. 409–422.

Elmquist, M., Fredberg, T. and Ollila, S. (2009), Exploring the field of open innovation, *European Journal of Innovation Management*, Vol. 12, No. 3, pp. 326–345.

Elmuti, D. and Kathawala, Y. (2001), An overview of strategic alliances, *Management Decision*, Vol. 39, No. 3, pp. 205–217.

Erikson, T. F., Magee, J. F., Roussel, P. A. and Saad, K. N. (1990), Managing technology as a business strategy, *Sloan Management Review*, Vol. 73, No. 3, pp. 73–302.

Ettlie, J. E. and Reza, E. M. (1992), Organizational integration and process innovation, *Academy of Management Journal*, Vol. 35, No. 4, pp. 795–827.

Ettlie, J. E. and Reza, M. (1992), Organisational integration and process innovation, *Academy of Management Journal*, Vol. 35, No. 4, pp. 795–827.

Ettlie, J. E., Bridges, W. P. and O'Keefe, R. D. (1984), Organization strategy and structural differences between radical versus incremental innovation, *Management Science*, Vol. 30, No. 6, pp. 682–695.

Evans-Pritchard, A. (2010), Vodafone joins the queue of firms to leave China, *The Daily Telegraph*, London, August 30, p. B2.

Ewaldz, E. B. (1990), Managing in an economic downturn, *Small Business Reports*, Vol. 15, No. 12, pp. 20–25.

Fan, Y. and Ku, E. (2010), Customer focus, service process fit and customer relationship management profitability: The effect of knowledge sharing, *The Service Industries Journal* Vol. 30, No. 2, pp. 203–223.

Fang, E. (2008), Customer participation and the trade-off between new product innovativeness and speed to market, *Journal of Marketing*, Vol. 72, pp. 90–104.

Fenby, J. (2008), *The Penguin Modern History of China: The Fall And Rise of a Great Power 1850–2008*, Penguin, London.

Ferguson, G., Mathur, S. and Shah, B. (2005), Evolving from information to insight, *Sloan Management Review*, Vol. 46, No. 2, pp. 51–62.

Ferlie, E. (2007), Complex organisations and contemporary public sector organisations, *International Public Management Journal*, Vol. 10, No. 2, pp. 153–165.

Fernández-Aráoz, C. (2005), Getting the right people at the top, *Sloan Management Review*, Vol. 46, No. 4, pp. 67–72.

Finkelstein, S. (2001), Internet startups: So why can't they win? *The Journal of Business Strategy*, Vol. 22, No. 4, pp. 16–21.

Finkelstein, S. (2005), When bad things happen to good companies: Strategy failure and flawed executives, *The Journal of Business Strategy*, Vol. 26, No. 2, pp. 19–29.

Fisher, M. L. (1997), What is the right supply chain for you, *Harvard Business Review*, March–April, pp. 105–116.

Flood, R. L. and Romm, N. R. A. (1996), Plurality revisited: Diversity management and triple loop learning, *Systems Practice*, Vol. 9, No. 6, pp. 587–603.

Ford, D., Gadde, L., Hakansson, H. and Snehota, I. (2003), *Managing Business Relationships,* 2nd ed., Wiley, Chichester.

Fox, J., Gann, R., Shur, A., Von Glahn, L. and Zaas, B. (1998), Process uncertainty: A new dimension for new product development, *Engineering Management Journal,* Vol. 10, No. 3, pp. 19–27.

Freel, M. (2006), Patterns of technological innovation in knowledge intensive business services, *Industry and Innovation,* Vol. 13, No. 3, pp. 335–359.

Freeman, T. (2002), Using performance indicators to improve health care quality in the public sector: A review of the literature, *Health Services Management Research,* Vol. 15, No. 2, pp. 126–138.

Frooman, J. (1999), Stakeholder influence strategies, *The Academy of Management Review,* Vol. 24, No. 2, pp. 191–205.

Fuchs, P. H., Mifflin, K. E., Miller, D. and Whitney, J. O. (2000), Strategic integration: Competing in the age of capabilities, *California Management Review,* Vol. 42, No. 3, pp. 118–148.

Fulmer, R. M. and Conger, J. A. (2004), *Growing Your Company's Leaders,* AMACOM, New York.

Galbraith, C. S. and Curtis, H. L. (1983), Firm profitability and relative firm power, *Strategic Management Journal,* Vol. 4, No. 3, pp. 237–248.

Garcia-Zamor, J. and Noll, S. (2009), Privatization of public services in Leipzig: A balancing act between efficiency and legitimacy, *Public Organization Review,* Vol. 9, No. 1, pp. 83–100.

Geer, J. F. (1997), Brand war on Wall Street, *Financial World,* New York, May 20, pp. 54–63.

Gilbert, N. (1990), The time trap: Short-term solutions needed for long-term problems, *Management Review,* Vol. 79, No. 7, pp. 28–33.

Giles, W. D. (1991), Making strategy work, *Long Range Planning,* Vol. 24, No. 5, pp. 75–91.

Gold, A. H., Malhotra, A. and Segars, A. H. (2001), Knowledge management: An organizational capabilities perspective, *Journal of Management Information Systems,* Vol. 18, No. 1, pp. 185–196.

Goodell, P. W. and Martin, C. L. (1992), Marketing strategies for recession survival, *The Journal of Business & Industrial Marketing,* Vol. 7, No. 4, pp. 5–17.

Grabher, G., Ibert, O. and Flohr, S. (2008), The neglected king: The customer in the new knowledge ecology of innovation, *Economic Geography,* Vol. 84, No. 3, pp. 253–281.

Graham, G. H. (1997), Correlates of perceived importance of organizational objectives, *Academy of Management,* September, pp. 292–303.

Greenley, G. E., Hooley, G. J. and Broderick, A. (2004), Strategic planning differences among different multiple stakeholder orientation profiles, *Journal of Strategic Marketing,* Vol. 12, pp. 163–182.

Gronroos, C. (1990), Relationship approach to marketing in service contexts: The marketing and organizational behavior interface, *Journal of Business Research,* Vol. 29, pp. 3–11.

Gronroos, C. (1994), Quo Vadis, marketing? Towards a relationship marketing paradigm, *Journal of Marketing Management,* Vol. 10, No. 5, pp. 347–360.

Guerrera, R. (2009), A need to reconnect, *The Financial Times,* London, p. 11.

Gunasekaran, A., Folker, L. and Koby, B. (2000), *Improving operations performance in a small company: A case study, Management Decision,* Vol. 20, No. 3, pp. 316–325.

Gunasekaran, A., Tirtiroglu, E. and Wolstencroft, V. (2002), Gap between production and marketing functions: A case study, *Management Decision,* Vol. 40, No. 5/6, pp. 428–436.

Guo, C. (2002), Market orientation and business performance: A framework for service organizations, *European Journal of Marketing*, Vol. 36, No. 9/10, pp. 1154–1164.

Gupta, A. and Singhal, A. (1993), Managing human resources for innovation and creativity, *Research Technology Management*, Vol. 36, No. 3, pp. 41–49.

Haberberg, A. and Rieple, A. (2001), *The Strategic Management of Organisations*, Pearson Education, Harlow.

Haeckel, S. H. (1999), *Adaptive Enterprise: Creating and Leading Sense-and-Respond Organizations*, Harvard Business School Press, Boston, MA.

Hagen, A. and Tootoonchi, A. (2006), Managing the barriers to strategic flexibility, *Competition Forum*, Vol. 4, No. 1, pp. 195–204.

Häikiö, M. (2002), *Nokia: The Inside Story*, Prentice Hall, London.

Hall, A. (2002), Curing a sickness called success, *Sunday Times*, London, December 15, p. 7.

Hall, W. K. (1980), Survival strategies in a hostile environment, *Harvard Business Review*, September/October, pp. 75–85.

Hambrick, D. (1983), High profit strategies in mature capital goods industries: A contingency approach, *Academy of Management Journal*, Vol. 26, No. 4, pp. 687–707.

Hambrick, D. C. and D'Aveni, R. A. (1992), Top team deterioration as part of the downward spiral of large corporate bankruptcies, *Management Science*, Vol. 38, No. 10, pp. 1145–1158.

Hambrick, D. C., MacMillan, I. C. and Day, D. L. (1982), Strategic attributes and performance in the BCG matrix—a PIMS-based analysis of industrial product businesses, *Academy of Management Journal*, Vol. 25, No. 3, pp. 510–532.

Hamel, G. and Prahalad, C. K. (1993), Strategy as stretch and leverage, *Harvard Business Review*, March/April, pp. 75–84.

Hamel, G. and Prahalad, C. K. (1994), Competing for the Future, *Harvard Business School Press*, Boston, MA.

Hammer, M. and Champy, J. (1993), *Re-engineering the Corporations*, Harper Business, New York.

Harari, O. (1992), You're not in business to make a profit, *Management Review*, Vol. 81, No. 7, pp. 53–58.

Harrinvirta, M. and Mattila, M. (2001), The hard business of balancing budgets: A study of public finances in seventies, *British Journal of Political Science*, Vol. 31, pp. 497–512.

Harris, M. (2010), Look, no hands—the Google car is coming, *Sunday Times, London*, October 24, p. 18.

Harrison, E. F. (1996), A process perspective on strategic decision making, *Management Decision*, Vol. 34, No. 1, pp. 46–53.

Hartley, P. R., Medlock, K. B. and Rosthal, J. E. (2008), The relationship of natural gas to oil prices, *The Energy Journal*, Vol. 29, No. 3, pp. 47–66.

Hatten, K. J. and Rosenthal, S. R. (1999), Managing the process-centered enterprise, *Long Range Planning*, Vol. 32, No. 3, pp. 293–310.

Hax, A. C. (1990), Redefining the concept of strategy and the strategy formation process, *Planning Review*, Vol. 18, No. 3, pp. 34–40.

Hayes, R.H. and Upton, D.M. (1998), Operations-based strategy, *California Management Review*, Vol. 40, No. 4, pp. 8—25.

Hearne, R. W. (1982), Fighting industrial senility: A system for growth in mature industries, *Journal of Business Strategy*, Vol. 3, No. 2, pp. 3–20.

Heikkila, J. and Carlos C. (2002), Outsourcing: A core or non-core strategic management decision? *Strategic Change*, Vol. 11, No. 4, pp. 183–194.

Hellman, T. and Puri, M. (2000), The interaction between product market and financing strategy: The role of venture capital, *The Review of Financial Studies*, Vol. 13, No. 4, pp. 959–974.

Helper, S. (1991), How much has really changed between U.S. automakers and their suppliers? *Sloan Management Review*, Vol. 32, No. 4, pp. 15–29.

Henning, G., Malte, G., Kolbe, L. and Brenner, W. (2003), Knowledge-enabled customer relationship management: Integrating customer relationship management and knowledge management concepts, *Journal of Knowledge Management*, Vol. 7, No. 5, pp. 107–123.

Heracleous, L. and Murray, J. A. (2001), Networks, interlocking directors and strategy: Towards a theoretical framework, *Asia Pacific Journal of Management*, Vol. 18, pp. 137–160.

Herrigel, G. (2004), Emerging strategies and forms of governance in high-wage component manufacturing regions, *Industry and Innovation*, Vol. 11, No. 1/2, pp. 45–79.

Higgins, J. M. (1995), Innovate or evaporate, *The Futurist*, Vol. 29, No. 5, pp. 42–49.

Hine, D. and Ryan, N. (1999), Small service firms—creating value through innovation, *Journal of Small Business and Enterprise Development*, Vol. 9, No. 6, pp. 441–456.

Hingley, M. K. (2005), Power imbalanced relationships: Cases from UK fresh food supply, *International Journal of Retail & Distribution Management*, Vol. 33, No. 8/9, pp. 551–569.

Hisrich, R. D. and Peters, M. P. (1992), *Entrepreneurship: Starting, Developing, and Managing a New Enterprise*, Irwin, Boston.

Hitt, M. A., Keats, B. K. and DeMarie, S. M. (1998), Navigating in the new competitive landscape: Building strategic flexibility and competitive advantage in the 21st century, *The Academy of Management Executive*, Vol. 12, No. 4, pp. 22–42.

Hitt, M. and Ireland, D. (2005), Achieving and maintaining competitiveness in the 21st century: The role of strategic leadership, *Academy of Management Executive*, Vol. 19, No. 4, pp. 63–77.

Hoang, H. and Antoncic, B. (2003), Network-based research in entrepreneurship: A critical review, *Journal of Business Venturing*, Vol. 18, No. 2, pp. 165–187.

Hofer, C. W. (1975), Towards a contingency theory of business strategy, *Academy of Management Journal*, Vol. 19, pp. 784–810.

Hoffman, N. P. (2000), An examination of sustainable competitive advantage concept: Past, present, and future, *Academy of Marketing Science Review*, Vol. 20, pp. 1–16.

Hoffman, N. P. (2000), An examination of the sustainable competitive advantage concept: Past, present, and future, *Academy of Marketing Science Review*, Vol. 2000, pp. 1–25.

Hogan, J. and Lucke, T. (2006), Driving growth with new products: Common pricing traps to avoid, *The Journal of Business Strategy*, Vol. 27, No. 1, pp. 54–59.

Hogarty, D. B. (1993), Beating the odds: Avoid these mistakes at all costs, *Management Review*, Vol. 82, No. 1, pp. 16–22.

Hojjat, T. A. (2009), Global food crisis—food versus fuels, *Competition Forum*, Vol. 7, No. 2, pp. 419–426.

Holmqvist, M. (2003), Intra- and inter-organisational learning processes: An empirical comparison, *Scandinavian Journal of Management*, Vol. 19, No. 4, pp. 443–467.

Hood, C. and Jackson, M. (1992), The New Public Management: A recipe for disaster, in Parker, D. and Handmer, J. (eds.), *Hazard Management and Emergency Planning Processes: Perspectives in Britain*, James and James, London.

Hook, L. (2011), China rare earth metals soar as Beijing curbs sales, *Financial Times London*, May 27, p. 33.

Hoskinson, R. E., Hitt, M. A. and Hillman, C. L. (1991), Managerial risk taking in diversified firms: An evolutionary perspective, *Organisation Science*, Vol. 2, No. 3, pp. 296–314.

Hu, W., Yang, C. T., Yeh, J. and Hu, W. (2008), Mobile and electronic commerce systems and technologies, *Journal of Electronic Commerce in Organizations,* Vol. 6, No. 3, pp. 54–73.

Huang, T., Wang, W. C., Ken, Y., Tseng, C. and Lee, C. (2010), Managing technology transfer in open innovation: The case study in Taiwan, *Modern Applied Science,* Vol. 4, No. 1, pp. 2–11.

Huber, G. P. (1991), Organizational learning: The contributing processes and the literatures, *Organization Science,* Vol. 2, pp. 88–115.

Hudson, R. (1997), Long-term care: The new risks of old age, *Challenge,* Vol. 40, No. 3, pp. 103–116.

Huff, A. S. (1982), Industry influences on strategy reformulation, *Strategic Management Journal,* Vol. 3, No. 2, pp. 119–132.

Huston, L. and Sakkab, N. (2006), Connect and develop: Inside Procter & Gamble's new model for innovation, *Harvard Business Review,* March–April, pp. 58–66.

Iansiti, M. (1995), Shooting the rapids: Managing product development in turbulent environments, *California Management Review,* Vol. 38, No. 1, pp. 37–58.

IBM (2008), *The Enterprise of the Future,* accessed via www.ibm.com/gbs/uk/ceostudy, January 2010.

Ibrahim, N. A., Anglidas, J. P. and Parsa, F. (2008), Strategic management of family businesses: Current findings and directions for future research, *International Journal of Management,* Vol. 25, No. 1, pp. 95–112.

Im, G. and Rai, A. (2008), Knowledge sharing ambidexterity in long-term inter-organizational relationships, *Management Science,* Vol. 54, No. 7, pp. 1281–1296.

Indridason, T. and Wang, C. L. (2009), Commitment or contract: What drives performance in public private partnerships? *Business Strategy Series,* Vol. 9, No. 2, pp. 78–86.

Jackson, T. W. (2007), Personalisation and CRM, *Journal of Database Marketing & Customer Strategy Management,* Vol. 15, No. 1, pp. 24–36.

Jacques, M. (2009), *When China Rules the World: The Rise of the Middle Kingdom and the End of the Western World,* Penguin, London.

Jain, R. and Jain, S. (2003), Measuring customer relationship management, *Journal of Services Research,* Vol. 2, No. 2, pp. 97–109.

James, G. (1999), Can big blue master some new steps? *Upside, Foster City* Vol. 11, No 5, pp. 96–104.

Jansen, M. (2009), Desert sun power pulls in the big guns, *The Sunday Times,* London, July 27, p. 11.

Jap, S. D. (1999), Pie-expansion efforts: Collaboration processes in buyer-supplier relationships, *Journal of Marketing Research,* Vol. 36, No. 4, pp. 461–475.

Jarillo, J. C. (1988), On strategic networks, *Strategic Management Journal,* Vol. 9, pp. 31–41.

Jarrett, K. and Wendholt, A. (2010), Transferring technology to transform China—is it worth it? *The China Business Review,* Vol. 37, No. 2, pp. 20–25.

Javalgi, R. G., Radulovich, L. P., Pendleton, G. and Scherer, R. F. (2005), Sustainable competitive advantage of internet firms: A strategic framework and implications for global marketers, *International Marketing Review,* Vol. 22, No. 6, pp. 658–673.

Jaworski, B. J. and Kohli, A. K. (1966), Market orientation: Review, refinement and roadmap, *Journal of Market Focused Management,* Vol. 1, No. 2, pp. 119–135.

Jennings, M. J. (2008), Some thoughts on ethics, governance and markets, *Corporate Finance Review,* Vol. 12, No. 4, pp. 40–46.

Jensen, S., Hougaard, E. and Nieksen, S. B. (1995), Population ageing, public debt and sustainable fiscal spending, *Fiscal Studies,* Vol. 16, No. 2, pp. 1–20.

Johnson, R. (2004), Economic policy implications of world demographic change, *Economic Review Federal Reserve Bank of Kansas City*, Vol. 89, pp. 39–65.

Johnson, R. A., Hoskisson, R. E. and Hitt, M. A. (1993), Board of director involvement in restructuring: The effects of board executives, *Strategic Management Journal*, Vol. 14, pp. 33–51.

Kahn, B. E. (1998), Dynamic relationships with customers: High variety strategies, *Journal of Academy of Marketing Science*, Vol. 26, No. 1, pp. 45–53.

Kak, A. (2004), Strategic management, core competence and flexibility: Learning issues for select pharmaceutical organizations, *Global Journal of Flexible Systems Management*, Vol. 5, No. 4, pp. 1–15.

Kalakota, R. and Whinston, A. B. (1996), *Frontiers of Electronic Commerce*, Addison Wesley, Reading, MA.

Kalling, T. (2003), Knowledge management and the occasional links with performance, *Journal of Knowledge Management*, Vol. 7, No. 3, pp. 67–81.

Kaplan, R. S. and Norton, D. P. (1996), Strategic learning & the balanced scorecard, *Strategy & Leadership*, Vol. 24, No. 5, pp. 18–25.

Kaplan, R.S. and Norton, D.P. (2001), Transforming the balanced scorecard from performance measurement to strategic management: Part II, *Accounting Horizons*, Vol. 15, No. 2, pp. 147- 161.

Kassicieh, S. K., Walsh, S. T., Cummings, J. C., McWhorter, P. J., Romig, A. D. and Williams, D. W. (2002), Factors differentiating the commercialization of disruptive and sustaining technologies, *IEEE Transactions on Engineering Management*, Vol. 49, No. 4, pp. 375–392.

Kay, J. A. (1993), *Foundations of Corporate Success: How Business Strategies Add Value*, Oxford University Press, Oxford.

Kazuhiko, K. (1993), Financial conglomerates: How big is beautiful? *The OECD Observer*, Paris, August/September, pp. 18–22.

Kearney, C., Hisrich, R. D. and Roche, F. (2009), Public and private sector entrepreneurship: Similarities, differences or a combination? *Journal of Small Business and Enterprise Development*, Vol. 16, No. 1, pp. 26–35.

Keen, A. (2008), Why Yahoo will be remembered as the most successful failure, *The Independent*, London, February 11, p. 12.

Kellerman, B. (2004), *Bad Leadership*, Harvard Business School Press, Boston, MA.

Kellerman, B. (2005), How bad leadership happens, *Leader to Leader*, Vol. 35, pp. 41–46.

Kennedy, P. (2009), Read the big four to know capitalism's fate, The Future of Capitalism, *Financial Times*, London, May 12, 18–20, accessed via www.ft.com/capitalism.

Kenney, M. and Von Burg, U. (1999), Technology, entrepreneurship and path dependence: Industrial clustering in Silicon Valley and Route 128, *Industrial and Corporate Change*, Vol. 8, No. 1, pp. 67–76.

Kenworthy, L. (1995), *In Search of National Economic Success: Balancing Competition and Cooperation*, Sage, London.

Kets de Vries, M. J. (1977), The entrepreneurial personality: A person at the crossroads, *Journal of Management Studies*, Vol. 14, No. 1, pp. 34–57.

Khadem, R. (2008), Alignment and follow-up: Steps to strategy execution, *Journal of Business Strategy*, Vol. 29, No. 6, pp. 29–35.

Khan, A. M. and Manopichetwattan, V. (1989), Innovative and non-innovative small firms and characteristics, *Management Science*, Vol. 35, No. 5, pp. 597–606.

Kim, W. and Mauborgne, R. A. (1993), Making global strategies work, *Sloan Management Review*, Vol. 34, No. 3, pp. 11–20.

Klaase, L. H. and Van der Vlist, J. A. (1990), Senior citizens a burden? *De Economist*, Vol. 138, No. 3, pp. 302–321.

Klein, J. (2002), Beyond competitive advantage, *Strategic Change*, Vol. 11, No. 6, pp. 317–327.

Kochan, T. A. (2006), Taking the high road, *Sloan Management Review*, Vol. 47, No. 4, pp. 16–19.

Koguchi, K. (1993), Financial conglomerates: How big is beautiful? *The OECD Observer*, Paris, August/September, pp. 18–26.

Kopczak, L. R. and Johnson, M. C. (2003), The supply-chain management effect, *Sloan Management Review*, Vol. 44, No. 3, pp. 28–34.

Kosa, M. and Lewin, A. (2000), Managing partnerships and strategic alliances: Raising the odds of success, *European Journal of Management*, Vol. 18, No. 2, pp. 146–151.

Kotzab, H., Grant, D. B. and Friis, A. (2006), *Supply chain management and priority strategies in Danish organisations*, Vol. 27, No. 2, pp. 273–302.

Krasner, J. (2001), Tech icon Polaroid files for bankruptcy, *Boston Globe*, Boston, October 13, p. A4.

Laforet, S. and Tann, J. (2006), Innovative characteristics of small manufacturing firms, *Journal of Small Business and Enterprise Development*, Vol. 13, No. 3, pp. 363–375.

Langford, R. and Brown, C. (2004), Making M&A pay: Lessons from the world's most successful acquirers, *Strategy & Leadership*, Vol. 32, No. 1, pp. 5–10.

Larsen, P. T. (2007), Victory formally declared in ABN tussle, *Financial Times*, October 9, p. 22.

Lawrence, A. T. (2010), Managing disputes with nonmarket stakeholders, *California Management Review*, Vol. 53, No. 1, pp. 90–113.

Lawton, T. C. (1999), Evaluating European competitiveness: Measurements and models for a successful business environment, *European Business Journal*, Vol. 11, No. 4, pp. 195–206.

Lawton, T. C. and Michaels, K. P. (2001), Advancing to the virtual value chain: Learning from the Dell model, *Irish Journal of Management*, Vol. 22, No. 1, pp. 91–112.

Lazzarotti, V., Manzini, R. and Pellegrini, L. (2010). Open innovation models adopted in practice: An extensive study in Italy, *Business Excellence*, Vol. 14, No. 4, pp. 11–23.

Learned, E. P., Christensen, C. R., Andrews, C. R and Guth, W. D. (1965), *Strategy, Policy and Cases*, Irwin, Homewood, IL.

Lei, D. and Slocum, J. W. (2005), Strategic and organizational requirements for competitive advantage, *Academy of Management Executive*, Vol. 19, No. 1, pp. 31–45.

Leonard-Barton, D. (1992), Core capabilities and core rigidities: A paradox in managing new product development, *Strategic Management Journal*, Vol. 13, pp. 111–128.

Leong, G., Snyder, D. and Ward, P. T. (1990), Research in process and content of manufacturing strategy, *Omega*, Vol. 18, No. 2, pp. 109–122.

Lesca, N. and Caron-Fasan, M. (2008), Strategic scanning project failure and abandonment factors: Lessons learned, *European Journal of Information Systems*, Vol. 17, No. 4, pp. 371–386.

Letza, S. R., Smallman, C. and Sun, X. (2004), Reframing privatisation: Deconstructing the myth of efficiency, *Policy Sciences*, Vol. 37, No. 2, pp. 159–171.

Lev, B. (2001), *Intangibles: Management, Measurement and Reporting*, Brookings Institution, Washington, DC.

Lewis, A. and Loebbaka, J. (2008), Managing future and emergent strategy decay in the commercial aerospace industry, *Business Strategy Series*, Vol. 9, No. 4, pp. 147–156.

Lichtenthaler, U. (2008), Open innovation in practice: An analysis of strategic approaches to technology transactions, *IEEE Transactions on Engineering Management*, Vol. 55, No. 1, pp. 148–157.

Lichtenthaler, U. (2009), Outbound open innovation and its effect on firm performance: Examining environmental influences, *R&D Management*, Vol. 39, No. 4, pp. 317–330.

Liedtka, J. (2000), In defence of strategy as design, *California Management Review*, Vol. 42, No. 3, pp. 8–31.

Lim, L. L. K. and Chan, G. C. A. (2004), The development and application of an organisational learning matrix, *International Journal of Management*, Vol. 21, No. 1, pp. 100–108.

Lindman, N. T. (2007), Remarks on the quality of the construction of business concepts, *European Business Review*, Vol. 19, No. 3, pp. 196–215.

Lindsay, J. and Hopkins, M. (2010), From experience: Disruptive innovation and the need for disruptive intellectual asset strategy, *Journal of Production Innovation Management*, Vol. 27, pp. 283–290.

Lindsay, V. J. (2005), The development of international industry clusters: A complexity theory approach, *Journal of International Entrepreneurship*, Vol. 3, pp. 71–97.

Llorca, R. (1998), Product differentiation and process R&D, *Proceedings of 25th Annual EARIE Meeting*, University of Copenhagen, August.

Loewe, P. and Chen, G. (2007), Changing your company's approach to innovation, *Strategy & Leadership*, Vol. 35, No. 6, pp. 18–26.

Lucas, L. (2011), View from the top, *Financial Times*, London, June 13, p. 18.

Lumpkin, G. T. and Dess, G. G. (1996), Clarifying the entrepreneurial orientation construct and linking it to performance, *Academy of Management Review*, Vol. 21, pp. 135–172.

Lumpkin, O. S. and Dess, G. D. (2004), Business strategies and internet business models: How the internet adds value, *Organizational Dynamics*, Vol. 33, No. 2, pp. 161–173.

Lundvall, B. (1998), Why study national systems and national styles of innovation? Technology Analysis and *Strategic Management*, Vol. 10, No. 4, pp. 407–421.

Luria, D. (1987), *Technology, work organization, and competitiveness: Automotive subsystem cost reduction, 1986–1992*, Center for Social and Economic Issues, Industrial Technology Institute, Ann Arbor.

Lynk, E. L. (1993), Privatisation, joint production and the comparative efficiencies of private and public ownership: The UK water industry case, *Fiscal Studies*, Vol. 14, No. 2, pp. 98–117.

MacKay, R. B. and McKiernan, P. (2004), Exploring strategy context with foresight, *European Management Review*, Vol. 1, No. 1, pp. 69–78.

MacMillan, I. C., Hambrick, D. C. and Day, D. L. (1982), The product portfolio and profitability—a PIMS-based analysis of industrial-product businesses, *Academy of Management Journal*, Vol. 25, No. 4, pp. 733–755.

Madsen, E. L. (2007), Significance of sustaining an entrepreneurial orientation on the performance of firms—a longitudinal analysis, *Entrepreneurship & Regional Development*, Vol. 19, pp. 184–204.

Mahoney, J. and Pandian, J. R. (1992), The resource-based view within the conversation of strategic management, *Strategic Management Journal*, Vol. 13, No. 5, pp. 363–380.

Mailliard, K. (1997), Linking performance to the bottom line, *HR Focus*, Vol. 74, No. 6, pp. 1–11.

Malhotra, P. and Lofgren, H. (2004), India's pharmaceutical industry: Hype or high-tech take-off? *Australian Health Review*, Vol. 28, No. 2, pp. 182–194.

Malhotra, P. and Lofgren, H. (2004), India's pharmaceutical industry: Hype or high-tech take-off? *Australian Health Review*, Vol. 28, No. 2, pp. 182–194.

Manchester, D. (1997), Smart cards: Key to cashless economy? *The Futurist*, Vol. 31, No. 1, pp. 29–32.

March, J. G. (1991), Exploration and exploitation in organisational learning, *Organisation Science*, Vol. 2, No. 1, pp. 71–87.

March, P. (2010a), Rail equipment group frets over being too successful, *Financial Times*, London, September 28, p. 20.

March, P. (2010b), John Guest nurtures a family approach to engineering, *Financial Tines*, London, September 29, p. 22.

Markides, C. (2004), What is strategy and how do you know if you have one, *Business Strategy Review*, Vol. 15, No. 2, pp. 5–12.

Marmor, T. R. (1998), Forecasting American healthcare: How we got here and where we might be going, *Journal of Health Politics*, Vol. 23, No. 3, pp. 521–542.

Marten, G. G. (2001), *Human Ecology*, Earthscan Publications, London.

Mason, R. B. (2007), The external environment's effect on management and strategy: A complexity theory approach, *Management Decision*, Vol. 45, No. 1, pp. 10–28.

Massingham, P. (2004), Linking business level strategy with activities and knowledge resources, *Journal of Knowledge Management*, Vol. 8, No. 6, pp. 50–62.

Mathews, J. A. (1997), A Silicon Valley of the east: Creating Taiwan's semiconductor industry, *California Management Review*, Vol. 39, No. 4, pp. 26–54.

Mayhew, K. and Neely, A. (2006), Improving productivity—opening the black box, *Oxford Review of Economic Policy*, Vol. 22, No. 4, pp. 445–461.

McAdam, R.A., Hazlett, S. and Casey, C. (2005), Performance management in the UK public sector: addressing multiple stakeholder complexity, *International Journal of Public Sector Management*, Vol. 18, No. 3, pp. 125—141.

Mccarthy, B. (2003), Strategy is personality-driven, strategy is crisis-driven: Insights from entrepreneurial firms, *Management Decisions*, Vol. 41, No. 4, pp. 327–340.

Miles, R. E., Snow, C. C., Meyer, A. J. and Coleman H. J. (1978), Organizational strategy, structure, and process, *The Academy of Management Review*, Vol. 3, No. 3, pp. 546–562.

Miller, D. (1986), Configurations of strategy and structure: Towards a synthesis, *Strategic Management Journal*, Vol. 7, pp. 223–249.

Miller, D. and Freisen, P. H. (1980), Momentum and revolution in organisational adaption, *Academy of Management Journal*, Vol. 23, pp. 591–614.

Miller, D. and Toulose, J. M. (1986), Strategic success, CEO personality and performance, *American Small Business Journal*, Vol. 10, No. 3, pp. 47–62.

Miller, D. (1993), The architecture of simplicity, *The Academy of Management Review*, Vol. 18, No. 1, pp. 116–139.

Miller, J. G. and Warren, H. (1989), Implementing manufacturing strategic planning, *Planning Review*, Vol. 17, No. 4, pp. 22–34.

Milmo, C. (2010), Precious metals that could save the planet, *The Independent*, London, January 2, p. 8.

Mintzberg, H. (1983), *Structure in Fives: Designing Effective Organizations*, Prentice Hall, Englewood Cliffs, NJ.

Mintzberg, H. (1990), The Design School: Reconsidering the basic premises of strategic management, *Strategic Management Journal*, Vol. 11, pp. 17, 1–19.

Mintzberg, H. (1990), The Design School: Reconsidering the basic premises of strategic management, *Strategic Management Journal*, Vol. 11, pp. 171–195.

Mintzberg, H. (1994), Rethinking strategic planning, part I: Pitfalls and fallacies, *Long Range Planning*, Vol. 27, pp. 12–21.

Mintzberg, H. (1999), Reflecting on the strategy process, *Sloan Management Review,* Vol. 40, No. 3, pp. 21–32.

Mintzberg, H. and Waters, J. A. (1982), Tracking strategy in an entrepreneurial firm, *Academy of Management Journal,* Vol. 25, No. 3, pp. 463–499.

Mishina, Y., Pollock, T. G. and Porac, J. (2004), Are more resources always better for growth: Resource stickiness in market and product expansion, *Strategic Management Journal,* Vol. 25, pp. 1179–1197.

Mitchell, A. (2001), Radical innovation, *BT Technology Journal,* Vol. 19, No. 4, pp. 60–71.

Mitra, J. (2000), Making connections: Innovation and collective learning in small businesses, *Education + Training,* Vol. 42, No. 4, pp. 228–237.

Moeller, J. O. (2008), Energy and the environment, *Regional Outlook: Southeast Asia, Singapore,* Vol. 13, pp. 74–68.

Mohr, J. J., Fisher, R. J. and Nevin, J. R. (1996), Collaborative communication in interfirm relationships: Moderating effects of integration and control, *Journal of Marketing,* Vol. 60, pp. 103–115.

Monaghan, A. (2010), China reassures foreign firms of a level playing field, *The Daily Telegraph,* London, September 8, p. B8.

Montoya-Weiss, M. M. and Calantone, R. G. (1994), Determinants of new product performance: A review and a meta-analysis, *Journal of Product Innovation Management,* Vol. 11, No. 5, pp. 397–417.

Moore, G. A. (1991), Crossing the Chasm, *The Free Press,* New York.

Morash, E. A. and Clinton, S. R. (1998), Supply chain integration: Customer value through collaborative closeness, *Journal of Marketing Theory and Practice,* Vol. 6, No. 4, pp. 104–119.

Morehouse, J., O'Meara, B., Hagen, C. and Huseby, T. (2008), Hitting back: Strategic responses to low-cost rivals, *Strategy & Leadership,* Vol. 36, No. 1, pp. 4–13.

Morgan, J. (2009), Customer information management (CIM): The key to effective CRM in financial services, *Journal of Performance Management,* Vol. 22, No. 1, pp. 36–53.

Morgan, R. E. (2004), Organisational learning—theoretical reflections and conceptual insights, *Journal of Marketing Management,* Vol. 20, No. 1, pp. 67–104.

Morgan, R. M. and Hunt, S. D. (1994), The commitment–trust theory of relationship marketing, *Journal of Marketing,* Vol. 58, No. 3, pp. 20–38.

Morris, M. H. and Jones, F. F. (1999), Entrepreneurship in established organizations: The case of the public sector, *Entrepreneurship Theory and Practice,* Vol. 24, No. 1, pp. 71–91.

Muafi, I. (2009), The effects of alignment competitive strategy, culture and role behaviour, *International Journal of Organizational Innovation,* Vol. 1, No. 4, pp. 74–101.

Mudambi, R. (2008), Location, control and innovation in knowledge-intensive industries, *Journal of Economic Geography,* Vol. 8, pp. 699–725.

Mukhopadhyay, S. K. and Gupta, A. V. (1998), Interfaces for resolving marketing, manufacturing and design conflicts: A conceptual framework, *European Journal of Marketing,* Vol. 32, No. 1/2, pp. 101–124.

Munk, W. P. and Shane, B. (1994), Using competitive analysis models to set strategy in the Northwest hardboard industry, *Forest Products Journal,* Vol. 44, No. 7/8, pp. 11–19.

Murray, A. J. and Greenes, K. A. (2006), In search of the enterprise of the future, *The Journal of Information and Knowledge Management Systems,* Vol. 36, No. 3, pp. 231–237.

Murray, A. J. and Greenes, K. A. (2006), New leadership strategies for the enterprise of the future, *The Journal of Information and Knowledge Management Systems,* Vol. 36, No. 4, pp. 358–370.

Musgrave, G. L. (1995), Health economics outlook: Two theories of health economics, *Business Economics*, Vol. 30, No. 2, pp. 7–14.

Nair, A. and Boulton, W. R. (2008), Innovation-oriented operations strategy typology and stage-based model, *International Journal of Operations & Production Management*, Vol. 28, No. 8, pp. 748–771.

Nakamura, L. (2003), A trillion dollars a year in intangible investment and the new economy, in Hand, J. R. M. and Lev, B. (eds.), *Intangible Assets*, Oxford University Press, Oxford, pp. 20–35.

Nguyen, H. and Kleiner, B. H. (2003), The effective management of mergers, *Leadership & Organization Development Journal*, Vol. 24, No. 7/8, pp. 447–454.

Nisar, T. M. (2007a), Risk management in public-private partnership contracts, *Public Organization Review*, Vol. 7, No. 1, pp. 1–20.

Nisar, T. M. (2007b), Value for money drivers in public private partnership schemes, *The International Journal of Public Sector Management*, Vol. 20, No. 2, pp. 147–166.

Noble, C. H. (1999), The eclectic roots of strategy implementation research, *Journal of Business Research*, Vol. 45, No. 2, pp. 119–134.

Noe, R. A., Hollenbeck, J. R., Gerhart, B. and Wright, P. M. (2006), *Human Resources Management*, McGraw Hill/Irwin, New York.

Nohria, N. and Eccles, R. G. (1992), *Networks and Organizations*, Harvard Business School Press, Boston.

Nolan, P. (2009), Raise a glass to Waterford Crystal—and pray it survives, *Daily Mail*, London, January 6, p. 12.

Nonaka, I. and Takeuchi, H. (1995), *The Knowledge Creating Company*, Oxford University Press, New York.

Norman, R. and Ramirez, R. (1993), From value chain to value constellation, *Harvard Business Review*, July–August, pp. 65–77.

Nuttall, C. (2010), IBM to buy Netezza for cash, *Financial Times*, London, September 21, p. 25.

O'Driscoll, A., Carson, D. and Gilmore, A. (2001), The competence trap: Exploring issues in winning and sustaining core competence, *Irish Journal of Management*, Vol. 22, No. 1, pp. 73–90.

Ogilvie, H. (1994), The big chill, *The Journal of European Business*, Vol. 5, No. 4, pp. 25–31.

Ohmura, A. and Watanabe, C. (2006), Cross-products technology spill over in inducing a self-propagating dynamism for the shift to a service orientated economy, *Journal of Services Research*, Vol. 6, No. 2, pp. 145–178.

Ojala, A. and Tyrvained, P. (2009), Impact of psychic distance to the internationalization behavior of knowledge-intensive SMEs, *European Business Review*, Vol. 21, No. 3, pp. 263–271.

Oliva, R. A. (1998), Playing the 'Web Wild Cards,' *Marketing Management*, Chicago, Vol. 7, No. 1, pp. 51–54.

Ortt, J. R. and Schoorman, J. P. I. (2004), The patterns of development and diffusion of breakthrough communication technology, *European Journal of Innovation Management*, Vol. 7, No. 4, pp. 292–301.

Osborne, S. P. (2010), Introduction: The (New) Public Governance: A suitable case for treatment?, in Osborne, S. P. (ed.), *The New Public Governance? Emerging Perspectives on the Theory and Practice of Public Governance*, Routledge, Abingdon, pp. 1–16.

Owen, L., Goldwasser, C., Choate, K. And Blitz, A. (2008), Collaborative innovation throughout the extended enterprise, *Strategy & Leadership*, Vol. 36, No. 1, pp. 39—47.

Owen, L., Goldwasser, C., Choates, K. and Blitz, A. (2008), Collaborative innovation throughout the extended enterprise, *Strategy & Leadership*, Vol. 36, No. 1, pp. 39–47.

Paap, J. and Katz, R. (2004), Anticipating disruptive innovation, *Research Technology Management*, Vol. 47, No. 5, pp. 13–23.

Palacios, D., Gil, I. and Garrigos, F. (2009), The impact of knowledge management on innovation and entrepreneurship in the biotechnology and telecommunications industries, *Small Business Economics*, Vol. 32, No. 3, pp. 291–312.

Parks, G. M. (1977), How to climb the growth curve—eleven hurdles for the entrepreneur manager, *Journal of Small Business Management*, Vol. 15, No. 1, pp. 25–33.

Parnell, J. A., Von Bergen, C. W. and Soper, B. (2005), Profiting from past triumphs and failures: Harnessing history for future success, S.A.M. *Advanced Management Journal*, Vol. 70, No. 2, pp. 36–47.

Parrish, E. D., Cassill, N. C. and Oxenham, W. (2006), Niche market strategy for a mature marketplace, *Marketing Intelligence & Planning*, Vol. 24, No. 7, pp. 694–707.

Pearce, J. A. and Zahra, S. A. (1991), Relative power of CEOs and boards of directors, *Strategic Management*, Vol. 12, pp. 135–154.

Perez, C. (2002), *Technological Revolutions and Financial Capital: The Dynamics of Bubbles and Golden Ages*, Edward Elgar, Cheltenham.

Perry, M. (1999), Clusters last stand, *Planning Practice & Research*, Vol. 14, No. 2, pp. 149–152.

Perry, M. (2007), Business environments and cluster attractiveness to managers, *Entrepreneurship & Regional Development*, Vol. 19, pp. 1–24.

Peters, T. P. (1984), Strategy follows structure: Developing distinctive skills, *California Management Review*, Vol. 26, No. 3, pp. 111–120.

Pickard, J. and Stacey, K. (2011), Huhne pressured to drop climate change targets, *Financial Times*, London, May 10, p. 4.

Piercy, N. F. (1991), Marketing implementation: The implications of marketing paradigm weakness for the strategy execution process, *Academy of Marketing Science Journal*, Vol. 26, No. 3, pp. 222–236.

Plant, T. (2009), Strategic planning for municipalities: Ensuring progress and relevance, *Performance Improvement*, Vol. 48, No. 5, pp. 26–35.

Poister, T. H. and Streib, G. (2005), Elements of strategic planning and management in municipal government: Status after two decades, *Public Administration Review*, Vol. 65, No. 1, pp. 45–58.

Polo-Redondo, Y. and Cambra-Fierro, J. (2008), Influence of the standardization of a firm's productive process on the long-term orientation of its supply relationships: An empirical study, *Industrial Marketing Management*, Vol. 37, pp. 407–420.

Popkin, B. M. (2008), Will China's nutrition transition overwhelm its health care system and slow economic growth? *Health Affairs*, Vol. 27, No. 4, pp. 1064–1077.

Popovich, M. (1998), *Creating High Performance Government Organizations*, Jossey-Bass, San Francisco.

Porter, M. E. (1980), *Competitive Strategy*, The Free Press, New York.

Porter, M. E. (1985), *Competitive Advantage*, The Free Press, New York.

Porter, M. E. and Millar, V. (1985), How information gives you competitive advantage, *Harvard Business Review*, Vol. 63, pp. 149–160.

Powner, E. T. and Yalcinkaya, F. (1997), Intelligent biosensors, *Sensor Review*, Vol. 17, No. 2, pp. 107–116.

PR Newswire (1999), *KPMG identifies six keys factors for successful mergers and acquisition; 83 per cent of deals fail to enhance shareholder value*, November 29, Vol. 9, No. 17, www.prnewswire.com.

Prahalad, C. K. and Hamel, G. (1990), The core competence of the corporation. *Harvard Business Review*, March/April, pp. 79–91.

Prahalad, C. K. and Hamel, G. (1994), *Competing for the Future,* Harvard Business School Press, Boston, MA.

Preble, J. F. (1992), Towards a comprehensive system of strategic controls, *Journal of Management Studies*, Vol. 29, No. 4, pp. 391–409.

Priem, R. L. and Butler, J. E. (2001), Is the resource-based 'view' a useful perspective for strategic management research? *Academy of Management Review*, Vol. 26, No. 1, pp. 22–41.

Prosser, S. J. and Schmidt, E. D. (1999), Smart sensors for industrial applications, *Microelectronics International*, Vol. 16, No. 2, pp. 20–23.

Pullen, W. (1993), Strategic shocks: Managing discontinuous change, *The International Journal of Public Sector Management*, Vol. 6, No. 1, pp. 30–40.

Pyhrr, P. A. (1973), *Zero-Based Budgeting: A Practical Tool for Evaluating Expenditure,* Wiley, New York.

Quinn, J. B. (1980), *Strategies for Change: Logical Incrementalism,* Irwin, Homewood, IL.

Quinn, J. B. (1993), Managing the intelligent enterprise: Knowledge & service-based strategies, *Planning Review*, Vol. 21, No. 5, pp. 13–20.

Quinn, J. B. (2000), Outsourcing innovation: The new engine of growth, *Sloan Management Review*, Vol. 41, No. 4, pp. 13–26.

Rachman, G. (2010), Sweep economists off their throne, *Financial Times*, London, September 7, p. 13.

Randall, D. (2004), The music industry vs. the file sharers, *Strategy & Leadership*, Vol. 32, No. 1, pp. 47–49.

Raps, A. (2004), Implementing strategy, *Strategic Finance*, Vol. 85, No. 12, pp. 48–53.

Raynor, R. E. (2008), Strategic options: A new tool for managing in turbulent environments, *Business Strategy Series*, Vol. 9, No. 1, pp. 21–29.

Reati, A. and Toporowski, J. (2004), An economic policy for the fifth long wave, Banca Nazionale del Lavoro *Quarterly Review*, Rome, Vol. 57, No. 231, pp. 395–437.

Reed, J. (2009), The future in his hands, *Financial Times Magazine,* London, July 25, pp. 23–27.

Rees, M. (2008), Just the facts, *The International Economy*, Vol. 22, No. 3, pp. 77–81.

Reitsperger, W. D., Daniel, S. J., Tallman, S. B. and Chismar, W. G. (1993), Product quality and cost leadership: Compatible strategies? *Management International Review*, Vol. 33, No. 3, pp. 7–22.

Rich, J. T. (1999), The growth imperative, *The Journal of Business Strategy*, Vol. 20, No. 2, pp. 27–31.

Rindova, V. P. and Kotha, S. (2001), Continuous morphing: Competing through dynamic capabilities, form and function, *Academy of Management Journal*, Vol. 44, No. 6, pp. 1263–1280.

Ring, P. S. and Perry, J. L. (1985), Strategic management in public and private organizations: Implications of distinctive contexts and constraints, *The Academy of Management Review*, Vol. 10, No. 2, pp. 276–288.

Riolli-Saltzman, L. and Luthans, F. (2001), After the bubble burst: How small high-tech firms can keep in front of the wave, *The Academy of Management Executive*, Vol. 15, No. 3, pp. 114–124.

Roberts, N. and Stockport, G. R. (2009), Defining strategic flexibility, *Global Journal of Flexible Systems Management*, Vol. 10, No. 1, pp. 27–32.

Roig, S. and Dobon, R. D. (2008), Exploring alternative approaches in service industries: The role of entrepreneurship, *The Service Industries Journal*, Vol. 28, No. 7, pp. 877–882.

Romano, C. A. (1990), Identifying factors which influence product innovation: A case study approach, *Journal of Management Studies*, Vol. 27, No. 1, pp. 75–95.

Rosen, S. and Shapouri, S. (2009), Global economic crisis threatens food security in lower income countries, *Amber Waves*, Vol. 7, No. 4, pp. 39–43.

Rowe, A. J., Mason, R. O. and Dickel, K. E. (1994), *Strategic Management*, Addison Wesley, Menlo Park, CA.

Rowe, W. G. (2001), Creating wealth in organizations: The role of strategic leadership, Academy of *Management Executive*, Vol. 15, No. 1, pp. 81–94.

Rowe, G. and Nejad, M. J. (2009), Strategic leadership: Short-term stability and long-term viability, Ivey *Business Journal Online*, September/October, pp. 1–6.

Rufat-Latre, J., Muller, A. and Jones, D. (2010), Delivering on the promise of open innovation, *Strategy and Leadership*, Vol. 38, No. 6, pp. 23–28.

Rycroft, R. W. and Kash, D. E. (2002), Path dependence in the innovation of complex technologies, *Technology Analysis & Strategic Management*, Vol. 14, No. 1, pp. 22–35.

Sakkab, N. Y. (2002), Connect and develop complements research at P&G, *Research Technology Management*, Vol. 45, No. 2, pp. 38–45.

Sanchez, R. (1993), Strategic flexibility, firm organisation, and managerial work in dynamic markets: A strategic options perspective, *Advances in Strategic Management*, Vol. 9, pp. 251–291.

Sanchez, R. (1997), Preparing for an uncertain future: Managing organizations for strategic flexibility, *International Studies of Management & Organization*, Vol. 27, No. 2, pp. 71–94.

Sanchez, R. and Mahoney, J. T. (1996), Modularity, flexibility and knowledge management, *Strategic Management Journal*, Vol. 17, Winter, pp. 63–76.

Santos, J., Doz Y. and Williamson, P. (2004), Is your innovation process global? *Sloan Management Review*, Vol. 45, No. 4, pp. 31–37.

Savory, C. (2006), Translating knowledge to build technological competence, *Management Decision*, Vol. 44, No. 8, pp. 1052–1075.

Saxenian, A. (1990), Regional networks and the resurgence of Silicon Valley, *California Management Review*, Vol. 33, No. 1, pp. 89–113.

Schmidt, G. M. and Porteus, E. L. (2000), Sustaining technology leadership can require both cost competence and innovative, Competence, *Manufacturing & Service Operations Management*, Vol. 2, No. 1, pp. 1–19.

Schumpeter, J. (1942), *Capitalism, Socialism and Democracy*, Harper Brothers, New York.

Schumpeter, J. (1950), *History of Economic Analyses*, Oxford University Press, New York.

Sehgal, S., Sahay, B. S. and Goyal, S. K. (2006), Re-engineering the supply chain in a paint company, *International Journal of Productivity and Performance Management*, Vol. 55, No. 8, pp. 655–670.

Senge, P. (1990), *The Fifth Discipline: The Art and Practice of the Learning Organisation*, Doubleday, New York.

Seuring, S. (2004), Industrial ecology, life cycles, supply chains: Differences and interrelations, *Business Strategy and the Environment*, Vol. 13, No. 5, pp. 306–315.

Shang, S. C., Lin, S. and Wu, Y. (2009), Service innovation through dynamic knowledge management, *Industrial Management & Data Systems*, Vol. 109, No. 3, pp. 322–337.

Sharke, P. (2003), Smart cars, *Mechanical Engineering*, Vol. 125, No. 3, pp. 50–52.

Sharma, R. S., Siddiqui, A., Sharma, A., Singh, R. and Sachin, R. A. (2007), Leveraging knowledge management for growth: A case study of Tata Consultancy, *Journal of Information Technology Case and Application Research*, Vol. 9, No. 4, pp. 29–39.

Sheehan, T. J. (2005), Why old tools won't work in the new knowledge economy, *The Journal of Business Strategy*, Vol. 26, No. 4, pp. 53–62.

Shimizu, K. and Hitt, M. A. (2004), Strategic flexibility: Organizational preparedness to reverse ineffective strategic decisions, *Academy of Management Executive*, Vol. 18, No. 4, pp. 44–58.

Simonet, D. (2007), Evaluation of downstream integration in the US pharmaceutical industry, *International Journal of Pharmaceutical and Healthcare Marketing*, Vol. 1, No. 2, pp. 143–158.

Simpson, C. (2000), Integration framework: Supporting successful mergers, *Mergers and Acquisitions Canada*, Vol. 12, No. 10, pp. 3–14.

Simpson, R. L. (2003), Today's challenges shape tomorrow's technology, part 2,
Nursing Management, Vol. 34, No. 12, pp. 40–44.

Singh, S. (2009), Global food crisis: Magnitude, causes and policy measures, *International Journal of Social Economics*, Vol. 36, No. 1/2, pp. 23–36.

Sirkin, H. L., Hemerling, J. W., Arindam, D. and Bhattacharya, K. (2008), Global-
ity: Challenger companies are radically redefining the competitive landscape,
Strategy & Leadership, Vol. 36, No. 6, pp. 36–41.

Slater, S. F., Olson, E. M. and Venkateshwar, K. R. (1997), Strategy-based performance measurement, *Business Horizons*, July/August, pp. 37–44.

Slevin, D. P. and Covin, J. (1990), Juggling entrepreneurial style and organisational
culture, *Sloan Management Review*, Vol. 31, No. 2, pp. 43–54.

Slowinski, G. and Sagal, M. W. (2010), Good practices in open innovation,
Research Technology Management, September–October, pp. 38–46.

Slywotzky, A. J. (1996), *Value Migration: How to Think Several Moves Ahead of
Competition*, Harvard Business School Press, Harvard.

Smith, A. D. (2008), Corporate social responsibility practices in the pharmaceutical industry, *Business Strategy Series*, Vol. 9, No. 6, pp. 306–315.

Smith, G. (2004), An evaluation of the corporate culture of Southwest Airlines,
Measuring Business Excellence, Vol. 8, No. 4, pp. 26–33.

Smith, W. E. (2009), Vitality in business: Executing a new strategy at Unilever,
Journal of Business Strategy, Vol. 30, No. 4, pp. 31–40.

Soliman, F. and Youssef, M. A. (2003), Internet-based e-commerce and its impact
on manufacturing and business operations, *Industrial Management + Data Systems*, Wembley, Vol. 103, No. 8/9, pp. 546–552.

Speier, C., Mollenkopf, D. and Stank, T. S. (2008), The role of information integration in facilitating 21st century supply chains, *Transportation Journal*, Vol. 47,
No. 2, pp. 21–30.

Spitzeck, H. and Hansen, E. G. (2010), Stakeholder governance: How stakeholders
influence corporate decision making, *Corporate Governance*, Vol. 10, No. 4,
pp. 378–391.

Stalk, G. Jr., (2006), Hardball innovation, *Research Technology Management*,
January–February, pp. 1–12.

Stone, M. (2009), Staying customer-focused and trusted: Web 2.0 and Customer
2.0 in financial services, *Journal of Database Marketing & Customer Strategy
Management*, Vol. 16, No. 2, pp. 101–131.

Stonich, P. J. (1990), Time: The next strategic frontier, *Planning Review*, Vol. 18,
No. 6, pp. 5–47.

Streeter, B. (2006), M&A: The deals just keep on coming, *ABA Banking Journal*,
Vol. 98, No. 2, pp. 50–54.

Sturgeon, T., Van Biesebroeck, J. and Gereffi, G. (2008), Value chains, networks
and clusters: Reframing the global automotive industry, *Journal of Economic
Geography*, Vol. 8, pp. 297–321.

Sushil, A. J. (2002), Sustainable competitive advantage with core competence: A review,
Global Journal of Flexible Systems Management, Vol. 3, No. 4, pp. 23–38.

Sveiby, K. E. (1997), *The New Organizational Wealth: Managing and Measuring
Knowledge-Based Assets*, Berrett-Koehler, San Francisco.

Szilagyo, A. S. and Schweiger, D. M. (1984), Matching managers to strategies: A review and suggested framework, *Academy of Management Review,* Vol. 9, No. 4, pp. 626–637.

Tan, C. W. and Pan, S. L. (2003), Managing e-transformation in the public sector: An e-government study of the Inland Revenue Authority of Singapore (IRAS), *European Journal of Information Systems,* Vol. 12, No. 4, pp. 269–281.

Tanabe, K. and Watanabe, C. (2005), Sources of small and enterprise excellent business performance in a service orientated economy, *Journal of Services Research,* Vol. 7, No. 1, pp. 5–21.

Tanabe, K. and Watanabe, G. (2005), Sources of small and medium enterprises excellent business in a service orientated economy, *Journal of Service Research,* Vol. 5, No. 1, pp. 5–21.

Tang, S. L. and Stylios, G. K. (2006), An overview of smart technologies for clothing design and engineering, *International Journal of Clothing Science and Technology,* Vol. 18, No. 1/2, pp. 108–128.

Taylor, W. A. and Wright, G. H. (2004), Organizational readiness for successful knowledge sharing: Challenges for public sector managers, *Information Resources Management Journal,* Vol. 17, No. 2, pp. 22–37.

Tellis, G. T., Prabhu, J. C. and Chandy, R. K. (2009), Radical innovation across nations: The pre-eminence of corporate culture, *Journal of Marketing,* Vol. 73, pp. 3–23.

Terwiersch, C. and Ulrich, K. (2008), Managing the opportunity portfolio, *Research Technology Management,* Vol. 51, No. 5, pp. 27–38.

Thietart, R. A. and Vivas, R. (1984), An investigation of success strategies, *Management Science,* Vol. 30, No. 12, pp. 1405–1424.

Thomas, A. R. and Wilkinson, T. J. (2006), The outsourcing compulsion, *Sloan Management Review,* Vol. 48, No. 1, pp. 10–14.

Thompson S., Teo, H. and Pian, Y. (2003), A contingency perspective on Internet adoption and competitive advantage, *European Journal of Information Systems,* Vol. 12, No. 2, pp. 78–89.

Tojo, Y. (2006), Creating value from intellectual assets, *OECD,* Paris, pp. 1–8, accessed via www.oecd.org/dataoecd/8/45/38194512.pdf, June 2010.

Tolstoy, D. (2010), Knowledge combination in networks: Evidence from the international venturing of four small biotech firms, *International Entrepreneurship and Management Journal,* Vol. 6, No. 2, pp. 183–202.

Tong, C. H. (2006), Formulating turnaround strategies for GM in the U.S. auto market, *Competition Forum,* Vol. 4, No. 1, pp. 106–109.

Tong, C. H. (2007), Strategy for transforming the corporation while delivering performance, *Strategy & Leadership,* Vol. 38, No. 3, pp. 35–43.

Treacy, F. and Wiersema, F. (1995), *The Discipline of Market Leaders,* HarperCollins, New York.

Treacy, M. and Wiersma, F. (1995), *The Disciplines of Market Leaders,* Addison-Wesley, Reading, MA.

Tripsas, M. and Gavetii, G. (2000), Capabilities, emotions and inertia, *Strategic Management Journal,* Vol. 21, No. 10/11, pp. 1147–1161.

Trompenaars, F. and Hampden-Turner, C. (1998), *Riding the Waves of Culture,* McGraw-Hill, New York.

Trott, P. (1998), Growing businesses by generating genuine business opportunities: A review of recent thinking, *Journal of Applied Management,* Vol. 7, No. 2, pp. 211–223.

Tyson, K. M. (1998), Perpetual strategy: A 21st century essential, *Strategy & Leadership,* Vol. 26, No. 1, pp. 14–18.

Van der Meer, H. (2007), Open innovation—the Dutch treat: Challenges in thinking in business models, *Creativity and Innovation Management,* Vol. 16, No. 2, pp. 102–207.

Venkatraman, N. and Prescott, J. E. (1990), The market share-profitability relationship: Testing temporal stability across business cycles, *Journal of Management*, Vol. 16, No. 4, pp. 783–805.

Von Krogh, G., Ichijo, K. and Nonaka, I. (2000), *Enabling Knowledge Creation: How to Unlock the Mystery of Tacit Knowledge and Release the Power of Innovation*, Oxford University Press, Oxford.

Vredenburgh, D. and Brender, Y. (1998), The hierarchical abuse of power in work organizations, *Journal of Business Ethics*, Vol. 17, No. 12, pp. 1337–1347.

Wagner, E. R. and Hansen, E. N. (2005), Innovation in large versus small companies: Insights from the US wood products industry, *Management Decision*, Vol. 43, No. 5/6, pp. 837–851.

Wallop, H. (2010), 1920s panic that led to a war on waste, *The Daily Telegraph*, London, April 28, p. 4.

Wanasika, I. (2009), In search of global leadership, *Journal of International Business and Cultural Studies*, Vol. 1, pp. 2–17.

Ward, A. (2010), New chief to make Nokia a little less Finnish, *Financial Times*, London, July 21, p. 23.

Warkentin, M., Bapna, R. and Sugumaran, V. (2001), E-knowledge networks for interorganizational collaborative e-business, *Logistics Information Management*, Vol. 14, No. 1/2, pp. 149–163.

Watanabe, C. (1972), *Industry-Ecology: Introduction of Ecology into Industrial Policy*, MITI, Tokyo.

Watanabe, C. and Fukuda, K. (2006), National innovation ecosystems: The similarity and disparity of Japan-US technology policy systems towards a service orientated economy, *Journal of Services Research*, Vol. 6, No. 1, pp. 160–171.

Watson, G. (2001), Sub-regimes of power and integrated supply chain management, *Journal of Supply Chain Management*, Vol. 37, No. 2, pp. 36–45.

Webster, E. (1992), The changing role of marketing in the corporation, *Journal of Marketing*, Vol. 56, No. 3, pp. 1–17.

Webster, F. E. (1992), The changing role of marketing in the corporation, *Journal of Marketing*, Vol. 56, pp. 1–17.

Wetherbe, J. C. and Montanari, J. R. (1981), Zero-based budgeting in the planning process, *Strategic Management Journal*, Vol. 2, No. 1, pp. 1–14.

Wheelen, T. L. and Hunger, J. D. (2006), *Concepts in Strategic Management and Business Policy*, Pearson-Prentice Hall, Upper Saddle River, NY.

White, L. H. (1989), Public management in a pluralistic arena, *Public Administration Review*, Vol. 49, No. 6, pp. 522–531.

Wikson, D. F. (1999), Competitive marketing strategy in a volatile environment: Theory, practice and research priorities, *Journal of Strategic Marketing*, Vol. 7, pp. 19–40.

Williams, J. R. (1992), How sustainable is your competitive advantage, *California Management Review*, Spring, pp. 31–41.

Williamson, O. E. (1975), *Markets and Hierarchies: Analysis and Antitrust Implications*, Free Press, New York.

Wincent, J. and Westberg, M. (2005), Persoanl traits of CEOs inter-firm networking and entrepreneurship in their firms, *Journal of Developmental Entrepreneurship*. Vol. 10, Iss. 3; pg. 271–285.

Wirtz, B. and Lihotzky, N. (2003), Customer retention management in B2C electronic business, *Long Range Planning*, Vol. 36, No. 6, pp. 517–532.

Witt, P., Schroeter, R. and Merz, C. (2008), Entrepreneurial resource acquisition via personal networks: An empirical study of German start-ups, *The Service Industries Journal*, Vol. 28, No. 7, pp. 953–971.

Womack, J. P. and Jones, D. T. (1966), *Lean Thinking,* Simon & Schuster, New York.

Wonglimpiyarat, J. (2004), The use of strategies in managing technological innovation, *European Journal of Innovation Management,* Vol. 7, No. 3, pp. 229–250.

World Economic Forum (2010), The Global Competitiveness Report 2010–2011, *World Economic Forum,* Geneva, Switzerland.

Worley, C. G. and Lawler, E. E. (2006), Designing organizations that are built to change, *Sloan Management Review,* Vol. 48, No. 1, pp. 19–23.

Wright, C. S. and Dawood, I. (2009), Information technology: Market success to succession, *The Review of Business Information Systems,* Vol. 13, No. 4, pp. 7–20.

Xu, M. and Walton, J. (2005), Gaining customer knowledge through analytical CRM, *Industrial Management + Data Systems,* Vol. 105, No. 7, pp. 955–971.

Yukl, G. and Falbe, C. (1990), Influence tactics and objectives in upward, downward and lateral influence attempts, *Journal of Applied Psychology,* Vol. 75, pp. 132–140.

Zack, M. H. (2003), Rethinking the knowledge based organisation, *Sloan Management Review,* Vol. 44, No. 4, pp. 67–71.

Zagotta, R. and Robinson, D. (2002), Keys to successful strategy execution, *The Journal of Business Strategy,* Vol. 23, No. 1, pp. 30–34.

Zahra, S. A. and Pearce, J. A. (1990), Research evidence on the Miles-Snow typology, *Journal of Management,* Vol. 16, No. 4, pp. 751–767.

Zanra, S. A. and Nielsen, A. P. (2002), Sources of capabilities, integration and technology commercialization, *Strategic Management Journal,* Vol. 23, No. 5, pp. 377–398.

Zimmerman, J. (2010), Corporate entrepreneurship at GE and Intel, *Journal of Business Case Studies,* Vol. 6, No. 5, pp. 77–81.

Zineldin, M. (2005), Quality and customer relationship management (CRM) as competitive strategy in the Swedish banking industry, *The TQM Magazine,* Vol. 17, No. 4, pp. 329–344.

Zuvekas, S. H. and Cohen, J. W. (2007), Prescription drugs and the changing concentration of health care expenditures, *Health Affairs,* Vol. 26, No. 1, pp. 249–257.

Index